A New Andalucia and a Way to the Orient

A New Andalucia and a Way to the Orient

The American Southeast During the Sixteenth Century

Paul E. Hoffman

Louisiana State University Press
Baton Rouge and London

Manufactured in the United States of America
First printing

99 98 97 96 95 94 93 92 91 90 5 4 3 2 1

Designer: Albert Crochet
Typeface: Linotron Trump Mediaeval
Typesetter: The Composing Room of Michigan, Inc.
Printer and binder: Thomson-Shore, Inc.

Publication of this book has been assisted by a grant from the Program of Cooperation of the Ministry of Culture of Spain and the Universities of the United States; the book has won a "Spain and America in the Quincentennial of the Discovery" Prize for 1987, which was sponsored by that program.

Library of Congress Cataloging-in-Publication Data

Hoffman, Paul E., 1943–
A new Andalucia and a way to the Orient : the American Southeast during the sixteenth century / Paul E. Hoffman.
p. cm.
Includes bibliographical references.
ISBN 0-8071-1552-5 (alk. paper)
1. Southern States—Discovery and exploration. 2. Explorers—Southern States—History—16th century. 3. America—Discovery and exploration—Spanish. I. Title.
F212.H64 1990
975'.01—dc20 89-13492
CIP

The paper in this book meets the guidelines for permanence and durability of the Committee on Production Guidelines for Book Longevity of the Council on Library Resources. ♾

This book about the neglected century of the history of the United States is dedicated with love to

Philip and Stephen

so that they and future generations can know what their parents did not when they were young,

and to

Barbara

in grateful remembrance of the fall of 1980 and many other falls and springs

Contents

Maps

Following page 21

Preface

One night in 1977, Eugene Lyon, Frank Aguilera, and I were sitting in a motel room in Saint Augustine, Florida, discussing Spanish Florida and its history. For some years, Gene and I had been working on a project for the Saint Augustine Restoration Foundation, Inc. (now the Saint Augustine Foundation), and Frank had just come aboard as a consultant on material culture. In the course of our discussion, we turned to the subject of the locations of Saint Augustine and her sister city, Santa Elena. We knew why the site of Saint Augustine had been selected for occupation: it was a protected port from which the Spanish could easily attack the French Fort Caroline. None of us knew why the Spaniards had moved onto the site of Santa Elena, although the attractions of Port Royal Sound seemed clear.

Curious about the why of Santa Elena, I undertook preliminary research in the secondary literature on Spanish Florida. I soon found a partial answer: Jean Ribault had left a colony at Santa Elena in 1562, an obvious enough reason for the Spaniards to move in during 1566. Digging deeper, I found that Ribault had been seeking Chicore and thought he had found it at Port Royal Sound. *Chicore?* More research showed that it was *Chicora* and suggested how Ribault had learned of the tale that Lucas Vázquez de Ayllón had spread in Spain in 1523. By then it was clear that there was a direct link between the earliest Spanish voyages to the American Southeast, in 1521–1526, and later French and Spanish colonial activity during the 1560s. Curiously, except for Johann Kohl, who in the nineteenth century noted Ribault's search, and Paul Quattlebaum, who in the 1950s produced a general history of South Carolina before 1670, no author had attempted to show how the early events were linked to the later, aside from simple chronological sequence. Too, the secondary literature revealed conflicting evidence and interpretations concerning where Ayllón had explored and settled (see the Appendix). What had looked like a simple answer to a basic question thus provoked a search for new facts and the testing of a hypothesis: that Ayllón's propaganda of the 1520s became a legend about the richness of the American Southeast which influenced later explorers and helped to direct them to particular parts of the southeastern coast.

With support from the Council on Research at Louisiana State University and from Joseph R. Judge, associate editor of the *National Geographic Magazine,* I was able to conduct research into the Spanish documents during the summer of 1978 and the fall of 1980. Confident that I had traced the story in the Spanish records and in all appropriate secondary literature, I set out to write, only to find when I got to the 1560s and Pedro Menéndez de Avilés that the story was more complex, and more exciting, than I had expected. Menéndez de Avilés knew not only the Chicora legend, as I had come to call Ayllón's tale, but also another: a variation on Verrazzano's report of what in the end turned out to be a false sea. That tale was also a product of the 1520s. On the one hand, my discovery required some additional research, which delayed the completion of my project; on the other, it provided the link to the English colonies at Roanoke Island which had eluded previous writers who discussed the sixteenth-century colonial rivalry in the American Southeast. I now saw that all the explorations and the attempts at colonization by the Spaniards, French, and English were linked by the belief of their leaders and promoters in these two legends from the 1520s as they had been altered over the decades.

This book argues that Ayllón's tale of Chicora, with its promised sylvan, agricultural, human, and mineral wealth, and Verrazzano's tale of an isthmus in North America at about 37° north led a generation of European explorers and colonizers, chiefly those of the second half of the sixteenth century, to search the southeastern coast for, respectively, the new Andalucia and a way to the Orient. The two legends were altered over time so that Chicora came to be associated with a place well to the south of the latitudes of Andalucia and Verrazzano's arm of the Pacific Ocean came to be associated with a place somewhat to the north of his supposed isthmus. The alterations explain why there was so much interest in the area around the Point of Santa Elena (Tybee Island, 32° north) after 1550, and later, in the 1580s and 1590s, in the area of the Outer Banks and the Chesapeake Bay. Ironically, the interest in the Chesapeake Bay, which arose from the alteration of Verrazzano's legend, led to a resurrection of the pure form of Ayllón's legend, which had placed Chicora at the latitudes of Andalucia, corresponding to those of Chesapeake Bay.

The book is also an account of how men's hopes and wishes for North America were contradicted by the difficult reality of the coastal zone of the southeast, and of reactions to that reality. Too, it is a study in how important it is to use sources in chronological sequence, assuming that differences between them may be part of some larger story rather than a result of confusions and mistakes by their authors—although that possibility has to be watched for as well. And finally, the book illustrates how important a new source can be in clearing up the mysteries left by other sources (see the Appendix).

I have not treated all parts of my story equally. Some, such as Menéndez de Avilés' conquest of La Florida, in 1565–1567, are well covered in the standard and the recent literature. Detailed repetition of what others have done ably is unnecessary. For those portions of the story, I have summarized, and suggested where the interested reader can learn more. My concentration has been on the story where it has not been told well heretofore. In particular, I have given the two Lucas Vázquez de Ayllóns disproportionate treatment. My bias reflects not only their treatment in the literature but also my own research strengths, which lie in Spanish archives. I trust that the result is not too unbalanced. I look forward to studies by scholars more familiar than I am with the French and, to a lesser degree, the English sources, studies that may revise parts of what I have said here on the basis of the secondary literature and the printed primary sources, much of the former well over half a century old.

A word about three words that I use. I construe a *legend* to be a story or report based on facts but altered over time by the human imagination so that only a part of its factual basis remains. I employ the term *La Florida* to refer to the whole of the Southeast, as the Spaniards did, and *Florida* to refer to the peninsula and the rest of the area occupied by the modern state of the same name.

Many persons have helped me along the way. Doña Rosario Parra, the director, and the staff of the Archive of the Indies provided friendly and prompt service with *legajos* and microfilms at times when the demands on their time and equipment were skyrocketing. The staffs of the Archivo General de Simancas, the Biblioteca Nacional of Madrid, the Archivo Histórico Provincial of Toledo, and the Archivo de Protocolos of Seville provided assistance with their collections and a welcome to an itinerant scholar. Elizabeth Alexander and her staff at the P. K. Yonge Library of Florida History, at the University of Florida, assisted me with access to their rich collections and answered a number of mail requests. The staff of the Troy H. Middleton Memorial Library, at Louisiana State University, in particular the interlibrary-loan staff, provided invaluable aid over the years.

I owe special debts to Howard E. Bond, of the LSU physics department; Gary Crump, of the LSU history department; Larry Rowland, of the University of South Carolina at Beaufort; the Reverend Charles E. O'Neill, S.J., currently head of the Jesuit Historical Institute of Rome; the late Samuel Elliot Morison; the staff of the Hispanic Society of America, in New York; and José Ignacio Avellaneda, of Colombia. Each provided special assistance at some point in the project, and that help is acknowledged further in my notes.

Joseph R. Judge, of the *National Geographic Magazine,* and Eugene Lyon merit special mention. For many years, Joe Judge has taken a lively interest in this project and assisted it with copies of maps and funds from his editorial office. I am deeply grateful. Eugene Lyon has been a friend, a critic, and my mentor in some aspects of the Florida documentation for the period of the 1560s, a period for which his studies are unsurpassed. He has supplied a number of notes on documents that he had used but that I had not, notes that I have employed in this study and acknowledged. It is safe to say that without his work, my own on the 1560s would have taken far longer than it did.

The dedication of this book is my final acknowledgment.

Abbreviations

AGI	Archivo General de Indias, Seville
PAT	Patronato
CD	Contaduría
CT	Contratación
JU	Justicia
SD	Santo Domingo
MEX	Mexico
GDA	Guadalajara
IG	Indiferente General
AGS	Archivo General de Simancas
EDO	Estado
DIE	*Colección de documentos inéditos para la historia de España*
DII	*Colección de documentos inéditos relativos al descubrimiento, conquista, y organización de las antiguas posesiones españoles de America y Oceanía, sacados de los archivos del reino, y muy especialmente del de Indias*
DIU	*Colección de documentos inéditos relativos al descubrimiento, conquista, y organización de las antiguas posesiones españoles de Ultramar*

PART ONE

The Spaniards and a New Andalucia

I

The Chicora Legend Created, 1521–1523

Pedro de Quejo was later to claim that he was the first to spot the thin dark line of land on the western horizon in the early hours of Monday morning, June 24, 1521, the day of the feast of Saint John the Baptist.[1] Elated but mindful of his agreement with Francisco Gordillo, who commanded the caravel that was sailing some distance astern, Quejo ordered his sails luffed so that the other ship, an older, slower sailer badly in need of a careening, might catch up and learn the good news.[2] By the time it had drawn abeam, however, Gordillo's lookouts had also spotted the land. Exchanging the exciting news, both captains laid a course to the west.

Quejo's caravel reached the coast first, just off the mouth of what he described as a river. Anchoring, he waited half an hour for his partner to come up and anchor. That done, the boats were let down into the sea, and landing parties were sent off to a beach. Twenty men from the crews went ashore before the commanders decided to move their ships into the comparative safety of the river. Sounding, they felt their way over the bar into what we know as the South Santee River (Map 1).

While the ships were being moved, the men on the beach encountered a group of Indians whose curiosity had drawn them from their village (or fishing camps?) along the river delta's shores. The landing party made peace with them by giving presents from among the few items of clothing they carried.[3]

Such is the story Quejo told. Peter Martyr recounts the events of that morning a bit differently in the seventh decade of his *De Orbe*

1. AGI, JU 3, No. 3, fols. 40v–41. The date of discovery is mentioned on fols. 29, 41v, 53, 62, 56v–60v, 62, 68, 70v. The sun rose at about 4:30 A.M. Eastern Standard Time, so they may have got underway as early as 3:00 A.M., when the first light was strong enough that they could see.

2. Pietro Martiere d'Anghiera, *Decadas del Nuevo Mundo,* ed. Edmundo O'Gorman (2 vols.; Mexico City, 1964–65), II, 595; AGI, JU 3, No. 3, fols. 40–41.

3. AGI, JU 3, No. 3, fol. 41.

Novo.[4] As he heard the story from the licenciado Lucas Vázquez de Ayllón, of whom more later, the Indians rushed to the edge of the sea, pushing and shoving one another in their excitement to see what the "monsters" were and to look at the men coming ashore in the boats. As soon as the Spaniards landed, the Indians fled, but the Spaniards ran after them. Some younger seamen sprinted ahead of their fellows and managed to catch a man and a woman, whom they took back to the boats. There the sailors dressed the captives in Spanish clothing, probably shirts and headcloths, attempted to convey by signs a desire to be friends, and then let them go. The Indians went to where the rest of their number had hidden and by showing off the new clothes induced them to return to the shore. There more Spanish clothing was given to the Indians, who soon went back to their village and showed the kerchiefs (*paños de cabeza*), linen shirts, and marvelous red caps (*gorras*) to their chief.[5] He sent the Spaniards fifty of his servants (*familiares*), carrying native foods. These last scenes were what Quejo noticed and described.

All the Spaniards must have appreciated the importance of discovering what to them was a previously unknown land north of the Bahama Islands. But none could have known that their reports about this land would plant the seed for one of the more important, if neglected, legends connected with North American exploration. Relocated and worked upon by men's imaginations until the discovery assumed the form of a new Andalucia flowing with milk and honey, not to mention laden with pearls, gold, silver, wine grapes, and olives, it was to spawn a legend that, together with another legend about the continent born three years later, would motivate Spaniards, Frenchmen, and Englishmen to explore and attempt to colonize the coast of North America between the latitudes of 32° and 39° north.

The Quejo-Gordillo voyage began as two separate ventures that merged in the Bahamas. Both had slaving as their objective. Each was commanded by a pilot and shipmaster with long experience in the Caribbean and in the Bahama Islands.

4. Anghiera, *Decadas,* Decade 7, Book 2 (II, 594).

5. Matienzo claimed that the Indians were given four red caps (*gorras coloradas*), three shirts of *precilla* and one of *ruan* (both types of linen), one shirt of hemp cloth (*cañamazo*), and six face or head cloths (*paños de cabeza*) worth four pesos, six tomines of fine gold (AGI, JU 3, No. 3, fols. 31–31v). Woodbury Lowery mistakenly asserts that the Indians were given "doublet and hose" (*Spanish Settlements Within the Present Limits of the United States* [2 vols.; New York, 1901–1911], I, 155–56).

For some years Quejo had worked as a pilot and shipmaster for Sancho Ortiz de Urrutía, a merchant born in Gordejuela, Vizcaya. Ortiz de Urrutía had first come out to Española about 1512 accompanying his perhaps distant kinsman the licenciado Juan Ortiz de Matienzo, judge (*oidor*) of the royal audiencia, whose partner he had been in earlier ventures.[6] Most of Quejo's sailing experience seems to have been in the greater Antilles in connection with trading.

Gordillo was an experienced pilot and slave trader. He had visited Babacoa (or Habacoa) Island, the Bahamas—modern Andros Island—during 1514–1517 as the agent of Ayllón and his occasional business associates, among others the licenciado Juan de Bezerra, Ayllón's father-in-law and a powerful land and mine owner on Española; Lope de Bardeci, a native of Palencia, in Spain, who represented many of the Italian firms doing business in the Antilles; and Juan de Manzorro, a member of the powerful Manzorro clan of Española. That expedition, and another fitted by some of the same men and directed by a Captain Toribio de Villafranca, had rounded up as many as nine hundred Indians, over half of whom died in pens in the Bahamas while awaiting supplies and ships so that they could be taken to Española for sale.[7]

In April or May, 1521, Urrutía again hired Quejo to pilot a ship, in which Urrutía planned to take merchandise to Cuba. Once that was accomplished, he intended to use a license granted by the son of Christopher Columbus, Diego Colón, admiral of the ocean sea and governor of Española from 1509 to 1527, to go to the Bahamas to hunt for slaves.[8] Clearing Santo Domingo late in May, they sailed to Cuba and then back to La Yaguana, Española (near modern Léogane), where they unloaded part of the cargo and left Urrutía. At La Yaguana, Urrutía gave Quejo his power of attorney for all matters during the rest of the voyage, in a transfer of authority common between owners and shipmasters.

Departing from La Yaguana, Quejo sailed to Baracoa, Cuba, where

6. Peter Boyd Bowman, *Indice geobiográfico de 40.000 pobladores españoles de América en el siglo XVI* (5 vols. projected; Bogotá and Mexico City, 1964–), I, 156, No. 4728.

7. AGI, JU 42, No. 1, fols. 229–32, 70–73.

8. The date is based on the salary payments for 4.5 months given in Matienzo's statement of expenses, AGI, JU 3, No. 3, fols. 30–32. Slaving in the Bahamas was authorized in cedulas of May 3, 1509, and June 25, 1511, as noted by Lesley B. Simpson in *The Encomienda in New Spain: The Beginning of Spanish Mexico* (Rev. ed.; Berkeley and Los Angeles, 1966), 22, 28. None of the witnesses in the lawsuit of 1526 except Quejo had seen the license, which was not put into the record.

he completely unloaded his ship and then put aboard a quantity of *cazabi* bread (bread made from flour prepared from cassava roots) and possibly other supplies as well. A large dugout canoe was also obtained for use as a tender. Quejo left Baracoa for the Bahamas about June 10. His plan seems to have been to take advantage of the waxing moon, which would be full on June 19, to aid navigation in the waters and reefs of the Bahamas.[9]

Gordillo's voyage seems to have begun in late January or in February, 1521. Ayllón and Diego Cavallero, secretary of the audiencia, also had a license from Governor Colón, which they claimed later was not only for slaving but also, and more important, for exploration and discovery. According to Cavallero, Ayllón had heard of a discovery made by Captain Pedro de Salazar, a slave raider who had been in the employ of Ayllón's fellow judge and occasional business partner, the licenciado Marcelo de Villalobos. Sometime between 1514 and 1516, Salazar had found land at a place to the northwest of the Bahama Islands.[10] Ayllón intended that Gordillo should check Salazar's report, but apparently only if he failed to find Indians in the Bahamas. Salazar had brought Indians of "giant" stature from his discovery and sold them as slaves, and that made his discovery doubly attractive to the ambitious and acquisitive judge.

Nothing is known of Gordillo's voyage until Quejo met up with him at the Yucayuelos, a group of keys near Andros Island. Apparently Gordillo spent as many as three and a half months systematically but fruitlessly searching the Bahamas for Indians. There were none; previous expeditions had picked the islands clean.[11]

Quejo reached Andros Island on the thirteenth of June. A landing party found only one Indian and signs—probably trash and the remains of cooking fires—that other Europeans had been there ten to twelve days earlier. Because the crew discovered no other Indians, it determined to sail for Bahama Island (present-day Grand Bahama Island) or Yucayoneque (Great Abaco Island) and, if no Indians were

9. AGI, JU 3, No. 3, fols. 67–68. *Cf. ibid.*, 39–40. Moon phases are calculated from Bryant Tucherman's *Planetary, Lunar, and Solar Positions, A.D. 2–1649* (Philadelphia, 1964), 778. I wish to thank Howard Bond, formerly of the Department of Physics and Astronomy at Louisiana State University, for his help in working out this information.

10. AGI, JU 3, No. 3, fols. 48v–49; Manuel Gimenez Fernández, *Bartolomé de las Casas* (2 vols.; Seville, 1953–60), I, 324, 327; Paul E. Hoffman, "A New Voyage of North American Discovery: The Voyage of Pedro de Salazar to the Island of Giants," *Florida Historical Quarterly*, LVIII (1980), 415–26.

11. AGI, JU 3, No. 3, fols. 40–41.

found on them, next to sail fifty leagues in search of land and, if they did not sight any, to turn west to peninsular Florida. Sailing the next morning, Quejo had not gone more than five leagues, or sixteen nautical miles, when his lookouts spotted a caravel at anchor. As they approached, a bark came away from it and met them. In that boat was Alonso Fernández Sotil, the master and pilot of the caravel and a relative of Quejo's. The kinsmen exchanged greetings, and Sotil persuaded Quejo to anchor and return to Andros Island the next day so that he and Gordillo, who was there, could work up an agreement to sail together.

On Andros Island, the two commanders compared notes and found that their crews were of equal size but that Quejo had three hundred *cargas* of *cazabi* biscuit whereas Gordillo had but one hundred. They agreed to redistribute the biscuit evenly between the ships and to divide evenly any slaves they found through Gordillo's information about the Salazar voyage.

On June 15, Quejo's and Gordillo's ships cleared Great Abaco Island on a northerly course. Riding at times along the eastern edge of the Gulf Stream and using the light airs of mid-June, the ships moved north for eight days, covering a distance later estimated to be between 110 and 115 leagues, or about 352 to 368 nautical miles. Because Quejo and Gordillo did not encounter land in those eight days as they expected they would on the basis of their knowledge about Salazar's voyage, they held a conference on June 22 and agreed to turn west, or more probably, southwest, for Florida. There they knew they would find Indians.[12] During that afternoon they were becalmed, but Quejo says he noted straw (*peje*) in the water and sharks. A sounding showed sixty-five fathoms. With evening, the land breeze sprang up, and the ships got underway again on a generally southwesterly course. Two hours after sunset (about 10 P.M.; the sun set about 8 P.M. Eastern Standard Time),[13] another sounding was taken at a point four to five leagues, or thirteen to sixteen nautical miles, beyond the first. Bottom was now at thirty fathoms. The ships continued to sail under a third-quarter moon.

12. Anghiera claims that a two-day storm drove them to land (*Decadas*, II, 594), but Quejo says nothing of a storm. Joseph R. Judge has shown that even a slow-sailing ship could have made the distance in question in eight days ("A Memorandum on the Voyage of Discovery of 1521 by Pedro de Quexo and Francisco Gordillo to South Carolina" [Washington, D.C., 1979; typescript in collection of the present author]).

13. That is, at "two hours of the night" (AGI, JU 3, No. 3, fol. 40v).

On the morning of June 23, they sounded again and found eighteen to nineteen fathoms. No land was in sight, and the wind dropped, leaving them becalmed until 3 P.M., when the wind again rose. They sailed until sunset, sounded again, and found eight to nine fathoms. The ships were anchored for the night. The next morning was the day of the feast of Saint John the Baptist, the day on which they discovered land.

The ships remained at anchor in the river for several days while the Spaniards explored their surroundings. This river was later called the Jordan because of the river associated with Saint John the Baptist.[14] Some exploration was apparently from the mastheads of the ships, but most was probably by ship's boat rowed up the river and into various meandering side channels, down the coast to at least modern Cape Romain, and up the coast past the mouth of the North Santee River and over the shoals on the western side of the entrance to Winyah Bay.[15] To the east, the shoals reached south and southeast for "two leagues," or about six nautical miles, from the south end of what is now known as North Island.[16]

North Island, along with Waccamaw Neck, forms part of the long

14. Diego Luís Molinari makes this obvious connection (*El nacimiento del nuevo mundo, 1492–1534: Historia y cartografía* [Buenos Aires, 1941], 124–26). Antonio de Herrera y Tordesillas is the source of the erroneous idea that the river was named for a captain or other crewman on the voyage (*Historia general de los hechos de los Castellanos en las islas y Tierrafirme del mar oceano* [17 vols.; Madrid, 1934–57], III, 327–34). John G. Shea mistakenly says that the river was named Saint John the Baptist ("Ancient Florida," in Justin Winsor [ed.], *Narrative and Critical History of the United States* [8 vols.; Boston and New York, 1884–89], II, 239*n*1), an error repeated by Lowery (*Spanish Settlements*, I, 155; *cf.* AGI, JU 3, No. 3, fol. 49).

15. On this point, Pietro Martiere d'Anghiera says, "Regiones p[er]lustrarunt paucorum dieru[m] intercapedine: plaerasque simul lo[n]ge protento in terra[m] adhaere[n]tes, vbi anchoras iecere, chicoram & Duhare primarias" (*De Orbe Nouo* [Compluti, 1530], fol. xcii verso; verification of text courtesy of the Hispanic Society of America, New York). Francis M. MacNutt renders this, "The exploration of the country occupied but a few days. It extends a great distance in the same direction as the land where [the Spaniards] anchored. The first [districts visited were called] Chicorana and Duhare" (*De Orbe Novo: The Eight Decades of Peter Martyr d'Anghera* [2 vols.; New York, 1912], II, 258; square brackets added to show his interpolations). My colleague Gary Crump suggests that a more faithful translation would be, "They thoroughly studied the regions for the space of a few days: most [of the regions] clinging together for a long space to the land where they cast anchor, Chicora and Duhare being the primary ones [*i.e.*, regions]." O'Gorman renders this into Spanish as, "En el espacio de unos pocos dias recorrieron [los nuestros] aquella región, quedandose en un golfo que penetra mucho en tierra" (Anghiera, *Decadas*, II, 596). O'Gorman's translation interpolates the existence of a "gulf" or bay into the Latin text, perhaps by a mistaken reading of *simul*, which presents problems of meaning, as *sinus*.

16. Andrés Gonzales Rutter, 1609, AGI, PAT 19, No. 31, fol. 5v.

curved strand that arches away to the northwest from the entrance to Winyah Bay before turning back toward the northeast about where modern Myrtle Beach is located. Approached close in along the shore from the south, North Island—and the shoals on that side of the entrance to Winyah Bay—would appear to be an "island stretching east-west."[17] The area was later to be described as a cape, that is, a place where the coast line abruptly changes direction from one arc to another.[18] The entrance to Winyah Bay is on the southwestern side of North Island, with the channel running northwest. On both sides of the entrance, the shoals were often covered by no more than nine feet of water even at nearly high tide. The coastal pilot of 1609 cautioned the mariner about them but added the significant detail that "within there is a very good port."[19] Up the bay lay various Indian villages, at least one of which came to be remembered as Chicora.

Having found the way into the estuary that they may have glimpsed as they approached the Santee from the northeast on June 23, the Spaniards moved their ships from the South Santee River to the better and safer anchorage of the bay. They went some distance up it to or near an Indian village. Indian sites of the period have been documented at Pawley's Island and inland from Debidue Beach, but they are on the Atlantic side of Waccamaw Neck and could be reached, if at all, only from the Waccamaw River. More likely, the Indian camp or village that the Spaniards visited was on the bay side of Waccamaw Neck, because Martyr is quite clear that "on the other side of the bay" lay the land that stretched to the dominions of a chief he called Duhare, whose real name seems to have been Du-a-e (Due-ah-eh), and who can be identified as the Datha about whom Francisco Fernández de Ecija inquired in 1609.[20]

Wherever the village or villages were that the Spaniards visited,

17. *Ibid.*

18. Anghiera says that the entrance to the river was marked by an "elevated promontory" (*Decadas*, II, 594). Paul Quattlebaum notes that before storms at the beginning of the twentieth century, Pawley's Island, which is some fifteen nautical miles north of the "cape," had twenty- to thirty-foot dunes (*The Land Called Chicora: The Carolinas Under Spanish Rule with French Intrusions, 1520–1670* [Gainesville, Fla., 1956], 10).

19. AGI, PAT 19, No. 31, fol. 5v.

20. Information provided by Robert L. Stephenson, formerly state archaeologist of South Carolina (Chicora-phase complicated stamped pottery of the period A.D. 1300–1600 has been found at these sites); Anghiera, *Decadas*, II, 596; "Journal of Francisco Fernández de Ecija on His Virginia Voyage," in David B. Quinn (ed.), *New American World: A Documentary History of North America to 1612* (5 vols.; New York, 1979), V, 144.

there is no doubt about what happened next. On the twenty-eighth or twenty-ninth of June, Gordillo and some of his men took possession of the land in the name of their employers. Upon learning of this, Quejo flew into a rage, visited Gordillo's ship to angrily denounce his underhanded act, and then went ashore with a party of his own and formally took possession for Urrutía and his associates. In sign of possession, Quejo had crosses cut in the bark of some red cedar (*savina*) trees. He also took a solar latitude reading, calculating that he was at about 33°30′ north. It was Sunday, June 30, 1521, a week after they had first seen the new land.[21]

The land having been claimed by both parties, the Spaniards settled into two weeks of trade and, according to Martyr's account, further exploration. Matienzo later asserted that besides the clothing initially given to the Indians, 4 axes, 300 "false pearls," 150 "fine diamonds," 3 very old hammers (*mazos de abolorio*), and a dozen combs were handed out, perhaps in exchange for the freshwater pearls and "other terrestrial gems" Martyr mentioned.[22]

Among the areas that Ayllón told Martyr his men had visited were "Arambe, Guacaya, Cuoathe, Tauzaca, and Pahor." These were said to be of small area (*corta extension*) and under the dominion of the chief Du-a-e. The five places in question can be identified as the Arande, Guacaya, possibly Huaque, Tancaca, and Pahor of the Ayllón contract of 1523 (see Chapter II). The only one of them whose location can be positively identified is Guacaya, the name of which is actually a reversing of the major syllables of *Cayagua,* which is the Spanish spelling of *Kiawa,* the English version of the name of the Indians who lived around Charleston Harbor. Charleston lies about forty nautical miles to the south of the South Santee, about a day's sail by small boat. It is of note that Martyr's statement that Charleston Harbor was visited contradicts testimony given in 1526 that explicitly says that there was little or no exploration in 1521 beyond the immediate area of the landfall. The other names mentioned by Martyr probably refer to villages or chiefs located up the Santee, Black, Peedee, and Waccamaw rivers at no great distance from the landing points of the Spaniards.

The people the Spaniards met at Winyah Bay and in its immediate

21. AGI, JU 3, No. 3, fols. 71v, 55–55v, 42.

22. *Ibid.,* fol. 31; Anghiera, *Decadas,* II, 597. *Mazos de abolorio* should probably read *mazos de abolengo* or *mazos de abalorio,* indicating hammers that came from one's ancestors or grandparents. That is, they were very old.

vicinity were "brown, like our peasants toasted in the summer sun."[23] The men let their black hair hang to the waist, and the women kept theirs even longer and gathered it in loops. Both sexes bound their hair. The men were without beards. Martyr was uncertain whether the absence of facial hair was natural or the result of pulling or the use of medications.

The real name of the Indians with whom the Spaniards had their principal dealings while anchored in Winyah Bay in 1521 does not appear in the sources. Martyr refers to their village by the name of Chicora, which derived from the nickname el Chicorano given to the Indian they called Francisco who came from these people and accompanied Ayllón to Spain in 1523. The origins of the nickname are not clear. Since no Chicora was ever encountered by later Spanish visitors to Winyah Bay, the surmise is that the name arose from a humorous wordplay by Ayllón or Martyr or combined a poorly understood Indian word with the Spanish word for *boy.* In the first case, Francisco was called the "little frog," *rana chica* in proper Spanish, here corrupted to *chico rano,* a form closer to *frog boy.* In the second case, *rano* was based on the *ya-a* grunt made by Indians rendering obeisance, a practice Juan Pardo found inland from the South Carolina coast. The nickname then meant "little ra," that is, "little ya-a." It may be that Ayllón or Martyr saw the droll possibilities in using *little ra,* or *ra boy,* in a form that was similar to *little frog.* Such speculation aside, the fact remains that Chicora was the name by which the homeland of Francisco ("el Chicorano") became known, and the name of the place about which a legend grew.

Across the bay from Chicora lay territories under the dominion of a place or tribe called Duhare, according to Martyr, or Du-a-e, in Ayllón's contract of 1523. The identification of this place is not certain, but James Mooney has suggested that the words are a corruption of the Cherokee name Duksai or Dukwsai for a town on the headwaters of the Keowee River which was later known as Toxaway.[24] Wherever the place was, it seems clear that it was an important hegemonic center of the proto-Cherokee Indians, whose control apparently extended as far as the coast at Winyah Bay and may even have reached as far as Charleston to the south.

The people of Du-a-e were said by Francisco to be "white" and to

23. Anghiera, *Decadas,* II, 596.
24. James Mooney, *The Siouan Tribes of the East* (Washington, D.C., 1894), 412.

have "blond hair to the heels." Their king, called Datha, was of "gigantic stature," and the queen of not much less. They had five children. Some tall young men carried the king about on their shoulders, according to the bachillero Alvaro de Castro, dean of the Cathedral of Concepción de la Vega, on Española (1523–?), who had known el Chicorano and Ayllón there but whose testimony, recorded by Martyr, is probably no more trustworthy than theirs. Ayllón, on the other hand, insisted that the Indians of Du-a-e had horses. Francisco did not help resolve Martyr's doubt whether these "barbarous and uncivilized" people could have such animals. Martyr gave it as his opinion that they could not.[25]

The chief of Du-a-e, or Duksai, had under his jurisdiction the inland provinces Martyr called Hitha, Zamunambe, and Tihe. These appear in the Ayllón contract as Yta tancal, Xamunanbe, and Anicatixe. Martyr offers no information on the first two but says that the residents of Tihe wore garments distinct from those of the "people" and, considered to be priests, were venerated by their fellow tribesmen. They cut their hair, leaving only two braids or pigtails hanging from the temples, and they tied the braids under the point of the chin. When the tribes went to war, both sides took the priests along to watch the battle. Just before the engagement, the priests had the combatants sit down or stretch out on the ground and sprinkled the warriors with the juice of herbs they masticated "like our priests do with Hissop to those who come to divine office." After the battle, the priests attended to the wounded of both sides and buried the bodies of the dead.[26]

Although Martyr gives only a part of the name, Tihe, there is no doubt from the list in Ayllón's contract that these people were the Anicatixe or, more probably, the Aní-kutánî or Aní-kuatánî, a group of shamans who the eighteenth-century Cherokee recalled had been killed for moral outrages a long time before.[27] Thus Martyr's account—however distorted it may be by his informants—is the only record of this group of shamans in the heyday of their power and influence among the proto-Cherokee and their neighbors.

Martyr spent the better part of Book Three of his seventh decade

25. Anghiera, *Decadas,* II, 597.

26. *Ibid.,* 597–98.

27. Mooney, *The Siouan Tribes,* 392–93, 501, 508; Raymond D. Fogelson, "Who Were the Aní Kutánî? An Excursion into Cherokee Historical Thought," *Ethnohistory,* XXXI (1984), 259.

describing the religious ceremonies of the people of Du-a-e and, possibly, of the coast as well. Other parts of the chapter relate their customs concerning widows, the calendar, justice, and the salutation of persons of high rank, and present a host of other unusual and amusing "facts." The chapter also includes el Chicorano's explanation of how the chief of Du-a-e came to be so tall. On the whole, this purportedly ethnographic material is entertaining and seems to be partially supported by the scant archaeological data currently available from along the coast in question.

Two other "provinces" figure in Martyr's account. Xapida (the Xapira of the Ayllón contract) was a land whence came pearls and "other terrestrial gems" similar in appearance to them. This province was on the border of Du-a-e's dominions but not subject to its chief. No identification is supplied by Spanish records. On the other hand, Inisiguanín (the Orista inisiguanín of Ayllón's contract) can be identified. *Orista,* rendered *Edisto* by the English, denominates the province of a group of Indians who lived along the Edisto River and the shores of modern Saint Helena Sound. The Spaniards had extensive dealings with these people after the founding of Santa Elena, on Parris Island, in 1566.

According to Martyr, the Chicorans told the Spaniards that they had heard from their elders that in "another time" men came to Orista who had immobile tails a palm (33 inches) long and as thick as a man's arm. The tails were of hard bone, like those of fish and crocodiles. In order to sit down, these men needed seats with holes in them or they had to dig holes in the ground. These men had fingers as long as they were wide and a dry, almost scaly skin. They ate only raw fish of a certain kind. When they exhausted that food, they died to the last man, without leaving descendants.[28]

The tale takes on ethnographic significance because Ecija found in 1609 that the language—or dialect—spoken at Orista was not understandable to Indians from Charleston north.[29] A linguistic frontier thus lay south of Charleston. The land on the south side of the frontier had once been inhabited by men who were not like other men. By implication, the then-current residents of Orista were also not like other men but were less than fully human.

28. Anghiera, *Decadas,* II, 598.

29. "Journal of Francisco Fernández de Ecija," in Quinn (ed.), *New American World,* V, 144–45.

With the passing of the new moon of July 3–4, and the approach of the full moon of July 19, the time had come for the Spaniards to consider their next moves. On Monday, July 15, they acted. By now on good terms with the local Indians, they invited some of them onto the ships with the promise of more presents. Once they had boarded some sixty, they raised the anchors, shook out and set the sails, and put the ships to sea, probably on a falling tide. The Spaniards took this action only after some argument, although it is unlikely that there was as much reluctance to seize the Indians as Quejo later claimed. In all probability, Martyr is correct when he says that the commanders did not want to return empty-handed to Santo Domingo and so become the objects of derision. They also may have feared the wrath of their employers if they returned without cargoes of slaves.[30] Both expeditions had, after all, been sent out to secure slaves wherever they could be found.

On the return voyage, Gordillo quarreled with Sotil and transferred himself, four or five of his crew, and all of his share of the Indians to Quejo's caravel. It was a fortunate decision, for Sotil's ship never returned to Santo Domingo.[31]

Exactly when Quejo reached Santo Domingo is not known. The evidence in a lawsuit of 1526 seems on first reading to suggest that he arrived on Sunday, September 22, the day the *real acuerdo* met to discuss what to do with the Indians and the petition of Ayllón, Matienzo, and Cavallero for an exclusive license to exploit the new discovery. That dating would have made the return trip a ten-week (seventy-day, July 15 to September 22) trip, which is quite long even allowing for a stop in the Bahamas. On the other hand, an entry in the records of the royal fifth—a tax—paid on pearls suggests a twenty-seven-day voyage, July 15 to August 11. Under date of August 12, a Monday, a "private person" presented a quantity of pearls for taxation. These might have been pearls from Chicora. If so, Quejo arrived on Sunday, August 11, 1521. An August arrival and a short trip seem more probable because of the distance, the sailing time, the limited supplies on the ship, and its crowded conditions. In any case, the arrival was on a Sunday.[32]

30. AGI, JU 3, No. 3, fol. 41v; Anghiera, *Decadas,* II, 594–95. Garcilaso de la Vega incorrectly says that more than 130 slaves were taken (*The Florida of the Inca,* trans. and ed. John G. Varner and Jeannette J. Varner [Austin, Tex., 1951], 10).

31. AGI, JU 3, No. 3, fols. 33, 49–50, 62v, 68, 70v; Anghiera, *Decadas,* II, 595.

32. Petition to the *real acuerdo,* September 22, 1521, copy in AGI, JU 3, No. 3, fols. 88–89v; payment of one peso, nine granos weight of round pearls as tax, AGI, CD 1050,

Once the ship had crossed the bar at the mouth of the Ozama River and worked its way past the tower fort on the bluff along the west side of the river's mouth and once it had been secured at one of the docks in front of Santo Domingo, Quejo set out to find Urrutía, who had returned to Santo Domingo earlier. Gordillo went to find Cavallero. Word of the arrival of the voyagers and their cargo of unusually tall Indian slaves spread quickly, reaching the treasurer of the crusade, Jerónimo de Medina, while he was at mass in the cathedral. A small crowd of the curious soon gathered at quayside.[33] Quejo formally gave the Indians to Urrutía, who seems to have divided them into two groups, as the agreement between Gordillo and Quejo required. Those belonging to Urrutía were then taken to the house of his heretofore silent partner, Matienzo, where a number of persons who were called to testify in 1526 saw them. Cavallero's heretofore silent partner, Ayllón, appeared, and he and Cavallero divided their thirty Indians. Everyone who saw these unhappy people agreed that the Indians were taller than those normally brought from the Bahamas and the South American coast. One witness recalled that the Indians were "white" and dressed in the skins of wild animals, including those of the mountain lion.[34]

What happened next is not clear. Apparently none of the Indians was offered for sale. All were put to work on the properties that the various principals—Ayllón, Matienzo, Cavallero—owned in and near Santo Domingo.[35] Ayllón and the others turned back to their normal business, although apparently spending some time in discussions about how to follow up on their discovery. They eventually agreed to form a company of sorts and to petition the crown for a contract to exploit the discovery.[36]

Among the matters occupying the judges of the audiencia was the ongoing question of Colón's claim to have the right under his father's contract with Ferdinand and Isabela to authorize exploratory expedi-

---

No. 1, Cargo de Perlas Comunes, fols. 69–76. A number of undated payments, all without names of the payee, follow this entry. Any of them could be the Chicora pearls.

33. AGI, JU 3, No. 3, fols. 42v, 43v, 49–49v.

34. Anghiera, *Decadas,* II, 595. Juan de Ampiés had seen a "muy señalada" Indian woman at Matienzo's house, as well as tall, well-formed Indian men; Francisco de Avila "knew" that Matienzo had some Indians at his house and was "curing them" of various illnesses; García Camacho said the same (AGI, JU 3, No. 3, fols. 36–36v, 38, 47).

35. Matienzo had a cattle ranch five leagues from Santo Domingo. Ayllón had a flock of sheep on the hacienda Santa Ana half a league from the city (AGI, JU 50, No. 1, fol. 49v).

36. AGI, JU 3, No. 3, fol. 50.

tions—and specifically one proposed by Cristobal de Tapía to Yucatán. The audiencia, consisting of Villalobos, Lebrón, Ayllón, and Matienzo as judges and Cavallero as secretary, met with the royal treasury officials and Colón in the chamber used by the audiencia in the Casas Reales, on Monday, September 2, to deal with this claim. This grouping of the crown's officials, known as the *real acuerdo,* met whenever important policy decisions had to be taken and served to restrict Colón's power. In the end, the majority—who would have been the judges (*oidores*)—decided to uphold a royal order prohibiting voyages that only Colón authorized and to send Ayllón to Spain at government expense to explain their action and the audiencia's opposition to Colón's continued governance.[37]

The accidental partners in the Quejo-Gordillo expedition now began to move to formalize their position. They agreed to prepare a memorial about the discovery and what Ayllón should request in all of their names. They seem also to have agreed to keep Quejo in Santo Domingo by offering him half pay until they could learn the fate of their petition for a contract.[38] To provide legitimacy for their continued possession of the Indians and to safeguard their discovery from claim jumpers as best they could, they took the matter to the *real acuerdo.*

The partners made their petition to the *real acuerdo* on Sunday, September 22, 1521. Because Matienzo and Ayllón were parties to the matter, they seem to have excused themselves, so that the *acuerdo* consisted only of Governor Colón, the licenciados Villalobos and Lebrón, and the royal treasury officials, with Cavallero as notary. The meeting agreed to grant an injunction prohibiting anyone from sailing to the new land, said by the petitioners to be at "about 34 degrees." That order the town crier duly proclaimed in the streets of the city.[39]

On the question of the Indians, the *real acuerdo* deferred action. The petitioners stated that these Indians were cannibals and sodomites, thereby providing the basis for a finding that they should remain slaves. At the same time, Ayllón and Matienzo bowed to the letter of the law that forbade slaving expeditions except to lands

37. Troy Floyd, *The Columbus Dynasty in the Caribbean, 1492–1526* (Albuquerque, N.Mex., 1973), 99–101, 143–45, 200–203, 215; AGI, JU 50, No. 1, fols. 232v–233. For complaints against Colón, see the memorial of the licenciado Lebrón carried by Ayllón [1521] (*DIU,* V, 106–109).

38. AGI, JU 3, No. 3, fols. 49–51.

39. *Ibid.,* fol. 88.

where they were specifically authorized. They also took account of the climate of opinion Ayllón was likely to find at the emperor's court, where there was opposition to the further enslavement of Indians except under unusual conditions. To accommodate all of these pressures, the petitioners said that the Indians, despite their abominations, should be returned to their homes when it was convenient. Official inaction in ordering an immediate return could thus be understood as agreement to hold the Indians in slavery until some later time when the petitioners might be able to send them.

The fate of these Indians is shortly told. Some of Matienzo's died from disease. As many as fourteen others fled into the interior of the island. Another survived as late as 1526, when, it was said, he was a pearl diver at Cubagua. Ayllón later liked people to think, though he never flatly said or tried to prove, that he took better care of his Indians. Only one, however, is known to have survived to 1526: Francisco ("el Chicorano"), the servant Ayllón took to Spain and then to North America. The fates of the other Indians can be surmised from what Martyr says on the basis of testimony by the dean of the Cathedral of Concepción de la Vega. Martyr reports that they were desperate and went about eating decaying garbage, especially dead puppies and donkeys.[40] Most must have died within a short time of their transfer from Santo Domingo to Concepción de la Vega, where Ayllón and his in-laws, the Becerras, had agricultural and other interests. Ayllón's suggestion that he took good care of his Indians looks to be largely a fiction intended to show that he was an upholder of royal policy whereas Matienzo was not.

Ayllón's preparations for his trip to Spain occupied him into October. On the eighth, he picked up five hundred pesos de oro from the royal treasury for his expenses. He also collected the fifty thousand maravedis due him as the second third of his salary for 1521. Then, on October 30, he registered two items with Juan Rodriguez de Zarco, master of the ship *San Nicolás,* on which he planned to travel as a passenger. One entry was for 2,200 pesos de oro, probably to be understood as a unit of account rather than the coin, and fourteen marks (about seven pounds) of pearls, both probably in one chest. A second entry was for 150 pesos that Ayllón was carrying for an unnamed third party. In addition, at about the same time, he registered 440 pesos de oro with Alonso de Algava, master of *La Madalena,* which

40. *Ibid.,* fols. 8, 35, 62v–63, 66, 69; Anghiera, *Decadas,* II, 595.

also was bound for Spain. It is not clear if he ever recovered that last shipment. *La Madalena* was captured by French privateers near Cape Saint Vincent, on the coast of southern Portugal, as it approached Spain.[41]

Even without the 440 pesos de oro shipped on *La Madalena,* Ayllón landed at Seville with a small fortune of 2,640 pesos de oro, and pearls worth several hundred ducats at least. Some of these assets were needed for his trip expenses, but many of them were probably bound for the avaricious hands of Charles V's principal Flemish advisers and for Ayllón and his partners' various patrons, who had shown themselves zealous in the pursuit of a share of the wealth in the Indies.

When Ayllón reached Spain is not known, but the sight of the sandy shores on each side of the entrance to the Guadalquivir River, and of San Lucar de Barameda's whitewashed houses and the church towers with their stork's nests must have been welcome indeed after the late-fall crossing.

At the time that Ayllón reached Spain, Charles V had not yet returned to the peninsula to reassert his royal authority in the aftermath of the Comunero and Germanía rebellions of 1520–1521. Royal control was secure, however, or being secured, in the spring of 1522. Because Ayllón's mission was to convey to court the complaints about the ways Colón was usurping royal power in taking cognizance of certain types of legal cases that were supposed to be heard by the audiencia, he seems to have proceeded directly from Seville to court to make the complaints known. Once there he became part of ongoing discussions about government in the Antilles and how the crown could bring an end to the relative chaos in the lines of authority which had resulted from the shifting politics of the period 1506–1520 and from Colón's resumption of his offices after 1520. No actions could be taken until the emperor was again in Spain, but in the spring of 1522 the groundwork was laid for the orders issued the next spring.

Charles V landed at Santander on July 16, 1522, accompanied by many of the Flemish advisers whose foreignness had offended the Castilians who took part in the rebellions of 1520–1521. He also brought an escort of four thousand German soldiers. That force, and the victories of his supporters in Castile during the previous two

41. AGI, CD 1050, No. 1, fols. 142v, 147, 169; register, *San Nicolás,* AGI, CT 5776, No. 2, R. 1, fol. 8v. On *La Madalena,* see AGI, IG 420, Book 9, fols. 27, 126, and AGI, IG 1202, No. 24.

years, meant that the consolidation of royal power and the union of the kingdoms of Castile and Aragon that the Catholic kings had won were secure after nearly seventeen years of political turmoil.[42] Once resident in Valladolid, Charles V turned his attention not only to peninsular affairs but also to the Indies, as the Spaniards called their empire in the Americas.

Besides the complaint that Ayllón carried on behalf of the audiencia, the crown had received many others about Colón's activities after his return to Española in November, 1520. Some represented the vengeance of disappointed seekers after benefits Colón could no longer bestow because the islands' economies were still in transition from their earlier mining phase, using native labor, to a phase based on sugar and hides, using imported black slaves. Some complaints arose from Colón's actions against persons long established in jobs or privileges but not of his political group. To all the grievances, Father Bartolomé de las Casas and his agents added their formidable voices. Las Casas believed that Colón had not adequately supported or defended the missions the Dominicans and Franciscans had established on the Venezuelan coast between 1516 and 1520.[43]

The outcome of the deliberations by the crown's officials was a reprimand directed to Colón and a series of orders overruling what the crown saw as actions exceeding his powers.[44] Other royal orders cleared up the lines of government authority by unambiguously establishing the audiencia's power and by ordering the completion of the various investigations that had been ordered in 1516 but that had not been concluded. Ayllón was selected to deal with Puerto Rico's government.

The first order to Ayllón regarding the Puerto Rican administration carried the date April 24, 1523. Styled a "commissioned judge," he was told to see that the heirs of the former royal treasurer Andrés de Haro received justice. He was also instructed to complete the residencia of Sancho Velázquez, justicia mayor from 1514 to 1519, take the accounts and residencia of the royal treasury officials, and take the residencia of the licenciado Antonio de la Gama, justicia mayor from 1519 to 1520.[45] In brief, he was to complete all pending investigations

42. John H. Elliott, *Imperial Spain, 1469–1716* (London, 1963), 149.
43. Floyd, *The Columbus Dynasty,* 215.
44. *Ibid.*
45. AGI, IG 420, Book 9, fols. 127v–128, 141v–142v, 147v–149v, 132v–133v. For background, see Floyd, *The Columbus Dynasty,* 108, 129, 147, 187–89, 210.

and audits and bring order to the untidy mess on Puerto Rico. The Ayllón mission to Puerto Rico, reinforced by similar actions for Cuba and by Colón's recall in August, 1523, helped to end Colón's quasi-seignorial regime and opened the way for the crown to exercise direct authority in the islands through the appointment of all officials. Ayllón's mission on behalf of the audiencia had borne the hoped-for fruit.

Equally fruitful was his quest on behalf of himself, Matienzo, and Cavallero for a license to explore further and to exploit the discovery Quejo and Gordillo had made in 1521. Thanks to Martyr's account, something is known about how Ayllón went about securing that license, although in the end his former partners were excluded and only he held the contract for the discovery.

Martyr says that he had Ayllón and his servant, Francisco, as house guests during at least a part of the licenciado's stay in Valladolid. Now and again, during a period of what must have been at least several months if not a year or more, Martyr talked about the new discovery with Ayllón and Francisco. He also discussed the voyage and discovery with the bachillero Castro, who was named dean of the Cathedral of Concepción de la Vega, on Española, at about this time. Castro had been on the island when the voyagers of 1521 returned. Martyr did not get to consult Ayllón's lengthy memorial but learned some of its contents from his other informants.[46] He made a set of notes about the discovery and the ethnography and geography of the area visited in 1521. His account provides important evidence of the way Ayllón altered the tale he was telling to make it support his appeal for a license to explore and settle the new discovery.

According to Ayllón's story at court in 1523, seven persons fitted two ships that sailed from Puerto Plata to search for Indians in the Bahamas, but they failed to find any because the islands had been picked clean by other Spaniards. Not wishing to be mocked for coming home empty-handed, the crews set off on a northwesterly course[47] but then were hit by a storm that lasted two days and blew them ashore near a "high promontory." There followed the scene on the beach, several days of exploration, the movement of the ships to a better anchorage, and finally, the capturing of the trusting natives by

46. Anghiera, *Decadas,* II, 595–96, 729.

47. Martyr says they sailed toward the constellation Orion, which would have been to the northwest.

the Spaniards who, to quote Martyr, "violated the faith due with hospitality."[48]

Ayllón told his hearers that his discovery was at the "height of the same degrees and identical parallels" as Andalucia.[49] In support of that, he described trees and plants similar to those in southern Spain, confirming what anyone who had read Ptolemy's *Geography* would believe: "that all animals, and all plants likewise, have a similarity under the same kind of climate or under similar weather conditions, that is when under the same parallels, or when situated at the same distance from either pole."[50] Although Ayllón did not say so, Martyr guessed that the new discovery formed part of a landmass connected with the cod fisheries, that is, Newfoundland and Nova Scotia, discovered in the 1480s and 1490s by the Bristol voyagers, including John Cabot.[51]

Ayllón completed his tale by recounting with his customary enthusiasm the region's potential human, sylvan, agricultural, and mineral resources. The point, quite clearly, was that this was a land just waiting for colonization. It could be settled by farmers, and the Spaniards could engage in trade with the Indians. A military conquest was unnecessary. Further, Ayllón had the financial resources to carry out a colonial enterprise. A man of the law with no prior military experience, he was less likely to stray from the king's commands and engage in military actions against the Indians like those of a Hernán Cortes or a Pedrárias. If he succeeded, the prize would be a new Andalucia, a new province rich in viticulture or at least the potential for it, olives (Ayllón even claimed, according to Martyr, that there were native olive trees that "once grafted" would grow as in Spain), gems, deerskins for the pelt trade, and pagans waiting to be converted. The lure was irresistible, especially if persons like Lope de Conchillos, the emperor's secretary, supported the petition. Matienzo and Cavallero were quietly dropped as partners. One man, Ayllón himself, would be the king's agent for the new venture.

48. Anghiera, *Decadas,* II, 593–95, with quotation from pp. 594–95.

49. *Ibid.,* 595–96. In Ptolemaic geography a "parallel" was an east-west band of varying north-south width determined by an arbitrarily selected interval between the lengths of the longest day as one proceeds north from the equator. Andalucia falls within Ptolemy's tenth parallel, which begins at 36° north and ends at 38°35′ north (Claudius Ptolemaeus, *Geography of Claudius Ptolemy,* trans. and ed. Edward Luther Stevenson [New York, 1932], 41).

50. Ptolemaeus, *Geography,* 31–32.

51. Anghiera, *Decadas,* II, 595. For the Bristol voyages, see David B. Quinn, *England and the Discovery of America, 1481–1620* (New York, 1974), 6–13, 18–22.

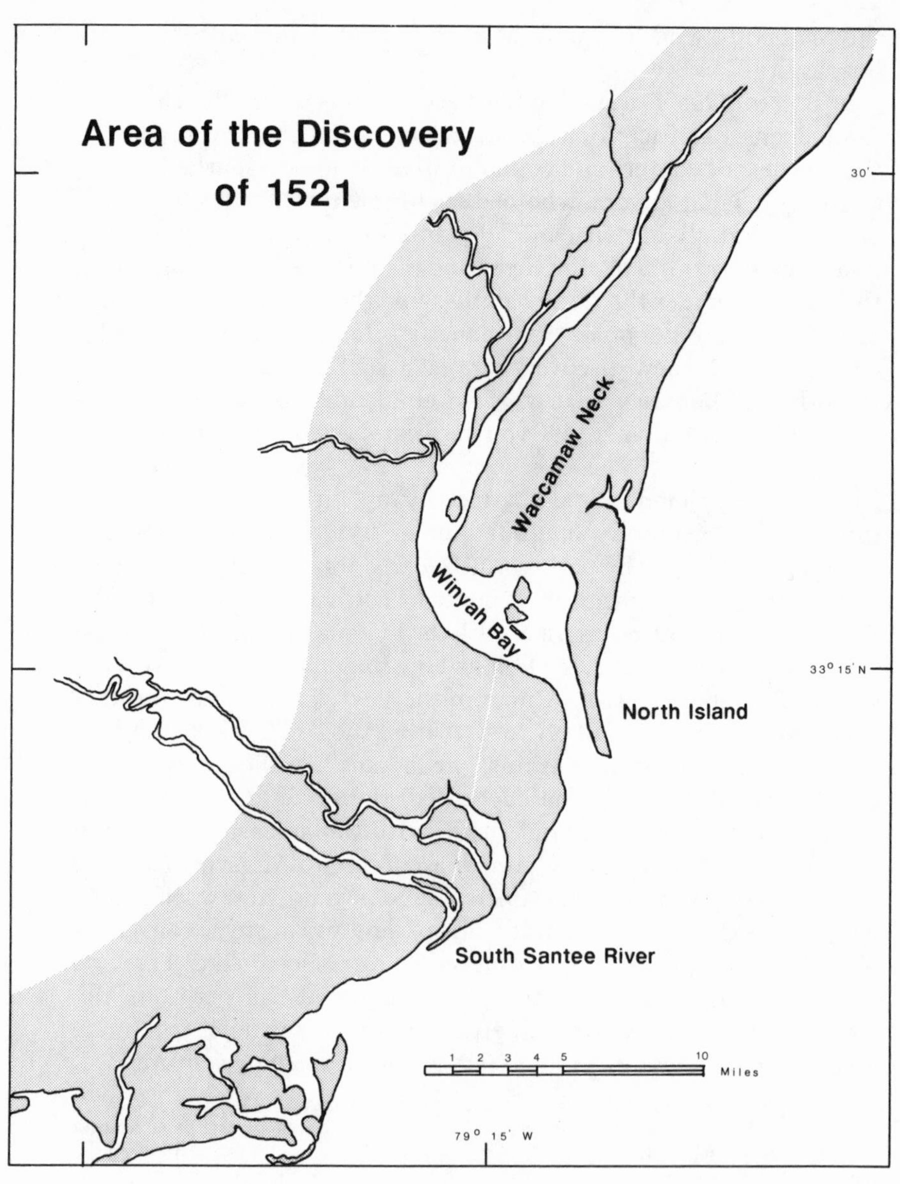

Area of the Discovery of 1521
30'
Waccamaw Neck
Winyah Bay
33° 15' N
North Island
South Santee River
1 2 3 4 5 10
Miles
79° 15' W

Map 1

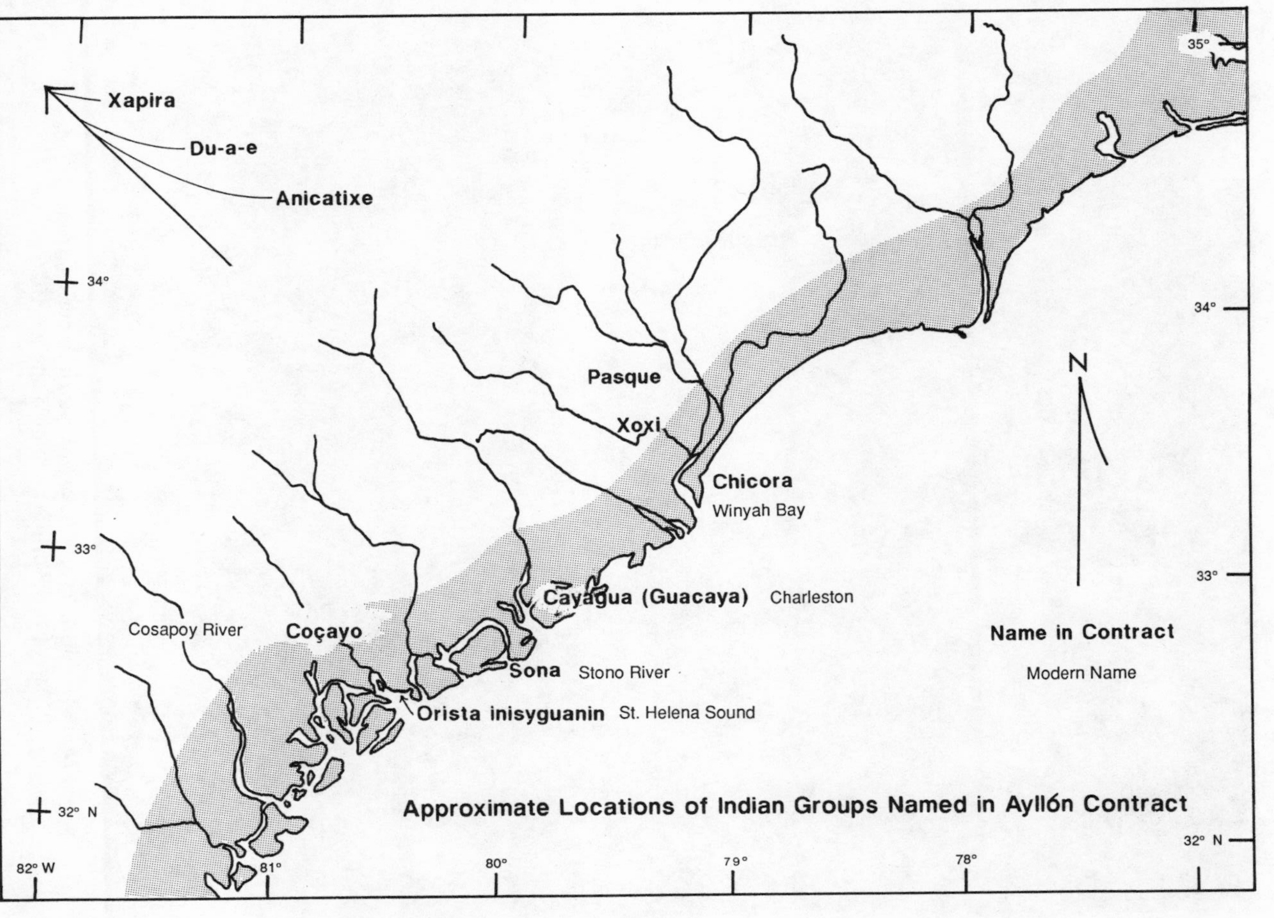
Xapira
Du-a-e
Anicatixe
34°
33°
32° N
82° W
81°
80°
79°
78°
35°
34°
33°
32° N
N
Pasque
Xoxi
Chicora
Winyah Bay
Cayagua (Guacaya)
Charleston
Cosapoy River
Coçayo
Sona
Stono River
Orista inisyguanin
St. Helena Sound
Name in Contract
Modern Name
Approximate Locations of Indian Groups Named in Ayllón Contract

MAP 2

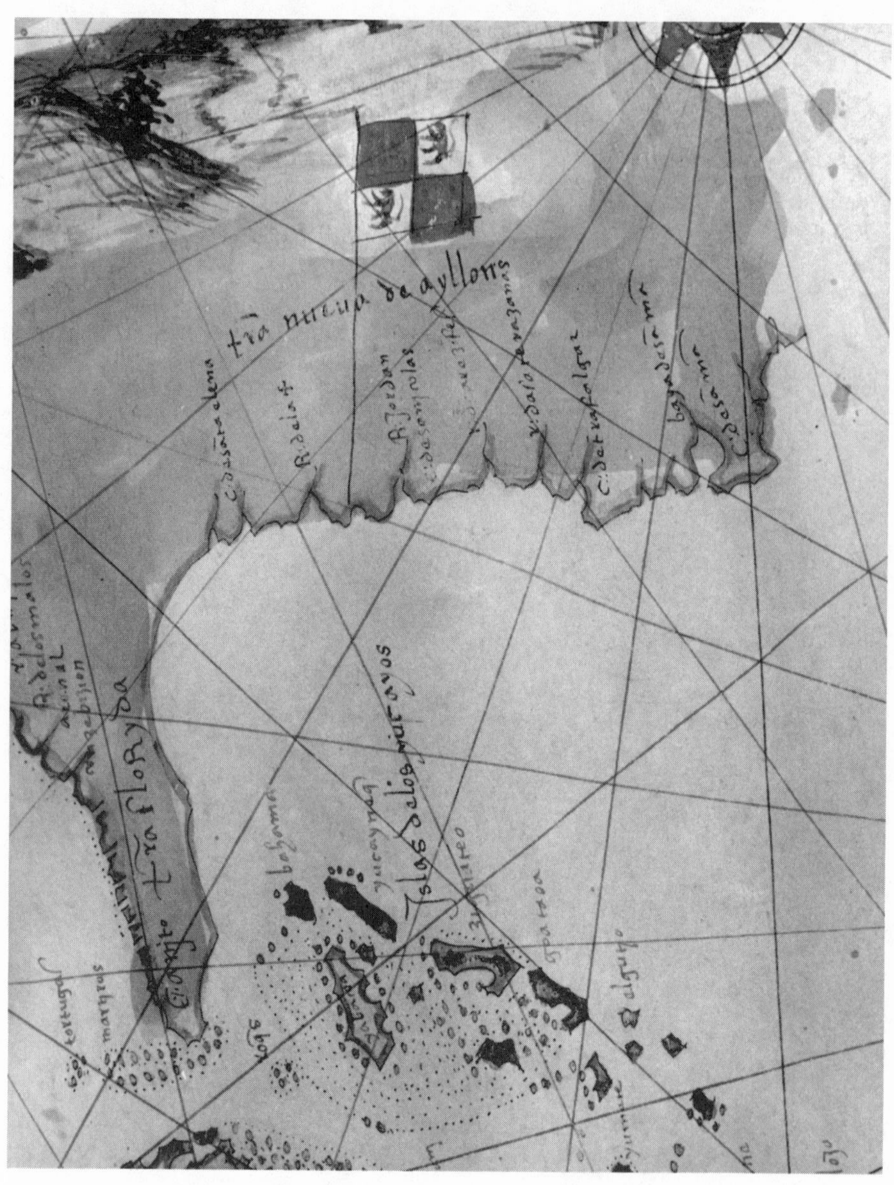

MAP 3 Southeastern Coast of North America, from "Map of the World," by Juan Vespucci, 1526.
Hispanic Society of America, New York

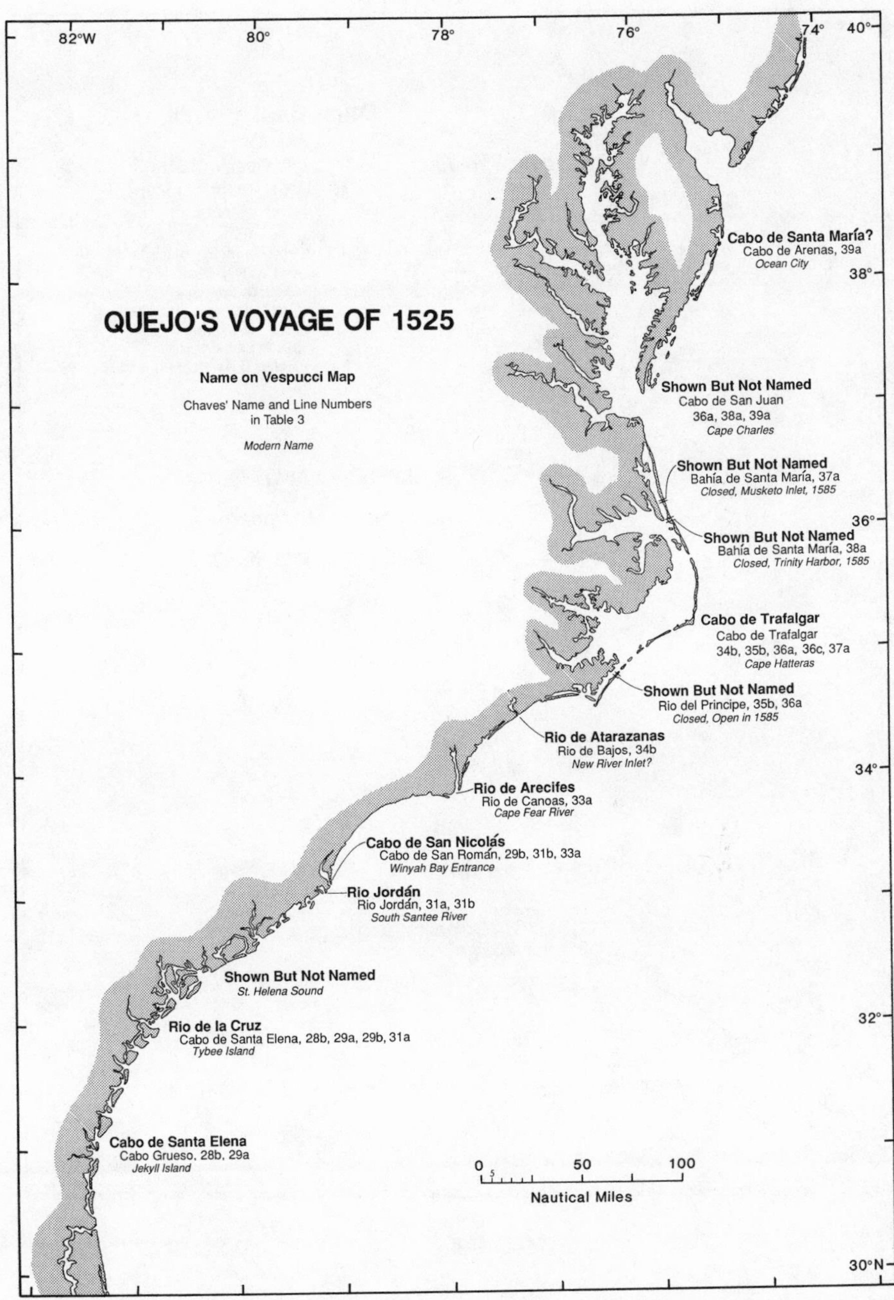
82°W
80°
78°
76°
74°
40°
38°
36°
34°
32°
30°N
QUEJO'S VOYAGE OF 1525
Name on Vespucci Map
Chaves' Name and Line Numbers in Table 3
Modern Name
Cabo de Santa María?
Cabo de Arenas, 39a
Ocean City
Shown But Not Named
Cabo de San Juan
36a, 38a, 39a
Cape Charles
Shown But Not Named
Bahía de Santa María, 37a
Closed, Musketo Inlet, 1585
Shown But Not Named
Bahía de Santa María, 38a
Closed, Trinity Harbor, 1585
Cabo de Trafalgar
Cabo de Trafalgar
34b, 35b, 36a, 36c, 37a
Cape Hatteras
Shown But Not Named
Rio del Principe, 35b, 36a
Closed, Open in 1585
Rio de Atarazanas
Rio de Bajos, 34b
New River Inlet?
Rio de Arecifes
Rio de Canoas, 33a
Cape Fear River
Cabo de San Nicolás
Cabo de San Román, 29b, 31b, 33a
Winyah Bay Entrance
Rio Jordán
Rio Jordán, 31a, 31b
South Santee River
Shown But Not Named
St. Helena Sound
Rio de la Cruz
Cabo de Santa Elena, 28b, 29a, 29b, 31a
Tybee Island
Cabo de Santa Elena
Cabo Grueso, 28b, 29a
Jekyll Island
0 5 50 100
Nautical Miles

MAP 4

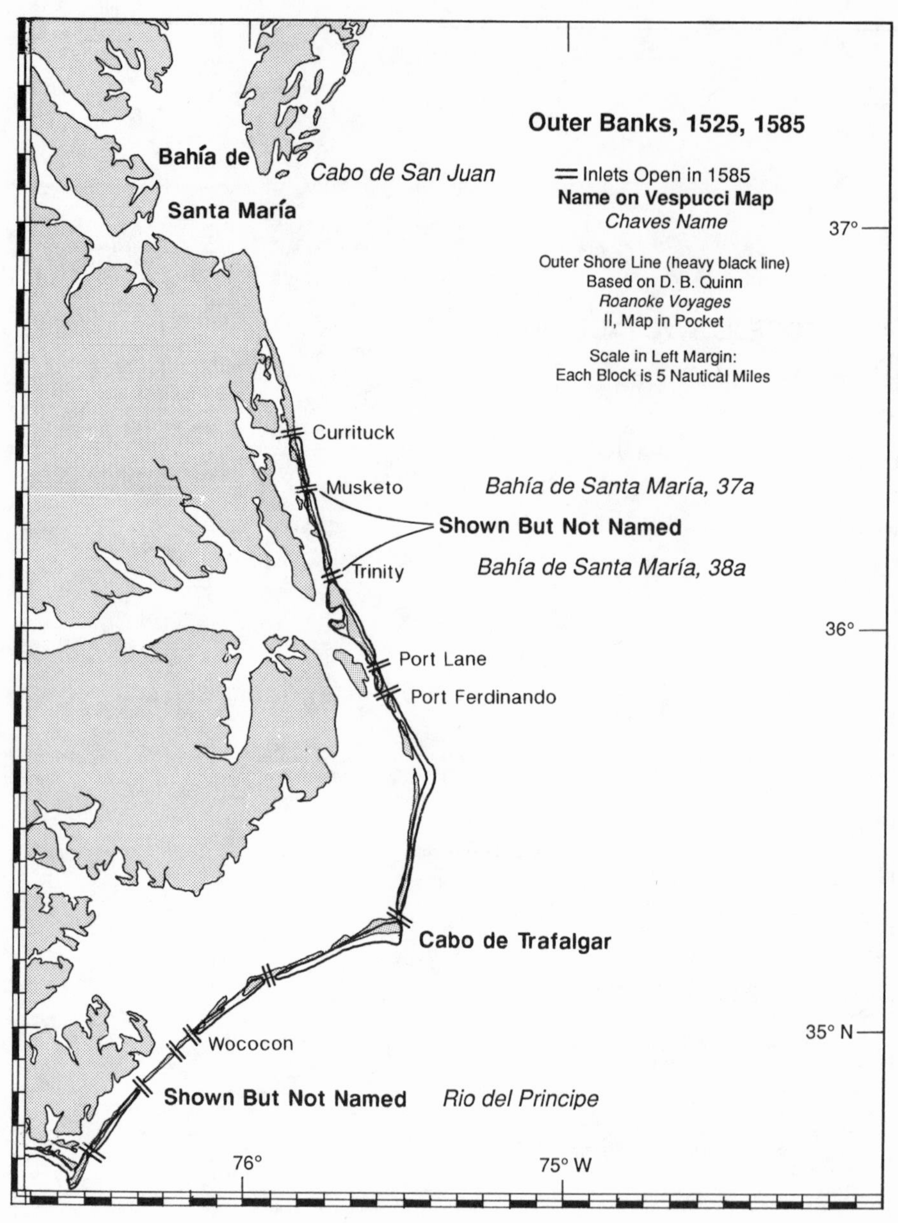
Outer Banks, 1525, 1585
═ Inlets Open in 1585
Name on Vespucci Map
Chaves Name
Outer Shore Line (heavy black line)
Based on D. B. Quinn
Roanoke Voyages
II, Map in Pocket
Scale in Left Margin:
Each Block is 5 Nautical Miles
Bahía de
Santa María
Cabo de San Juan
37°
Currituck
Musketo
Bahía de Santa María, 37a
Shown But Not Named
Trinity
Bahía de Santa María, 38a
36°
Port Lane
Port Ferdinando
Cabo de Trafalgar
35° N
Wococon
Shown But Not Named
Rio del Principe
76°
75° W

MAP 5

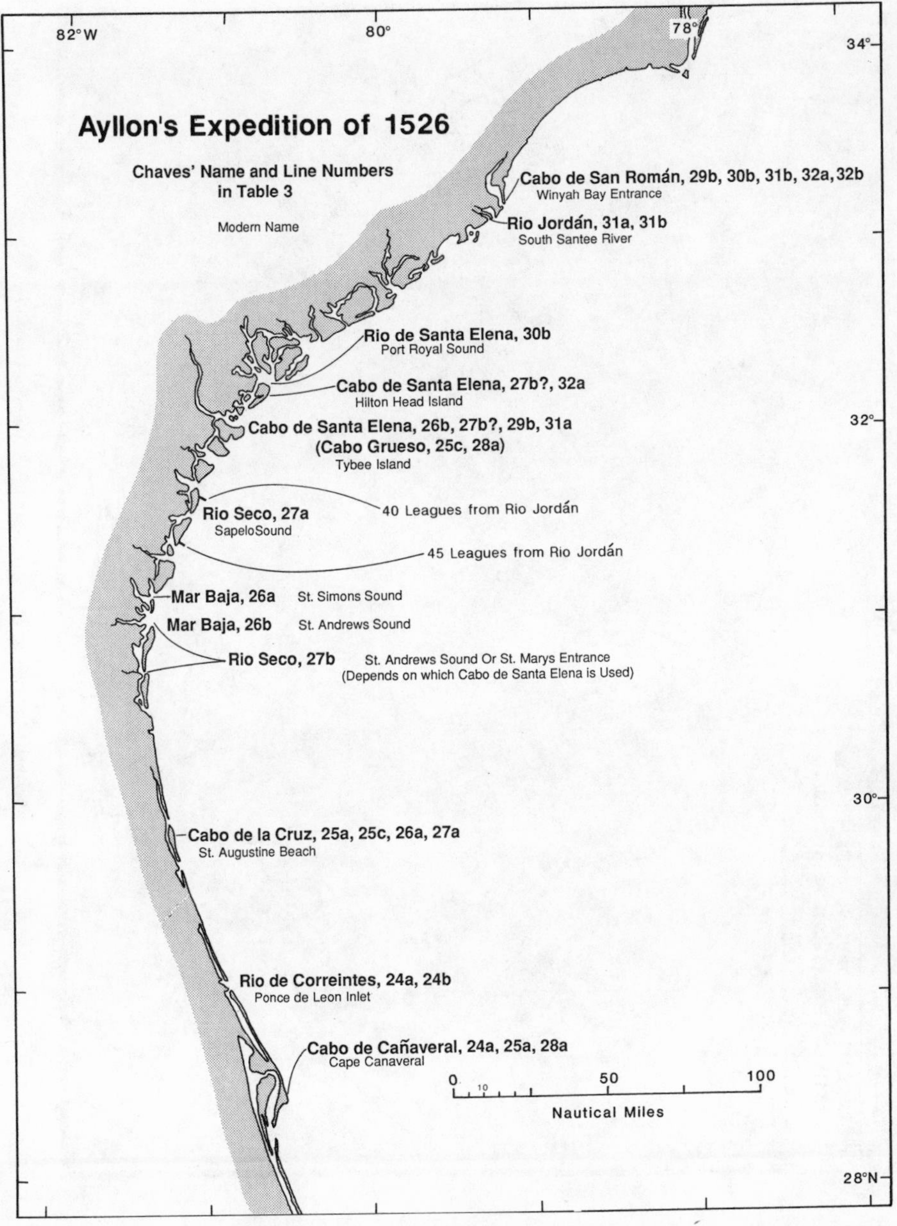

82° W
80°
78°
34°
32°
30°
28°N
Aylln's Expedition of 1526
Chaves' Name and Line Numbers in Table 3
Modern Name
Cabo de San Román, 29b, 30b, 31b, 32a, 32b
Winyah Bay Entrance
Rio Jordán, 31a, 31b
South Santee River
Rio de Santa Elena, 30b
Port Royal Sound
Cabo de Santa Elena, 27b?, 32a
Hilton Head Island
Cabo de Santa Elena, 26b, 27b?, 29b, 31a
(Cabo Grueso, 25c, 28a)
Tybee Island
40 Leagues from Rio Jordán
Rio Seco, 27a
SapeloSound
45 Leagues from Rio Jordán
Mar Baja, 26a
St. Simons Sound
Mar Baja, 26b
St. Andrews Sound
Rio Seco, 27b
St. Andrews Sound Or St. Marys Entrance
(Depends on which Cabo de Santa Elena is Used)
Cabo de la Cruz, 25a, 25c, 26a, 27a
St. Augustine Beach
Rio de Correintes, 24a, 24b
Ponce de Leon Inlet
Cabo de Cañaveral, 24a, 25a, 28a
Cape Canaveral
0 10 50 100
Nautical Miles

Map 6

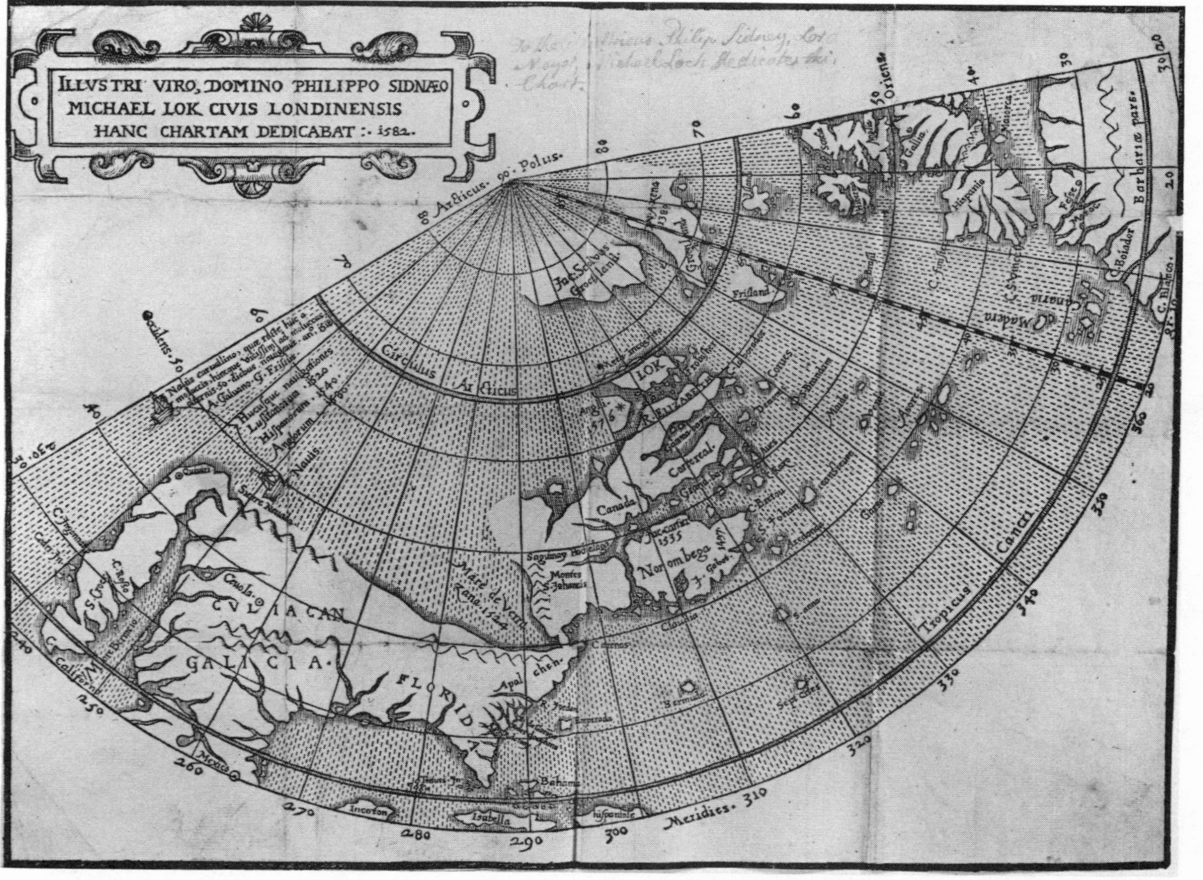

MAP 7 North America, by Michael Lok, Printed, 1582
John Carter Brown Library at Brown University

MAP 8 Western Hemisphere, from "World Map," by Battista Agnese
John Carter Brown Library at Brown University

MAP 9 "Novae Insulae, XVII, Nova Tabula," by Sebastian Münster, 1544
Newberry Library, Chicago

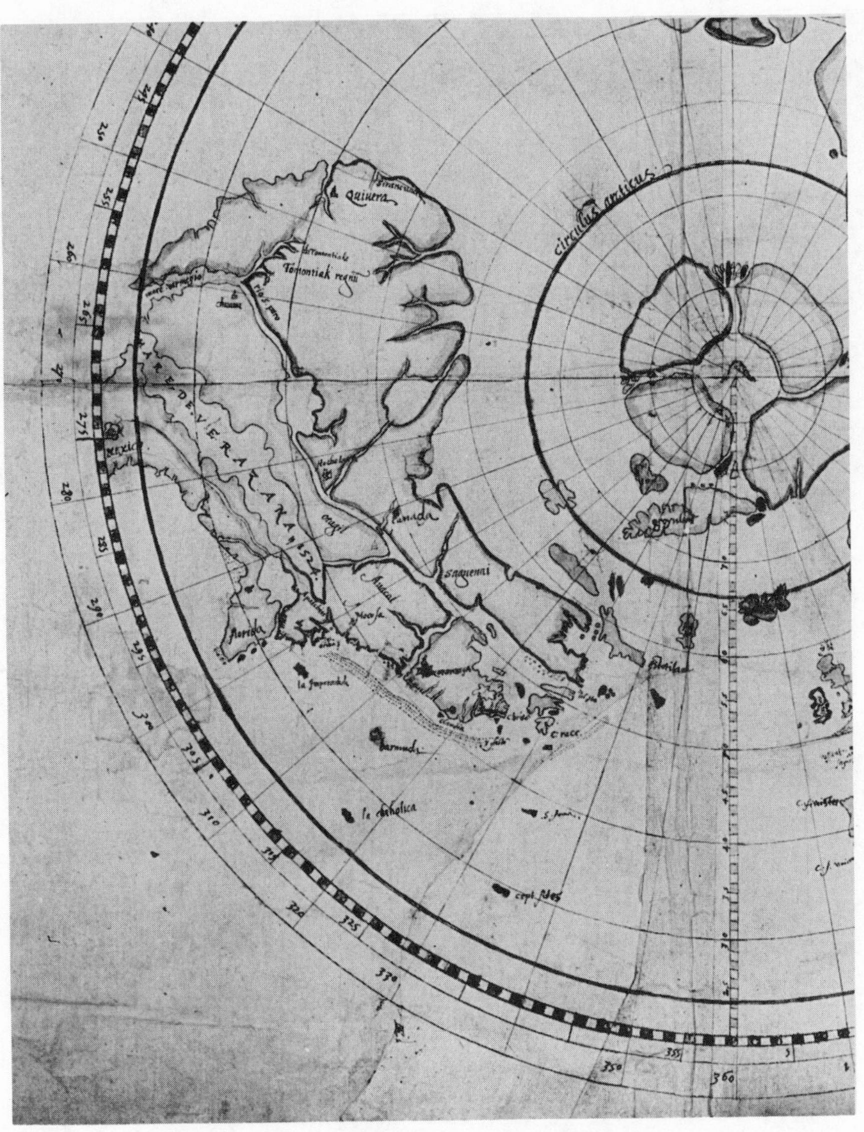

Map 10 "Humfray Gylbert knight his charte"
[by John Dee, *ca.* 1582–1583].
Rare Book Department, Free Library of Philadelphia

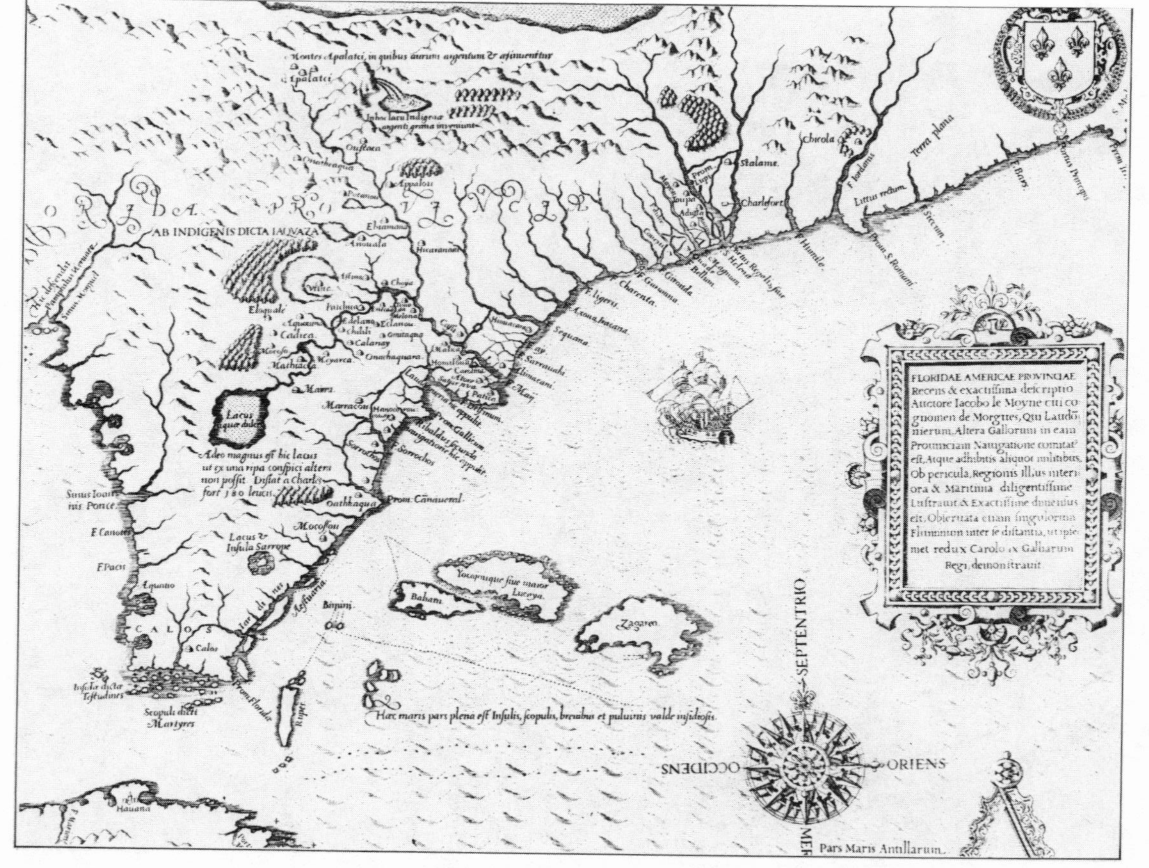

MAP 11 "Floridae Americae Provinciae," by Jacques Le Moyne, engraved by Theodore de Bry, 1590.

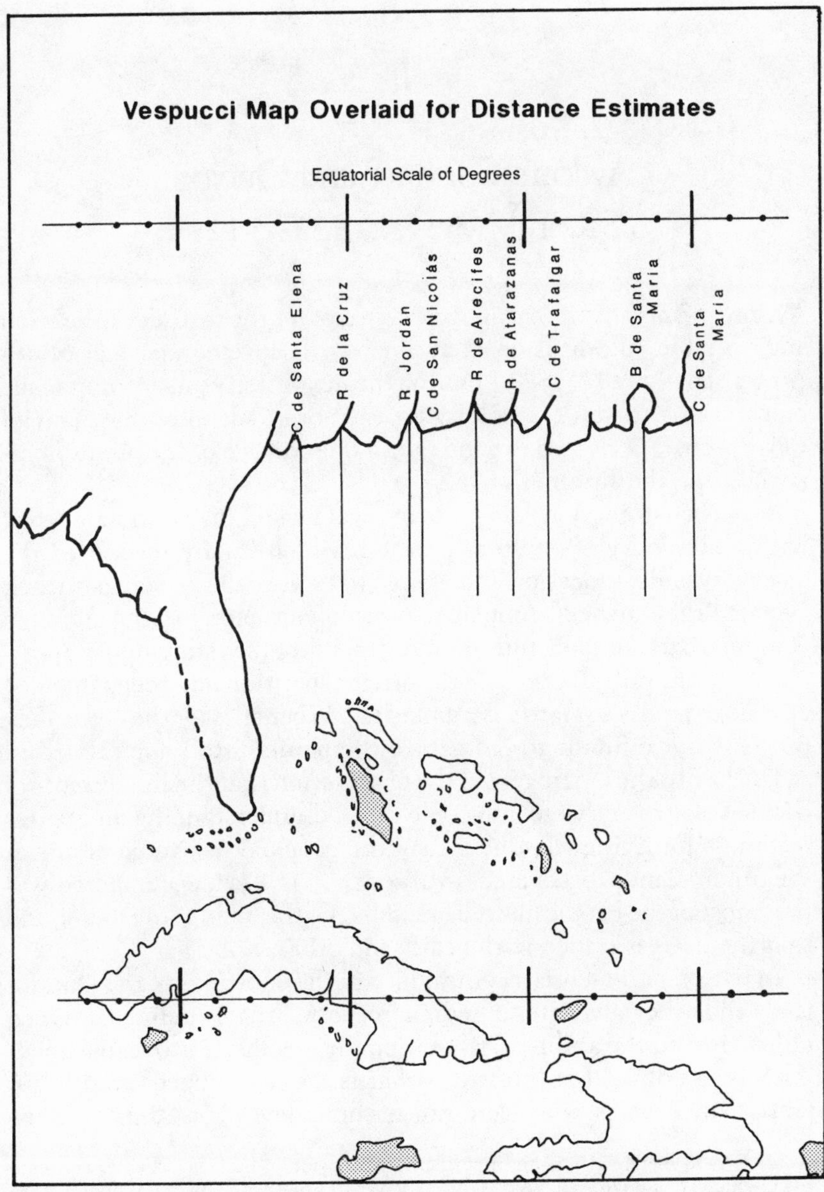

Vespucci Map Overlaid for Distance Estimates
Equatorial Scale of Degrees
C de Santa Elena
R de la Cruz
R Jordán
C de San Nicolás
R de Arecifes
R de Atarazanas
C de Trafalgar
B de Santa María
C de Santa María

MAP 12

II

Ayllón's Contract and Quejo's Second Voyage, 1523–1525

Ayllón and his sovereign signed a contract for the further exploration and possible colonization of the newly discovered coast of North America on June 12, 1523.[1] During the next three years, Ayllón made preparations to settle a colony on the coast. An important part of those preparations was to send Quejo on a voyage of further exploration during the summer of 1525.

As was customary with grants of royal favors, the contract opened with a summary of Ayllón's petition, which briefly recounted the discovery and its location and offered to explore the new area further. The text then moved to consider a variety of topics, mixing grants to Ayllón, statements of intent, and general policy statements apparently haphazardly, rather as if the original petition had been amended at various points to clarify items and to add benefits for the petitioner. But it is not difficult to reorganize the points into a logical series.

The key to the entire text is the observation that the inhabitants of the new discovery were a "people of good understanding and better readiness for living *en policía* than the people of Española or any of the other islands discovered until today."[2] The evidence offered was that most of the people obeyed one ruler, Datha, "king" of Du-a-e, and that the natives traded with pearls and other things.

To live *en policía* was a central idea in the doctrines of the Dominicans and other advocates of Indian freedom. Broadly defined, *vivir en policía* meant the ability to live rationally (*i.e.*, like Europeans) under one's own political authorities—that is, to be civilized, even if not Christian. Peoples who were not natural slaves according to Aris-

1. *DII*, XIV, 504–515, is an imperfect transcription of the 1541 copy of this contract, which is found in AGI, PAT 21, No. 2, R. 4, Pieza 8. Another printed version of the same manuscript is in *DII*, XXII, 79–93. Other manuscript copies (and their dates): AGI, JU 3, No. 3, fols. 9v–17 (1526), AGI, SD 11, No. 43 bis, fols. 2–10 (1562), AGI, IG 415, Book 1, fols. 32–35 (*ca.* 1565). I have used *DII*, XIV, 504–15, but checked it against the manuscript copies, preferring those in JU 3, No. 3, over the later copies.

2. *DII*, XIV, 504.

totle's definitions were able to live *en policía* and thus were entitled to treatment as equals, not as inferiors. The applicable law was the *jus gentium*, or the law of nations, the intermediate of the three levels of law recognized in medieval jurisprudence. As Francisco de Vitoria was later to make clear, the law of nations required that Spanish contacts with sovereign native states be by peaceful trade and peaceful preaching of the gospel. The natives could not decline such approaches although they might deny Europeans the right to acquire land.[3] It was precisely overtures of this nature to the Indians of North America that Ayllón's contract enjoined him to make, because the objectives that the emperor had in mind were the conversion of their souls, their willing acceptance of his dominion, and trade.

For that reason and because little was known about the new area, Ayllón's chief job was to explore the discovery further and to acquire more information about its inhabitants, their resources, and the missionary and commercial activity that would be effective for bringing them into the Spanish empire. He was given a term of one year, to the summer of 1524, to begin explorations that were to stop when his people had traversed eight hundred leagues (about 2,560 nautical miles, if the maritime league of 3.1998 nautical miles is meant) or when they reached areas already explored by other Spaniards or areas that, if to the north, fell within the demarcation of the king of Portugal under the terms of the Treaty of Tordesillas of 1494. Making reference to a then-current controversy with the Portuguese over possession of the Spice Islands, Charles V instructed Ayllón to guard completely what the crowns had agreed.[4] In the event that Ayllón or his agents found a strait, they were to explore it thoroughly. The contract provided a term of three years from the beginning of exploration for those activities and for the preparation and submission of a report on the land, its peoples, and its resources.

The contract said that the area Ayllón's men had discovered in 1521 was at 35°, 36°, and 37° north latitude. Thirty-seven degrees north

3. J. Lechner, "El concepto de 'policía' y su presencia en la obra de los primeros historiadores de Indias," *Revista de Indias,* XLI (1981), 398–99, 408; Francisco de Vitoria, *De Indis (1539); as, On the Indians Lately Discovered,* trans. John Pawley Bate, in James B. Scott, *The Spanish Origin of International Law, Part I, Francisco de Vitoria and His Law of Nations* (Oxford, 1934), Appendix A, xli–xlii.

4. Frances G. Davenport (ed.), *European Treaties Bearing on the History of the United States and Its Dependencies* (4 vols.; Washington, D.C., 1917–37), I, 118–20. For the controversy with the Portuguese, see *El tratado de Tordesillas y su proyección* (2 vols.; Valladolid, 1973), I, 119–84.

passes through the center of Andalucia; 36° north marks the southern boundary of Ptolemy's tenth "parallel," within which Andalucia falls.[5] Ayllón had deliberately moved the area of the discovery from 33°30′ north to higher latitudes in order to impress his Spanish hearers with its potential. He thus completed the process begun before the *real acuerdo* at Santo Domingo in September, 1521, when the location was given as "toward 34°," *en treintaquatro grados.*

Almost as interesting as this bit of fraud was the list of Indian "provinces and islands" included in Ayllón's grant. It implicitly extended his grant southward to 32°30′ north and gave the lie to his stated latitudes. In place of the sketchy twelve names mentioned to Peter Martyr, Ayllón provided the king with nineteen, two of them linked to other words in phrases. The first province Ayllón listed was Du-a-e, under the rule of Datha, the gigantic king who dominated the rest of the provinces, if Martyr had his facts correct. The others were Chicora, Xapira, Yta tancal, Anicatixe, Cocayo, Guacaya, Xoxi, Sona, Pasqui, Aranbe, Xamunanbe, Huaque, Tancaca, Yenhohol, Pahor, Yamiscaron, Orista inisiguanin, and Anoxa.

By using clues supplied by Martyr's account and the twentieth-century work of John Swanton, it is possible to locate many of these places approximately on a modern map.[6] From south to north, there were Orista inisiguanin, which was near the mouth of the modern Edisto River; Cocayo, which was on the upper Edisto or Cosapoy River just to the west of Orista; Sona, which was near modern Stono Inlet; Guacaya, which should be called Cayagua, that is, what the English recorded as Kiawa, and was in the Charleston area; and Chicora, which was on Winyah Bay. Upriver from Chicora was Xoxi, and beyond that Pasqui. Northwest of the bay lay Du-a-e and Anicatixe. Near them was Xapira, the place where gems and pearls were to be found (Map 2).

To support Ayllón's exclusive privileges, the king agreed that he would issue no permits to explorers or traders for the area covered by the contract during the year that the contract allowed for preparing explorations. The king promised that if he issued permits for explora-

5. Ptolemaeus, *Geography,* 41.

6. John R. Swanton, *Early History of the Creek Indians and Their Neighbors* (Washington, D.C., 1922), 37–38. A number of Swanton's identifications are not valid. He based the spelling of names on the imperfect copies of Ayllón's contract found in the *DII.* My study of the manuscripts has established the spellings and phrases given here.

tion during the following six years, they would be for the "last" (*i.e.*, the most distant?) two hundred leagues, or 640 nautical miles, that Ayllón discovered under the contract. But in an escape clause, the king also said that should other persons be authorized to go to the areas where Ayllón was working, that would be construed as being without prejudice to Ayllón's contractual rights. The licenciado could not have been very pleased. He had asked for a six-year monopoly on exploration and trade, on the grounds that others might undo the arrangements he made with the Indians. Evidently he did not want other Spaniards moving in on his trade or causing the sorts of trouble with the Indians that slave raiders had brought the Franciscan and Dominican missions on the coast of Venezuela in 1520.[7] Charles V, on the other hand, did not wish to tie his own hands or, one might guess, those of his principal ministers, who were important patrons to lesser officials in the New World.

Ayllón received permission to build one or more forts or strong houses to protect the persons he left to develop trade with the Indians. A son could be named the warder of one fort, at a salary of 100,000 maravedis per year (267 ducats per year, roughly). Ayllón, however, was under no obligation to create any posts or settlements.

Another right, which was also a duty, was to send clergy to the new land to preach the gospel. Ayllón could choose whom he wished but had to supply them with the appropriate equipment for saying mass. He also had to see that each ship he sent to explore the area had a chaplain. The king provided for the use of the tithe on the produce of the new land to support the missionaries and the construction of churches and of a Franciscan monastery. According to the contract, no bishops would be established until all this had been achieved.

A final obligation was to see that no division (*repartimiento*) of the Indians took place and that they were well treated and paid for any labor they performed. On March 18, 1520, the king had ordered the Indians in the Antilles freed from the encomienda system as current holders died.[8] He was trying, as well, to undo Cortes' distribution of encomiendas in New Spain. Royal policy was to keep the Indians under their own rulers and directly under the crown, especially Indians able to live *en policía.* To do that was both morally correct accord-

7. *DII,* XIV, 507–508. For the Venezuelan affair, see Floyd, *The Columbus Dynasty,* 155, 172, 204–207.

8. Floyd, *The Columbus Dynasty,* 183.

ing to the Dominicans and politically and economically to the crown's advantage in that it prevented the creation of quasi-seignorial territories and assured the crown of tribute revenues.

Set against Ayllón's duties, some of which—like the building of forts and the selection of clergy—were also privileges, was a long list of noneconomic and economic privileges. Ayllón's noneconomic privileges began with the use of the title of *alguazil mayor* (high sheriff) by him and his heirs forever. He and a successor could take the title of adelantado in commemoration of his service in advancing the frontiers of empire. Ayllón was to be governor during his lifetime and, with the concurrence of the king's treasury officials, judge in the distribution of water and lands. In the awareness that he might die before the terms of the contract were carried out, he could name an heir or other successor to complete them, with that person enjoying full rights under the contract. The king promised to issue all necessary orders to allow Ayllón to implement the contract.

Among his economic privileges was the right of duty-free export from Spain of all ships, men, materials, weapons, and the like that he might need for exploration and trade, or for his own household. For the three years of the exploration period and an additional three beyond, he received the exclusive right to trade or barter with the Indians *"if they were willing"* (emphasis added) for gold, silver, pearls, and gemstones and any other gems and things of value, paying only a tenth as a tax. Were he to get the natives to cultivate silk—and he planned to introduce what was needed for that, along with masters to teach the art—he would receive five hundred ducats a year from the king's revenues from the industry. Silk was a royal monopoly in Granada, which provided the model for Ayllón's anticipated production.

Ayllón had exclusive rights to the fisheries of the new discovery for his lifetime. The king promised to award two more limited fisheries to his heirs forever. Clearly Ayllón envisioned his discovery to carry title to areas similar to the cod fisheries, then already well known off Newfoundland. The fisheries privilege also covered pearl beds, which existed at Xapira.

Ayllón's grant included a square of land fifteen leagues, or as many as forty-eight miles, on a side over which he might exercise complete economic control but possess no rights of jurisdiction, that is, no seignorial rights. He could select his tract of land without any temporal or other conditions; at least none are spelled out in the contract.

Ayllón could also trade for slaves found among the natives, and the slaves could be shipped to Española for work on his estates there or sold. At first glance, this provision was a peculiar inclusion in a contract that reflected the Dominican notions of Indians as free persons, but it took into account the possibility that under native custom there might be slaves. Most Spanish thinkers considered anyone who by native custom was a slave legally to be a slave and held that the thrall might be bought and sold at the same time that the free native owner was exempt from the encomienda and from any obligation to give personal unpaid service to Spaniards.

There were privileges, too, to be paid for from the revenues generated by the new land once it came under Spanish control. Ayllón's salary as governor, 375,000 maravedis or 1000 ducats per year, and the salary of a son as warder of a fort (100,000 maravedis per year), fell into this category even though the contract did not specifically name the source from which the monies were to be drawn. The contract did stipulate that all of Ayllón's expenses in the exploration would be repaid to him upon presentation of certified bills. Other provisions directed that the revenues of the land were to be applied to securing clergy and equipping them with vestments, ornaments, and other supplies for their conduct of the sacred offices, to constructing forts, to sending chaplains on ships, and to seeing that each expedition had a surgeon and a pharmacist. A final charge against the revenues of the new land was the fifth part of all royal revenues which Ayllón and his heirs were to receive in perpetuity.

The king reserved three things to himself. First, he was to decide how best to develop contacts with the peoples of the new land once he had Ayllón's report on the exploratory phase of the project. Second, he would name treasury officials to watch over his own interests both in the exploration fleet or fleets and in any colonies. Finally, he reserved the rights of jurisdiction (the seignorial rights) within the fifteen-leagues-on-a-side square of land Ayllón was to have for his estate.

Save for the land grant, there was nothing in the contract incompatible with the Dominican view that the Spaniards should approach the one known native state, Du-a-e, as if it were an Old World state. Trade, exploitation of fisheries, and mission work could all proceed with little or no Spanish settlement. One or more fortified posts might be built to support those activities, but the contract was vague on that point and did not contain the explicit demand for the establishment of settlements that is in the later contracts concerning La Florida.[9] In 1523, the Spaniards were not concerned about possible settlement by other Europeans and hence could take the position that their own settlements might not be needed if the Indians really did live under a native state that could be brought to acknowledge the emperor's sovereignty. The Spaniards thought that Du-a-e, with its pearl fishery, apparent herds of tame deer, and agricultural potential, would no doubt be duplicated by other native states in the parts of the continent that Ayllón had not yet explored.

Exploration was, let it be noted, the primary intention of the contract. The numerous commissions that Ayllón already had in connection with the officials of Puerto Rico meant that he would have time to organize and would send out only exploring parties during the year for beginning his project. There would be time later to consider what further steps he might wish to take and what the crown might wish to allow.

Seen in this context, Ayllón's deception about the location of the areas explored in 1521 was unimportant. For Ayllón, further exploration would prove whether he was right about the new Andalucia at 35° to 37° north or whether the known reality of Du-a-e's domain, which lay north of approximately 33°30′ north but apparently did not reach much beyond 35° north, was what he wanted to exploit. In 1523, no one could know that Martyr's account of the new land, given without latitudes, would see print in 1530 and become a basis for a legend that was to influence a later generation of Spanish, French, and even English explorers and dreamers to seek to create empires in North America.

Whatever the future might reveal about the new territory, in the immediate present Ayllón wanted to obtain benefits for his services both as a judicial official since 1504 and as the patron of the exploring voyage that had opened up a new area for imperial control. Of immediate concern was a time limit on a land grant he had received from the town of Azua, on Española, in 1519, for developing a plantation and sugar mill. Ayllón's service in Cuba and New Spain in 1520, however (see below), and then his journey to Spain had prevented him, he claimed, from carrying out his intention. On June 21, the crown

9. For the comparison of contracts, see Eugene Lyon, *The Enterprise of Florida: Pedro Menéndez de Avilés and the Conquest of 1565–1568* (Gainesville, Fla., 1976), Appendix 2.

granted an extension of the term, which would now *begin* at Christmas, 1523.[10]

Of greater consequence were two requests approved, one on June 26 and the other on an unknown but presumably similar date. By an order of June 26, Ayllón and his wife, Ana Bezerra, were authorized to create a *mayorazgo,* or entail.[11] They thus had the instrument to form an estate for one of their children and to protect its contents from sale, seizure to pay debts or other judgments, and so forth. It was a valuable privilege not often given, but there is no evidence that Ayllón or his wife used it. To do so, they would have had to appear before a notary and set up the *mayorazgo* in proper legal form and then make provision for it in their wills. Had Ayllón succeeded in his North American venture and realized the promise of a square of land fifteen leagues on a side, in all likelihood he would have established the *mayorazgo* with that land as its central property.

Equally important, and of even more immediate prestige value, was the concession of the right to have an inquiry made to see if Ayllón qualified for the habit of the military order of Santiago. Only a part of the file recording that inquiry has survived. As a result, nothing is known about the dates of its authorizing order and of the investigating officers' ruling that Ayllón qualified. What is known is that they took testimony at Valladolid on July 28 and August 25. All witnesses agreed that Allyón came from a distinguished Mozarabic family and was considered to be a hidalgo. Further, an older brother, Pedro, was a member of the order. No witness knew if Ayllón then owned a horse, but all believed him wealthy enough to do so. With other testimony now lost, that was enough to convince the authorities of the order that Ayllón qualified. Sometime in the fall of 1523, perhaps in November, he became a *comendador* of the order of Santiago.[12]

While Ayllón was thus engaged, the crown granted him yet another privilege: it paid passage for him, his servants, a riding mule, and ten toneladas of goods from Seville to Santo Domingo.[13]

Who was this man upon whom Charles V was loading these privileges? Ayllón was born in Toledo in about the year 1480. He was a

10. AGI, IG 420, Book 9, fol. 51.

11. Copy, AGS, Registro General del Sello, 26 junio 1523, No. 355.

12. Archivo Histórico Nacional, Madrid, Ordenes, Santiago, Expediente 8565, Lucas Vázquez de Ayllón. Ayllón's title is given in AGI, JU 13, No. 1, R. 4, fols. 3–4.

13. AGI, IG 420, Book 9, fol. 166.

younger son of Inés de Villalobos and Juan Vázquez de Ayllón, nicknamed the good because of his distinguished service as a member of the city council. On his father's side, he claimed descent from Estevan Yllan and Per (Pedro) Alvarez de Toledo, in his time judge (*alcalde*) of the Mozarabs of Toledo, holding perhaps the most important office possible for a person of his ethnic group in the city. Nothing is recorded about his mother's lineage.[14]

To his distinguished heritage, Ayllón added a solid education in the law and politics. Antonio de Herrera y Tordesillas, the historian, reported many years after Ayllón's death that he was a man of "great learning and gravity";[15] nothing else is known about his formal education. Growing up in Toledo provided Ayllón with a sound education in the political arts. Toledo was the seat of the cardinal primate of Spain and the sometime seat of the royal court.

Heritage, knowledge, and political skill came together in 1504 to secure the young lawyer the post of second *alcalde mayor* for the new colony of Española.[16] He was about twenty-five years old. Once in the colony, Ayllón was assigned the difficult task of bringing royal justice to the turbulent gold-mining districts of the interior and the northern coast of the island. The litigious residents of the then splendidly rich towns of the mining districts, Concepción de la Vega, Santiago de los Caballeros, Puerto Plata, Puerto Real, and Lares de Guahaba, offered the judge ample opportunities to use his knowledge of the law and to acquire wealth and political connections.

Skilled as he apparently was in building relationships with the powerful and wealthy, Ayllón did not escape the changing fortunes of

14. Gimenez Fernández says he was born in 1470 (*Bartolomé de las Casas*, I, 323), but the facts of his life suggest a later date; see responses to question 11 of the interrogatory of Pedro Vázquez de Ayllón, Santo Domingo, 1560, AGI, PAT 63 (Stetson), and Archivo Histórico Nacional, Madrid, Ordenes, Santiago, Expediente 8565, Lucas Vázquez de Ayllón. The Mozarabs were Christians who remained in Toledo after its conquest by the Muslims in the eighth century. They retained a Visigothic form of the Christian liturgy, as well as Visigothic laws. The position of judge was created after the Christian reconquest of the city, because of objections by the newly arrived Christians to being judged under a form of law they did not understand, and by the Mozarabs to being judged under the laws of their new lords. See Antonio Martín Gamero, *Historia de la ciudad de Toledo* (2 vols.; Toledo, 1862), 819–26; and Pedro de Alcoçer, *Historia o descripción de la imperial ciudad de Toledo* (Madrid, 1554), fols. 39–39v, 54v.

15. Herrera, *Historia general,* III, 81–82.

16. Bartolomé de las Casas (*Historia,* trans. André Collard [New York, 1971], 147) and Herrera (*Historia general,* III, 81–82) said 1506, but Ayllón, in testimony recorded on April 16, 1517, stated that his appointment was in 1504 (AGI, IG 1624). See also Ursula Lamb, *Fray Nicolás de Ovando, gobernador de las Indias, 1501–1509* (Madrid, 1956), 184.

court politics during the first two decades of the sixteenth century. Fray Nicolás de Ovando had been appointed governor of Española in 1502 during Isabela the Catholic's reign. A practitioner of a kind of evenhanded justice, the governor had by 1508 angered many residents of the island and the men who controlled colonial affairs at court. When Ferdinand the Catholic returned to power in late 1508, pending the arrival in Spain of Charles of Hapsburg—who was then a boy residing in the duchy of Burgundy—these men had Miguel de Pasamonte sent to the island as royal treasurer. He quickly began to build the network of partisans that became known as the Pasamonte faction, and he gathered evidence against Ovando. Ayllón, although identified with Ovando's regime, seems to have made a discreet shift in allegiance. Still, when Ovando was recalled to Spain in 1509, Ayllón and the licenciado Alonso de Maldonado, the other *alcalde mayor,* were both subjected to a review, or residencia, of their conduct in office and sent back to Spain for a final decision on the charges made against them.[17]

The record of the residencia of 1509 has not survived, but its principal charges against Ayllón were recorded by Bartolomé de las Casas. Ayllón was found to be less of a friend of justice and less pious than Maldonado. Ayllón's use of his economic opportunities produced the charge that he had acquired a fortune unjustly. How serious the charges were is not known. Ayllón's family remembered that he had given a good account of himself and so escaped punishment. Las Casas ascribed his escape to his relationship with Lope de Conchillos, the rapidly rising protégé of Bishop Fonseca, the virtual ruler of the American empire since 1493.[18] In either case, Ayllón's service as *alcalde mayor* did not hinder his subsequent advancement in the royal service.

Ovando's replacement as governor was Diego Colón, the legitimate son of Christopher Columbus, the discoverer. Colón's attempt to build his own power base on the island by appointing justices and by favoring locally resident married men over absentees such as Ferdinand, Fonseca, and Conchillos in the distribution of Indian labor gangs and mines soon brought him into conflict with Pasamonte and Pasa-

17. Lamb, *Nicolás de Ovando, passim,* esp. 215, 218–19, 222–25; Carl O. Sauer, *The Early Spanish Main* (Berkeley and Los Angeles, 1966), 196; *DII,* XXXI, 446–48.

18. Herrera, *Historia general,* III, 146; testimony in reply to questions 3 and 4 of the interrogatory of Pedro Vázquez de Ayllón, Santo Domingo, 1560, AGI, PAT 63, R. 24, fols. 3v–4, 7, 15, 17. Las Casas' view is noted in Gimenez Fernández' *Bartolomé de las Casas,* I, 324.

monte's patrons at the royal court. Then, in May, 1511, Colón won his lawsuit against the crown over his rights as his father's successor. Among the limited powers the crown retained in the Antilles was the right to appoint appeals judges. That was enough. In October, 1511, Ferdinand created an audiencia for the Indies. Among the three judges selected to staff that appeals court and to become the legal and political rein on Colón's pretensions was Ayllón, now boasting the title of licenciado, apparently obtained through a quick course of additional legal studies at the University of Salamanca.[19]

Ayllón rapidly became an important figure in the Pasamonte faction's efforts to reduce Colón's power. His marriage to Ana de Bezerra, the daughter of a wealthy miner, shortly after his return to the island (*ca.* 1514) further increased his power and wealth by allying him with the Bezerra-Manzorro clan, also members of the faction.[20] If he did not already own a half interest in a sugar plantation near Puerto Plata from his previous period of service, he soon acquired it. He may have had other properties as well. Trading and slave-trading ventures soon added to his wealth and produced complaints that he and other judges were muscling in on the slave trade and extorting high prices. Ayllón's slaving expeditions were especially notorious for poor provisioning—which caused the starvation of many of the captured Indians—and for abusing seamen who wanted the payment of fair wages. Too, Ayllón and his fellows seem to have been guilty of adultery. Ayllón was said to have had at least one illegitimate child and to have kept a neighbor's wife as a concubine in his own house.[21] In sum, in matters personal,

19. Floyd, *The Columbus Dynasty,* 131–32, 145–47; *DII,* XI, 546–55. Gimenez Fernández said the University of Valladolid (*Bartolomé de las Casas,* I, 324), but a debt Ayllón owed to the bachillero Francisco de Prada, of Salamanca, and the *esposales* of his son Pedro, a child by his first wife, with a girl from Salamanca suggest that he studied there (Power of attorney from Francisco de León to Pedro de Aguilar on behalf of the bachillero Francisco de Prada, of Salamanca, Seville, March 7, 1517, AP-SVQ, Oficio XV, 1517, libro 1, fols. 211–211v, and power of attorney from Ayllón to Pedro Alvarez de Ayllón, Seville, March 9, 1511 [*sic*], AP-SVQ, Oficio V, 1511, libro único, first third).

20. Memorial to Cisneros [*ca.* 1517], *DII,* I, 259, dated by Sauer and ascribed to the licenciado Alonso Zuazo, who was investigating the audiencia in 1517 (Sauer, *The Early Spanish Main,* 205). For the Bezerra-Manzorro clan, see Floyd, *The Columbus Dynasty,* 229; and Hoffman, "A New Voyage of North American Discovery," 418–19. The date of Ayllón's marriage to Ana is based on Ana's testimony about their children's ages in 1526 (AGI, JU 13, No. 1, R. 4, fols. 31v–35). *Cf.* Floyd, *The Columbus Dynasty,* 229. Apparently Ayllón was married prior to his appointment in 1504 but was a widower by 1512.

21. Gimenez Fernández, *Bartolomé de las Casas,* I, 325, 328–29. Regarding the Pasamonte faction: residencia of the audiencia, 1517 (AGI, JU 42, No. 1, fols. 15v, 31,

professional, and economic, the judges quickly created what some contemporaries viewed as a tyranny of their own, especially once Colón returned to Spain in 1514 to defend his prerogatives. That, at least, is what the highly partisan record of the residencia of 1517 says. According to the evidence there, Ayllón was the foremost tyrant of the three.

Just as the tyranny was reaching new heights, Ferdinand the Catholic died, on January 23, 1516. Cardinal Francisco Jiménez de Cisneros once again, as in 1504 and 1508, assumed a regency. Stirred by the Dominicans' denunciations of the exploitation and destruction of the Indians, which were little checked by the legislation issued in 1512 in response to their first outcries, Jiménez de Cisneros determined to send three Hieronymite friars to investigate conditions on Española, and the licenciado Alonso de Zuazo to take a residencia of the audiencia and of other officials whose conduct Father Las Casas and others so complained of.[22]

Zuazo suspended the judges from the exercise of their duties in May, 1517, when he began to take testimony about their conduct in office. They might well have lost their positions had not the political winds again changed in Spain. When Charles V arrived in Spain in the fall of 1517, his chief minister, William of Croy, Sieur de Chievres, quickly took Fonseca under his protection. In March, 1518, Fonseca and Conchillos were restored to their old positions as controllers of policy and patronage for the Indies. When news about that arrived in the Antilles in the summer of the year, the residencia was suspended and Zuazo was put under scrutiny.[23] The formal restoration of the audiencia's powers was ordered on August 24, 1518, but did not become effective until the spring of 1520.[24]

Throughout all this change, Ayllón seems to have remained a central political figure, second in importance only to Pasamonte. One mark of his importance is that, in the spring of 1518, in the election of

---

101). Regarding Ayllón's trading: fols. 53, 101, 250, 262v. Regarding the slave trade: fols. 84, 70–73, 102–104v, 230–31. "Querella . . . por García de Roales contra su muger Catalina de Salas por adulterio . . . con . . . Ayllón" (Santo Domingo, September 9, 1523, AGI, PAT 295, No. 110, which includes evidence first taken in 1515).

22. Lewis Hanke, *The Spanish Struggle for Justice in the Conquest of America* (Boston, 1965), 17–45; Simpson, *The Encomienda in New Spain,* 37–44.

23. Floyd, *The Columbus Dynasty,* 175–76, 184; AGI, JU 42, No. 1, fols. 336–39; Sauer, *The Early Spanish Main,* 205*n*14.

24. Simpson says August 22 (*The Encomienda in New Spain,* 53), but Floyd gives August 24 (*The Columbus Dynasty,* 175, 262–63*n*49).

an agent to represent the towns of Española before the new monarch, he won after protracted maneuvering by the Colón and Pasamonte factions. Ayllón never went to Spain, however, because Zuazo stepped in and began investigating the election.[25] Still, Ayllón's selection by powerful interests on the island indicates that his special talents and connections were considered superior to those of other officials.

A second mark of Ayllón's importance in the politics of the Antilles was the role he was given in the attempt to prevent a civil war between Hernán Cortes, on the one side, and Pánfilo de Narváez and Diego Velásquez, on the other. Cortes' assumption of independent authority after the establishment of Veracruz became known to his erstwhile superior, Velásquez, the governor of Cuba, in late August, 1519, when a ship carrying the news and a large bribe for officials in Spain stopped in a Cuban port for water and supplies before sailing across the Atlantic. Velásquez at once hastened the preparations for a reinforcing expedition he had been organizing. Narváez was named its commander and given orders to depose Cortes and assert Velásquez' authority. Hearing of this, the *real acuerdo* of Española agreed to send Ayllón to try to prevent fratricidal strife by interposing the audiencia's authority and forcing the parties into court, a move that would favor Cortes in the short term but preserve royal power in the long run.[26]

Armed only with the audiencia's decree—itself of doubtful legality because the audiencia was still suspended from office—along with the side arms of his *alguazil* and the pen of his notary, Ayllón went to Cuba. Confrontations with Narváez and Velásquez produced nothing but a denial by them of the audiencia's authority to intervene in the matter. Velásquez did agree to remain in Cuba to ensure its safety against Indian uprisings, but he would not stay Narváez's departure. Ayllón had no choice but to sail with the fleet. At Veracruz, he attempted again to establish his authority, was approached by representatives of Cortes, and then was arrested and deported by Narváez. Allyón claimed that once he was at sea, he overawed the crew of his ship with his authority and had them land him at Española, but it is

25. *DII*, XXXV, 29–37; "Relación de lo obrado en la isla Santo Domingo," 1518, *DII*, I, 359–61; Floyd, *The Columbus Dynasty*, 182.

26. *DII*, XXXV, 29–37, 41–55. The story of Ayllón's mission is told in Anghiera's *Decadas*, II, 490ff.; in Francisco Lopez de Gómara's *Historia general de las Indias* (2 vols.; Barcelona, 1954), II, 176–79; and in Herrera, *Historia general*, V, 370–74.

likely that Narváez gave orders to let him go on his way once the ship reached Cuban waters.[27]

Back at Santo Domingo, Ayllón reported his experiences. The audiencia, newly restored to power, immediately undertook actions to establish the guilt of those who had disobeyed Ayllón's orders. It also turned to other problems, including the attempts of the reinstated governor, Diego Colón, to extend his power and claims by unlawfully sponsoring expeditions of discovery and conquest. Ayllón's voyage to Spain in 1521 was a result of that problem.

In sum, Ayllón was someone who had risen rapidly in the king's sevice while lesser men had fallen by the wayside in the political intrigues of the time. He had amassed a considerable private fortune and was back in office with every prospect of remaining there for some time. Yet he also was in his late forties, if not early fifties, and had a house full of small children. He had seen Mexico. His pilot had made a new discovery and brought back Indians whose stories of their homeland offered a basis for the dream of even greater achievements in a time when novelties and wonders were being turned up by nearly every voyage westward from the Antilles. The restless intelligence that had taken him to the top of Antillean society and his profession once more seems to have seized him. His contract with his king to exploit the new discovery, but in a new way, offered an opportunity to satisfy still unfulfilled ambitions.

The crown evidently expected Ayllón to be on his way to Española by the end of August, 1523, because on the thirty-first it ordered the House of Trade to release to him Cristobal Barroso, who was to be sent into exile at Santo Domingo.[28] Ayllón did not immediately go to Seville, however. Instead, it seems that he went to Toledo, perhaps to complete the investigations required for his admission to the order of Santiago and to be invested with his knighthood of that order in the presence of his relatives in the imperial city. From there, he headed toward Seville, pausing for the night at Guadalupe in late December, 1523, or early January, 1524. As it happened, Goncalo Fernández de Oviedo, later to be the official chronicler of the Indies and the author of the principal source for the voyage of 1526, was on his way to court

27. *DII*, XXXV, 83–139, XIII, 339–46, XXXV, 342–51.
28. AGI, IG 420, Book 9, fols. 176v–177.

at the same time. Like many travelers on that road, both men had stopped at the ancient shrine of Guadalupe to venerate its statue of the virgin Mary.[29]

Writing many years later with all the benefit of hindsight and a moralizing purpose, Oviedo recounted their meeting:

> As we were friends, he told me of his trip and for certain I was sad to hear him say where he went. He told me the great trust he had in that slave [Francisco ("el Chicorano")] and that he had made him a Christian and that he was a very good person and of very excellent [*gentil*] judgment. . . . He said to me that that Indian had told him that there were excellent, large [pearls] in his land. . . . He told me much more and I took his [self-]deception to be certain. I believed that that Indian lied in everything he had told him, that the desire to return to his homeland had made him say all of that which he knew pleased the licenciado, and that as an astute [person] he piled up tales [*novelas*] that ought not to have been believed. I said this to the licenciado. He replied that the Indian was now very apt with the language [*ladino*] and a very good Christian and had as much love for the licenciado as if he were his son and he [Ayllón] treated him as if he had procreated him.[30]

Oviedo's assessment of the degree to which his acquaintance had fallen under the spell of his deceitful servant ought not to be taken at face value. Ayllón had deliberately altered the story of the discovery with respect to latitude and potential, using the idea of similar climates at similar latitudes, an idea that Francisco could not have known. No doubt Ayllón came to believe at least partially what he was saying when he praised the possibilities of the new land. He did no more than many later explorers, almost all of whom, even when they had seen North America at first hand—as Ayllón had not up to this time—tended to see it not as it was but as it could become once developed by European hands.[31] In talking with Oviedo, Ayllón continued his deceptions, perhaps even of himself. Yet the more-experienced Oviedo was right: the new land was not so rich and so easy to occupy as Ayllón wanted the world to believe.

By mid-February, 1524, Ayllón had reached Seville. He took up lodgings in the parish of Espiritu Santo, the area around the cathedral.

29. Gonzalo Fernández de Oviedo, *Historia general y natural de las Indias* (4 vols.; Madrid, 1851–55), I, 112. Oviedo's text implies that he was with Diego Colón's party as it made its way from Seville to court to answer the charges that Ayllón and others had brought against Colón's government. Regarding the Virgin of Guadalupe, see Alcoçer, *Historia,* fols. 55–55v.

30. Oviedo, *Historia general,* III, 626.

31. Wayne Franklin, *Discoverers, Explorers, and Settlers: The Diligent Writers of Early America* (Chicago, 1979), 69.

There on February 29 he authorized a power of attorney for his old associate Hernán Vázquez, of Toledo, allowing Vázquez to use Ayllón as a bondsman for fifteen hundred ducats to secure Vázquez' contract for the bulls of the Crusade and Saint Peter's in the bishoprics of Cuenca, Sigüenza, Osuna, and Avila, and the kingdom of Valencia. The next day he had the House of Trade register the cedula informing Diego Colón—still governor of Española although he was then at court in Spain—and the audiencia of the contract he had with the crown and of its terms.[32]

For the next month, Ayllón spent his time preparing for the trip. During that period, the king issued an order, dated March 23, allowing him to postpone for one year, until 1525, the time by which he had to begin exploration.[33] Ayllón gave his jobs in Puerto Rico as the reason for the delay, but the real reason was that he would not return to the Antilles until the beginning of the summer of 1524 and so would not be able to arrange for an exploring voyage that year.

By March 30, Ayllón had loaded his goods and his mule and servants into the ship of Lope Sanchez, *La Magdalena,* which was at San Lucar awaiting favorable weather. Completing one last piece of business, which he may not have had time to take care of in Seville, Ayllón appeared before the notary Pedro Fernández and signed a general power of attorney for his nephew Francisco de Vargas, giving him complete control over all his peninsular affairs, both in Toledo and outside it. Some days later, and perhaps before April 18, when the House of Trade registered the extension on when he had to begin exploration, Ayllón sailed.[34]

He reached Puerto Rico in June. On June 30, he formally opened the residencia of Sancho Velázquez and the treasury officials. He seems to have remained on the island at this business until late in the year, only reappearing as a signatory of documents at Santo Domingo in December.[35] At some point in the fall, perhaps in September, but surely no later than December, he sent instructions to Vargas to buy

32. Power of attorney in AP-SVQ, Oficio V, 1524, Book 1, fol. 192; note on copy of the cedula in AGI, JU 3, No. 3, fols. 17v–18v.

33. AGI, CT 5090, No. 3, R. 5, fols. 26–26v.

34. AGI, CT 4675 B, Datas, 1525–30, fol. [8v] (old fol., 69v); power of attorney, San Lucar de Barameda, March 30, 1524, copy, AP-SVQ, Oficio V, 1526, Book 1, fols. 619–619v; note of entry on the House of Trade's books, AGI, JU 3, No. 3, fol. 19.

35. Residencia, Puerto Rico, 1524 (AGI, JU 48, No. 1, R. 1, *passim;* AGI, IG 1202, No. 3 [item 6], fol. 7). His presence in Santo Domingo during December is taken from the date of a *libranza* he signed that was charged against his estate in the audiencia's residencia of 1528 (AGI, JU 50, No. 1, fol. 770).

weapons, olive oil, and other necessities for the fleet he expected to fit in 1526.[36]

From December, 1524, until the end of March, 1525, Ayllón stayed at Santo Domingo, dispatching various matters as a member of the audiencia and preparing for the expedition of 1525, which was to carry out his obligation to explore a portion of the coast and gather the data upon which the crown could formulate policies for the annexation of the new land into the Spanish empire.[37] As part of his preparations, he had his exclusive license cried in the streets of Santo Domingo, much to the anger of his former partner, Juan Ortiz de Matienzo, who said he heard Ayllón's disclosure of this turn of events one morning while shaving. Ayllón also took over payment for the services of Quejo, whom Matienzo, Diego Cavallero, and Ayllón had been maintaining on partial salary at Santo Domingo during the previous three and a half years. Pilots being in high demand, that had been the only way to keep him available to the partnership and possibly also the only way to prevent him from returning to the discovery of 1521 in someone else's pay.[38]

Neither the date nor the place of sailing of the new expedition under Quejo's command is known. If it sailed from Santo Domingo, it is possible that it carried Ayllón to San Germain, where he passed sentences in the residencia of the Puerto Rican officials on April 6 and 8.[39] In that case, the departure would have been in late March or on the first day or two of April. Alternatively, Quejo may have taken his departure from Puerto Plata, leaving Ayllón to get to San Germain by some other means. In any case, Ayllón was back at Santo Domingo on May 27 and remained there for the rest of the year and into 1526, until he left for Puerto Plata and the sailing of the expedition of 1526.[40]

Probably about the same date Ayllón returned to Santo Domingo, Matienzo completed his letter to the crown complaining that his man, Quejo, had made the discovery, that he, not Ayllón, had the

36. AGI, JU 3, No. 3, fol. 81.

37. For examples of his official actions, see *DII*, XIII, 471–78.

38. AGI, JU 3, No. 3, fol. 30; Juan Ortiz de Matienzo to crown, Santo Domingo [Spring, 1525], in AGI, PAT 174, No. 1, R. 60 (and in *DII*, XXXIV, 563–67). Matienzo claimed he had made the payments to Quejo, but the lawsuit of 1526 suggests that the arrangement was on behalf of the partnership set up in 1521 (AGI, JU 3, No. 3, fols. 30, 32v, 43, 44v, 51v).

39. Sentences, AGI, JU 48, No. 1, R. 1.

40. On May 27, he signed a letter found in *DIU*, I, 209–13.

audiencia's authorization to follow up on the new discovery, and that only circumstances had prevented him from doing so. Specifically, he said that the House of Trade had prevented ships of the right size for the venture (those under eighty toneladas in capacity?) from sailing because of the war with France.[41] He claimed to have spent over six hundred pesos de oro on the 1521 voyage and in maintaining Quejo and others at Santo Domingo during the previous two (*sic*) years. Further, he claimed that he had two caravels ready when Ayllón appeared and had his contract proclaimed. He demanded that Ayllón be prohibited from sailing, that evidence in the matter be taken by the audiencia, and that he himself receive justice.[42] Matienzo's petition probably went to Spain at the same time as Ayllón's report on his audit and investigation of the Puerto Rican officials.

The expedition of 1525 consisted of two caravels, some sixty crewmen, and Quejo as pilot.[43] Ayllón's instructions to Quejo are not known, but certain inferences are possible from Ayllón's later claims. Quejo was to explore at least two hundred leagues, or 640 nautical miles, of coast, take such soundings and bearings as might be necessary to allow a retracing of his steps, take possession of the land in the king's name and Ayllón's, erect stone markers with Charles V's name and the date, obtain Indians who might serve as interpreters once they learned some Spanish, introduce European food plants in at least a few places, and establish peaceful relations with the natives by giving gifts and treating them well, notwithstanding that the caravels were "well armed."

Quejo made landfall on May 3, 1525, the day of the festival of the Invention of the Cross in the Spanish calendar of the sixteenth century.[44] Accordingly, Quejo named the river he entered the Rio de la Cruz (river of the cross). By using the Juan Vespucci map of 1526 (Map 3), which incorporates a report of the voyage, and Alonso de Chaves' rutter (see the Appendix), which also incorporates that report but with a different nomenclature for the places in question, it is possible

41. On July 14, 1522, the crown prohibited ships under eighty toneladas in the Atlantic trades (AGI, IG 420, Book 9, fol. 17).
42. AGI, PAT 174, No. 1, R. 60, and *DII,* XXXIV, 563–67.
43. AGI, JU 3, No. 3, fol. 7.
44. The dates for saints' days are taken from Jerónimo de Chaves' *Chronographía o reportório de los tiempos* (Seville, 1581), fols. 162v–173v.

to determine that this was the Savannah River (Map 4).[45] Quejo apparently had orders not to go directly to the river visited in 1521, and probably came upon the coast at the Savannah by the pure coincidence that it lies at 32° north latitude. Latitude sailing was standard navigational procedure at the time.

Upon landing at the Savannah's mouth, Quejo found that his Indian interpreters, survivors from among the slaves captured in 1521, could not speak the local language. He had thus encountered the second of the four linguistic groups he was to meet (his "Chicoran" interpreters were from the first). The Indians of the Savannah area spoke a form of Muskogean, whereas the Chicorans spoke another language, thought by some scholars to be a form of Siouan.[46]

Quejo did not tarry on the Savannah but did succeed by some means in getting several Indians from that area aboard his ships. The plan was to teach them Spanish so that they could serve as interpreters for later voyages and, possibly, as informants about the nature of their own societies.

From the Savannah River, the expedition sailed north looking for the combination of river, bay, and "cape" that figured in the discovery of 1521. It is unsurprising that Vespucci's map shows no distinct coastal features for this stretch, because except for the entrances to Port Royal and Saint Helena sounds and Bull's Bay, no major features were readily visible from an offshore course. Charleston Harbor was then entered from the south. Shoals covered the area that is now its dredged entrance.

45. Alonso de Chaves, *Alonso de Chaves y el libro de su "Espejo de navegantes,"* ed. Pablo Castañeda, M. Cuesta, and P. Hernández (Madrid, 1977), 124–25. The Vespucci map is owned by the Hispanic Society of America, New York. The relevant portion of it is reproduced in William P. Cumming's *The Southeast in Early Maps* (Princeton, 1958), plate 2. The saints' days used here are from the Juan Vespucci map of 1526, which seems to have been based on the now-lost report Ayllón sent to the emperor with his letter of September 9, 1525, acknowledged by Charles V in a letter to Ayllón from Toledo dated December 1, 1525 (AGI, IG 420, Book 10, fols. 190–190v).

46. AGI, JU 3, No. 3, fol. 7. For a linguistic map of the southeastern United States, see Charles F. Voegelin, *Map of North American Indian Languages* (New York, 1944). For a review of what little is known about the coastal groups in question, see James M. Crawford, "Southeastern Indian Languages," in James M. Crawford (ed.), *Studies in Southeastern Indian Languages* (Athens, Ga., 1975), 1–120. The Siouan thesis was proposed by James Mooney (*The Siouan Tribes*) but was challenged by Carl F. Miller ("Revaluation of the Eastern Siouan Problem, with Particular Emphasis on the Virginia Branches—the Occaneechi, the Saponi, and the Tutelo," in *Anthropological Papers*, No. 52, Bureau of American Ethnology Bulletin 164 [Washington, D.C., 1957], 115–212). Miller's views have been rejected by other scholars.

On May 9, the festival of San Nicolás, the sailors spotted the cape in question, naming it the Cape of San Nicolás. The river of 1521 was now given the name River Jordan, a name perhaps already in use by Ayllón and his men. Chaves described the cape, which is called Cape San Roman in his book (see Chapter III for an explanation): "This cape has before it some shoals that run about three leagues into the sea, and to the west it has a bay and it has the Jordan River."[47]

Having found their landfall of 1521, the Spaniards proceeded to seek contact with the Indians of the area, probably by again entering Winyah Bay. At first the Indians were hostile toward the kidnappers of their friends and relatives, but through the interpreters, Quejo convinced the natives that this time he came in peace and that those taken in 1521 would soon be returned to their kin. He also made a liberal distribution of gifts—clothing is mentioned by Ayllón—which probably went as far as anything to calm the understandable anger of the Indians. Ayllón later claimed that Quejo had success with the Indians at least partly because he told them of the grandeur of Charles V, but that may be regarded as flattery. In addition, according to Ayllón, Quejo gave the Indians seeds for various Spanish plants that Ayllón hoped they would cultivate. The Spaniards even showed the Indians how they should grow them.[48]

After several days or possibly a week at Chicora, the Spaniards again set sail. The available sources fail to show what they did next. The Chaves materials indicate that at some point in the expedition Quejo went northeast from the Winyah Bay area to the vicinity of Cape Fear, whose river, or a nearby inlet, is called the Río de Arrecifes (river of reefs) on the Vespucci map. It is not clear exactly where the Spaniards entered this river, whether on the western or the eastern side of Cape Fear. Since, curiously, the cape does not appear in identifiable form on the Vespucci map and is not mentioned in the Chaves materials, the inference is that the landing was most likely on the western side. But if the Spaniards entered the river to the east of the cape, they would have seen the shore curving away to the northeast and concluded that it went on for some distance. If the winds were blowing at force four on the Beaufort scale (12–16 miles per hour) from the north and northeast quadrants, as they do for about a third of the time in May, the view up the coast may have been enough for

47. Chaves, *Espejo de navegantes,* 124.
48. AGI, JU 3, No. 3, fols. 21v–23.

Quejo and his masters.[49] Although tacking into such winds was not beyond their skill, it would have been time-consuming. Thus they may have shifted the direction of their course to the south, to take advantage of the following wind.

Alternatively, the leg of the trip from Cape San Nicolás to the Río de Arrecifes could have been made as the Spaniards returned north after having sailed south from Cape San Nicolás. There is no way to know the order of events until additional sources come to light.

Once the expedition turned south, it rapidly retraced its course as far as the Río de la Cruz and the great cape (*cabo grueso*) that marked its entrance but to which no name was attached at the time, if Vespucci is followed. Today the cape is known as Tybee Island. From that point south, Quejo probably ran fairly close to shore because he was to be on the lookout for a possible strait. The Chaves materials suggest even more strongly than the Vespucci map does that the fleet put in at Saint Simons Sound, still in the territory of the Muskogean speakers. Again putting to sea, the caravels ran southward until May 22, the festival of Santa Helena, virgin martyr of Auxerre, France.[50]

On that day the Spaniards made a landfall at the northern end of Amelia Island, at Saint Mary's Entrance, near where Fernandina Beach, Florida, is today. The northern end of the island, seen from a ship coming south close to the shore appeared to be, and was named, a cape, the Cape of Saint Helena. Here Quejo seems to have again taken interpreters. The Indians spoke Timucuan, the third of the languages he encountered.

Having reached approximately latitude 30°40′ north, Quejo seems to have come to a point familiar to him or at least close enough to Ponce de Leon's Florida that he knew that no further exploration to the south was necessary, because no strait would be found. Consequently he turned north once again, this time with the intention of running up the coast to at least 37° north, the northern limit Ayllón claimed for his discoveries.

49. U.S. Department of Commerce, NOAA, *Pilot Chart for the North Atlantic, June, 1966* (Washington, D.C., 1966).

50. *The Book of Saints: A Dictionary of Servants of God Canonized by the Catholic Church,* comp. the Benedictine Monks of Saint Augustine's Abbey, Ramsgate (4th ed.; New York, 1947), 284. Jerónimo de Chaves erroneously lists May 22 as the festival of Saint Helen the empress (*Chronographía,* fol. 166v); the correct date is August 18. The empress' festival was celebrated on May 21 in the Eastern Orthodox calendar but on August 18 in the West after the eighth century.

From May 22 until June 24, the voyage cannot be reconstructed with certainty because, with two exceptions, none of the points visited north of Cabo de San Nicolás, the Winyah Bay entrance, were given saints' names; there is thus no chronological basis for a narrative. Nor does Chaves help very much for points north of Cabo de Trafalgar, that is, Cape Hatteras. His text ceases to use the two-point referencing system employed south of Cape Trafalgar and goes instead to a south-to-north system that is essentially point to point and could as easily have been a north-to-south system in the original report from which Chaves took his data.

Two possibilities exist for the voyage between May 22 and June 24. Quejo could have worked his way back up to the Jordan–Cape San Nicolás area, perhaps with a following wind, and then taken the coast up to the Río de Arrecifes, near Cape Fear, whence he swung out into the Atlantic until he reached the entrance to Delaware Bay. He would then have sailed south. Or he could have sailed up the Gulf Stream until he cleared Cape Hatteras and then continued north offshore until he was at approximately 39° north, when he would have sailed west along that latitude until he encountered land. The end result would be the same, a landfall on the Delmarva peninsula sometime before June 24. With good weather there was more than enough sailing time for either course, and the prevailing winds of June would have made either one relatively easy.

The northernmost section of the Vespucci map's southern coast shows exploration along the western side of a westward-curving shore with two rivers running down to it. South of that shore, the name Cabo de Santa María is put on a peninsulalike land area just east of a round bay labeled the Bahía de Santa María (bay of Saint Mary), which is in turn separated from the Cabo de Trafalgar by two inlets that are unnamed (Map 3). In Chaves' rutter, the northern point of the peninsular is called Cabo de Arenas and is said to be twenty-five leagues, or eighty nautical miles, northeast, a quarter to the north, from the Cabo de San Juan. This distance and direction put one at Ocean City rather than Cape Henlopen. Even so, it appears that Quejo entered Delaware Bay and coasted much of its western side, then passed down the east coast of the Delmarva peninsula to Cape Charles, where he arrived on June 24, the festival of Saint John the Baptist, for whom he named the cape.

The Vespucci map shows that the Spaniards entered the lower portion of Chesapeake Bay far enough to see a river running westward into the continent. They did not stay long or explore very fully.

Continuing on south on July 2, the festival of the Visitation of Our Lady, they entered an estuary that lay twenty leagues, or about sixty-four nautical miles, south of Cabo de San Juan.[51] It is the first of two unnamed entrances on the Vespucci map, moving west from the great bay. Chaves shows that it, not Chesapeake Bay, should be named Bahía de Santa María. That entrance is now closed but corresponds to one shown on John White's map from 1585 of the Outer Banks area (Map 5). The inlet, like its companion on the Vespucci map, gave entrance to Pamlico and Albemarle sounds. The companion seems to have been visited a few days later but does not appear in the Chaves materials. In 1585, the English named it Trinity Harbor.

From these entrances into the sounds of North Carolina, Quejo sailed south to Cabo de Trafalgar, modern Cape Hatteras, which became his reference point for all the places he had visited on the run south from Cabo de Arenas and all the places he was yet to visit as he turned west-southwest along the coast toward Cape Lookout.

Apparently the next landfall was at a river that is unnamed on the Vespucci map but in Chaves is called the Río del Principe, following Diogo de Ribeiro, who in 1527 named it in commemoration of the birth of the boy who became Philip II.[52] The river lay fourteen leagues, or 44.8 nautical miles, west of Cabo de Trafalgar. It too is an entrance now closed, but it existed in 1585 and is shown on the White map (Map 5).

From there a course was shaped around Cape Lookout, which, like Cape Fear, is curiously omitted from Chaves and from obvious inclusion on the Vespucci map. The course carried the Spaniards thirty-six leagues, or 115 nautical miles, west, a quarter southwest, of Cabo de Trafalgar, to a river the Vespucci map calls the Río de las Aterazanas, that is, the Río de las Atarazanas (river of the boat sheds).[53] That no distance or direction to the next river, the Río de Arrecifes, is given suggests that at this point Quejo believed he had completed his survey and closed the map, as the Vespucci map shows. He was at either

51. This distance is a bit too great, but Chaves' other distance for Santa María, putting it twenty leagues north of Cabo de Trafalgar, is correct within five nautical miles (Chaves, *Espejo de navegantes,* 125).

52. Philip was born on May 21, 1527. The name first appears on the Ribeiro *mappamundi* of that year.

53. Louis-André Vigneras, "Is There a 'Verrazano River' on Juan Vespucci's 1526 Mappemonde?" *Terrae Incognitae,* VII (1976), 65–67.

Bogue Inlet, in the case of coast-hugging travel, or at New River Inlet, if he sailed straight courses across the insides of the arcs Cape Hatteras–Cape Lookout–New River. The date was perhaps the tenth of July, at the latest. Having completed his survey of the coast from approximately 30°40′ north to approximately 39°40′ north, and having run a total of almost 215 leagues, or approximately 688 nautical miles, along the coast but over double that in actual distance sailed, Quejo turned for Santo Domingo.[54]

At some point in his explorations north of Winyah Bay, he had picked up yet a fourth group of prospective interpreters, for the languages spoken north of Cape Fear were Algonkian, like Muskogee and Timucuan unintelligible to his Chicoran interpreters. At several points, Ayllón later claimed, Quejo had erected stone markers bearing the name of Charles V and the date and had had his notary record the event. Equally important, Quejo had compiled a rutter (*derrotero*) of his voyage, with soundings and bearings for the points along the coast that he had visited.[55] He had surveyed the resources of the coast and attempted to add certain European food plants to them, at least at the Jordan River. His only disappointment may have been that he did not find a strait. That aside, it was a brilliant reconnaissance during a little under two and a half months of sailing along the coast.

What Quejo found, especially at latitudes 35°, 36°, and 37° north was not what Ayllón's propaganda had said would be there. In place of a new Andalucia, Quejo saw only the sand dunes of the barrier islands and Outer Banks area, with unpromising sounds behind them beyond which lay more pine barrens, oak hammocks, and old and new Indian fields. Chesapeake Bay, whose clayey soil was different from the sandy ground found farther south, seems not to have impressed him enough to warrant a full exploration. What he saw from the lower bay probably suggested that its shores were not much different from the coast to the south nor more heavily populated than other coastal districts. Indeed, Quejo must have been disappointed not to have met with any large concentrations of Indians. Thus, he passed the Chesapeake by.

Probably at the beginning of the second week of July, Quejo ordered a course to the south-southeast. That would have carried the caravels

54. Chaves' data suggest that, exclusive of the exploration of the Delaware and Chesapeake bays, Quejo covered not less than 207 leagues and not more than 220, with 213 being the likeliest figure.

55. AGI, JU 3, No. 3, fol. 7. None of these stone markers has ever been found.

across the Gulf Stream and then to the east of the Bahama Islands on a long reach across the face of the prevailing winds until they came upon Puerto Rico and the Mona Passage. Thence Quejo would have steered to Santo Domingo, or less likely, Puerto Plata. It was a fast passage; the ships were in port by the end of the month.[56] One can imagine the sensation that Quejo's report and the strange Indians he brought must have caused even in Santo Domingo, long jaded with exotic peoples from the far corners of the Caribbean.

Quejo's return to Santo Domingo at the end of July, 1525, set in motion preparations for the next phase of the project. Ayllón paused in his activities to write a report to the king, dated September 9, in which he gave a full account and apparently included a copy of Quejo's rutter. The document was received in Spain no earlier than late October, and its duplicate must have arrived in November. Ayllón's news received warm welcome and elicited a royal letter expressing pleasure at the discovery and report and informing Ayllón that the newly created Council of the Indies (1524) had on November 10 authorized an investigation of the licenciado Matienzo's complaint. Charles V expressed his desire that Ayllón not be bothered by the matter, but he told Ayllón that, because it was a "matter of justice," the inquiry had been ordered.[57]

Matienzo's complaint was not the only challenge to Ayllón's contract that summer. Even as Quejo was turning his helm back toward Santo Domingo, a letter was on its way from Toledo to the audiencia of Santo Domingo, telling it to advise Ayllón that he had to make his voyage of discovery within the time limit as extended or the concession would be given to another. The audiencia was to certify that Ayllón had begun, if he had. Behind the reminder was not just royal interest in getting the job done but also the maneuvering of no less a rival than Narváez, Ayllón's opponent from 1520. Although Narváez did not receive his contract until May, 1526, and then for the Gulf of Mexico's northern coast (Rio de Palmas to La Florida and all of La Florida, still defined as the peninsula), it is clear that for at least a year before 1526, he had been after a concession; whether Juan Ponce de Leon's or Ayllón's or Francisco de Garay's seems not to have mattered. In the end, he got Ponce de Leon's and Garay's for his own.[58]

56. *Ibid.*, fols. 7, 81, 82v–87v.

57. AGI, IG 420, Book 10, fols. 190–190v, 151v–152, 172v–173.

58. AGI, IG 420, Book 10, fols. 23v–24; petition of Pánfilo de Narváez, Seville, May 27, 1526, AGI PAT 18, No. 3, R. 2. The only account of his expedition is Alvar Núñez

Ayllón had made good on his contract by sending Quejo in the summer of 1525, thereby blocking Narváez's grab for the coast north of peninsular Florida.

Matienzo's complaint had results that will transpire later. The next task facing Ayllón was to follow up on Quejo's discoveries of 1525 by founding a settlement from which the friars could spread the gospel and he and his agents could trade with the Indians of the Southeast.

Cabeza de Vaca's *The Narrative of Alvar Núñez Cabeza de Vaca,* trans. Fanny Bandelier, with Oviedo's version of the lost joint report presented to the audiencia of Santo Domingo translated by Gerald Theisen (Barre, Mass., 1972).

III

The Ayllón Expedition of 1526

Quejo's report that the coast from 35° to 37° north was similar in appearance to the coast at 33°30′ north probably made up Ayllón's mind about where to found a colony, if he still had any doubts. He would take his colonists to the Jordan River, the access to Du-a-e, the only Indian "kingdom" known to the Spaniards.

Events soon showed that sending Quejo was the easiest part of Ayllón's fulfillment of his contract. Preparing a major expedition to follow up on Quejo's discoveries was much more difficult and ended in Ayllón's running up large debts that took years for his widow to pay. What Ayllón encountered on the expedition itself quickly overwhelmed him and the plans he had made. In the reality of a late summer and fall spent on the sandy and marshy shores of coastal estuaries, Ayllón and his dream both died, but the Chicora legend he had created did not.

Whatever Ayllón's plans for his third, colonizing expedition to the new land, he carried six hundred or so persons with him, including some women, some children, and a number of black slaves. Perhaps 100 to 150 were seamen of the six ships that made up his fleet. The other five hundred or so were people drawn from Spain, especially the provinces of Badajoz and Toledo, and from the Indies.[1] Men who had not succeeded in the conquests of Honduras, New Spain, and Tierra Firme (Panama and the coast of modern Colombia) or who had grown restless once domination of the Indians had been achieved in those places, seem to have come to Santo Domingo and Puerto Plata when word got around that Ayllón wanted able men for his venture. Others left the declining economy of Española. From Puerto Rico, Ayllón

1. Boyd Bowman's lists allow identification of only five men: Cristobal Gallego was from Seville (*Indice*, II, 283, No. 9237); Antonio de Aller from Leon (*ibid.*, 178, No. 5890); Alonso de Villanueva from Villanueva del Fresno, Badajoz (*ibid.*, 57, No. 2063); Juan de Avila from Avila, New Castile (*ibid.*, 13, No. 357); and Goncalo Martín from Cartaya, Huelva (*ibid.*, 152, No. 5085).

recruited a number of married men, presumably with their families.[2] Black slaves, probably the personal servants of the more affluent members of the expedition, also formed part of the force. Secular clergy, doctors, and surgeons in unknown numbers joined the group. The spiritual axis of the expedition was provided by the Dominican friars Antonio de Montesinos and Antonio de Cervantes and a Dominican lay brother named Luís.[3] All the people had to be "entertained" prior to sailing, although probably only the more important persons actually received very much food from Ayllón's establishments at Santo Domingo and Puerto Plata. The ordinary folk would have got only occasional gratuities as they waited. Most seem to have gathered at Santo Domingo.

If manpower was the first requirement for an expedition, ships were the second. Eventually six ships sailed. Francisco de Vargas, Ayllón's nephew and agent in Seville, apparently sent out a caravel from Spain, which was in all likelihood one of the last ships to join in.[4] Allyón himself bought *La Trinidad* from the royal treasury for 225 pesos de oro, payable over six months.[5] How Allyón obtained the other ships is not known. Goncalo Fernández de Oviedo's list, although difficult to clarify, appears in Table 1, which also gives data on the fates of the six ships that returned from the expedition. The ships, like the people, were divided between Santo Domingo and Puerto Plata. Three of the six vessels were at Santo Domingo on March 5, 1526; another was at Puerto Plata.[6]

To supply this fleet, which probably grew rapidly in the spring of 1526, Ayllón had to strip his own estates of foodstuffs and buy supplies in Española as well as from nearby islands and Spain. The basic starches the voyagers were to eat while under way and during their initial months on land were some three thousand *cargas* (276,000 kilograms) of *cazabi* bread drawn from Jamaica, Mona Island, San Germán (Puerto Rico), and Higuey and Puerto Plata (both on Española). One thousand fanegas (roughly a bushel each) of maize were

2. Cedula, Seville, March 16, 1526 (AGI, IG 420, Book 10, fol. 282v), forbade this recruitment from Puerto Rico.

3. AGI, JU 3, No. 3, fols. 81–87v (and in *DII*, XXXV, 547–62); AGI, SD 11, No. 43 bis, fols. 24–25; testimony of Diego de Herrera in reply to questions 8–10 of the interrogatory of Pedro Vázquez de Ayllón, Santo Domingo, 1560, AGI, PAT 63 (Stetson).

4. AGI, JU 3, No. 3, fols. 82v–83v; and *DII*, XXXV, 548. This statement cannot be verified from other sources.

5. It had been purchased by the audiencia earlier in 1525 for a voyage to Honduras on official business (Cargo, October 8, 1525, AGI, CD 1050, No. 2, fol. 102).

6. AGI, JU 3, No. 3, fol. 80v.

Table 1. Ships of the Ayllón Fleet, 1526

Name	*Type*	*Fate*
El Bretón Grande a.k.a. (?) *Capitana*	Nao	Returned to Puerto Rico after voyage of fifty days; one source says four months (Oviedo, *Historia,* IV, 537). If *Capitana,* sank at Jordan River in August, 1526 (called *Capitana ibid.,* III, 627).
La Chorruca	Nao (?)	Still active in October, 1526 (*ibid.,* III, 632).
El Bretón	Nao (?)	Returned to Puerto Plata with Dominicans in voyage of twenty-one days; sank upon anchoring (*ibid.,* IV, 537).
Santa Catalina	Caravela (?)	One of these last three made port at Anegada Island, one at Cape Tiburon, one at Puerto San Francisco, Puerto Rico (*ibid.*). Cannibalism on one during return. *La Gavarra* was built on the Jordan River in August, 1526 (AGI, Santo Domingo 11, No. 43 bis, fol. 28v).
La Trinidad (?)	Brigantine or caravela	
La Gavarra	Patache (?)	

gathered, 350 to 500 from Jamaica and 600 to 700 from Ayllón's own estate in Puerto Plata. Live cattle, sheep, and pigs were taken along both for meat and as breeding stock for the colony. The sheep, at least, probably came from an estate, Santa Ana, that Ayllón owned half a league from Santo Domingo.[7]

To get about a hundred horses, it was necessary to comb the island, since horses were few, not generally reproducing well in the island's climate. Francisco de Vargas purchased olive oil in Spain beginning in December, 1525, and continuing as late as early March, 1526, with shipment probably later that month. In all, about 1,300 arrobas (about 16,332 liters) can be traced at a cost of 577 pesos de oro payable over a period of a year.[8]

7. *Ibid.,* 80v, 82–87v; AGI, JU 50, No. 1, fol. 49v.

8. Debt obligations and related documents of December 14, 23, 1525, and March 5, 1526, AP-SVQ, Oficio 5, 1525, Book 4, fols. 506v–507, 600, and 1526, Book 1, fols. 621v, 619, 615v–616.

Lucas Vázquez de Ayllón the Younger later estimated the cost of all the preparations at more than 100,000 ducats (83,334 pesos de oro), but that appears to be an exaggeration. Witnesses who were called in 1560, at about the same time, in support of the petition concerning the merits and services of his brother Pedro Vázquez de Ayllón could remember expenditures totaling about twenty thousand pesos, still a vast fortune for the 1520s.[9]

Known investments in the venture suggest that the figure of twenty thousand pesos de oro is closer to the truth. To raise that money, Ayllón resorted to a number of loans. He bought *La Trinidad* on credit. He mortgaged his half of the Puerto Plata sugar plantation for a million maravedi, or about 2,222 pesos de oro. The loan (*censo*) carried 15-percent interest per annum. Hernán Vázquez, of Toledo, Ayllón's business agent and trading partner, put at least 4,500 ducats into the venture, monies possibly secured by Ayllón's properties in Spain. Vargas, Ayllón's nephew and agent in Seville in 1525–1526, spent 73 pesos for serge cloth in addition to the at least 577 pesos de oro for olive oil. Both debts were guaranteed for Ayllón by his partner, Francisco Cavallos, who owned the other half of the Puerto Plata plantation.[10] These known investments total 7,372 pesos de oro, suggesting that the figure of twenty thousand pesos de oro is closer to the real total than that of 100,000 ducats. In short, Lucas the Younger's estimate of his father's expenditures is exaggerated. On the other hand, his statement that his father spent all of his fortune and the dowry goods of his wife, Ana de Bezerra, is probably close to the truth.

Intruding into these preparations, which were going ahead at Santo Domingo and Puerto Plata and probably elsewhere on the island, was the hearing of Juan Ortiz de Matienzo's lawsuit over his right to the new discovery. On March 28, 1526, Matienzo presented the king's cedula authorizing the inquiry to the licenciados Marcelo de Villalobos and Cristobal de Lebrón. The essence of his claims has been noted in Chapter II.

9. AGI, SD 11, No. 43 bis, fol. 1; testimony by Lope de Bardeci and Diego de Herrera in reply to questions 8–10 of interrogatory of Pedro Vázquez de Ayllón, Santo Domingo, 1560, AGI, PAT 63 (Stetson).

10. Copy of entry in books of Bautista Justinian for his purchase of the censo from the licenciado Francisco de Prado, April 3, 1529, AGI, JU 13, No. 1, R. 4, fols. 87v–88v; testimony of Diego de Herrera in interrogatory of Pedro Vázquez de Ayllón, Santo Domingo, 1560, AGI, PAT 63 (Stetson); obligation by Francisco de Cavallos to Ayllón and Francisco de Vargas, Seville, March 5, 1526, AP-SVQ, Oficio 5, 1526, Book 1, fols. 621–621v, and debt of Vargas and Cavallos to Alonso de Nebreda, Seville, March 5, 1526, fols. 615v–616.

The thrust of Ayllón's defense was to point out that he too had sponsored a voyage, Francisco Gordillo's, which like Matienzo's had as its object the seizure of Indians. He then went on to recount the voyage of 1525, whose expense and discoveries he implicitly set against Matienzo's claim for six hundred pesos de oro in expenses incurred in the voyage of 1521 and an undisclosed amount in maintaining Quejo at Santo Domingo on partial salary. In any case, Ayllón held the royal contract and, although he did not say so, knew that the king had agreed to Matienzo's complaint's being heard only because it was a "matter of justice."

Motions and countermotions occupied the litigants from March 28 to April 19, when Lebrón ordered both sides to present evidence. Matienzo began to do so on April 20, with his last witness sworn on April 27. Ayllón did not present his interrogatory and witnesses until May 2 and did not conclude the preliminary taking of testimony until June 9. Even then he had not got all his witnesses, notably Gordillo, to testify. In fact, by June 9, Ayllón had turned the case over to an advocate (*procurador de causas*), Diego de Alcántara, under a power of attorney signed May 26. His defense was largely pro forma.

The final publication of the evidence, when each side got to see what the other had collected, was ordered on June 12. On June 15, Matienzo's motion accepting Ayllón's admission that Matienzo's caravel, piloted by Quejo, had made the initial discovery was entered without protest. The judges concluded the case on June 18, although Ayllón's lawyer protested that he had not had time to obtain testimony from key witnesses. Rejecting that protest, the judges decided on June 25 to send the record of the case to the emperor for final determination. A note on the document shows that Matienzo carried it with him when he went to Spain that spring, presenting it at Granada on November 26, 1526.[11]

11. AGI, JU 3, No. 3, *passim.* Matienzo went to Spain to seek redress of his grievances in June, 1526, aboard the ship *La Victoria,* whose master was Lope Sanchez. Besides 1,660 pesos of his own funds, he carried various amounts for four other officials resident in the Antilles (Register, *La Victoria,* June 12, 1526, AGI, IG 1801). In the fall of 1527, fifteen marks of pearls were sent to him ("Relación del oro y perlas . . . nao, Santa María de Regla," Seville, October 13, 1527, AGI, IG 1801). He arrived at court in September, 1526, when Charles V was still at Granada on his honeymoon with Isabel of Portugal. He followed the court, giving a power of attorney at Burgos in December, 1527, but shortly afterward departing for Seville and his new post as *oidor* of the audiencia of Mexico. Characteristically, he got out of Spain without paying the 115 pesos Hernán Vázquez, of Toledo, claimed he owed him, even though Vázquez had tried to obtain payment while Matienzo was at court, and had secured a cedula ordering

The testimony for both parties—Quejo testified for both sides!—is the chief source of information about the voyages of 1521 and 1525 and reveals that Matienzo was after a monetary settlement as much as anything else. He had, it is true, helped to support Quejo during the years of waiting and he had thought to have his version of the discovery put on record on June 30, 1523, probably in response to a private letter from Spain advising that, as Diego Cavallero, the secretary of the audiencia, said in testimony during the lawsuit, the king had selected Ayllón alone to carry out further discovery in spite of Ayllón's initial petition on behalf of the three partners (Ayllón, Matienzo, and Cavallero). Matienzo also seems to have got a permit from the audiencia to go to the new land. In other regards, however, Matienzo did not show that he had any better right to the discovery than Ayllón did. It was Ayllon's man, Gordillo, who had known about the voyage of Pedro de Salazar, and Gordillo who had first taken possession of the new land for his employer.[12]

Nor was it true, as Matienzo claimed, that suitable ships had not been available between 1521 and 1525 for him to continue the exploration under the license he claimed to have from the audiencia (which was not put on record). Testimony by Quejo showed that he had in fact participated in an expedition in 1523 that traded for low-karat gold objects with the natives of Jamaica using a small ship of the size Matienzo apparently wanted for the North American voyage.[13] In further contradiction of this claim, Cavallero and Pedro Ortiz de Matienzo, a kinsman of the licenciado Matienzo, indicated that the ships Matienzo claimed to have on standby awaiting others from Spain had been prepared under the partnership agreement, not as a personal venture. There is a suggestion in this testimony that Matienzo may have tried to turn them to his own account in 1523 but lacked sufficient funds to send an expedition north or perhaps thought better of it because he had heard that the crown was going to grant Ayllón an

Matienzo to post bond that he would make payment (Power of attorney, Burgos, December 6, 1527, AGI, JU 42, No. 4, item 3; petition, n.d., and power of attorney, April 23, 1528, with cedulà, Madrid, March 13, 1528, and documents of May 2–4, at Seville, all AGI, IG 1202, No. 58). Matienzo served in Mexico until 1533, when he again returned to Spain and again succeeded in getting a new appointment, this time back to Santo Domingo (Cedulas, March 23, 1535, AGI, CT 5009). He served at Santo Domingo until his death.

12. AGI, JU 3, No. 3, fols. 53–60v, 48v–51v, 42.

13. *Ibid.*, fol. 69v. For the 1523 voyage to Jamaica, see AGI, CD 1050, No. 1, fols. 59v–60.

exclusive license.[14] Prudence in the latter circumstance would have dictated preparations and actions to establish a claim but no action in contravention of the royal will.

In sum, Ayllón was not far off the mark when he stated that Matienzo had tried in various ways to keep him from carrying out the contract.[15] The harassment failed. Sometime between May 27 and June 1, Ayllón left Santo Domingo for Puerto Plata and the final preparations of his fleet without having offered Matienzo any settlement for his claims.

The fleet that Ayllón gathered at Puerto Plata's round, shallow harbor under the shadow of Mount Isabel La Torre consisted of at least five ships; later witnesses uniformly mentioned six. Four of these ships had been in Ayllón's command from before March 5. The fifth (or sixth) was likely the long-awaited ship with oil, wine, and other goods that Vargas dispatched from Spain in March. Its arrival was probably the signal for Ayllón's departure from Santo Domingo.

By mid-July, the ships' crews had stowed final provisions and fresh water and had boarded the animals along with enough fodder for the few weeks of voyage to the Jordan River. Among those who gathered to watch the fleet depart was Father Bartolomé de las Casas.[16] Ayllón, the adelantado, was to try to prove that peaceful means would draw Indians into the empire. As an advocate of such means, Las Casas had every reason to see the fleet off, and no doubt to offer many prayers for its success.

The departure from Puerto Plata was in mid-July; no exact date has been preserved. The course was probably north-northwest along the eastern side of the Bahamas and then across the Gulf Stream and up the coast to latitude 33° north, where the ten-fathom curve would have been crossed to the east of modern Cape Romain. The smaller craft would have gone ahead to scout the way, but within hours the tops of the shore's first pine trees would have become visible. The appearance of the "cape"—North Island and its shoals—was final proof, if it was needed, that the ships had come again to the Jordan River and its cape. To commemorate the landfall, Ayllón and his pilots changed the name of the cape from San Nicolás to San Román,

14. AGI, JU 3, No. 3, fols. 46, 51.
15. *Ibid.*, fols. 34–35.
16. AGI, SD 11, No. 43 bis, fol. 19.

for the saint whose festival it was (Map 6). The date was Thursday, August 9, 1526.[17]

According to Oviedo, as the ships were being worked in over the bar at the entrance to the Jordan River, the *capitana* grounded and was lost along with all its cargo but not the crew or Ayllón, who was a passenger. On the other hand, Father Cervantes and Alonso de Espinosa Cervantes, also a member of the expedition, said only that the *capitana* was lost at the "entrance" to the new land. Espinosa Cervantes added that this happened at night during a storm, perhaps a squall that drove the ship into shallow water where it opened up.[18] Wherever it sank, whether entering the river or on a bar or shallow off the coast, its loss was keenly felt and helps to account for much of the starvation that the expedition's members experienced.

Given the vagueness of Oviedo's narrative and his evident errors concerning geography he had not seen and the details of which were not important for the story he was telling, there is no way to know whether the Spaniards entered the South Santee River or Winyah Bay on or after August 9, 1526, but there is no doubt that they were in the Santee-Winyah area. Chaves' materials make that clear.

Whether up the Santee River or up Winyah Bay, Ayllón soon found that the site was not suitable for the sort of colony he had in mind. Within a matter of days, Francisco ("el Chicorano") and the other Indian translators had fled from the camp, never to be seen again. Scouting parties sent inland returned to say that they had found no land suitable for settlement, which probably meant they had found few Indian villages. That is not surprising, because the soils of this area are mostly highly acid sands that are not good for growing corn and other crops. Only a few pockets of clay loams or sandy loams exist in the river valleys. They are often poorly drained today, and may have been at that time too. Pasturage is also poor because of the soil characteristics.[19] Whatever Spanish-style farming Ayllón intended for his colony, the absence of Indians in numbers meant that it could not

17. As for the 1525 voyage, so for that of 1526, dates have been derived from the saints' days, using Jerónimo de Chaves' *Chronographía.* The details of the course and of what he saw are conjectural because no account survives.

18. Oviedo, *Historia general,* III, 628; AGI, SD 11, No. 43 bis, fols. 25v–26, 28–28v. The accounts of Cervantes and Espinosa Cervantes are the only source aside from Oviedo and the not entirely reliable word of the chroniclers of the Soto expedition, whose knowledge of the event in question was that the *capitana* had sunk and deprived the expedition of its stores, with resulting hardship and failure.

19. U.S. Department of Agriculture, *Soil Survey, Georgetown County, South Carolina* (1982), *passim.*

succeed at such a location. Moreover, missions and trade with the Indians were as important as Spanish farming, perhaps more important.

Probably even before he sent the first scouting parties inland and down the coast, Ayllón decided to build a boat to replace the lost *capitana.* Accordingly, men were set to cutting pine and oak trees to build a ship that became known as *La Gavarra.* Its construction seems to have taken much of August and possibly part of September.[20]

Realizing that the area where they were would not do for settlement, Ayllón sent out scouting parties by sea, as well as by land, to see if there was a more suitable area on the coast that Quejo had somehow missed in his all too quick reconnaissance of 1525. Both Father Cervantes and Espinosa Cervantes mention these expeditions, with Father Cervantes noting that the expeditions went more than two hundred leagues *costa a costa,* which probably means that the round trip was over two hundred leagues in length. The approximate distance from the Jordan River (South Santee River) to Cabo de la Cruz, Florida (Saint Augustine Beach), was ninety leagues, according to Oviedo.[21] Ten leagues south of it is Ponce de Leon Inlet, known to the Spaniards as Río de Corrientes. It is just such a voyage, from the Río de Corrientes or a bit below it to the Jordan River, that Chaves records in his rutter, along with two others that reached as far south as the old Cabo de Santa Elena, now renamed the Río Seco (dry river) in the Chaves terminology.[22] Chaves once again is a record of voyages otherwise known only in barest outline.

The ship that sailed south to below Río de Corrientes worked its way north along the coast past Cabo de la Cruz until it put in at Saint Simon's Sound, named the Mar Baja (shallow sea) by the pilot on this voyage. From Mar Baja, the ship went north to a new Río Seco, modern Sapelo Sound. From there, the next leg of the trip was to Tybee Island—or Cabo Grueso, as it was called by the pilot on this voyage. From Cabo Grueso, it was a short and familiar run north to the Jordan River.

A second expedition went down the coast from the Jordan River to

20. AGI, SD 11, No. 43 bis, fol. 28v. The timetable is based on the events of the expedition as given in Oviedo and on the saints' days used by Chaves (*Espejo de navegantes,* 124–25).

21. Oviedo, *Historia general,* I, 444.

22. Chaves, *Espejo de navegantes,* 124–25.

modern Port Royal Sound, which was entered on August 18, the festival of Santa Elena, the mother of the Roman emperor Constantine. The sound accordingly was named the River of Santa Elena, suggesting that the Spaniards explored it deeply enough to see that the Broad River was in fact a river and not a bay. Next the party made landfall at Tybee Island, which they or the cosmographer Diogo de Ribeiro named the Cape of Santa Elena.[23] The evidence from the third scouting party of 1526 (see below) suggests that this cape was not seen on August 18, unless it was seen along with the "river" from five or six miles out at sea, where they appear side by side without other coastal features being distinguishable.[24] In any case, logic may have suggested that these two very prominent and proximate features of the coast be given the same name.

From the Cape of Santa Elena, the second scouting party sailed south to a Río Seco, which seems to have been Saint Mary's Entrance, but may have been Nassau Sound, just to the south, depending on how Chaves' materials are plotted. Having reached the southern limit specified in their orders, the second scouting party turned back for the Jordan River, apparently without having discovered anything more interesting than Port Royal Sound, which would have appeared uninhabited because most of the Indian communities were well back up the rivers or inland from them. No Indian villages would have been visible to men on a ship anchored in the bay. Parris Island, site of the later Spanish town of Santa Elena (1566–1587), was uninhabited.[25]

The third scouting party indicated by Chaves' materials followed basically the same route as the second except that it made landfall on Hilton Head Island, on which it bestowed the name Cabo de Santa Elena, indicating a landfall on August 18. From there the party sailed on south to the Río Seco, apparently not entering any of the bays along the way. Thus it, too, had little of value to report when it

23. The name first appears on the Ribeiro maps of 1529. It is used by Chaves. The Santa Elena in question was said to have discovered the true cross near Jerusalem; thus her name was appropriate for a cape initially named for the true cross.

24. I am indebted to Larry Rowland, of the University of South Carolina at Beaufort, for this information.

25. Stanley South shows that the only Indian ceramics found on the south end of the island are from the Deptford Period, A.D. 100–300 (*Exploring Santa Elena, 1981* [Columbia, S.C. (1982)], 70–71). There is a site (Chester Field Site) on Port Royal Island, but it is eight nautical miles from the lower bay and is from a Stalling's Island culture, which is of the pre-Irene (or pre-Chicora) phase. See Regina Flannery, "Some Notes on a Few Sites in Beaufort County, S.C.," in *Anthropological Papers*, No. 21, Bureau of American Ethnology Bulletin 133 (Washington, D.C., 1943), 143–53.

returned to the Jordan River. Of all the places inspected during these reconnaissances, the most interesting for Ayllón was probably Sapelo Sound. Here the Guale Indians lived in settlements at what is now Pine Harbor and on the barrier islands, especially Saint Catherine's Island, site of the seventeenth-century Spanish mission of the same name. Archaeologically classified at this time in their history as Irene Phase peoples, the Guale lived in individual family homesteads spread along the shores of the Sapelo River (at Pine Harbor) and over the surface of the islands, wherever suitable soils for maize, bean, and squash agriculture existed. The center of each community was a great house and a burial ground.[26] Because of the richness of Guale agriculture and the marine and faunal resources of the estuary, the people there may not have been quite as seasonally migratory as their neighbors to the north around Port Royal Sound, of whom the Jesuits complained so much in the 1560s.[27] The Guale supplemented the products of the field with fish, shellfish, and various animals, especially deer, taken in the hunt in the estuarine environment. Assuming that the populations of the 1560s reflected long-established settlements, it appears that there were very large, if somewhat dispersed, populations in the area around Sapelo Sound in the 1520s. That was exactly the sort of place the Spaniards were seeking. Sapelo Sound lacked, perhaps, only the pearls and quartz crystals that had been obtained from the Chicorans in 1521 and 1525.

Sapelo Sound also offered a "fine" and "very powerful" river, the Sapelo River. The United States Coastal Pilot indicates that since the beginning of records, in 1859, the entrance to Sapelo Sound has been open through the natural action of the currents. The 1609 rutter says that the bar had fourteen *palmos* (about three meters) of water at low tide and up to three fathoms of water at high tide.[28] This agrees with Oviedo's description of the "very powerful" river on whose shore Ayllón settled, but it contradicts the rest of his description, which says that the river's mouth had a bar that could not be crossed even at high tide. Given available evidence, the apparent inconsistency cannot be resolved unless it is hypothesized that what Oviedo did was mix two reports: one of the entrance to the sound (the "very powerful

26. The Irene culture was first defined by Joseph R. Caldwell and Catherine McCann in *Irene Mound Site, Chatham County, Georgia* (Athens, Ga., 1941).

27. Felix Zubillaga, *Monumenta Antiquae Floridae, 1566–1572* (Rome, 1946), 476.

28. Oviedo, *Historia general,* III, 628; U.S. Department of Commerce, NOAA, *United States Coast Pilot, Atlantic Coast: Cape Henry to Key West* (16th ed.; 1978), 137–38; Andrés Gonzalez Rutter, 1609, AGI, PAT 19, No. 31, fol. 2v.

river") and one of the entrance to the "river" on whose shore the Spaniards built their town. Any of the smaller streams or channels feeding into the Sapelo River and Sound could well have had bars that prevented the ships from entering them. That is certainly the case today. That the sound possessed a fine, powerful river suitable for a settlement seems certain, whatever is made of the statement about an entrance too shallow to be crossed even at high tide. In sum, Sapelo Sound had almost all the things that the Spaniards wished for.

The return of the three scouting parties toward the end of August, coupled with further reports from scouting parties sent inland, and the people's discontent because of the humidity and insect life—mosquitoes, chiggers, and deerflies are common—caused Ayllón and his advisers to decide definitively to go south, to Sapelo Sound (his Río Seco).[29] There they would find Indians and soils better suited to the agriculture Ayllón intended to establish. Why Ayllón did not decide to strike inland in search of Du-a-e and its resources is not indicated in any of the sources. Perhaps he felt that he lacked guides to reach that place, whose location had been but vaguely reported in 1521, or perhaps he no longer believed it existed. He may also have been reluctant to leave the coast and the possibilities it offered for resupply and reinforcement from Española.

Rather than simply loading the people and the animals on ships and going south, Ayllón decided to take the men who were fit for fighting—many were already sick—the horses, and possibly the livestock, and go overland. That not only reduced the risk of losing valuable horses but also allowed the land party both to scout the interior, fulfilling one of the requirements of Ayllón's contract, and to forage through the countryside, reducing the drain on the already seriously diminished food stores aboard the ships.

None of the sources say much about the move except that the women, children, and the ill went by ship while Ayllón, the able men, and the horses went by land. Ayllón probably took only a small party with him, since some of the able men had to be on hand to begin the new settlement and to protect the women and the sick until Ayllón and his team arrived.

The two groups bade each other farewell early in September. By sea

29. Oviedo says that after a few days the party was "discontented with the land" (*Historia general,* III, 628). Espinosa Cervantes says that they saw that the land where they had first disembarked "was not good" and so decided to go to the better land the scouting party claimed to have found (AGI, SD 11, No. 43 bis, fol. 28v).

the forty to forty-five leagues that Oviedo says the ships covered before reaching Gualdape would have required but a few days' journey. The distance Oviedo gives is additional evidence that Gualdape was at Sapelo Sound, whose entrance is nicely bracketed by forty and forty-five leagues measured from the South Santee River. Once in the sound, the sea party probably located a site for settlement and began to build houses.

The land travelers may have required as many as three weeks to work their way down the Indian trails to the fork that carried them back out to the coast where the Guale lived. In the eighteenth century, there was an Indian trail that described a long arc inland from near Winyah Bay to cross the Santee, Ashley, Cooper, Edisto, and Broad rivers well back from the coast, where they are smaller and shallower and the land is higher, and where the ground was probably drier than it is now.[30] United States alternate route 17 seems to follow the general path. The crossing point on the Savannah is uncertain. If it was close to the present city of the same name, the Spaniards might have had to construct rafts to traverse the deep, swift flowing stream. If it was farther upstream, they might have found a ford. Once they were over the Savannah, the only major river they faced was the Ogeechee.

The objection is possible that a march down the coast, even by the arcing Indian trail, would have been nearly impossible because of the many rivers and their swampy margins. But though some of this route involves swampy areas today, it may have been drier in late summer in the sixteenth century, when the sea was about a meter lower than in present times, promoting drainage along the coast. Where the pine forests were climax stands of virgin woods, there must have been little underbrush to impede the movement of the men and horses. In any case, not knowing what they would encounter and being possessed of the peculiar and amazing sixteenth-century Spanish ability to confront and overcome obstacles from which lesser men would retreat, Ayllón and his party may simply have pressed on until they made their objective. Their contemporaries in Mexico, Central America, Colombia, and within a decade, Peru did equally if not more astounding things in plunging into the geographical unknown. Unlike many of those Spaniards, Ayllón and his marchers probably had

30. William E. Myer, "Indian Trails of the Southeast," in *Forty-second Annual Report, 1924–1925,* of the Bureau of American Ethnology (Washington, D.C., 1928). Plate 15 shows coastal trails on the basis of a map of 1755 (numbers 117, 83, 84).

little to worry about concerning potential armed resistance. Archaeological evidence suggests relatively light Indian populations along the coast except for the Guale area. The Indians did not live where the soils would not support maize agriculture, although they seem to have hunted and collected acorns in areas they did not otherwise use. Inland, the climax long-needle pine forests were devoid of human settlement except for a few small villages along some of the rivers that come down from the piedmont.[31]

Once reunited at Sapelo Sound, the parties set out to organize their settlement formally and to establish wider contacts with the Indians of the area. None of the sources say much about this, but one date is suggested by the name attached to the town: San Miguel de Gualdape. The festival of Saint Michael the archangel is on September 29. That was probably the date the town was created in juridical form and judges (*alcaldes*) elected. It is probably also the date that the church, perhaps with the same name, was dedicated.

The Spaniards set about building houses as well as a church because, says Oviedo, there were only a few scattered Indian houses, like rural farmsteads in Spain (*caserías*), distant one from another. He also says that the settlement (he uses the military term *real* to indicate a fortified place, but there is no other evidence that any defenses were built) was on the coast (*costa*), or shore, of the River of Gualdape. Taken together, these two bits of information—and another to be noted—suggest that the settlement may have been on one of the islands bordering the sound, although a mainland location cannot be excluded if it was opposite one of the coastal islands. Oviedo admitted that Gualdape was not on any map, and his comments on its location show only that it was south of the Jordan River and the River of Santa Elena.[32]

Oviedo accurately described the area in which the Spaniards found themselves as flat (*llana*) and having many marshes (*cienagas*) and a powerful river. Its resources included pine trees, live oaks (*robles*) that produced gullnuts, holm oaks (*encinas*) that gave acorns, wild grapevines, chestnut trees, willows, reeds, walnut trees, bramble berries (*zarzamoras*) that the Indians made into raisins for winter food, blackberry bushes, service trees (*servos,* i.e., *serbales*), laurel trees, sumac, palmettos, sorrels, and sow thistles (*cerrajas*). Faunal re-

31. Lewis H. Larson, *Aboriginal Subsistence Technology on the Southeastern Coastal Plain During the Late Prehistoric Period* (Gainesville, Fla., 1980), 43–47.

32. Oviedo, *Historia general,* III, 630.

sources included mountain lions (*tigres*), tapirs perhaps (*dantas o beoris*), deer, rabbits, spotted jackals (hyenas?) that cried at night, sometimes all night, "little cats" that were probably bobcats, and what must surely be opossums (*monillos pardillos con solos dos dientes altos*). The birds included cranes, crows, thrushes, sparrows, partridges, turtledoves, geese, and ducks.

By far the most abundant forms of wildlife Oviedo's informants had seen and dined on were fish and shellfish. No fewer than eighteen types were noted. Using a chinchorro net (like a long seine net), the Spaniards caught more than six hundred bream (*mojarras*) on one occasion; on another they caught over seven hundred small flatfish (*lenguados*) in a creek.[33] Most of the other species named were also estuary-dwelling or migratory into the estuaries in the cooler weather of the fall. Many were caught using hook and line rather than nets.[34] The region's resources, if not matching exactly those Ayllón had promised in his vision of a new Andalucia, were substantial and, with certain exceptions among the animals, are still to be found along the Georgia–South Carolina coast.

Wherever the settlement on Sapelo Sound and however rich the area's natural resources, the Spaniards faced serious problems not unlike those of every pioneering colony. It was too late in the year to plant maize or almost any other cultigen. The food supplies brought from Española that remained after the loss of the *capitana* were almost gone. Oviedo says that the people died for want of bread even though fish were abundant for those with the strength to catch them.[35] Ayllón may have intended to use his estates on Española to supply maize and *cazabi* bread, but there is no record that any ships were sent back to the Antilles for food. In any case, the Ayllón estates seem to have been stripped just to outfit the expedition. Additional supplies would have had to be purchased with credit Ayllón may not have had after his earlier expenses. Too, supplies of maize and other foods rounded up from the local Indians were probably quickly exhausted, especially if the Indians took the precaution of hiding some of their grain from the Spaniards.

Drinking water must also have been a problem if an artesian source

33. *Ibid.*, 631–33.

34. Elizabeth Reitz, "Availability and Use of Fish Along Coastal Georgia and Florida," *Southeastern Archaeologist*, I (1982), 65–68. Larson's *Aboriginal Subsistence Technology* is a general discussion of Indian foodways; on the overall characteristics of the coastal strand, see p. 20 of that volume. Larson does not use Oviedo's data in his discussion.

35. Oviedo, *Historia general*, III, 631.

was not located. Barrel wells sunk into the freshwater lens just below the surface of most of the islands along the Georgia coast could yield very pure water but at low hydrostatic pressures. Contamination of such wells by carelessness in the placement of manure piles and garbage pits probably occurred almost at once.[36]

Deaths from diseases given their opportunity by hunger and, probably, contaminated water supplies, seem to have mounted rapidly in the weeks following the establishment of the colony. The padres and the gravediggers did not want for work.

One solution to the food problem which was also consistent with Ayllón's obligations and self-interest was to scout inland in the hope of finding denser populations with food surpluses that could be bought by barter, taken as tribute, or otherwise appropriated, whatever the Dominican friars might say. Hence, Ayllón sent more parties inland, even going himself on some, and in the process exhausting himself so that he too fell ill.[37] His scouts apparently never crossed the pine forests to the piedmont, where there were prosperous Indian towns, as Hernando de Soto was to discover fourteen years later.

On top of the hunger, exhaustion, and disease, the Spaniards suffered through several early-fall cold fronts that may have dropped temperatures from the high seventies or low eighties into the low forties or even the upper thirties in a matter of hours. Because the Spanish calendar was still on the Julian system and thus was at least ten days behind the solar seasons, the Spaniards established San Miguel on the solar equivalent of October 8, and so had their residence there well into October and November, the months when the cold season's frontal movements begin. Whether they experienced temperatures like the modern record low of twenty-eight degrees Fahrenheit cannot be known, but Oviedo records that they did suffer from the cold.[38]

36. David Hurst Thomas, director of the Saint Catherines Island Project, American Museum of Natural History, to the author, May 29, 1984.

37. Oviedo, *Historia general,* III, 628; Fray Cervantes in AGI, SD 11, No. 43 bis, fol. 26.

38. Oviedo, *Historia general,* III, 628. Modern data show average maximum temperatures of about 80 degrees Fahrenheit for Sapelo Island in October and 70 degrees for November. The average monthly temperatures for Savannah are 67.1 degrees for October and 57.1 degrees for November; the record lows are 28 degrees for October (1952) and 15 degrees for November (1950). The average temperatures are based on the period 1941–1970; the Savannah records go back into the 1880s (U.S. Department of Commerce, NOAA, Environmental Data Service, *Climatological Data, Georgia,* 75, Nos. 9–11 [1971]; U.S. Department of Commerce, NOAA, *Comparative Climatic Data for the United States Through 1978* [1979], 8, 71).

Exhaustion, hunger, cold, and disease took a heavy toll. Ayllón died of an unnamed illness on Thursday, October 18, the festival of Saint Luke (a nice irony). As a good Catholic, he had received the sacraments and was duly buried, perhaps before the high altar of the church of San Miguel. News of his death reached Santo Domingo about a month later.[39]

The adelantado's death opened a period of perhaps two weeks, at most a month, about which more is known than is known about the previous three weeks or indeed the previous three months.

Ayllón designated as his successor a nephew, Juan Ramirez, royal treasurer of the island of Puerto Rico. Ramirez was on that island, so command at Gualdape fell to Captain Francisco Gómez. Gómez and the *alcaldes* of the town intended to remain at San Miguel to await their receipt of orders, and possibly supplies, from Ramirez. Others in the Spanish community, however, wanted no more of the hardships and the difficulties of living on short rations in a strange land. For some, the obvious answer was to impose themselves on the Indians, demanding food and, probably, personal services on the pattern long familiar to Spaniards in the Caribbean. Others sought only some avenue of escape to the Antilles. Actions by both groups soon produced a crisis that caused Gómez and the *alcaldes* to evacuate the surviving colonists to the Antilles.

According to Oviedo, the self-appointed leader of those who wanted to leave at once was one Ginés Doncel, *vecino* of Santo Domingo and native of Gibraltar. He skillfully played on the discontent of others by promising that if he and they took over the government of the town, he would see that all who wished to leave could do so on the ship (or ships?) being readied to sail to the Antilles and Ramirez. Probably within a week of Ayllón's death, he had enough supporters to carry out his plan. Among his lieutenants was Pedro de Bazán, who was just as restless as Doncel.[40]

Once assured of enough followers, Doncel gathered a group of armed men who arrested Gómez and the *alcaldes* and, for a time, cowed all other potential opposition. They locked up Gómez and the

39. Oviedo, *Historia general,* III, 628; AGI, SD 11, No. 43 bis, fols. 26, 28v. Tutorship, Santo Domingo, December 22, 1526, notes Ayllón's death "about two months" earlier (AGI, JU 13, No. 1, R. 4, fols. 31v–35).

40. Oviedo, *Historia general,* III, 629. The first brief published account of these events is that by Alonso de Santa Cruz in *Crónica del Emperador Carlos V* (5 vols.; Madrid, 1920–25), III, 480.

alcaldes in Doncel's house. It was said that thereafter the captives were poorly treated, probably meaning that they were given little food and water and were kept under lock.

At about the same time, some of the other men, who could no longer see treating the Indians with the respect the Dominicans demanded, seem to have moved in with a village three leagues, or 9.6 nautical miles, from the main settlement. The Indians tolerated them for a time but soon grew tired of the unwanted and impudent guests. According to the version that Garcilaso de la Vega ("el Inca") heard in Peru many years later from Hernándo Mogollón, the Indians feasted their guests for three or four days, gave them every assurance of loyalty, and then slew them all on a single night. The next day, the Indians attacked the settlers "on the coast" who were guarding the ships. According to the account, the majority, including Ayllón, were killed or wounded. The expedition pulled out and left the land to its owners.[41]

Mogollón's version of events is not accurate on several points. For example, Ayllón was already dead, and Mogollón seems to place these events shortly after the arrival of the Spaniards, which is incorrect according to Oviedo's chronology. Still, the point of Mogollón's story —that the presence of Spaniards in some numbers in an Indian town led to an attack on them because they overstepped native concepts of hospitality—can be accepted as accurate. Furthermore, the killing of the renegades was probably the signal for general Indian hostility toward the rest of the Spaniards and possibly for harassing raids against them by small bands. Oviedo notes that the Indians had arrows made of chestnut wood that made nasty wounds but were not poisoned like those used by many South American forest tribes.[42] His comment suggests that harassment was delivered against small companies of Spaniards out foraging and perhaps by showering the settlement with arrows from a distance.

Doncel's seizure of power quickly became the object of resentment by men who "loved good" and were not part of Doncel's clique. Among those men were two hidalgos, named Oliveros and Monesterio, who emerged as leaders. The group went to Doncel to protest his actions and to suggest that the prisoners be freed. Oviedo reports

41. Garcilaso de la Vega, *The Florida of the Inca,* 11. Oviedo mentions trouble with the Indians in one sentence, saying only that they killed some unruly or impudent Spaniards (Oviedo, *Historia general,* III, 629).

42. Oviedo, *Historia general,* III, 629.

that from the date of the interview that the group received, Doncel had it in for Oliveros for being a real man (*un hombre de hecho*) who would not long accept Doncel's tyranny. Accordingly, Doncel began to discuss with Bazán how Oliveros and Monesterio might be killed. They finally agreed on night attacks.

On the night chosen, as Bazán was making his way toward Monesterio's dwelling, some of the black slaves set fire to Doncel's house, or perhaps to some buildings in his compound. Oviedo does not say what moved them to do that, except to remark that they had their reasons.[43] His intimation is that they too resented Doncel's high-handed ways. The fire drew most of the rest of the population to the scene. In a town built of huts with thatched roofs and wooden, cane, or wattle-and-daub walls, a fire was a major danger. Doncel, who had armed himself that night, apparently fled the scene and hid under a bed made by sticking poles in the ground. In short, he showed himself a coward.

When Bazán appeared outside Monesterio's door, Monesterio stepped into the street and began to treat him rather roughly because Bazán was armed. Oliveros was at that very moment seeking out Doncel to arrest him. Hearing the commotion Monesterio and Bazán made, he intervened, eventually cutting Bazán on the leg with his weapon after a sword fight of some duration. When Bazán fell to the ground, he was subdued and arrested.

Monesterio and Oliveros then went to Doncel's dwelling, where they freed Gómez and the *alcaldes.* Doncel was eventually found and put under arrest. The people apparently extinguished the fire without major damage to the rest of the town. The rightful government had been restored, and Doncel's partisans arrested. The *alcaldes* tried Bazán and ordered him degraded, that is, publicly scorned, and then beheaded. Oviedo excuses this by saying that he would have died from his wounds anyway.

With the leader and the major members of the insurrection in jail, the city government and the leadership of the expedition had to con-

43. *Ibid.* Most of the slaves on the expedition were probably household servants or skilled craftsmen, not field hands fresh from Africa. For people of their station to rebel, the cause had to be extreme personal provocation rather than their unwillingness to adjust to slavery. The bald refusal to submit more often underlay rebellion among field hands, especially those fairly recently arrived from Africa. See Richard Price (ed.), *Maroon Societies: Rebel Slave Communities in the Americas* (New York, 1973), 24.

sider what to do next. They decided to remove the surviving colonists to the Antilles. They put their plan into effect toward the end of October, perhaps within two weeks of Ayllón's death. In any case, they had abandoned San Miguel de Gualdape by mid-November.

Nothing is known about the loading of the ships or even the date of their departure. Oviedo says it was very cold on the return voyage—that on the *Santa Catalina* seven men froze to death, and on the *Choruca* a man lost the flesh from his legs when he tried to take his pants off. In another place, he tells of an apparent miracle in which the virgin Mary provided water to the seamen of one ship.[44] Each reader will judge for himself whether these stories are to be believed. That the trip home was stormy and at times cold and that the men were thirsty as well as hungry cannot be doubted.

Oviedo also says that Ayllón's body was put into a skiff and towed behind one of the ships until it was lost at sea. Father Cervantes and Espinosa Cervantes, however, are both quite explicit in saying that Ayllón had been buried at San Miguel.[45] It is unlikely that a body at least two weeks into the decay of death would have been exhumed and carried in a skiff, even at some distance from a ship. Cervantes and Espinosa Cervantes would surely have commented on a procedure that unusual.

The first of the ships to make port in the Antilles was the *Bretón.* It brought the three Dominicans to Puerto Plata on a voyage of twenty-one days, probably on the southeast course around the Bahamas. The ship sank shortly after making port (Table 1). The *Bretón Grande* took at least fifty days to reach Puerto Rico, although Oviedo records other estimates of up to four months. Only fifteen or twenty of its original complement of seventy survived the journey; the rest died of hunger or thirst.[46]

The other three ships made various ports. One landed at Anegada, in the Bahamas. The story of the virgin Mary's miracle in supplying water on a dry little island probably came from that ship. A second

44. Oviedo, *Historia general,* III, 631–32, IV, 537–38. Bernardo de Fuentes heard that Ayllón died and was buried at sea, according to his answer to question 7 of the interrogatory of Pedro Vázquez de Ayllón, Santo Domingo, 1560, AGI, PAT 63 (Stetson).

45. Oviedo, *Historia general,* III, 630; AGI, SD 11, No. 43 bis, fols. 26, 28v.

46. Oviedo, *Historia general,* IV, 537. Twenty-seven years later, the licenciado Juan de Vadillo said that by the time the *Bretón Grande* reached Puerto Rico almost all of the hundred persons aboard had died (AGI, SD 11, No. 43 bis, fol. 16).

ship landed at Cape Tiburon, on the western end of Española; the third ended up in the port San Fermín, in Puerto Rico.[47]

Wherever the survivors landed in the Antilles, they probably counted themselves fortunate. Of the five or six hundred men, women, and children who had set out, only about 150 returned to the Antilles four months later.

Some of them remained on Española into the 1530s and 1540s, but most drifted off to other places and to obscure deaths. Oviedo mentions some who remained on Española: the Dominican fathers Montesinos and Cervantes, Captain Gómez, Quejo, and Juan Rodriguez Malaver. Doncel returned to Española for a time, apparently none the worse off for his part in the rebellion. In 1529, he was a shipowner engaged in trade with Mexico.[48]

Something is known about the later lives of nine of the survivors of the Ayllón expedition who went to other places. Diego Rodriguez, the licenciado Francisco de Prado, and Juan Muñoz moved on to Cuzco, where the last two testified to the merits and services of the first (1539). They remembered the great labors and hunger of the expedition of 1526.[49] Mogollón and Cristobal Gallego also ended their lives in Peru, Gallego after spending time in Honduras and Nicaragua before going to Peru around 1531. Mogollón was the old man from whom Garcilaso de la Vega heard a bit about the expedition.[50]

Others of the survivors went to New Spain. Antonio de Aller, who had been an ensign with the expedition, went on to settle in Tenochtitlan (Mexico City) and participate in the expedition of 1541 against the Indian rebels of New Galicia. He may well have spent his later years reminiscing with Alonso de Villanueva, who also settled in the capital of New Spain. Juan de Avila was there in the late 1520s. Gonzalo Martín settled at Puebla, Mexico, in the 1530s.[51]

Two of the Dominican friars who had gone with Ayllón have left little trace of their subsequent lives. Brother Luís disappears from the

47. Oviedo, *Historia general,* IV, 537.

48. *Ibid.,* III, 627; AGI, SD 77, No. 52, fols. 20v–21.

49. *Probanza* de Diego Rodriguez, Cuzco, March 10, 1539, AGI, Lima 204; testimony, Madrid, May 17, 1553, AGI, SD 11, No. 43 bis, fol. 17v. Alvar Núñez Cabeza de Vaca, who only met survivors as they came to Santo Domingo in 1526, recalled that these were the topics they spoke of.

50. Boyd Bowman, *Indice,* II, 283, No. 9237; Garcilaso de la Vega, *The Florida of the Inca,* 11.

51. Boyd Bowman, *Indice,* II, 178, 57, 13, 152, Nos. 5890, 2063, 357, 5085 respectively.

record completely. Father Cervantes seems to have remained on Española until at least 1541 but then disappears from the record until the fall of 1561, when as a very old man he was at the Monastery of San Pablo, in Seville. There he gave a deposition about the expedition at the request of Ayllón the Younger.[52]

Father Montesinos continued to play a visible role in Caribbean history until his death in 1540. In 1528, he and Father Tomás de Verlanga, vicar and vice-provincial of the Dominicans on Española, went to Spain to see the emperor on matters of "great importance" not otherwise specified.[53] Out of this trip came Montesinos' appointment as protector of the Indians in Venezuela. Charles V had just granted that province to Ambrosio Alfinger and Bartolomé Sayller, representatives of the Welser Company, one of his German creditors. Montesinos sailed with the German expedition. He was murdered on June 27, 1540, by an officer of the expedition, because he tried to prevent the wholesale exploitation of the Indians.[54]

Ayllón's widow, Ana Bezerra, was left to deal with a pile of debts from the expedition, to account for a period of Ayllón's service as judge for which no accounting had been rendered, and to raise Ayllón's children. Her actions cannot be followed in any detail, but a few glimpses of this remarkable young woman—she was probably not yet thirty in 1523—are possible.

Ana's first step was dictated by the law and her husband's will naming her the tutor and curator for their children. On December 22, 1526, she legally assumed those capacities toward her minor children, under the age of twelve: Juan de Ayllón, later to take his father's name; Fernando de Bezerra; Pedro Alvares de Ayllón; Constanca de Ribera; and Ynés de Villalobos. Because the enabling legal act was not properly executed, a new tutorship document was drawn up on November 8, 1527, but this time Ana swore an oath to care faithfully and carefully for the children and to administer the property according to an inventory to be made.[55] She seems to have moved her family to Puerto Plata soon afterward.[56]

52. Register entry, *Santa María de la Antigua*, Santo Domingo, August 29, 1541, copy in AGI, IG 1562, Book for 1559–1562, fol. 323; AGI, SD 11, No. 43 bis, fol. 23.

53. Constable of Castile to emperor, Verlanga, August 3, 1528, AGS, EDO K1643, No. 91. For other details of this trip, see instruction, Puerto Plata, March 10, 1528, AGI, IG 1382 (moved from IG 3088), and payment, March 20, 1528, AGI, CD 1050, No. 2, fol. 269.

54. Mirtha A. Hernández, "Fray Antonio de Montesinos and the Laws of Burgos" (M.A. thesis, Louisiana State University, 1977), 97–100.

55. AGI, JU 13, No. 1, R. 4, fols. 31v–35, 5v–7v respectively.

56. AGI, JU 50, Pieza 1, fols. 10–11, 14–14v.

To help pay Ayllón's debts, Ana's agents sold bronze artillery weighing fifteen hundred pounds to the royal treasury for 166 pesos, 5 tomines, and 4 granos of gold.[57] They also sold Ayllón's house in Santo Domingo to the licenciado Alonso de Zuazo for seventeen hundred pesos de oro payable over ten years. In November, 1533, after Zuazo had failed to pay his semiannual installments, Ana sued him, eventually regaining title to and occupancy of the house.[58]

Ana thus returned to Santo Domingo. Debts probably still remained for her to pay, but she had made significant progress toward discharging them in the decade after her husband's death. The half-interest in the sugar plantation and mill at Puerto Plata and help from her late husband's business associates, to most of whom the estate owed something, coupled with her own shrewdness—witness the suit against Zuazo—had accomplished a great deal.

When Ayllón's service as *oidor* from the time of his restoration to office in 1520 until his departure for the new land came under scrutiny in 1527–1528, Ana had to provide an attorney to represent his estate. The secret inquiry (*pesquisa secreta*) and the formal charges that the licenciado Gaspar de Astudillo, inspector (*veedor*) of the audiencia, filed affirmed that Ayllón, in common with his fellow judges, had spent as much as two months in each year away from Santo Domingo tending to his estates, had neglected to sentence certain cases, had engaged in trade, had failed to see that equal numbers of men and women were imported by the slave contractor, had not taken the royal accounts and those of the towns, and had not checked yearly on the accounts of curators of minor children and their property. Ayllón himself was said to be guilty of trading in Bahamian slaves and not paying what he owed people, even those who worked for him.

Although there was considerable evidence to support these accusations, the *juez de residencia,* the licenciado Gaspar de Espinosa, absolved Ayllón of all charges. Ayllón's death and Espinosa's desire to enjoy some of the same liberties while in office—he was to become a judge himself—placed the adelantado beyond any but divine judgment, as Espinosa himself observed.[59] There seems to have been a

57. AGI, CD 1050. Cited by Emilio Rodriguez Demorizi in *Los dominicos y las encomiendas de indios en la isla Española* (Santo Domingo, 1977), 85–86.

58. AGI, JU 13, No. 1, R. 4.

59. *Cargos* from the *pesquisa secreta,* with sentence, March 5, September 16, 1528, AGI, JU 50, No. 4.

similar outcome to an order from the Council of the Indies, in September, 1528, for Ayllón's heirs to respond to certain charges of trade in Indian slaves left over from the residencia of 1517.[60] The slaving voyages of the teens and the trading ventures of men then dead were left to history, as was the expedition of 1526.

Reflecting on the fate of the Ayllón expedition, Oviedo offered not only an observation that men not of the sword ought not to undertake such essentially military tasks but also the more insightful comment that captains like Ayllón failed because they did not know the conditions they would encounter and so did not make preparations appropriate to the conditions. The rules that had worked in the Caribbean were not valid, he saw, for the northern areas where the Indians were more warlike and the climate colder.

Yet for all that had been suffered by Ayllón's people, "some liked the shape [*la forma*] of the region they had seen and said that, doing what was requisite for settling in that place, and with enough foods to last until the land was understood, [settlement] would not be a bad thing, because the climate there was better suited for Spaniards."[61]

Fourteen years later, some of Soto's men made the same judgment about the area they knew as Cofitachequi, a province on the Wateree River, a tributary of the Santee River (Ayllón's Jordan). Both groups brought experience and reality to bear on Ayllón's propaganda about the land of Chicora and did not disagree with his hope that it could be a new Andalucia. In their own ways, the persons who reached an optimistic conclusion in spite of the hardships they endured in the new land helped to perpetuate the Chicora legend for the next generation of explorers and would-be colonizers. That next generation was Hernando de Soto and his men.

60. Cedula, September 4, 1528; AGI, JU 50, No. 3; notifications, Santo Domingo, February 22, 1529, *ibid.*; declaration of rebellion, Valladolid, July 10, 1529, *ibid.* Nothing further seems to have been done about the matter.

61. Oviedo, *Historia general,* III, 630.

IV

The Chicora Legend Discounted Among Spaniards, 1526–1551

In the quarter century that followed the death of Ayllón, his positive assessment of the Southeast, especially its Atlantic coast, lost its appeal for most Spaniards even though it found literary form in the writings of Peter Martyr and the captions on some copies of the official Spanish map of the world. A number of events account for that development. The experience of Ayllón's colony did much to diminish belief in the picture he had painted of a verdant new Andalucia on the southeastern coast of North America. Hernando de Soto's explorations failed to find another part of the legend: Xapira, the inland district that supposedly produced gemstones. What is more, the hardships and failure of Soto's expedition reinforced negative images of the Southeast. Still, some Spaniards' hopes that the Southeast was a new Andalucia did not die but were displaced from Ayllón's Chicora to the interior, where Soto had discovered large Indian populations and apparently abundant agricultural resources. Action on this form of Ayllón's legend was postponed, however, because of a renewed royal commitment to peaceful conversion of the Indians in all of the Americas. La Florida became a test of this approach to empire. The failure of that test further tarnished the region's reputation but did not alter the hopes that attached to the interior.

During the dozen years between Ayllón's death and Soto's peregrination, only Pánfilo de Narváez' ill-fated expedition carried on the exploration of the Southeast. Restricted because of Ayllón's grant to the peninsula of Florida and the Gulf Coast—that is, to Ponce de Leon's and Francisco de Garay's grants, now invalid because of the deaths of those men—Narváez disappeared without a trace after leaving Cuba in 1528. Only when Alvar Núñez Cabeza de Vaca reached Mexico in 1536 was the expedition's fate revealed.[1] Narváez' disappearance pro-

1. Lowery, *Spanish Settlements,* I, 172–209.

vided yet more evidence in support of the idea that the southeastern part of North American was not the new Andalucia that Ayllón had claimed it to be.

Yet even as a negative image of the reality of the Southeast was settling into Spanish consciousness, Ayllón's legend was taking the literary form that would excite and deceive a later generation of would-be colonizers. Martyr turned his notes on Ayllón into a story to amuse Francesco Maria Sforza, the duke of Milan (1521–1535). That manuscript became Books 2 and 3, and most of Book 4, in Martyr's seventh decade when all eight decades were published posthumously in Latin in 1530 at Alcalá de Henares.[2] Martyr has always been better known for the numerous editions of the first three decades, originally published in 1516, which contained accounts of Columbus' and Amerigo Vespucci's voyages, among others. But the edition of all of the decades in 1530 was more important for the history of North American discovery. Here alone, in all the pre-1550 printed books, could be found a complete account of Ayllón's expedition of 1521. Here, too, was the fullest description of the supposed resources and customs of the Indians of the Southeast to see print prior to Thomas Harriot's account of Virginia (Roanoke) and the engraved versions of the John White–Jacques Le Moyne drawings, published in 1588 and the 1590s respectively.[3] But most important, here was the claim that a part of the southeastern coast of North America was a new Andalucia, rich not only in the agricultural products Europeans associated with that Spanish region but also in pearls and gems.

Equally important for keeping the memory of Ayllón's work alive, if less explicit about what had happened and what could be expected from the new land, were the Ribeiro maps. Diogo de Ribeiro was a Portuguese first employed in 1525 to make the master map, or *padrón general,* kept by the House of Trade at Seville. The *padrón general* of

2. Anghiera, *De orbe nouo.* See Bibliography for information on other editions and the Spanish and English translations.

3. Oviedo's *Historia general* (Seville, 1535), which was incorporated into the 1851 edition, noted that Ayllón had gone to his "government," but Oviedo provided no other details (1851 ed., I, 111–12). Thomas Harriot's *A Briefe and True Report of the New Found Land of Virginia* (London, 1588) is reproduced in David B. Quinn (ed.), *The Roanoke Voyages, 1584–1590* (2 vols.; London, 1955), I, 317–87. For the engravings, see Jacques Le Moyne de Morgues, *The Work of Jacques Le Moyne de Morgues, a Huguenot Artist in France, Florida, and England,* ed. Paul H. Hulton (2 vols.; London, 1977), and Stefan Lorant (ed.), *The New World: The First Pictures of America, Made by John White and Jacques LeMoyne and Engraved by Theodore de Bry . . .* (Rev. ed.; New York, 1965).

the sort of Ribeiro's became the standard Spanish map until Alonso de Chaves modified it in the early 1530s.[4] Prominently displayed on it was the legend "land of Ayllón" near the Jordan River and the Cabo de San Román. On the 1529 Weimar Ribeiro, the legend under that title says,

> The country of Ayllón which he discovered and returned to settle, as it is well suited to yield breadstuff, wine and all things of Spain. He died here of disease.[5]

The legend on the 1529 Rome Ribeiro map is more informative. It says,

> Here the licenciado Ayllón went to settle. He departed from Santo Domingo or Puerto de Plata where he embarked his men. They carried very few supplies, and the people of that land fled inland out of fear so that when winter came many persons died from hunger and cold. And thus, being in this labor, they agreed to return to Española.[6]

In short, even if other Europeans were not aware of the details of Ayllón's tale as found in Martyr, they could learn something of the promise of the land and the history of his colony by reading one or more copies of the Ribeiro map. In combination, Martyr's account and the Ribeiro maps promised much to the explorer and colonizer who could again locate the land of Chicora. Thus did Ayllón inadvertently establish a legend, a report based on facts but exaggerated in the telling until there was little relationship to the original reality.

Even though Ayllón's expedition had ended in failure and his death, his legend of Florida's potential retained its attractive power at least so far as the interior was concerned. Xapira's pearls and "other ter-

4. Louis-André Vigneras, "The Cartographer Diogo Ribeiro," *Imago Mundi,* XVI (1962), 76–83. For reproductions of Ribeiro's maps, see William P. Cumming, R. A. Skelton, and David B. Quinn, *The Discovery of North America* (New York, 1972), plates 74 (1527 Rome), 115 (1529 Rome); and E. L. Stevenson, "Early Spanish Cartography of the New World with Special Reference to Wolfenbüttal-Spanish Map and the Work of Diego Ribero," *Proceedings of the American Antiquarian Society,* n.s., XIX (1909), 369–419 (1533 Weimar), The east-coast portions of both 1529 copies of the map (Rome and Weimar) are reproduced in I. N. P. Stokes's *The Iconography of Manhattan Island, 1498–1909* (1915–28; rpr. New York, 1964), II, plate 10.

5. Stevenson, "Early Spanish Cartography," 394*n*79.

6. Translated by the author from the reproduction of the map legend in Stokes's *Iconography,* II, plate 10, as checked by the Reverend Dr. Charles E. O'Neill against the reproduction in Roberto Almagia's *Monumenta Cartographica Vaticana* (4 vols.; Rome, 1944), I, tav. xxii. I want to thank Dr. O'Neill for this assistance.

restrial gems" had not been found by any of Ayllón's parties. But the North American continent was clearly very large and many believed that it ought to contain other, even higher, Indian civilizations than those Ayllón had found or heard about. The long string of Spanish discoveries and conquests on the mainlands of Central and South America was creating a widely held belief that every unexplored part of the Americas might contain additional Mexicos or Perus. By 1535, the largest unexplored part of the Americas was North America.

What was needed was an entrepreneur with the military experience Ayllón had lacked who would thoroughly explore the Southeast before reaching any conclusions. Soto was such a man.

Born in 1500 of parents who were themselves the children of hidalgos on both sides, Soto grew up in Villa Nueva de Barcarrota, Badajoz Province, Spain, not far from the Portuguese frontier and deep in the heart of Extremadura, the mother of conquistadores.[7] As a youth, he had served with Pedro Arias de Avila (Pedrárias) in Nicaragua. He married Isabel de Bobadilla, Pedrárias' daughter. From Nicaragua, he went to Peru, where he served with Francisco Pizarro in the capture of Atahualpa, the last Inca to rule prior to the Spanish conquest. Alone of the major Spanish captains, he opposed the execution of Atahualpa. If Antonio de Herrera y Tordesillas is correct, Soto and some sixty companions left Peru about 1535 because of the incipient struggle between Pizarro's and Diego de Almagro's followers that caused that execution.[8] Soto's goal was the court at Valladolid, where favors were dispensed to those who, like him, knew how to seek influence and share the wealth they had gained from their New World adventures. Garcilaso de la Vega ("el Inca") says that Soto's share of the loot from Cajamarca, the gifts given him at Cuzco when he and Pedro del Barco were sent there, and Atahualpa's gifts to him amounted to over 100,000 ducats, an immense fortune.[9]

The prize upon which Soto cast his eye was the North American continent. Ayllón's death and Narváez' disappearance were already known. Accordingly, none of the former grants were any longer valid, and the way was open for a new grant. After some preliminary negotiations, the emperor and Soto signed a contract on April 20, 1537. Soto fell heir to Narváez's contract area, which had included Garay's

7. Lowery, *Spanish Settlements,* I, 213*n*4.

8. John Hemming, *The Conquest of the Inca* (New York, 1970), 71–79; Herrera, *Historia general,* III, 160; Lowery, *Spanish Settlements,* I, 214.

9. Garcilaso de la Vega, *The Florida of the Inca,* 4.

grant from Pánuco to Ochese (Achuse) and Ponce de Leon's grant for peninsular Florida, and to Ayllón's grant for the areas north of the peninsula. Thus consolidated, the three areas were now named the province of La Florida by royal order.[10] That is, the region from at least 37° north, the stated northern limit of Ayllón's grant, to the Pánuco River was now to be known as La Florida, whereas formerly that name had applied only to the area Ponce de Leon had discovered, roughly from Ponce de Leon Inlet, Florida, on south and then up the west coast of the peninsula to perhaps Apalachee Bay. If the limits of Pedro de Quejo's exploration of 1525 are taken into account, La Florida reached from the Delaware Bay on the north (roughly 39° north) to the Pánuco River on the west. In sum, Soto took as his stage the whole of what is now the United States Southeast, in addition to Texas and parts of northern Mexico.

Like Ayllón's and Narváez' contracts, Soto's called for a period of exploration before he was obliged to create settlements. That often-overlooked provision largely accounts for his long peregrination throughout the Southeast. Once he had explored his domain, he was to select two hundred leagues of coast, or about 640 nautical miles, to settle and populate. Three forts were to be built at Soto's expense; he could name the warder for one. To attract Spanish settlers, he was allowed to grant encomiendas, in a radical departure from the terms of Ayllón's and Narváez' contracts and in tacit acknowledgment of the bad reputation La Florida had acquired. He won remissions of any royal taxes on gold and all import and export fees for goods destined for residents of the new settlements, for a period of six years following settlement. Goods from graves and precious objects from temples and other native religious places would be assessed a 50-percent tax. Soto could keep one-sixth of ransoms and any other loot he obtained from the Indians, with the other five-sixths going to his followers, after deduction of the king's fifth off the top of the whole. He also got a grant of land twelve leagues on a side wherever he might wish. Like his predecessors, he was awarded the governorship for life and the title of adelantado. Like Narváez, he was named captain general for life, but the administration of, and appointment of judges for, judicial affairs was reserved to the crown.

To help pay the costs of the expedition, Soto was accorded fifty slave

10. AGI, CT 3309, Book of Florida, fol. 127. The contract is in AGI, IG 415, Book 1, fols. 38–41 (and in *DII*, XV, 354–63, XXII, 534–46).

licenses free of duties and taxes, with a promise of fifty more later. As with Ayllón, so with Soto, all salaries and all expenses for the religious establishment would be paid from the ecclesiastical revenues generated by the province. Unlike Ayllón's contract, however, Soto's made no provision to repay other expenses. Those expenses would have to be recouped in other ways.

By no means least, Soto was named to the governorship of Cuba, an appointment that provided him with an income and a base of supply.[11] Like his predecessors Ayllón and Narváez, he knew that he would have to support the new settlements for a time from the resources, especially the food resources, of the Antilles. In sum, his contract combined the plans and experiences of the earlier explorers of La Florida with Soto's own experiences in Peru and Nicaragua.

The conquest promised to be peaceful only to the extent that the Indians did not resist. If they resisted, the Spaniards had implicit authorization to use the iron hand of war to bring them into obedience to the emperor. At court, Charles V's absence apparently meant that Dominican influence, although still strong, was not so dominant as it had been in the early 1520s and as it would become again in the early 1540s, when Charles was back in Spain. The more pious probably hoped that the show of force that Soto's army would make would be enough, especially once the Indians understood the Christian message and the grandeur of the emperor. Men who thought of themselves as realists probably laughed at such hopes, which had yet to be proved in practice anywhere in the Americas.

Three months after Soto signed his contract, Cabeza de Vaca landed at Lisbon. He had been preceded by sensational, if sketchy, accounts of his travels and what he had found in Texas and northern Mexico. Soon at court, he began to tell his story to anyone who would listen; many persons were eager to hear him. Some details, he said, were only for the emperor's ear, but what he could say was that the Indians among whom he had lived had cotton cloth, and gold and silver and precious stones of great value. With what must have been a certain malicious glee, he advised some of his kinsmen that they ought to sell all they owned and join Soto in his expedition to this "richest country in the world."[12] That word, too, got around, as did information that

11. Contract, AGI, IG 415, Book 1, fols. 38–41. See also Lyon, *The Enterprise of Florida.* Appendix 2, [220–23].

12. Gentleman of Elvas, quoted in Lowery's *Spanish Settlements,* I, 216.

Cabeza de Vaca had accepted Soto's invitation to join the expedition. (In the end he did not join it.)

A sort of hysteria to accompany Soto developed in the minds of many men, especially among the restless returnees from the conquests of Peru and Central America who had gathered at court and in many villages in Extremadura and Andalucia. These men and others convinced themselves that new Perus and new Mexicos lay in the interior of the Southeast. Soto had no trouble finding volunteers eager to pay their own way.

Rendezvous was set for Seville in the spring of 1538. Some six hundred soldiers assembled, bringing with them numerous servants and even a few wives. Three Dominican friars went along, led by Father Juan de Gallegos. The emperor's representatives were Luís Hernández de Biedma, royal factor and one of the chief narrators of the expedition; Juan de Añasco, royal accountant; and Juan Gaytán, royal treasurer.

Soto's fleet of seven large and three small ships sailed from San Lucar de Barameda on April 6, 1538, as the escort for twenty merchantmen bound mostly for Mexico. Although Spain was officially at peace with France, French commerce raiders, or corsairs, had been reported on their way to the Canary Islands with the aim of intercepting shipping bound for the New World.[13]

The crossing was uneventful. Port was made at Santiago de Cuba, still the capital of the island, on June 9. While Soto attended to the defense of Santiago—it had just been raided by French corsairs—and gathered foodstuffs and more men, Añasco was sent to Florida to find a suitable port on the west coast. On his second trip, he came back with Indians whom the Spaniards planned to train as interpreters.

From Santiago, the fleet moved on to Havana, which, like Santiago, was open to French raids. Following royal orders, Soto contracted for the construction of a tower fort, more a symbol of the emperor's sovereignty than a defense.[14] The expedition gathered supplies and made arrangements for the forwarding of additional supplies once the

13. Lowery, *Spanish Settlements*, I, 217–18. For the military situation, see Paul E. Hoffman, *The Spanish Crown and the Defense of the Caribbean, 1535–1585: Precedent, Patrimonialism, and Royal Parsimony* (Baton Rouge, 1980), 24–26.

14. The construction at Santiago is reported in *DIU*, VI, 73–74. The work at Havana is discussed in Irene A. Wright's *Historia documentada de San Cristobal de La Habana en el siglo XVI* (2 vols; Havana, 1927), I, 14–17.

army was in La Florida. Juan de Rojas was named lieutenant governor of Cuba, and Isabel de Bobadilla, Soto's wife, was left at Havana to see that her husband's personal interests were protected.

Soto sailed for La Florida on Sunday, May 18, 1539. He reached the coast on the twenty-fifth and landed on the twenty-eighth. The location of the landing has been open to controversy for most of the twentieth century, but the most recent reexamination of the evidence has placed it near Ruston, on Tampa Bay.[15] Soto now had six hundred men, eight secular priests, four friars, a surgeon, assorted skilled tradesmen such as coopers and blacksmiths, 213 horses, probably hundreds of pigs, and mastiff dogs (*gallgos*) for hunting down Indians as well as game. In addition, the fleet carried a supply of neck chains for the slaves they expected to capture and ship back to Cuba. A portable forge allowed the repair of the chains and other iron equipment.

Most of the Indians had fled before the Spanish reached shore. Three exploring parties sent inland reported swamps and rivers and little food. The last party, however, returned with an account, apparently concocted by Soto to encourage his army, of a rich province "to the west" called Cale.[16] At a council of the officers it was decided to seek out this province by moving inland and away from the coast. The council agreed to send the ships back to Cuba for supplies, with a rendezvous appointed for Apalachee Bay. A garrison of thirty horse and fifty foot soldiers was left at the landing port.

The main body of the exploring army set off to the east on August 1, 1539. By stages and with many adventures, Soto took his men north to Anica Apalache, an Indian town that was near modern Tallahassee. They arrived there at the end of October. The fall harvest was in, and the residents had stores of maize, pumpkins, and other foods. Here Soto determined to make his winter stop. From his camp he sent back to his landing port for the garrison left there. He sent a second party west, which discovered Pensacola Bay. A third party went down to the coast at Apalachee Bay and found what they took to be the remains of

15. Jerald T. Milanich, *Hernando de Soto and the Expedition in La Florida* (Gainesville, Fla., 1987), 9; Lowery, *Spanish Settlements,* I, 219; *Final Report of the United States De Soto Expedition Commission,* 76th Congress, 1st Sess., House Document No. 71, p. 137. Cf. Robert S. Weddle, *Spanish Sea: The Gulf of Mexico in North American Discovery, 1500–1685* (College Station, Tex., 1985), 214, 230–31.

16. Lowery, *Spanish Settlements,* I, 220–21.

Narváez' camp, where he had built his horsehide-covered boats for the desperate trip along the Gulf coast.[17]

Among the Indians that Soto had with him was a youth captured at Napetuca, the scene of a battle on the march north. The youth told the Spaniards of a land to the east and north governed by a woman. It was a large town that held many other chiefs under its sway. When shown gold, silver, gemstones, and pearls, the youth "replied that in the last province he had visited [he was a servant to traveling merchants], a place called Cofachiqui [*sic*], there was much metal like the yellow and the white, and that the principal business of the merchants whom he served was that of buying and selling such metals in other lands. Moreover, he said, great quantities of pearls were to be found there."[18] Because this was what the Spaniards had been hoping to find, Soto determined to use this boy and another of about the same age and background as guides to the province of Cofitachequi.

The march to Cofitachequi began on March 3, 1540. Like most legs of Soto's route, his crossing of Georgia is much in dispute. Five days were needed to leave the province of Apalache and get to the province of Altapaha. Crossing that province occupied the next two weeks, including ten days spent marching toward the north along a river. The next province was Achalaque, a poor place with few inhabitants that the Spaniards hastened across in five days, such, says Garcilaso, was their desire to reach Cofitachequi and its riches. Anyway, they were on level land with no rivers to cross. The next province was Cofa. After a four days' march into it, they came to the chief town, which received them as well as Altapaha had done. They found the region rich in agricultural and sylvan resources. For five days the army rested at the principal town.

Resuming the march, the Spaniards went six or seven days to the edge of the province of Cofaqui, ruled by a brother of the cacique of Cofa. Here, too, they were welcomed, especially once Soto revealed his intention to go to Cofitachequi, which turned out to be the hereditary enemy of the people of Cofaqui. The cacique promised warriors, supplies, and bearers for the campaign, and informed the marchers

17. *Ibid.*, 225–26. Garcilaso de la Vega uses pp. 59–260 of *The Florida of the Inca*, or about 33 percent of his narrative, getting to this point. For the geography and geology of the likely route in Florida, see Alan Blake, *A Proposed Route for the Hernando de Soto Expedition from Tampa Bay to Apalachee Based on Physiography and Geology* (University, Ala., 1987).

18. Garcilaso de la Vega, *The Florida of the Inca*, 254.

that there were five or more days of uninhabited country to cross. Here, too, the boy—now called Pedro—who had promised to lead the Spaniards to Cofitachequi seems to have realized that he did not know the way. To cover his quandary, he claimed to be attacked by devils and sought and received baptism. His reason became plain after another seven days or so of marching: the trail ended in a host of small paths in a forest. Wandering through it, the army came to a great river, larger than two they had crossed in the deserted area. Both Spaniards and Indians were now lost without food, there being, according to Garcilaso, no Indian among the several thousand who had accompanied Soto from Cofaqui who had ever been that far.

Exploring parties were sent out, one upriver and the other downriver, to the southeast. The explorers going upriver finally found a town with rich supplies of food and, from the top of its highest building—probably a temple mound—a view that showed that other towns lay farther up the river. They sent word by horseman to Soto. It was mid-April, 1540.

Within four days, the army had reached this village. Here Soto rested for a week, allowing parties that had been out seeking Indians and settlements to rejoin the main body and to rebuild their strength after so many days without food. During this period, Soto's Indian allies raided their enemy's towns round about, killing any Cofitachequians that they could capture and desecrating the burial mounds and temples.[19] Soto soon put a stop to that and sent the Cofaquians home, loaded with presents and happy, says Garcilaso, because they had avenged past wrongs suffered at the hands of the Cofitachequians.

Several additional days of marching brought Soto to Cofitachequi, the object of his search. Recent scholarship has established that this town was on the Wateree River, near modern Camden, South Carolina.[20] Here the Spaniards demanded and got yellow metals, which

19. *Ibid.*, 294–95. This differs from Ranjel's account, which fails to mention these details. See also Luís Hernández de Biedma, "Relación de la isla de la Florida," in Buckingham Smith (ed.), *Colección de varios documentos para la historia de la Florida y tierras adyacentes* (London, 1857), 51 (and in *DII*, III, 414–20). See also Lowery, *Spanish Settlements*, I, 228.

20. Chester DePratter, Charles Hudson, and Marvin Smith, "The Route of Juan Pardo's Exploration in the Interior Southeast, 1566–1568," *Florida Historical Quarterly*, LXII (1983), 138. Stephen Baker locates Cofitachequi close to Columbia (Cofitachequi: Fair Province of South Carolina" [M. A. thesis, University of South Carolina, 1974]). For a location at Silver Bluff on the Savannah River, see Lowery, *Spanish Settlements*, II, 228; and *Final Report of the United States De Soto Expedition Commission*, 180–83.

turned out to be copper, and white metals, which were iron pyrites. They also got pearls, mostly by looting mortuary temples of the various towns they visited around Cofitachequi.[21] In the same temples they found great bundles of deerskins (chamois, in Garcilaso's account) and mantles made of dressed furs from "animals both great and small. . . . Many were of different species and colors of cats, and others, of very fine marten, each of them being so well dressed that among the best of Germany or Muscovy one could not have found better. . . . They would bring a high price in our Spain."[22]

At Talomeco, a town a league from that in which the queen of Cofitachequi lived, they found two Spanish woodcutting axes (possibly hatchets), a rosary of *cuentas de azebache,* and some *margaritas,* or trade beads. The trade goods, they surmised, had come from the Ayllón expedition. One of the men with Soto had been with Ayllón, for Biedma says that "one who had been there (with Ayllón) told us that of six hundred men Ayllón had landed in that land no more than fifty-seven had escaped," most having perished because of the loss of supplies carried in the "large ship."[23] This man also said that the Ayllón party had stayed on the coast and that Ayllón's death had been followed by a period of internal troubles in the colony which led to its abandonment. Learning from the Indians that the river entered the sea thirty leagues downstream (two or three days' journey), the "gentleman of Elvas," Biedma, and others concluded, as Biedma said, that this was "the River of Santa Elena, where the licenciado Ayllón had been."[24] The conclusion that this was a river visited by Ayllón is correct if Cofitachequi was on the Wateree River. The Wateree River feeds into the Santee River, Ayllón's Jordan. But the Wateree River was not the same as the River of Santa Elena, which most maps showed at or very near the Point of Santa Elena, which was well to the south of the mouths of the Santee River. Nor had Ayllón attempted to settle on that river.

21. Garcilaso de la Vega, *The Florida of the Inca,* 311.

22. *Ibid.,* 311, 313.

23. Hernández de Biedma, "Relación," in Smith (ed.), *Colección,* 52 (and in *DII,* III, 422).

24. Hernández de Biedma, "Relación," in Smith (ed.), *Colección,* 51,; Rodrigo Ranjel, "Relación," in Oviedo, *Historia general,* I, 558–62; gentleman of Elvas, *True Relation of the Hardships Suffered by Governor Fernando de Soto and Certain Portuguese Gentlemen During the Discovery of the Province of Florida,* trans. and ed. James A. Robertson (2 vols.; Deland, Fla., 1932–33), II, 57–58.

Rich as Cofitachequi and Talomeco were in pearls, Soto decided to move on—to seek gold, silver, and gems and to leave a province that had been devastated by an epidemic the previous year. Disease had killed many persons and caused the survivors to flee their villages, and thus not to plant crops, producing a local food shortage. Provinces not so afflicted, and thus possessing abundant food supplies, were farther on, the Indians said. In any case, Soto had not yet finished exploring his domain, nor had he found the source of the "terrestrial gems" that the Chicora legend promised. If he knew as much about it as would seem likely from Elvas', Biedma's, and Rodrigo Ranjel's brief notes, he would have recognized that Cofitachequi was but a part of the province of Xapira, the land of pearls and terrestrial gems in Ayllón's tales. Quite correctly, Soto guessed that the gems might be found farther north and northwest, in the mountains of whose existence the Indians probably spoke.

After two weeks at Cofitachequi, Soto resumed his march. The army seems to have followed at least a part of the same northward-running Indian trail that Juan Pardo was to follow twenty-six years later. Soto, like Pardo, eventually turned westward and crossed the Appalachian Mountains into the Tennessee River valley but missed the quartz crystal mines that Pardo found on that leg of his journey. Precious metals, too, eluded Soto, although gold exists in small amounts in the hills of northern Georgia. Soto did find Coosa, the rich Creek Indian area identified by Hudson and others as near Carters, in the northwestern corner of Georgia.[25] So rich and fertile was this land that it became part of a new legend, one that drew Tristan de Luna and others to the coast of the Gulf of Mexico in the 1550s.

In sum, Soto's exploration of Xapira showed that the only items of value to be found there, aside from the Indians and their lands, were furs and freshwater pearls, most of the latter small and blackened because the mussels were opened by heating them in fires. Soto, however, "had no wish to content himself with good land or with pearls."[26]

25. DePratter, Hudson, and Smith, "The Route of Juan Pardo's Exploration," 139–50; Charles Hudson, Marvin Smith, David Hally, Richard Polhemus, and Chester DePratter, "Coosa: A Chiefdom in the Sixteenth-Century Southeastern United States," *American Antiquity,* L (1985), 726–27. *Cf. Final Report of the United States De Soto Expedition Commission,* 206–207.

26. Gentleman of Elvas, *True Relation,* II, 96.

Encountering nothing to cause him to abandon his search for yet richer Indian provinces, Soto went on not only to Coosa but from there to the southwest, to Mavilla, near modern Montgomery, Alabama. To avoid meeting supply ships at Pensacola when he had nothing of importance to report about Florida and when he suspected his men of plotting to desert, he veered to the northwest into the modern state of Mississippi. Soto reached the Mississippi the following April. Once across it, his expedition spent the winter of 1541 in Arkansas before returning to the Mississippi River, near which Soto died on May 21, 1542. He had not found the rich kingdom he sought.

Luís de Moscoso, named to carry on the exploration, did so for another year by going westward and southwestward on a trail vaguely reported by the survivors' accounts. Finally returning to the Mississippi, Moscoso and the remaining men, now only about half their original number, determined to build boats and sail down the river to the sea, which they correctly guessed was the Gulf of Mexico or, at least, some body of water that would take them to New Spain. They did that in the spring of 1543, arriving at the Pánuco River and the city of Tampico on September 10, 1543.[27]

In the summer of 1543, as in two previous summers, Diego Maldonado and Gómez Arias sailed along the Gulf coast seeking Soto, who had sent them to Havana in 1539 with orders to prepare supplies and meet him in the summer of 1540 at Achuse (Pensacola?) Bay. They had rendezvoused at the bay as ordered but, failing to find Soto, had cruised the Gulf coast and then sailed up the east coast of the continent as far as the cod fisheries without seeing any sign of Soto. In 1542 and again in 1543, they made "similar efforts," spending as long as seven months in their searches, each time setting out from Havana with a load of supplies for the adelantado. Finally in October, 1543, they put into Veracruz, where they learned the fate of the expedition.[28]

The arrival of the survivors of the Soto exploration at Pánuco in the summer of 1543 caused a revival of interest in La Florida among Spaniards which both strengthened a negative assessment of the region and its potential and, paradoxically, added the discoveries of Soto in the interior to earlier favorable reports. The result was a shift in

27. Lowery, *Spanish Settlements*, I, 230–44, 247–50.
28. Garcilaso de la Vega, *The Florida of the Inca*, 632–34.

emphasis from the Atlantic coast to the interior as the possible location of the new Andalucia.

Persons who saw the Soto survivors when they arrived in Mexico witnessed the negative effects of La Florida at first hand in the survivors' physical condition and in the loss of so many of their companions and their fortunes on the vain quest. The Mexicans were the first to hear the negative reports that many of Soto's argonauts gave of La Florida and their experiences there.

Yet in those reports were some grounds for a positive assessment of what Soto's men had found. Garcilaso says that the viceroy Antonio de Mendoza and his court at Mexico City were impressed by the stories about the Indians, by their courage and skill in combat, by the wealth of provinces like Cofitachequi and Coosa, and by similar evidence of advanced Indian cultures. The Mississippi was also of interest. Mendoza was pleased to hear that the land was rich in fruit trees like those of Spain, in oaks, in mulberry trees, and in wild grapes. According to Garcilaso, "It made him very happy to hear of the spaciousness of that kingdom, the opportunity that it holds for raising all kinds of livestock, and the fertility of the land in corn, grains, fruits, and vegetables. And because of these things, his desire to make the conquest increased."[29] From that desire eventually grew the idea of sending a new expedition to the Southeast, but one that would use a Gulf-coast port for its base.

In Spain, too, reports on the Soto expedition were mixed. Some of the surviving soldiers and officials, such as the accountant Añasco, the treasurer Gaytán, and the captains Baltasar de Gallegos, Alonso Romo de Cardeñosa, Arias Tinoco, and Pedro Calderon, returned to Spain filled with a "hatred" for the Indies because of what they had suffered and of the losses to their estates occasioned by the expedition.[30] They undoubtedly had little good to say about the land or its peoples, although even they must have mentioned the pearls, marten skins, deerskins, and other furs found at Cofitachequi and elsewhere. Information about such resources was also contained in Ranjel's and Biedma's manuscript reports to the Council of the Indies in 1544, and in other accounts, now lost.[31] Optimistic men could draw from these

29. *Ibid.*, 629.
30. *Ibid.*, 630.
31. Ranjel's report is in Oviedo's *Historia general,* I, 544–77, and is translated in *Narratives of the Career of Hernando de Soto in the Conquest of Florida,* trans. Buckingham Smith, ed. Edward Gaylord Bourne (2 vols.; New York, 1904). Garcilaso de

stories conclusions not only about the great hardships and the difficulties of taming the natives, who fought back at every opportunity, but also about the riches waiting to be exploited.[32] In Spain, as in Mexico, there were men who were excited rather than discouraged by the reports brought back by the veterans of the Soto expedition.

Francisco Lopez de Gómara says that in 1544 many persons petitioned for the right to take up Soto's contract. Among them were Julian de Samano and Pedro de Ahumada, brothers of Juan de Samano, the secretary of the Council of the Indies. Gómara, who knew Ahumada well, says he was very learned and virtuous.[33] Andrés Gonzalez de Barcía Carballido y Zuñiga, writing two centuries later and with the benefit of Garcilaso's narrative as well as Gómara's, and perhaps of documents not now known to exist, says that the brothers knew why Soto had failed and believed that once they had pacified the land it could be made to yield not only the pearls and fine furs that Soto had found but also mines of gold, silver, and other metals. They promised to use their authority judiciously, if given the grant.[34]

If what Barcía reports was in fact what Samano and Ahumada said in their petition, then the brothers meant to return to the River of Santa Elena, identified by Biedma and others as Ayllón's river. The river led to Cofitachequi and its pearls and fine furs, and it gave access to the mountains where minerals could be found. Indeed, the copper presented at Cofitachequi when gold was shown to the Indians augured well for the discovery of precious metals. Given Juan de Samano's position in the king's council, it would not have been hard for the petitioners to determine approximately where the River of Santa Elena—their "river of Ayllón"—was, even if they did not gain access

la Vega tells of several reports he used but that are now lost (*The Florida of the Inca,* 622). Eugene Lyon has noted the existence of a fragment of a Soto narrative, by Sebastián de Cañete in AGI, PAT 19, No. 1, R. 15. My citation of it is courtesy of him. The date for Hernández de Biedma's account is given by Juan Bautista Muñoz on the copy he made for his collection (Smith [ed.], *Colección,* 64).

32. Cabeza de Vaca's reports also led to a lawsuit between Soto, Hernán Cortes, and Núño de Guzmán, which is found in AGI, PAT 21, No. 2, R. 4, and printed in part in *DII,* XV, 300–408. The Coronado expedition is discussed by Herbert E. Bolton in *Coronado: Knight of Pueblos and Plains* (New York, 1949).

33. Gómara, *Historia general,* I, 72. Ahumada may also have been related to the licenciado Antonio de Ahumada, who had been the late empress' chaplain and claimed a reward at this time (AGS, Cámara de Castilla 275, Nos. 31, 60).

34. Andrés Gonzalez de Barcía Carballido y Zúñiga, *Chronological History of the Continent of Florida,* trans. Anthony Kerrigen (Gainesville, Fla., 1951), 25.

to Chaves' manuscript rutter, which gives exact latitudes for both the Point and River of Santa Elena.

The crown made no grant.[35] Instead, the Dominicans prevailed upon it to leave La Florida to them. On the key questions of Spanish titles to the Indies—as the Spaniards called the Americas—and the policies that should be followed in areas already conquered and in areas that might be looked toward for conquest in the future, the friars finally persuaded Charles that his possession was valid only if the Indians asked for his government.[36] There were no important examples of Indian societies asking to be ruled by Charles and his Spanish agents, but the Dominicans seemed confident that that would change if they were only given a free field on which to preach the gospel. Its self-evident truth would, they believed, be accepted by the Indians, who would then also welcome rule by the "universal monarch," Charles V. Few free mission fields remained, that is, ones not already occupied by the Spaniards. But La Florida was one, and Soto had shown that there were large, well-ordered native polities there.

Given that background, the rejection of the request by Samano and Ahumada to undertake an aggressive "pacification" of La Florida is not surprising. Nor is it surprising that permission was granted, if reluctantly, three years later, when Father Luís Cancer, of the Dominican order, requested authorization to undertake mission work on the western side of peninsular Florida. The reluctance reflected an unwillingness to launch any costly new ventures in a time when the crown's finances were still recovering from the emperor's last round of wars and from paying for Charles's new campaign in the Holy Roman Empire against the German Protestants. Too, there had been a waning of enthusiasm for the extreme position of the reformers, a waning that—as before—correlated with Charles's absence from the peninsula.

A student under Las Casas in Guatemala during the 1530s and a

35. AGI, GDA 51, fols. 171–72, 262v–263; Fray Pedro de Ayala to SM, Mexico City, March 15, 1562, AGI, MEX 280. For Pedro de Ahumada's subsequent biography, see Andrés de Tapía to the licenciado Chaves, Mexico City, March 11, 1550, AGI, MEX 168.

36. Vitoria, *De Indis,* xli–xlii. For a narrative of the debates at this time, see Juan de Manzano y Manzano, *La incorporación de las Indias a la Corona de Castilla* (Madrid, 1948), 95–120; and Hanke, *The Spanish Struggle for Justice,* 72–105. The New Laws of 1542, which were the direct outgrowth of these debates, and their application in Mexico are discussed by Simpson in *The Encomienda in New Spain,* 126–44.

veteran of his successful campaign to bring peace and the gospel to the Indians of the "land of war" (1537–38), Cancer had accompanied Las Casas to Spain in 1539–1542 before returning to Vera Paz (true peace), as the former "land of war" was now called. There he remained until 1546, when he went to Mexico City determined to preach the gospel in La Florida. Some evidence exists that he may have been moved to his project by contact with Indians taken to Central America by some of the Soto survivors. Whatever the source of his inspiration, he soon linked up with Father Gregorio de Beteta, another Dominican, who also had a restlessness that could not be stilled by the routine work of the convent or by preaching in the more settled parts of New Spain.[37]

Again joining Las Casas for a journey to Spain in 1547, Cancer eventually obtained royal permission to preach the gospel at a point on the Gulf coast of Florida that had not been visited by Spaniards. Florida Indians repatriated from their captivity in Mexico and Central America were to be used as traders to attract their fellows. The crown agreed to pay the expenses, which would be slight.

Returning to Mexico, Cancer secured a ship and pilot and sailed for the Florida coast accompanied by Father Beteta and Juan García, Father Beteta's companion on earlier missions, and a Father Diego de Tolosa. They made landfall at about 28° north, but did not attempt a landing until the ship had run north to 28°30′ north. After scouting and finding the Indians hostile, the party returned to near their previous anchorage. While again scouting the shore, they met Indians, who appeared very friendly, especially once the Spaniards offered them trade trinkets. Their friendliness was a deception, however. Three members of the party sent ashore disappeared, and an effort to find them at a harbor the Spaniards understood the Indians to have spoken of proved fruitless.

Just as the remaining friars and their ship were preparing to depart, Indians appeared on shore, calling to them in broken Spanish to say that they were friends. The encounter brought the news that the three who had disappeared earlier were still alive, and one of the Indians, a woman known as Magdalena, even spoke with Father Cancer. The

37. Agustín Davila Padilla, *Historia de la Fundación y discurso de la provincia de Santiago de Mexico de la orden de Predicadores por las vidas de sus varones insignes y casos notables de Nueva España* (Madrid, 1596), 215–31; Lowery, *Spanish Settlements*, I, 411–27. Hanke briefly covers the Vera Paz experiment, in *The Spanish Struggle for Justice.*

news, however, was given the lie by a Spaniard named Juan Muñoz, one of Soto's men long held captive by the Indians. He reported that the friar among the three had been killed.

Beteta and Juan García declared they would land the next day, as agreed with the Indians, regardless of the danger. Father Cancer decided that it was his duty, as leader of the remaining friars, to try to resolve the situation by landing and seeing if he could speak with the Indians through Magdalena. He was killed in his attempt. The remaining members of the party fled. They set course first for Havana and then for New Spain, where they arrived on July 19, 1549.[38]

Father Cancer's death, admired by the pious as a martyrdom, served to remind those who knew of it that after several decades of slave raiding, the Florida peninsula's coastal Indians were very hostile to the Spaniards. Only restless souls like Father Beteta could find working with such people interesting, mostly because it promised the crown of martyrdom. For the rest of the clergy and for most laymen, La Florida was a graveyard of hopes.

By the midforties, La Florida's east coast had been written off officially as "unfruitful" and as lined only with deserted islands. Its Gulf coast was almost unknown except for a few features like Miruelo's Bay and the Bay of the River of the Holy Spirit, both of uncertain location. The experiences of Narváez, Soto, and Cancer suggested that both coasts were wastelands full of hostile Indians and difficult geographical and climatic conditions. Soto's survivors remembered Coosa, the rich land in the interior not too far from the Bay of Ochuse and the great river that they had used to escape from their migratory hell, but almost everyone else was more impressed by the hardship stories of Cabeza de Vaca and the Soto survivors and by the tale of Father Cancer's violent death on a sand beach on the central west coast of Florida.

A final proof that Ayllón's legend held little interest for most Spaniards by the mid-1540s may be found in the fact that when Lucas Vázquez de Ayllón the Younger, went to court in 1547 to press for a reward because of his father's services to the crown, he asked neither for his rights as the heir mentioned in his father's contract nor for a contract of his own but for an extension of time during which to pay off the debts his dead father-in-law, Esteban de Pasamonte, and Es-

38. Lowery, *Spanish Settlements*, I, 411–27.

teban's father, Miguel de Pasamonte, owed the crown from their periods as treasurer of Española.[39]

In sum, by 1550, Ayllón's glittering promises of a new Andalucia had faded in the light of Spanish experience in La Florida and with the deaths of men who had believed the sanguine assurances. A few, like some of the Soto survivors, were able to see beyond their own difficult experiences to the potential that the land held, but their vision took in a different part of the Southeast from Ayllón's. When Spaniards next became interested in colonizing La Florida, they focused on the Gulf coast. Only as the threat grew of a French occupation of one or more Atlantic ports of the Southeast was Spanish attention restored to the east coast. The circumstances of the threat made the Spanish aware of a French legend about North America's geography, a legend that in turn drove a brief new wave of Spanish interest in the area of Ayllón's contract, above 35° north. When that interest, too, receded, the way was open for the English, who inherited and acted upon Ayllón's and Verrazzano's legends in the closing twenty years of the sixteenth century.

39. AGI, PAT 150, No. 8, R. 1, fol. 1.

PART TWO

The French and a Way to the Orient

V

Verrazzano's Sea and Franco-Spanish Claims to North America and the Caribbean

Even as Ayllón and his captains were exploring and trying to settle the part of North America they had discovered and as Soto was questing in the Southeast, two of Spain's neighbors, England and France, were beginning to show interest in what lay across the Atlantic from their western coasts. Most of their early interest focused on trying to find a strait or other passage that would carry the voyager to the Orient and its spices at a latitude between those of peninsular Florida and the cod fisheries at Nova Scotia and Newfoundland.[1]

The principal result of the first English and French voyages of exploration was the legend that Giovanni da Verrazzano began when he fancied that he saw the Pacific Ocean on the other side of the Outer Banks of North Carolina. Although enshrined in some maps, the pure Verrazzano legend soon was modified by reports of Jacques Cartier's discovery of an "arm of the sea" at the western end of the Saint Lawrence River valley, an arm thought by some to be Verrazzano's sea but separated from the Atlantic Ocean by several hundred miles of land. Both versions of the legend confirmed the academic geographers' theories that such an arm of the Pacific Ocean existed. As late as the 1580s, the legend in both its forms gave Spain's rivals reasons to renew their explorations of North America's east coast.

English and French voyages of exploration along the western shores of the Atlantic Ocean brought diplomatic conflict with the Spaniards because of their claim that the Papal Donation of 1493 gave them an exclusive sphere of missionary and colonial activity west of the line of Tordesillas. Adhering to this claim in rhetoric, the Spaniards increasingly abandoned it in practice after 1534 in favor of a more

1. For the origins of this myth, see Marcel Destombes, "La Cartographie florentine de la Renaissance et Verrazano," in *Giovanni da Verrazzano: Giornante commemorative, Firenze—Greve in Chianti, 21–22 ottobre 1961* (Florence, 1970), 31–32.

limited demand that the French, and later the English, accept and be governed in time of peace by Spanish navigation laws. Those laws forbade anyone not holding a license from the House of Trade of Seville from sailing in waters the Spaniards considered theirs by virtue of having colonies along their shores. For Spain, this meant that the entire Caribbean and the sea approaches and exits from it were closed to nonlicensed shipping.

Except for a mild protest over the Bristol voyages in 1496, the Spaniards did not raise their claims in diplomatic discussions until the late 1530s.[2] By then Verrazzano and Cartier had sailed and given France a claim to North America based on discovery and formal, *de jure,* taking of possession.

Verrazzano's voyage of 1523–1524 was part of a spate of voyages sponsored by several European governments in the middle 1520s. All aimed at reaching the Orient, and most aimed at discovering a way there through a supposed western or northwestern passage. Ayllón's charge to explore a strait if his pilots found one, the voyage of Esteban Gómez from north to south along the North American coast from the sixties to the forties north latitude, Verrazzano's voyage, and the Englishman John Rutt's voyage of 1527 were all part of the effort to find a way west by a route other than the one Magellan had pioneered around South America. The classical geographers seemed to promise such a route, according to many then-contemporary scholars.[3]

Verrazzano's voyage was jointly sponsored by Francis I, king of France, and certain Florentine merchants from Lyon. The merchants may have been inspired by the publication in 1523 of Antonio de Pigafetta's account of his trip around the world in the Magellan–El Cano fleet. Francis I was motivated by his war with Charles V.[4]

2. Paul E. Hoffman, "Diplomacy and the Papal Donation, 1493–1585," *The Americas,* XXX (1973), 154. Quinn covers English voyages before 1500, in *England and the Discovery of America,* 6–23, 93–110. Franklin T. McCann discusses later English voyages (to 1536), in *English Discovery of America to 1585* (New York, 1952), 63–68; Quinn discusses them in *England and the Discovery of America,* 162–89.

3. Samuel E. Morison covers the Rutt and Gómez voyages, in *European Discovery of America: The Northern Voyages* (New York, 1971), 233–37, 326–31. See also Quinn, *England and the Discovery of America,* 171–82. Ayllón's activities have been described above, and an account of Verrazzano's will follow. For an excellent discussion of what Verrazzano might have learned from the geographers, see Lawrence C. Wroth, *The Voyages of Giovanni da Verrazzano, 1524–1528* (New Haven, 1970), 17–56.

4. Marcel Trudel, *Les Vaines Tentatives, 1524–1603* (Montreal, 1963), 34–42,

French commerce raiders had captured one of the ships Cortes had sent home in 1521 with a rich cargo of silver, gold, and featherwork from the Mexica-Azteca empire. The French reasoned that should a voyage to the west succeed in reaching Asia, they might be able to compete with the Spaniards for its trade by the western route, but with the advantage of a more direct course than Magellan's. Even if the voyage failed to reach the Orient because there was a continent between peninsular Florida and the cod fisheries, it might still yield something—maybe a way of tapping the riches of the New World by direct contact with the native cultures or by providing a base from which to raid Spanish shipping.

Verrazzano's preparations over the winter of 1522–1523 are poorly documented, but it is known that four ships were prepared at Rouen and that merchants were investing in the venture as late as the end of March, 1523. One of the ships was the king's *Dauphine,* a caravel thought to have had a capacity of about a hundred tons.[5]

Hearing of the French preparations and believing that Verrazzano might intend yet another in the series of voyages by France to Brazil, which had begun in 1504, or new attacks on Portuguese shipping, the Portuguese sent a special ambassador to France in what proved to be a vain attempt to obtain an order staying the voyage. All that the agent could secure was the assurance that the voyage was directed against the interests of Spain, not those of Portugal.[6]

In May or June, 1523, Verrazzano's fleet departed Rouen but encountered a storm in the Bay of Biscay that sank two of the ships and forced the *Dauphine* and the *Normanda* to seek shelter and repairs in Breton ports. While repairs were under way, Francis I ordered the ships to the Spanish coast for several months of commerce raiding. Upon completion of that duty, Verrazzano was allowed to prepare again for his voyage of discovery. Only the *Dauphine* remained for the voyage. It seems to have left France no later than the end of December, 1523.[7]

Vol. I of Trudel, *Histoire de la Nouvelle France,* 3 vols. to 1983; Wroth, *Verrazzano,* 59–62, 65–67; Jacques Habert, *La Vie et les Voyages de Jean de Verrazzane* (Montreal, 1964), 46.

5. Wroth, *Verrazzano,* 67–70; Norman J. W. Thrower, "New Light on the 1524 Voyages of Verrazzano," *Terrae Incognitae,* XI (1979), 59–66, esp. 61.

6. Habert, *Verrazzane,* 58–59, and Wroth, *Verrazzano,* 67–69.

7. Wroth, *Verrazzano,* 70; Thrower, "New Light," *passim.*

On January 17, 1524, the *Dauphine* set a course westward from some rocks off Madeira Island, sailing roughly along the thirty-second parallel until a storm caused a slight deflection toward the northwest. Fifty days after leaving European waters, the lookouts sighted land.[8] It was early March, 1524.

The exact point of Verrazzano's landfall on the Carolina coast has been a matter of discussion among scholars for some time. Lawrence Wroth has reviewed the evidence and concludes that Verrazzano came upon the coast to the west of Cape Fear, perhaps near the modern boundary between the Carolinas. That would place him in or near the angle where the coast turns southward. Later French maps designated this point as Daraflor or Unaflor and located it at 34° north.[9]

Verrazzano's report indicates that he made no landing once the coast was in sight but instead shaped a course to the south for about fifty leagues. The place reached, which was the southernmost point of the voyage, seems to have been marked in the later French cartography as Dieppe. If Verrazzano came upon the continent at about the modern boundary of the Carolinas and then ran south for fifty leagues, he would have sailed about 2.86 degrees of latitude, assuming he was figuring his leagues at 17.5 to the degree. That would have carried him to about 31°10′ north latitude, roughly at Saint Simon's Island, rather short of the extreme limit suggested by some of the French maps, which put Dieppe at 30° north, or just north of Saint Augustine, Florida.

Assuming that Verrazzano did run as far south as Saint Simon's Island, it is curious that he failed to see at least Port Royal Sound, the one major harbor on the coast that would have been readily observable to seamen going south. The others—especially Winyah Bay and Charleston Harbor—were partially hidden by the extensive shoals that used to exist on the northeastern side of their entrances, shoals that often ran south-southeast all the way across the entrances. Verrazzano probably kept fairly well offshore for fear of such shoals. Perhaps following information derived from Verrazzano, Jean Alfonse, the French cosmographer whose manuscript *La Cosmographie* was completed in 1545, said of this stretch of coast that "one should not approach closer to the land than three leagues because of

8. Wroth, *Verrazzano,* 71–72.

9. *Ibid.*, 79, 80, 133–34. For the text of the voyage, see *ibid.* and Giovanni Battista Ramusio, *Navigationi et Viaggi: Venice, 1563–1606* (3 vols.; Amsterdam, 1967), III, fols. 350–50 [*sic;* 352].

the shoals [*baptures*] and dangers that are on it at the foot of the rocks [*rochiers*]."[10] If these are Verrazzano's notes, it is clear why he failed to find a harbor anywhere along the coast south of 34° north: he was sailing as much as ten nautical miles offshore and keeping land barely visible on the western horizon.

Having run south to a point where he knew that the coast would continue on to latitudes that had been explored by the Spaniards—who had not found a strait—Verrazzano turned back to the north and regained his point of encounter with the continent. There, near Cape Fear, the *Dauphine* anchored off the coast and sent a small boat to land. The natives who had been on the shore watching the ship now fell back as the French approached but were eventually persuaded to return to where the French had landed. The shore was

> completely covered with fine sand xv feet deep, which rises in the form of small hills about fifty paces wide. After climbing further, we found other streams and inlets from the sea which come in by several mouths, and follow the ins and outs of the shoreline. Nearby we could see a stretch of country much higher than the sandy shore, with many beautiful fields and plains full of great forests, some sparse and some dense; and the trees have so many colors, and are so beautiful and delightful that they defy description. . . . They are adorned and clothed with palms, laurel, cypress, and other varieties of tree unknown in our Europe. And these trees emit a sweet fragrance over a large area.[11]

Today, the coast near Cape Fear still has sand dunes, cabbage palms, cypress trees, and pine trees. The latitude Verrazzano gave was 34°.[12]

The Verrazzano narrative describes with some care the Indians who came to the shore. They wore animal skins ("like martens") with a narrow belt of grass around the body at the waist, but, they were otherwise naked. Some had garlands of bird's feathers in their thick black hair, which was tied back in a "small tail" behind the head. To Verrazzano, they appeared dark in color, "not unlike the Ethiopians." Their bodies were well proportioned and of medium height. The men on the average were taller than the French—Pedro de Salazar's giants! These Indians had broad faces and were good runners. The French did not stay long enough to learn of their customs.[13]

10. Jean Alfonse [Jean Fonteneau], *La Cosmographie, avec l'espere et regime du soleil et du Nord,* ed. Georges Musset (Paris, 1904), 508.

11. Verrazzano, translated in Wroth, *Verrazzano,* 134.

12. *Ibid.,* 135: "questa terra i gradi 34." Wroth's commentary notes that this is a general rather than a precise latitude.

13. *Ibid.,* 134.

Instead, the French sailed along the eastward-trending coast, noting the fires that the Indians lit and the fact that the bottom dropped off quickly within four or five paces of the shore (about ten to fifteen feet—rather an exaggeration) so that there was little danger to ships if they had good anchors and cables to hold them against storms. Needing water, the French halted in the open sea and sent their ship's boat to shore, but its crew found the surf too rough for a safe passage and turned back. A sailor who, swimming close to shore, was swept to the beach by the waves made contact with the local Indians but could not bring any fresh water with him when he swam back to the ship's boat.[14] This place was called Annunciata, for the day of arrival, March 25, 1524, the feast of the Annunciation of the virgin Mary. Scholars believe that Annunciata was near Cape Lookout.

At Annunciata, the French thought they saw the isthmus that became a feature of the cartography based on the Verrazzano voyage. Verrazzano described it in his annotations of the Cèllere Codex of his report as

> one mile wide and about two hundred miles long, in which we could see the eastern sea from the ship, halfway between west [originally written as east] and north. This is doubtless the one which goes around the tip of India, China, and Cathay. We sailed along this isthmus hoping all the time to find some strait or real promontory where the land might end to the north, and we could reach those blessed shores of Cathay.

The "isthmus" was named by the discoverer Varazanio, just as "all the land we found was called 'Francesca' after our Francis."[15]

From Annunciata the coast veered "somewhat to the north." It actually runs northeast to Cape Hatteras, then almost due north to New York, with only a slight tendency to the northeast. The French went fifty leagues until they reached another land that seemed much more beautiful, and full of great forests. At what they named Arcadia, they anchored and sent twenty-five men ashore. The narrative recounts in some detail the people they found and their manner of life, and it is thus the earliest account of the Indians who lived on the Delmarva peninsula. What Verrazzano mostly commented on, however, were the rich floral and sylvan resources of the area, which ranged from trees to herbs and "fragrant flowers different from ours."[16]

14. *Ibid.*, 135.
15. *Ibid.*, 135*n*8 (which is the Cèllere annotation).
16. *Ibid.*, 136–37.

After three days at Arcadia, the French sailed on, not wishing to remain anchored off the coast. Their course was to the northeast for a hundred leagues. Sailing by day and anchoring by night, they came in time to a "very agreeable place between two small but prominent hills: between them a very wide river, deep at its mouth, flowed out into the sea." They had reached New York Harbor.

From this river mouth, the coast turned to the east. Running fifty to eighty leagues (depending on the manuscript), the French followed it to Refugio (Narragansett Bay) and the sheltered harbor that became Newport, Rhode Island. There the crew rested for fifteen days. The Verrazzano narrative is more extensive in its description of this area and of the local Indians than it is for any other part of the coast. Its description was later to play a role in promoting English interest in New England, even as early as 1578.[17]

After refreshing themselves at Refugio, the sailors set their course to the east. Once around a cape (Cape Cod), the course seems to have been west to the shore, then north and northeast along the coast to Maine. A brief landing there, with unfriendly contact with the Indians, and the ship again sailed north until the French saw that they were in waters already familiar to Breton seamen. By then short on naval stores and other provisions, Verrazzano steered for home. He had discovered, he said, over seven hundred leagues of coast. He reached Dieppe in early July, 1524.

Verrazzano addressed several questions at the end of his report that show that the French were at least partially aware of the argument about the "nature" of the Indians, that is, about the state of their culture. Admitting that the lack of a common language prevented certainty, Verrazzano recorded that he and his companions had nonetheless concluded that the Indians had neither religion nor laws and that they did not know of the First Cause, did not worship celestial bodies, and did not practice any sort of idolatry. They lived in "absolute freedom" and "everything they do proceeds from Ignorance."[18] That would have said to the Spanish that the North American Indians did not live *en policía,* although the defenders of Indian rights could have noted that Verrazzano never visited an Indian settlement and so did not know what they did on many of these points.

Concerning his mission, which had been to seek a way to Cathay, he said, "I did not expect to find such an obstacle of new land as I have

17. *Ibid.,* 88.
18. Verrazzano in *ibid.,* 141.

found; and if for some reason I did expect to find it, I estimated there would be some strait to get through to the Eastern Ocean. This was the opinion of all the ancients, . . . but this opinion . . . has been proven false by experience."[19] He *had* found, he claimed, an arm of the Pacific Ocean reaching to within an insignificant distance of the Atlantic. That body of water is known as the false Verrazzano sea.

Verrazzano tried to follow up on his discovery in 1524, but Francis I could not spare ships from his naval war with Spain. Disappointed, Verrazzano approached Henry VIII, of England, and João III, of Portugal, but received no support. In 1526–1528, France sent him on two voyages to Brazil. He died on the second of these.[20]

Verrazzano's understanding of the geography of North America was incorporated into a number of maps, some of which gained wide circulation in the half century that followed his voyage, but especially in the years prior to 1555. It is possible to link one of these maps directly to the later English voyages.

Wroth and others have interpreted statements by Richard Hakluyt the Younger to indicate that Verrazzano himself drew a map of his discoveries in 1525, or possibly early 1526, and sent or presented it to Henry VIII (it is not clear whether he was in England in those years). That earliest map is now lost except insofar as elements of it are incorporated into Michael Lok's printed map in the first edition of Hakluyt's *Diveres Voyages* (1582; Map 7). Whether or not Hakluyt is correct that this lost map was the work of Giovanni da Verrazzano rather than his brother, Gerolamo, who made a number of maps with this geography, its impact on the thinking of Hakluyt and his contemporaries was clearly very great, because it provided them with a direct link to the Verrazzano concept of North America, a link whose antiquity and propinquity to the original voyage likely inspired more confidence than printed and manuscript copies of later maps in the series.[21]

The supposed original Verrazzano map aside, most Europeans learned of the body of water that Verrazzano believed an arm of the Pacific from either the widely distributed manuscript atlases of Battista Agnese (Map 8) or the even more widely distributed printed

19. Verrazzano in *ibid.*, 142.

20. *Ibid.*, 155–64, 220–35, and Habert, *Verrazzane*, 309–36.

21. Raleigh A. Skelton, "The Influence of Verrazzano on Sixteenth Century Cartography," in *Giovanni da Verrazzano: Giornante commemorative, Firenze—Greve in Chianti, 21–22 ottobre 1961* (Florence, 1970), 55–69.

maps of Sebastian Münster (Map 9). Agnese's oval world map and the derivative Atlantic hemisphere map (found in some but not all of the surviving copies of his atlas) have been shown to be based on a manuscript map made by Gerolamo da Verrazzano in 1529. The key feature of that map is that it puts the false Verrazzano sea at 40° north and shows an isthmus that a legend on the map says is six miles wide, rather than the one mile Giovanni's annotation of the Cèllere manuscript mentions. Agnese's maps show a relatively thick isthmus but place it at nearly 45° north.

Münster's maps, on the other hand, seem to reflect the work of Vesconte Maggiolo, who was a cartographer at Venice in the 1530s, 1540s, and early 1550s. Maggiolo placed the false sea below 40°, and his maps were used to illustrate editions of Ptolemy and of his own *Cosmographia Universalis,* which went through thirty-five editions in various languages—but not Spanish—from 1544 to 1578. Münster's map carries no latitude scale, but the location of the isthmus and false sea can be estimated by their positions due west of the Iberian peninsula, that is, in the upper thirties north latitude. Even though the two widely distributed maps—Agnese's and Münster's—seem to be derived from rather different originals, their representations of the latitude of the isthmus and false sea are similar. In addition, they both show a rather wide isthmus.

Other versions of the Verrazzano cartography also circulated.[22] Examples are the globes ascribed to Robertus Bailly (1530 and later) and an anonymous map variously dated between 1536 and 1544 and known as the Harlien Mappemonde. In spite of its name, which refers to an owner it once had, the map seems to have been made in Dieppe and appears to be based on Alonso de Chaves' 1536 revision of the Spanish *padrón general* as well as on the Verrazzano cartographic tradition. Bailly places the isthmus below 40°. On the Harlien Mappemonde, it is at about 34° north, where Verrazzano's annotations to the Cèllere Codex placed it. Uniquely for its period, however, the Harlien map shows a river called the Santa Elena running from the Atlantic to the false sea. The reappearance of that feature in Dr. John Dee's manuscript map of 1582–1583 (Map 10) and John White's map of 1585 (*Virginea pars*) suggests that they had access to the Harlien map or to one of similar design.

22. For a full discussion of the Verrazzano cartography, see Wroth, *Verrazzano,* 178–216.

However understood by cartographers who followed the Verrazzano-Dieppe tradition, Verrazzano's concept of North America embodied a legend that caused later explorers to risk their lives and treasures on the Atlantic coast of North America. The legend that made the false Verrazzano sea into a part of the Pacific, like Ayllón's legend of a new Andalucia, was based on and seemed to prove the ideas of the academic geographers. Once an account of Verrazzano's voyage was published in 1556, it became possible to link the two legends with the upper thirties north latitude as well as with 40° north, the apparent latitude of the isthmus. By then, too, Europe knew of Cartier's discoveries, which seemed to offer additional proof of the existence of the passage to the Orient, although along a route that did not entirely agree with the cartographic tradition stemming from the Verrazzano maps.

Because Verrazzano's voyage occurred during a Franco-Spanish war, Spanish officials may not have known of it until some years after the Peace of Cambray, of 1529. They did know of the voyage in 1528 of the first French commerce raider to enter the Caribbean. Guided by a Portuguese pilot, the French ship appeared first at the pearl fishery of Margarita and then off Mona Island between Española and Puerto Rico.[23] Its voyage indicated that France was no longer respecting Spain's monopoly over the Americas west of the line of Tordesillas any more than it was over Brazil. The appearance of an English ship off Santo Domingo in 1527 suggested that the English, too, had little respect for Spain's prerogatives. Despite the clear challenges to the Iberian claims, the issue of Spain's exclusive possession of the New World under terms of the Papal Donation of 1493 did not come up in the negotiations for the Peace of Cambray. Instead, general trade provisions were inserted into the treaty that gave free, peaceful access to the dominions of each party by the others' subjects under such restrictions as the laws of each kingdom imposed.

As long as the Peace of Cambray held and French merchants accepted their virtual exclusion from trade with the Spanish empire under the terms of Spain's navigation laws, the question of French access to the New World seems to have attracted little attention in Spain.[24] The Portuguese, on the other hand, had reason for concern

23. Hoffman, "Diplomacy and the Papal Donation," 157*n*18; *DII*, XXXX, 407–17.

24. The provisions of Spanish navigation laws are discussed in Hoffman's "Diplomacy and the Papal Donation," 155; Richard Konetzke's "Legislación sobre immigración de extranjeros en América durante la época colonial," *Revista internacional de*

because French captains, including Verrazzano, continued to sail for Brazil and India. Portugal's response was not to press her supposed rights under the papal donation but to use military and monetary power to correct the situation. After 1529 Portugal undertook the definitive occupation of Brazil. Using monetary power, the Portuguese arranged in 1531 to "pension," that is, bribe, Philippe Chabot, admiral of France, to use his influence to restrict if not eliminate French voyages to Brazil and the Indian Ocean.[25]

Once France recovered from the wars of the 1520s and found that it was unable to reach India by following the Portuguese route around the Cape of Good Hope or to occupy a part of Brazil without challenge, the backers of exploration seem to have returned their attention to the idea of a strait or other route across or through North America.

Notwithstanding the Verrazzano cartography that showed an isthmus at the middle to high thirties north latitude, new French explorations aimed to continue Verrazzano's discoveries but beyond the northern limit of his voyage of 1524. It seems probable that the French sponsors of voyages of exploration had heard fishermen's reports of a great river that lay west and northwest of the cod fisheries. Thus in April, 1534, they sent Cartier to look for a northwest passage by way of that river, which was the Saint Lawrence. Cartier's voyage set the stage for a series of Franco-Spanish diplomatic discussions of Spain's claims upon the Americas, especially upon North America, which was then unoccupied by any European power.

There is no documentation that the Spaniards at the time knew of Cartier's first voyage (April 20–September 5, 1534) or of his second (from May 18, 1535).[26] Nor is it certain that they knew of Francis I's

---

sociología (Madrid), XI–XII (1945), 279–81; Clarence H. Haring's *Trade and Navigation Between Spain and the Indies in the Time of the Hapsburgs* (Cambridge, Mass., 1918), 98–100; and *DII*, XXI, 91, items 7, 8, 10.

25. Wroth, *Verrazzano*, 236–52; Habert, *Verrazzane*, 350–53; Edward G. Bourne, "The History and Determination of the Line of Demarcation Established by Pope Alexander VI Between the Spanish and Portuguese Fields of Discovery and Colonization," *Annual Report for 1891* of the American Historical Association (Washington, D.C., 1892), 127 (based on Henri Pigeonneau's *Histoire du commerce de la France* [2 vols.; Paris, 1885–97], II, 150–54). For events of 1522–1531, see August A. Thomazi, *Les Flottes de l'or: Histoire des galions d'Espagne* (Paris, 1937), 28–32. On the voyage into the Indian Ocean in 1528, there is Lope Hurtado de Mendoza to Los Cobos, Lisbon, March 31, 1529, in AGS, EDO 368, No. 186.

26. *Cf.* Henry Folmer, *Franco-Spanish Rivalry for North America* (Glendale, Calif., 1953), 38, 43.

effort to obtain a pronouncement on the subject of territories overseas from Pope Leon XII, a hater of Spaniards. Leon reportedly asserted in his bull that the Alexandrine bulls of 1493–1495 did not apply to areas not actually occupied by Spain.[27]

Whatever the Spaniards knew, Antoine Perrenot Cardinal de Granvelle, one of Charles V's chief advisers, recognized that the French interest in colonies and in trade with the New World was a long-term threat to Spain's empire there. Accordingly, when war over the possession of Milan became a probability in late 1535, he suggested a compromise in which France would give up its interests in the New World and the Holy Roman Empire would abandon its rather weak claim to Milan. That is, a major territorial concession by Charles V in Italy was to be matched by a French agreement to cease all exploration and trade in the western Atlantic, north and south.[28] War broke out before Cardinal de Granvelle's idea could be explored, however, and the problem of France's royal sponsorship of voyages to claim land and establish colonies awaited another time. Also left for a later diplomatic round was the implicit suggestion that the established commerce of the Indies might be opened to Frenchmen sailing as private persons rather than as agents of the French monarchy.

Cartier returned to France in 1536 after wintering over in Canada. French corsairs appeared in unprecedented numbers in the waters off Spain and the Azores and began to appear in the Caribbean after 1537. They also raided Portuguese shipping and seem to have returned to Brazil, causing the French government once more to prohibit such activity against the Portuguese, with whom they remained at peace during the war with Spain.[29] Clearly, French raiding and the French interest in colonies needed to be addressed during the next peace negotiations. Accordingly, when Charles V sent his preliminary instructions for negotiations with the French to Francisco de Los Cobos and Cardinal de Granvelle in November, 1537, he asked whether

27. Morison, *European Discovery of America*, 341 (based on Baron de La Chapelle's "Jean Le Veneur et le Canada," *Nova Francia*, VI [September–December, 1931], 342, which is "extrait de la Généalogie de la Maison le Veneur, Comtes de Tillières de Carrouges, Par le Président Hénault, Membre de l'Académie Francaise, 1723," a source whose claim cannot be further substantiated; the late Admiral Morison kindly provided the citation).

28. Antoine Perrenot de Granvelle, *Papiers d'état du cardinal de Granvelle d'après les manuscrits de la bibliothèque de Bessançon*, ed. Ch. Weiss (9 vols.; Paris, 1841–52), II, 404.

29. Folmer, *Franco-Spanish Rivalry*, 38–41; Hoffman, *The Spanish Crown*, 24–27; Bourne, "The Line of Demarcation," 127.

"something might not be agreed about the Indies, to the end that the King of France will not try anything in the future that is prejudicial to His Majesty."[30]

The best terms the imperial negotiators could get in the Treaty of Nice (1538), which established a truce for ten years between Francis I and Charles V, were the vague clauses that read, "During that [peace] neither side will work, attempt, or move anything directly or indirectly; all things will remain in the state they are in, and the possession [and] usufruct will remain with each as he has it, where they have them [*sic*], respectively," and, "During the said ten years the lords . . . may not directly nor indirectly damage each other in any location or place that may be, for their own account or that of others."[31]

Written with European affairs in mind, these clauses could be applied to colonial disputes as well, although there *possession* was harder to define. For example, what did it mean in North America, long since discovered and "possessed" through formal legal acts but not occupied by the Spaniards, the French, or the English? Too, many parts of the Caribbean and Brazil, where the Iberian states had settlements, were unoccupied but long "possessed" by Spain and Portugal. A definition of the "Indies" of both Spain and Portugal would be needed to clarify this question. Spanish interest in such a definition was patent since at least 1535. Portuguese interest in the question developed after Admiral Chabot's disgrace in 1539 for receiving Portuguese bribes caused the French crown to lift the prohibitions on voyages to the Portuguese Indies, especially to Brazil, which Chabot had obtained in 1531 and again in 1537 and 1538. Shortly after these events, the Spanish ambassador in France learned of the preparations for the Cartier-Roberval expedition, the third in the series begun in 1534.[32]

Iberian reaction to the news about Cartier and Roberval was swift. Charles V instructed his ambassador to protest the license as a violation of the Treaty of Nice and had his ministers speak to the French ambassador at the Spanish court in the same sense. The Portuguese, for their part, tried to find someone to bribe to secure a revocation of

30. Quoted in Davenport (ed.), *European Treaties*, I, 205*n*2.

31. "Tregua firmada en Niza," June 18, 1538, in Pedro de Girón, *Crónica del Emperador Carlos V*, ed. Juan Sánchez Montes (Madrid, 1964), 268–69.

32. Henri P. Biggar (comp.), *A Collection of Documents Relating to Jacques Cartier and the Sieur de Roberval* (Ottawa, 1930), 102–103.

the license. Neither approach worked. Indeed, Cartier received his license at the very time that the Spanish ambassador was protesting to the French royal council. The constable of France, Henri de Montmorency, replied to Spanish protests that Cartier was not going to any of Charles V's or João III's domains but rather had the aim of discovering new lands. He concluded by adding that "to uninhabited lands, although discovered, anyone may go."[33]

Although rebuffed with a clear statement of the doctrine of effective occupation, which said that only lands actually occupied by a European power could be considered its possessions, Charles V did not drop the diplomatic attack. He instructed his ambassador in France to protest again that the license to Cartier was contrary to the Treaty of Nice and the papal donation. The result was an explicit French rejection of the donation, delivered both directly and in the report that Francis I had scoffed that "the sun also warmed him" and that "he much desired to see Adam's will to learn how he had partitioned the world."[34] Although the Spaniards and Portuguese continued their diplomatic protests during 1540 and 1541, Francis I refused to forbid voyages by his subjects to any part of the world.[35]

While diplomacy was running its course, the Spaniards were considering and then finally rejecting more drastic measures. Their deliberations provide glimpses of what the king's chief ministers thought at the time about the Atlantic coast of North America.

As early as December, 1540, the Council of the Indies initiated purchases of supplies for a fleet to attack Cartier either in his ports or where he landed. If he escaped from France or failed to land, the fleet might be used to convoy home any monies that had collected at the ports of the Caribbean. It had to be assumed that Cartier and the other captains arming in France intended to raid Spanish commerce, whatever Francis I's government claimed was their purpose. In late March, 1541, the Council of State reviewed the situation and decided that a fleet large enough to deal with the number of ships and men Cartier was taking—the men reportedly coming to 2,500—would cost more

33. Charles V's instructions are not in Biggar's collection, but their substance is reported by Charles V in a letter to his Spanish ministers that is paraphrased in Biggar (comp.), *Documents Cartier,* 104–107; the quotation from a letter of Bonvallot to Charles V, [November 8–10, 1540], is on p. 136.

34. *Ibid.,* 141, 169–71. These phrases, often inaccurately given as verbatim quotations, were reported in a letter from the cardinal of Toledo to Charles V, January 27, 1541, *ibid.,* 190.

35. *Ibid.,* 197–98, 242–43, 268–71, 283–84, 329–30, 404.

than was available besides undermining Charles V's posture as the last to break the truce. The council chose to accept the official French position that only six ships were sailing for Brazil and Guinea, which were not the emperor's possessions. If the French had other plans, such a small force was likely to be insufficient for capturing any part of the Spanish empire in America that was occupied. If the French went to the uninhabited north—to Canada—that was no cause for alarm, because there was nothing there to be coveted. The more immediate danger was that the French were going to attack commerce; for that the councillors recommended sending soldiers to various ports in the Caribbean and using a convoy to guard cargoes bound for Europe. Charles V agreed to the council's recommendation and ordered a caravel to shadow Cartier. Once Spain knew where Cartier settled, the council reasoned, a fleet could be fitted to attack him during the summer of 1542.[36]

In advocating the policy of spying out the French settlement, the Council of the Indies and its president, Cardinal Loaysa, spelled out Spanish fears about the use to which a Canadian settlement might be put, as well as the Spanish assessment of the east coast of the continent. Reports from France were that the fleet was heading for a point on the continent 760 leagues west of San Malo. That, the council said, had to be the cod fisheries, or Newfoundland. From there the French were expected to go an additional six hundred (or in some versions, seven hundred) leagues, presumably to the south, that is, as far as peninsular Florida, where they could intercept shipping coming out of the Bahama Channel. "This must be their chief interest in going to settle on that coast," the council concluded, for otherwise the land in question was "useless." Cardinal Loaysa added that the French thought that Canada was "rich in gold and silver" and expected to duplicate the Spanish experience in South America. He believed them deceived, for apart from the fishery the coast all the way to Florida was completely unfruitful (*unfrutuosa*), and the French would get lost there or have to return to Europe after expending a few men and most of the supplies they brought from France.[37]

36. *Ibid.*, 158–62; AGI, IG 1963, Book 7, fols. 253v–254v; *consulta* of Consejo del Estado, in Biggar (ed.), *Documents Cartier,* 248–53; Charles V to the cardinal of Toledo, May 7, 1541, in Biggar (ed.), *Documents Cartier,* 287; "Relación de su viaje por Francisco Sanchez," Seville, January 19, 1542, in Smith (ed.), *Colección,* 116–18.

37. AGI, PAT 267, No. 13 (and in Smith [ed.], *Colección,* 109–11, as well as in Biggar [ed.], *Documents Cartier,* 324–26).

Alonso de Santa Cruz, the chief cosmographer of the House of Trade from 1540 to 1567, had the same opinion of the Atlantic coast of North America. He wrote in his *Islario General,* of the period, that once past the Río de las Gamas (the Penobscot River), on the way south as far as Florida, "many islands are found, all deserted and of little benefit [*provecho*], which were seen and discovered by the licenciado Ayllón, who was from the chancery of Santo Domingo. Going to settle the continent, he died there, he and many of the people whom he took with him, and all his fleet was lost."[38]

On what to do about Cartier, the Council of the Indies recommended that if the French were at the cod fisheries or in Canada and if the emperor decided to attack them, he should commission a "good Spaniard" to conduct a mission of discovery and settlement. The mission could hide Charles V's hand and make it appear that he had not broken the truce.[39]

The points the council touched on endured in Spanish discussions of the Atlantic coast of North America: The coast was "useless"—clearly echoing Ayllón's experience rather than his legend. Danger from foreign occupation arose if the enemy moved into peninsular Florida, because that place would afford a position from which to attack shipping leaving the Caribbean. In a time of peace with Spain's European enemies, the way to remove potentially hostile colonies established by its enemies was through a private contractor empowered to settle the same area in the name of the Spanish monarchy.

Because Spain thought Cartier represented a threat to its commerce, it made preparations during the summer of 1541 to send out a fleet in the spring of 1542. Gradually, however, Spain's purpose for the fleet changed. It was clear by late summer that the French were in Canada. With war looming on the European horizon, the receipt of the bullion collecting at the various ports of the Caribbean became more important than pursuing Cartier. Too, the Spaniards were unable to persuade the Portuguese to furnish ships and men for a joint expedition against the French in Canada. There was some talk at the Portuguese court about a joint effort, but the Spanish ambassador judged the discussions nothing but "smoke." The attitude of the Portuguese was

38. Alonso de Santa Cruz, *Islario general de todas las islas del mundo . . .* (2 vols.; Madrid, 1918), I, 441–42.

39. AGI, PAT 267, No. 13 (and in Smith [ed.], *Colección,* 109–11, as well as in Biggar [ed.], *Documents Cartier,* 324–26).

captured in their king's blunt opinion that the French "could not have gone to any place which would be less prejudicial to [Charles V] or him."[40] Accordingly, the Spaniards decided that the fleet they were preparing should go to Panama to bring the bullion accumulating there safe to Spain.[41]

A new Franco-Spanish war broke out in 1542 and raged until 1544. French commerce raiders attacked in record numbers off the Iberian peninsula and the Azores and in the Caribbean. Cartier's settlement lasted the winter of 1541–1542 and then broke up. Roberval's colonists stayed in Canada the winter of 1542–1543 but withdrew in the spring of 1543. By the time negotiations began again in 1544, there was no doubt that there would have to be a resolution of the questions of French desires for New World colonies and of French demands for commercial access to the Spanish empire.

Spain's territorial claim to North America proved to be a consideration in the negotiations because of the renewal in 1544 of Spanish enthusiasm for North American colonization, brief though it was, following the return to Mexico and Spain of the survivors of the Soto expedition (see Chapter IV). Too, Spain realized that North America could be used as a base for raids on its commerce in the Caribbean and in the Bahama Channel. Yet in the negotiations of 1544, the Spaniards were willing to surrender their territorial claim to the hemisphere west of the Tordesillas line—including North America—if that would secure French agreement on matters affecting Spain's commerce with its empire. The Spaniards wanted the French to accept Spanish navigation laws and agree not to engage in smuggling in the Caribbean nor to raid Spanish ships in time of peace. The Spaniards' new negotiating position arose in large part because the defenders of Indian rights had persuaded Charles V that Spain should obey the *jus gentium* in its relationship with the Indians of the Americas. That meant that Spain could not deny other nations commercial access to its empire's peoples, although it might impose regulations. Similarly, the *jus gentium* meant that Spain's title to any part of the Americas had to rest on occupation, not discovery or a papal donation.

The details of the negotiations of 1544 are unknown, but it is evident from the treaty terms and the separate article on the Indies

40. Luís Sarmiento to emperor, Lisbon, January 22, February 16, 1542, both AGS, EDO 373, No. 12, fols. 31, 44–48.

41. AGI, IG 1963, Book 8, fols. 65–66; Hoffman, *The Spanish Crown*, 31.

that the Spanish negotiators brought up the question of French voyages of discovery. They obtained agreement to terms that were highly favorable to Spain and Portugal: in effect France would abandon colonial activity in return for what amounted to a waiving of the requirement in Spain's and Portugal's law that only native or naturalized residents could trade with their American empires.[42]

When the proposals were sent to Portugal and Spain, they were rejected. The Portuguese were unwilling to admit the French to the spice trade with India, then the principal source of the Portuguese crown's revenues from overseas and a trade in which many persons at the Portuguese court and in the Low Countries had interests. Freedom from French colonial ventures in Brazil—Canada had been written off—was not worth the price the Spanish negotiators were prepared to have the Portuguese pay. In the end, the Portuguese negotiated a separate treaty with the French on the subject of reprisals.[43]

In Spain, the Council of the Indies, the Council of State, and the House of Trade refused to believe that the French would obey Spanish laws if granted trading rights. Nor were the Spaniards favorable to giving them commercial access to an empire won with Castilian blood and treasure.[44]

Faced with the opposition of their councils and the House of Trade, the emperor and Prince Philip did not ratify the additional article. They approved the general treaty, which dealt mostly with European affairs, and thereby accepted a trade clause that granted the French access to *all* Spanish territories.

To prevent the French from using the language of the general treaty as a legal cover for sailing to and raiding in the Caribbean, Charles V demanded and got a French prohibition on sailing to the Americas. On August 5, 1545, Francis I issued an order to the duke of Etampes, governor of Brittany, that forbade him to allow any ship to sail to the

42. "Traité de paix," September 18, 1544, in Jean Dumont (ed.), *Corps universal diplomatique du droit des gens . . .* (8 vols.; Amsterdam, 1726–31), IV, Part 2, 280–81, and additional clause in Davenport (ed.), *European Treaties,* I, 208–209. For naturalization laws, see *DIU,* V, 74–78, and Konetzke, "Legislación sobre immigración de extranjeros," 277–79.

43. AGS, EDO 373, Nos. 187, 210, 185, 147, 219. The Portuguese position is summarized *ibid.,* No. 234, dated at Evora, December 26, 1544. See also Manuel Francisco de Barros, Vicount de Santarém, *Quadro elementar das relações políticas e diplomaticas de Portugal com as diversas potencias do mundo, desde o principio da monarchia portugueza até aos nossos dias* (18 vols. in 13; Paris, 1842–76), III, 308–309.

44. Davenport (ed.), *European Treaties,* I, 205–209; AGI, CT 5103, Book of Drafts, fols. 2v–3v. Loaysa's views and those of the Council of the Indies are in AGI, PAT 2?? (2–5–1/26), R. 1.

Spanish or Portuguese Indies.[45] The Spaniards had protection for their commerce, although the means were less than ideal, in that they consisted of a royal letter to a lieutenant and were not backed by a treaty.

The failed attempt at resolving the problem of French commerce raiding in the New World by obtaining France's agreement not to colonize there, in exchange for trade rights in the Spanish and Portuguese empires, did not, of course, lessen the interest of Spain's European rivals in North America and the other parts of the Americas. In France, Alfonse compiled his *Cosmographie* about 1545. It contained a fairly detailed description of the North American coast northward from a cape at 36° north, and a less detailed description of the coast below that point. Among the features Alfonse noted is a bay at 38° north with four islands at its mouth. Some of this geography is from Spanish maps, but some of it seems to be from the Verrazzano voyage, particularly the materials for the coast south of 35° north. That Alfonse dismissed that coast as bordered by islands and having no anchorages suggests that he may have been following Verrazzano's narrative rather than the Spanish maps of the period that show many river mouths, and therefore possible anchorages, between Cabo de Trafalgar and Florida. Whatever his sources, the significant detail is that Alfonse had a fairly good knowledge of the coast, especially the parts north of 35° north.[46]

By 1545, too, the Agnese and Münster maps had gained wide circulation. On the Münster map, the land north of the Verrazzano isthmus was clearly labeled Francesa, using Verrazzano's name for the area he had surveyed. That is, the French claim to areas north of about 40° north was clearly stated on widely available maps even as the French were, temporarily, renouncing their rights to explore or settle there.

In England, Richard Eden was at work on his early translations of travel and discovery literature, while at sea an English ship that had left Dartmouth in 1546 to raid commerce during the Anglo-French war was blown by a storm to the coast of La Florida at about 37° north. There the English entered a "good bay," where they anchored and traded with Indians who came out to the ship in thirty canoes and exchanged marten skins for metal objects. The English then sailed

45. Charles G. M. B. de La Roncière, *Histoire de la marine française* (6 vols.; Paris, 1899–1932), III, 302–303; Davenport (ed.), *European Treaties*, I, 207.

46. Alfonse, *La Cosmographie*, 506.

south for two days, coming to a place at 33° north that the teller of this story, in the 1550s in Mexico, thought was the Point of Santa Elena. Again they traded with the Indians, for marten skins and pearls. The English were at a point near a river that had little water in it, probably because of low tide. From there, they returned to Europe.[47]

But aside from Alfonse, Eden, and this English voyage, the late forties were generally a time of little interest in the Atlantic coast of North America south of the cod fisheries. Veterans of Cartier's expedition circulated reports of what they had found along the Saint Lawrence River and of the supposed arm of the sea at its western end, but the general reaction to Canada seems to have been unfavorable except for the cod fisheries, which continued to be visited by Spanish, Portuguese, Basque, French, and English fishermen. As a result, when French energies were released in October, 1547, by the lifting, following Francis I's death, of his restrictions on sailings to the Indies, French seamen concentrated on voyages to Brazil and Africa and on building a clandestine commerce with the Antilles, a commerce punctuated by occasional armed attacks.[48] The English, for their part, began to seek the northeast passage around Scandinavia to Asia. They never got through, because of the ice pack in the Arctic, but they did establish contact with Muscovy and begin a trade that greatly enriched them.[49] For the Portuguese and the Spaniards, the main focus of naval activity was on the defense of commerce off the Iberian peninsula and in Caribbean waters, especially during the brief flare-up of naval warfare during 1548–1550.[50] The Atlantic coast of North America south of the cod fisheries was left to its inhabitants and to the occasional shipwreck victim who reached shore, there to die or to be enslaved by the Indians.

47. Richard Eden, *Decades of the Newe Worlde or West India . . .* (London, 1555); narrative of an Englishman signed by the viceroy [1560], in Herbert I. Priestley (ed.), *The Luna Papers: Documents Relating to the Expedition of Don Tristan de Luna y Arellano for the Conquest of La Florida in 1559–1561* (2 vols.; Deland, Fla., 1928), II, 176–79 (taken from AGI, JU 13, fol. 186).

48. Henri II authorized his subjects to sail to the Portuguese Indies on October 20, 1547, although they had been doing so regularly since the spring of 1546 (Roncière, *Histoire de la marine,* III, 303–305).

49. McCann, *English Discovery,* 102–106. For the Muscovy voyages, see Thomas S. Willan, *The Early History of the Russia Company, 1553–1603* (Manchester, Eng., 1956).

50. On attacks, see Hoffman, *The Spanish Crown,* Tables 3, 11, pp. 26, 68; on defense in the 1540s, see pp. 27–39, 71–77.

VI

A Renewal of Interest in the Southeast, 1552–1557

In Zaragoza, Spain, on Christmas Eve, 1552, Augustín Millan finished printing the first edition of Francisco Lopez de Gómara's *Historia general de las Indias.* Five years later, the "gentleman of Elvas" published his account of the Soto expedition. In combination with the cartography available for twenty years, these literary works, especially Gómara's widely read book, provided the curious with a location for Ayllón's activities, and therefore for Chicora's and Xapira's potentials and Cofitachequi's pearls. Ayllón's Chicora legend was thus revived, with important additions.

For the French, the new form of the Chicora legend seems to have been particularly important, because during the same period that Gómara's and Elvas' books were appearing, Verrazzano's narrative—but not the annotations of the Cèllere Codex—was published along with André Thevet's account of his voyage along the Atlantic coast of North America. These works gave histories and geographies to the French to back up the cartography shown in Münster's and Agnese's maps. That is, the French claim to the Southeast gained a place in the literary record and was extended southward, from 40° north, to Cape Florida.

Whether by design or coincidence, the publication of Verrazzano's and Thevet's accounts fitted nicely with wider French activities that were challenging Iberian claims and possessions in the Americas. Throughout the 1550s, the French gathered pilots for and geographical information about the Spanish empire in the Americas and attacked Spain's Caribbean settlements and their commerce. In Brazil, they founded a colony in 1555 that was not only a challenge to Iberian claims of exclusive spheres under the Papal Donation of 1493 but was also a flanking position from which they could threaten the Caribbean and the Rio de la Plata and, beyond them, Peru.

In such circumstances, the southeastern coast of North America also came to have considerable importance, because it, like Brazil, was an area to which the French had some historical claim, and it too was a flanking position, one even more menacing to Spanish commerce than Brazil. Furthermore, the revival of the Chicora legend promised great wealth to the successful colonizer of the Southeast.

The Spaniards did not let French activity go unopposed. In addition to diplomatic and military moves intended to deal broadly as well as specifically with French military deeds during these years, the Spanish government issued orders in 1557 for the effective occupation of the threatening section of the Brazilian coast and of the Southeast. Effective occupation was the condition the French had earlier asserted was necessary before they would recognize a claim of possession or exclusive trading rights. The stage was set for the Franco-Spanish showdown of 1559–1565 over possession of the Southeast.

Gómara's *Historia general* was the first comprehensive account of Spanish activities in the Americas since the 1530 edition of Peter Martyr's *Decades.* Part One of the book is a systematic survey of Spanish explorations and conquests from Columbus' time to Gómara's. Part Two is a history of the conquest of Mexico. In the fashion of the time, Gómara borrowed freely from Martyr's *Decades,* Goncalo Fernández de Oviedo's *Sumario,* and some manuscript sources. He also included a complete copy of the bull of donation *Inter Caetera (II).*

Probably because of the book's comprehensiveness, Gómara's *Historia general* became a best seller in several languages during the next twenty years. The Zaragoza edition of 1552 was quickly followed by editions at Medina del Campo and Antwerp in 1553. The decree of November 17, 1553, banning the book, apparently because the history of the conquest of Mexico was critical of Charles V's treatment of Cortes, seems to have spurred interest.[1] Indeed, in 1554 there were no fewer than five printings, one at Zaragoza and four at Antwerp. The Antwerp editions were shipped to Spain and its colonies in the Americas. An Italian translation appeared at Rome in 1556, with the first part—the general history—receiving a separate edition at Venice in the same year. Other Italian editions followed in 1560 and 1565. The first French translation came out in 1569. Richard Eden used Gómara in his *Decades of the Newe Worlde or West India,* published in 1555,

1. AGI, IG 425, Book 24, fol. 8v. Reading it carried a fine of ten thousand maravedis, or about a month's wages for a soldier or for many a skilled craftsman.

but an English translation, of the second part only, was not available until 1572.[2] The lag in translation into French and English does not mean that the book was unknown in the countries of those languages before the translations. In the case of France, statements made in 1563 by Jean Ribault indicate that he had read and understood it by the time of his remarks.

The sixth and seventh subsections of Gómara's survey of the Americas are a history of the "Jordan River in the land of Chicora" and an account of the "customs of the Chicoranos," both derived from Martyr's *Decades.* Gómara devoted roughly twice as much space to the customs—religious rituals, for the most part—of the Chicorans as to the voyage of discovery of 1521. There are only two sentences on the colony of 1526, which Gómara incorrectly dated to 1524. Ayllón, he said, went to the new land with a will to settle and with the dream of great treasures but soon lost his *capitana* in the Jordan River, along with "many Spaniards." In the end, Ayllón perished "without doing anything worthy of memory."[3]

As to the richness of the land, Gómara stressed the portable forms of wealth while saying little about the sylvan and agricultural possibilities that figured in Martyr's account. Thus in telling the story of the initial landing of 1521, he noted that the Spaniards got small amounts of mother of pearl (*aforos*), small, irregular pearls (*aljófar*), and silver in trade and that they were impressed by the "richness and garb of the land." At the end of his description of the customs of the Chicorans, he reminded his readers that the land of Chicora yielded silver, small irregular pearls, and "other stones," and that the many deer raised in the houses and herded by shepherds were a source of milk from which cheese was made. Nowhere did he describe the trees and plants that Martyr mentioned in his description of Ayllón's new Andalucia.

What Gómara did note, and what makes his brief account of the Ayllón expedition so important, was where Ayllón had been. The voyagers of 1521 had gone, he said, to a "land that they called Chicora and Gualdape, which is at 32° and is what is now called the Cape of

2. Bibliographic particulars on the various editions are listed in Antonio Palau y Dulcet's *Manual del librero hispano-americano: Bibliografía general español e hispano-americana desde la invención de la imprenta hasta nuestros tiempos . . .* (28 vols.; 2nd ed.; Barcelona, 1948–77), VII, 640–42. See also Juan Canter, "Notas sobre la edición principe de la Historia de López de Gómara," *Boletín del Instituto de Investigaciones Históricas* (Buenos Aires), I (1922), 128–45.

3. Gómara, *Historia general,* I, 66–67.

Santa Elena and the Jordan River."[4] Those names had been on the better Spanish maps and their derivatives for thirty years, with the cape accurately shown at 32° north. What had not been known previously to anyone but the survivors of the Ayllón expedition and persons to whom they spoke was that the Jordan River was the site of Chicora. Ayllón's legend now had a definite location on the southeastern coast instead of being placed only by the vague "land of Ayllón" label found on some printed maps of the period.

The publication of Gómara's *Historia general* was a signal literary and political event, at least in Castile, but its consequences, aside from the royal decree banning it in the Spains, were slow in appearing. Only later, starting in 1555 with Eden's *Decades of the Newe Worlde or West India,* did Gómara's information begin to show up in the works of writers from states actually or potentially hostile to Spain.[5] But whether read in the original, in an Italian translation, or mediated through a work like Eden's, Gómara's new information about the Spanish colonies in the Americas served to kindle the avarice of merchants and courtiers who outfitted commerce raiders and dreamed of setting up their own empires in the vacant spaces of the Americas.

One apparent reason for the time it took for Gómara's information to get into the writings of others was that Europe plunged into war again in the spring of 1552. During the war's first phase, 1552–1555, the French attacked the Caribbean and Brazil. In both places they began with raids on commerce and settlements by one- and two-ship expeditions. But the raids soon grew into carefully planned multiship attacks. So nearly ubiquitous were the French in the Antilles—where they made forays against thirteen ranches, plantations, and small towns and seized more than nineteen ships—that one official wrote home to Spain in 1553 that "a bird cannot fly without being seen" by a Frenchman.[6] Spanish commerce around the island of Española stopped. Continued smuggling by the Portuguese and renewed smuggling by the French replaced it.

The French achieved a high point in the Caribbean on July 10, 1555, when Jacques de Sores captured Havana after raiding other settlements. He remained in Havana for nearly a month, until August 5.

4. *Ibid.,* 66.

5. Richard Eden, *Decades of the Newe Worlde.*

6. AGI, SD 49, No. 150 and AGI, SD 71, Book 2, fols. 28–30v; Hoffman, *The Spanish Crown,* Table 11, p. 66.

When he left, the tower fort begun by Soto was a burned-out shell. The French had spiked its artillery—and also the Spanish government's assumption that militias could defend the key towns of the Caribbean without the help of paid, professional soldiers. Another French corsair, on his way home to Europe, took Havana in September.[7]

In short, by 1556, Spain had almost lost control of the waters of the Caribbean and of the port that was the assembly point for Spanish ships returning to Europe with the treasures of the Americas. It had not implemented the defensive measures it planned in 1552; in their place, it depended on convoying on the main commercial routes.[8]

In Brazil, the French attempted to seize a portion of the coast. Beginning in 1504, they conducted a trade in brazilwood with the Indians even though the Portuguese had driven them out on a number of occasions. With the breakdown of earlier understandings between the two powers because of the Hispano-Portuguese alliance of 1552, the way opened for Nicolas Durand, Sieur de Villegaignon, who seems to have become excited in 1553 by the possibility of a Brazilian colony. A Catholic nobleman who had made a reputation in the Mediterranean as a knight of Malta, he enlisted the support of both Catholics and Protestants in his enterprise. Sailing from France on July 12, 1555, Villegaignon's fleet of three ships had to put back into port twice before finally clearing French waters on August 14. The passage to Brazil was slow and marked by an outbreak of scurvy. The fleet did not enter Guanabara Bay until November 10.

The site chosen for the settlement was Segeripe Island, also called Palmeiras Island. One of three islands in the entrance to the bay of Rio de Janeiro, it offered excellent defensive possibilities but lacked the soils to grow enough food for the garrison. Trade with the local Indians provided food in the short term. Villegaignon set about converting his tropical island into a new Malta, complete with strict military discipline.[9]

At the same time that the French were sending raiding parties and Brazilian colonists across the Atlantic, they were endeavoring to

7. Saturnino Ullivarri, *Piratas y corsarios de Cuba: Ensayo histórico* (Havana, 1931), 61–78, Roncière, *Histoire de la marine,* III, 579–84, and Wright, *The Early History of Cuba,* 235–41.

8. Hoffman, *The Spanish Crown,* 79–88.

9. Charles-André Julien, *Les Voyages de découverte et les premiers établissements: XVe–XVIe Siècles* (Paris, 1948), 161–221, and Robert Southey, *History of Brazil* (3 vols.; 1810–19; rpr. New York, 1969), I, 280–94.

learn by other means as much as they could about the Americas, especially about the Spanish empire and its trade routes. Little is known about this effort before 1556, but what is known suggests that it was directed primarily to securing pilots with experience on the routes to and from the Caribbean. For example, in 1551, before the war in Europe broke out, the Spanish ambassador at the French court reported that one Sancho, a Vizcayan, was there and had been asked to serve the French king in "these things of the sea" but had refused unless the expeditions were against the English. The ambassador encouraged Sancho to enter the emperor's service. It is not known if he did.[10]

Even if Sancho did not join the French against his sovereign, they were successful in recruiting Portuguese pilots. One was said to have guided Sores, and others were occasionally mentioned in reports from the Caribbean.

Another way the French tried to obtain information about the Caribbean was by sending spies. Again little is known, but one case can illustrate how the French probably went about it. In 1555, the officials at Seville heard that a certain Guillermo Hamel, said to be a French cosmographer and merchant, was shipping to Santo Domingo with Benito Sanchez in order to learn about the ports of that island and others, and the secrets of navigation to the Caribbean. An attempt to arrest Hamel failed when the Spaniards could not find him, but their inquiry disclosed that Sanchez was not properly licensed to be a pilot.[11] It is not known what became of Sanchez nor if Hamel ever made his trip. In the nature of the case, successful spies of his type left no traces in the Spanish documentation.

Even as Sores was sailing from France for the largest raid into the Caribbean that the French had mounted up to that time and Villegaignon was trying to get his Brazilian expedition to sea, French and Spanish diplomats were opening negotiations for a truce. Early in April, 1555, Charles V pressed the Council of Castile for its opinions on issues that might come up in the negotiations, the last of which was the safety of the commerce of the Spanish empire in America. The council replied that the only thing that Spain could ask by way of remedy for French attacks on its commerce in the Caribbean was that

10. AGS, EDO K1489, Book 8, No. 30.
11. Francisco Mexía to SM, Seville, January 30, 1555, AGI, IG 1561.

no Frenchmen go there. For in both peace and war, when the French sailed on pretext of conducting trade they conducted raids. Moreover, the papal bulls granted Spain possession and prohibited anyone from going to the region without the Spanish king's license, even for commerce. (The last reminder was an oblique reference to, and rejection of, the Dominican position that the laws of nations allowed other nations to trade with the American Indians.) Further, Spanish laws and ordinances forbade voyages without a license. The council held that the French who went to the Indies without Spanish licenses should be punished. But it recognized that if Spain sought an absolute prohibition of French voyages in the negotiations, it might meet refusal or a demand for things "in prejudice to the right and possession that Your Majesty has."[12]

Because the main issues between Henri II and the emperor were European, not colonial, the negotiations proceeded to the conclusion of a truce, signed at Vaucelles on February 5, 1556. Most territorial issues were still unresolved; the body of the treaty dealt with the establishment of commercial relations during the period of the truce. The wording of the clauses restoring commerce to its prewar terms was necessarily broad, so broad that the Spanish delegates insisted that the French accept a separate article forbidding French subjects or their agents from navigating, trafficking, or trading with "the Indies belonging to the King of England" unless licensed by him. The "King of England" was Mary Tudor's husband, Philip, who had become Philip II of Spain on January 16, 1556. If that article was violated, the Spaniards were free to proceed against the Frenchmen they caught. The French objected that *navigation* of the seas had formerly been permitted, but they signed the additional article anyway.[13]

Neither side seems to have tried to define the extent of Spain's dominions in the New World or their territorial waters. For the Spaniards, the broader the implicit definition, the better. The French, too, had little incentive to work out a definition, since the truce would not last forever and French captains once at sea did more or less what they wished or had been instructed to do. Besides, the new French colony in Brazil gave France a legitimate destination in the Americas and thus a point of argument should one of their ships be seized within the Spanish sphere: they could claim that it was off course because of

12. AGS, EDO K1642, No. 70, and AGS, EDO K1643, No. 1.
13. Davenport (ed.), *European Treaties,* I, 217; Granvelle, *Papiers d'état,* IV, 541.

storms and invoke the ancient rule of assistance to seamen in distress.

In negotiating the additional article to the Treaty of Vaucelles, the Spaniards had arrived at the negotiating posture they would assume for most of the next 120 years: that of defending their commerce by advancing a territorial claim based on the papal donation which deprived the French—and later the English and the Dutch—of any legitimate destination near the Spanish New World trade routes. By denying that their rivals had legitimate business on the western side of the Atlantic, they could hold that any ship found there belonging to subjects of those states had to be intending to rob or smuggle if it was without Spanish permits. Thus they could seize it without further proof. In time of peace, they could put the crews to death as pirates. All that Spain needed to do was make certain that no one besides itself and Portugal created colonies anywhere close to the Caribbean and its trade routes. The approaches to the Caribbean, including Brazil and La Florida, consequently took on even more strategic importance for Spain.

The proclamation of the truce in Europe in March, 1556, did not relieve Spain's concern for the security of its Caribbean commerce. News traveled slowly, and there was no guarantee that French ships might not still sail to the Caribbean under pretext of a voyage to some part of Africa or to the French colony in Brazil. Watchfulness, the gathering of intelligence about French preparations, and continued defensive measures in the Caribbean were all necessary for the immediate future.

The sluggishness with which news traveled and the sorts of fears that Spaniards in the Caribbean had of new French attacks in the spring of 1556 are illustrated by a letter Pedro Menéndez de Avilés, captain general of the New Spain convoy of 1555, wrote from San Juan de Ulua on April 29, 1556. Menéndez de Avilés expressed the fear that the French might have seized Havana again or might be lying in wait for his convoy. He spoke of the precautions he was taking to deal with those possibilities. He was especially concerned about the network of French spies he was certain existed at Lisbon, Ceuta, and even San Juan de Ulua. To prevent news of his departure from reaching France by way of them or because of the interception of the newsboat he was sending, he had ordered Diego de Mazariegos, the new governor at

Havana, to hold the newsboat and all other shipping until his convoy arrived there. That would also, he wrote the crown, provide the governor with additional men and equipment for the defense of the port.[14]

Menéndez' concerns, expressed with typical prolixity and justifications, were not without some foundation. Spanish intelligence reports reaching the crown at Brussels in April, 1556, showed that at least four French ships were preparing for the Indies voyage, although subsequent information revealed that with the signing of the truce, France had canceled the raid in force that it had planned for the summer of 1556—about which Menéndez was concerned.[15]

Whether because of Spanish diplomatic protests to the admiral of France, Gaspard de Coligny, or because the French crown had already suspended all voyages to the Caribbean, none of those ships sailed to attack Spanish shipping except the one commanded by a "Captain Guilligres" (Gilchrist?), an English renegade. He captured two ships in the English Channel before the English captured him. Interrogated, tortured, and then interrogated again, Guilligres confessed that prior to the conclusion of the truce the French crown had ordered the fitting of ten ships for "Peru" (the Caribbean, specifically the Isthmus of Panama) but that it had ended the preparations upon the signing of the truce. Guilligres, however, had decided to take Henri II's *Le Secret,* in addition to a ship belonging to Guilligres' brother and two ships belonging to other men, to attack shipping coming from the Indies—probably when it was off the capes of the Algarve—and then to sail to Guinea.[16] He had sailed no farther than the English Channel when he was captured.

Hard on the heels of the first reports from the ports of France came others of French ships arming in Holland and even in England for attacks on the Spanish colonies and their commerce. French ships in Norman and Breton ports were said to be preparing for fishing voyages or to go to China.[17] An agent sent to Normandy reported in early July that eleven ships, including the "great hulk" belonging to the admiral of France, were being prepared there for a voyage to the Indies. Another six ships were arming in Breton ports for the same journey. Six

14. Pedro Menéndez de Avilés to House of Trade, San Juan de Ulua, April 29, 1556, AGI, MEX 168.

15. AGS, EDO 511, Nos. 116–17.

16. Granvelle, *Papiers d'état,* IV, 626–27; Regent Figueroa to Philip II, queen to Philip II, both London, September 10, 1556, AGI, IG 1561 (copies regarding Guilligres).

17. AGS, GA 62, No. 35; Granvelle, *Papiers d'état,* IV, 590–91.

ships belonging to the king of France were not going on the journey, as had once been planned. A certain Fontaine and one "Gascon" and his brother were said to be leading the troops being assembled. This was, in fact, a fleet to reinforce Villegaignon's colony at Rio de Janeiro, as reports received in early August finally made clear. Specifically, the ambassador Simon Renard reported to Philip II that Villegaignon had established himself in a port "in the passage to the Indies" and had asked for three thousand to four thousand soldiers with which to conquer a part of the Spanish Indies. The Rio de la Plata was what he had in mind. By mid-September, Renard knew that the French colony was "near" the Cape of Three Points (Cape Verde).[18]

While Renard and his agents were keeping Philip II, who was in Brussels, and the peninsular authorities informed of what the French were doing to prepare ships for the Indies, Philip II and the Spanish ambassador in Lisbon were providing details to the peninsular authorities of French efforts to recruit Spanish pilots or at least to get the information they had about the Spanish colonies. Spaniards who had sided with Hernando Pizarro in his war against the viceroy Blasco Núñez Vela (1545–1546) and then against the licenciado Pedro de la Gasca (1547–1548) were beginning to reach Portugal as early as 1554, although most of them seem to have arrived in the spring and summer of 1556. Such men were potential recruits for the French service.

One of the earliest of the Peruvian rebels to reach Lisbon, and one in whom the Spanish diplomatic service displayed a great interest, was Julian de Solorzano. He arrived in Lisbon in October, 1554, and soon was in contact with Francisco Mexía, *fiscal* of the House of Trade, then in Lisbon on official business. For transmittal to the crown, Solorzano gave Mexía a petition for a pardon and certain paragraphs relating to maps he showed Mexía but would not surrender to him. Eventually Solorzano got to Brussels but was refused the pardon he sought. He then went to France, in March, 1556, with the intention of offering the French king "some things touching on the Indies." By early August, Renard could report that Solorzano had spent two hours with the king and the constable of France discussing the Indies, the "passes" and "sites" there. Solorzano, he had heard, was offering to help the French take a port that all ships had to pass going from Spain to the Indies. He needed only two ships and three hundred soldiers, he

18. Granvelle, *Papiers d'état,* IV, 626–27, 700–701; AGS, GA 62, No. 11.

said. The proposal pleased Henri II and his constable, and the rumor was that they intended to do what Solorzano had suggested.[19]

Other refugees from Spanish justice who arrived in Lisbon in the summer of 1556 had interviews with the French ambassador to the Portuguese court or with Lucas Grenaldo, a Genoese merchant who, according to one account, was "very French" and a "great friend of the constable of France."[20] The Spanish ambassador monitored the conversations as well as he could and sent word that a "bad friar" named Godoy was soliciting French help to return to Peru by way of the Strait of Magellan and that Grenaldo had got Lope García de Isasi, a Vizcayan pilot knowledgeable about the Caribbean, out of Portugal before the Spaniards could have the pilot arrested for failing to account for all the funds entrusted to him in the Indies. Isasi seems to have reached France in August.[21] Again the French had recruited a knowledgeable Spanish renegade.

To counter French activities during the spring and summer of 1556, the Spanish made a diplomatic effort in the fall of 1556 to get the Portuguese to do something about the French colony in Brazil. In November, Philip II wrote to João III asking the Portuguese to hear Juan Hurtado de Mendoza, who could relate what the Spaniards had learned about the French in Brazil and would explain what the Spaniards hoped the Portuguese might do about it. Hurtado de Mendoza was to offer Spanish help in dealing with the problem.[22]

When Hurtado de Mendoza spoke with the Portuguese, they told him that they were trying to get more information since the Portuguese royal council and its experts were not convinced that the French colony represented any long-term danger to Portuguese Brazil. They said they were going to send a ship to Brazil with an order to officials there to gather information on the French. They thanked Spain for offering help but declined it for the moment. Still, Hurtado de Mendoza could say that "all who know the place agree on how bad this is for the Portuguese now and how much worse it would be in the

19. Francisco Mexía to king, Seville, March 17, 1555, AGI, IG 1561; AGS, EDO 511, No. 105; Ambassador Renard to princess, August 17, 1556, AGI, IG 1561, with original in AGS, GA 62, Nos. 55–57.

20. Luís Sarmiento to Juan Vázquez, Lisbon, July 9, 1556, AGS, EDO 378, No. 48.

21. AGS, EDO 378, Nos. 51, 59, 198; AGI, IG 2001, fols. 30v–31; AGS, EDO 511, No. 237; AGS, GA 62, Nos. 12–14.

22. AGI, IG 425, Book 23, fols. 257v–258v.

future." According to him, they dared not speak openly because of the king's position.[23]

João III's temporizing was consistent with his long-standing policy of avoiding open confrontation with the French if he could. Negotiations and bribery usually secured an accommodation; he probably hoped that that would again be the case. So long as he lived, the Portuguese did nothing except gather facts. After his death, in 1557, pressure from the Jesuits in Brazil, rather than from Spain, persuaded the queen regent to authorize Mem de Sá's attack on the French, which he delivered in 1559.

The year 1556 ended without any resolution of the growing threat to the Spanish Caribbean. The French still held Rio, they were still preparing ships for voyages there and elsewhere in the Atlantic, and they had gathered a large body of information about the Caribbean and other parts of the Spanish empire.

Complementing these events in the Americas and Europe was the publication during the years 1555–1557 of five books that helped spark a revival of interest in the Southeast. The first, and at the time the least important for the history of the Southeast, was Eden's *Decades,* published at London in 1555. Eden's purpose was not to lay claim to any particular area for the English but rather to stimulate interest in voyages to distant places. As a broad geographical survey of the world outside Europe, Eden's book relied heavily on Martyr's first four decades, on Oviedo's *Sumario,* and above all, on Gómara's *Historia general.* Eden also used other Spanish authors and some who had written in Italian or been translated into other languages to compile the description of the general geography and resources of the Americas, Asia, and Africa.

One commentator has said that Eden's brief description of Florida and the east coast of North America as far as Canada—taken from Gómara—would not have given a reader unfamiliar with the maps of the time a good idea of peninsular Florida's geography.[24] On the other hand, the reader would have learned of the failures of Ponce de Leon and Soto and of the decision by the crown to send only friars to the areas de Leon and Soto had explored—friars like Luís Cancer who fared no better than the military men who preceded them.

23. AGI, EDO K1489, Book 8, No. 97, p. 3. Southey notes the order to find out what the French were about, in *History of Brazil,* I, 291.

24. McCann, *English Discovery,* 137.

Eden paid more attention to, and gave far better information about, the land of the cod fisheries. Following Martyr, he located this part of the Americas from the latitude of the Straits of Gibraltar (36° north) on to the north. Most of Eden's geographical description of the area, however, referred to Canada and the fisheries, that is, to the area north of about 43° north. Martyr, Gómara, Oviedo, and Galeatus Butrigarius were quoted to give an essentially negative image of the land, exclusive of the fisheries, with only Jacques Cartier's views, as Butrigarius presented them, quoted to positive effect. For Cartier, Canada was "fair and fruitful, with plenty of all sorts of corne, herbes, frutes, woode, fishes, beasts, metals, and rivers of such greatness that ships may sail more than 180 miles upon one of them, being on both sides infinitely inhabited."[25]

On the whole, then, Eden's readers got only a vague and essentially negative geography of North America. His information on failed Spanish expeditions into the interior reinforced the negative image. He was sure that far richer fields for commerce lay in Muscovy—to which voyages were just beginning—and other parts of the Old and New Worlds.

Given this portrayal, it is not surprising that, except for English schemes during the 1560s, the Spanish claim to North America was secure from English challenges for another generation. In the long run, however, Eden's book prepared the way for Sir Humphrey Gilbert and Sir Walter Raleigh by spreading knowledge of North America and of the authors whose works gave fuller descriptions of its potential riches.

The second book to help kindle interest in the Southeast was the third volume of Giovanni Bautista Ramusio's collection of voyages, published at Venice in 1556. That book contained the texts of both Giovanni da Verrazzano's report to Francis I on his voyage of 1524 and the "Discourse of the Great Captain," which mentioned a French voyage "of 1539" (it was really in 1529) to 40° north latitude.[26] Verrazzano said that he made landfall at 34° north and then sailed both north and south from that point. The French thus had a published claim to the North American coast at least north of 34° north.

25. Quoted *ibid.*, 135.

26. Ramusio, *Navigationi et Viaggi*, III, fols. 350v–358 [*sic;* 352v–354]. Bernard G. Hoffman provides an English translation and dates and identifies this voyage as Parmentier's ("Account of a Voyage Conducted in 1529 to the New World, Africa, Madagascar, and Sumatra, Translated from the Italian, with Notes and Comments," *Ethnohistory*, X [1963], 1–79).

That claim extended six degrees of latitude farther south than what the widely circulated Agnese and Münster maps showed. And it came very close to the Spanish claim centered on the Cape of Santa Elena, at 32° north, which had first appeared in Gómara's *Historia general,* of 1552.

The Italian translation of Gómara's work, the third of the five books to trigger renewed interest in the Southeast, was issued at Rome in 1556, with a second translation of the general-history section—the part containing the story of Ayllón—appearing at Venice in the same year, perhaps with Ramusio's help. Spanish cartography, and woodcut maps based on it, had laid claim for many years, of course, to all of North America south of the cod fisheries. Gómara's history gave that claim substance in the form of specific events and a specific attempt to colonize. He also brought the supposed riches of the Southeast once more to the attention of anyone who might be interested in them.

In sum, anyone who was able to read Italian could, after 1556, learn a great deal about early French and Spanish exploration on the southeastern coast of North America and about what that area might provide to a colonizing expedition. Henri II's queen, Catherine de Medicis, and her court were one avenue by which Ramusio's collections and the translation of Gómara might have come to French attention. There were undoubtedly others.

Further information about the Southeast and its supposed riches became available in 1557 when the "gentleman of Elvas" published his account of the Soto expedition at Evora.[27] That same year, a new French claim to North America was also published, one even more sweeping than that in Verrazzano's report.

Elvas gave the most detailed account of the interior of North America to appear in the sixteenth century. Of special interest are what he said of Cofitachequi and its relationship to Ayllón's landing place. The apparent source of Ayllón's pearls could be located using Elvas, just as the place that he had been could be located using Gómara. A quick check of Martyr would have completed the picture by linking the pearls of Cofitachequi, apparently on the Jordan River, with the vague report of Xapira. Chicora and the riches Ayllón had claimed for it were not far from 32° north. Documentation is lacking, but later

27. [Gentleman of Elvas,] *Relaçam verdadeira dos trabalhos q[ue] ho Governador dõ Fernãdo de souto e certos fidalgos portugueses passarom no descobrimẽto da provincia da Frolida, Agora nouamẽte feita per hũ fidalgo Deluas* (Evora, 1557).

events suggest that both the French and the Spaniards made the linkages between the Spanish sources and Elvas' account. The result was that the Cape (or Point) of Santa Elena became an important place in North American geography and a focus for imperial conflict.

A second French claim to the southeastern coast of North America was published in 1557 when Thevet's *La France Antarctique* came off the press.[28] In the course of recounting his trip to Brazil, Thevet at first claimed that on his way home, in 1556, his ship sailed along the North American coast from Cape Florida to the cod fisheries, although he later stated that the actual voyage along the coast was from about 40° north to Newfoundland. Nonetheless, he laid claim to the Florida peninsula as "our Florida" and provided a description derived from other authors.[29] His claim probably reflected the views of at least some people at the French court and was the first manifestation of the idea that led to Ribault's voyages and to the claim to the Southeast that the French made in connection with them.

These five books—by Eden, Ramusio, Gómara (in Italian), the "gentleman of Elvas," and Thevet—provided all the information about the Southeast and the European exploration of it that was available outside secret government and private archives. The composite picture they presented included the Chicora legend, the record of Spanish failures, and French claims to the entire coast from Cape Florida to the cod fisheries. The publication of the information was a sign that the neglect of the Southeast was about to end. A new Franco-Spanish war hastened that end.

The truce of February 5, 1556, had hardly been proclaimed when, in July, 1556, the papacy negotiated a treaty with France aimed at restoring papal power in Italy and depriving the Spaniards of their claim to Naples, a kingdom to which the French royal house also had hereditary claim. War between papal and Spanish forces followed over the summer, to be compounded in January, 1557, when the duke of Guise, leader of the ultra-Catholic party in France and strongly anti-Spanish at this point, moved an army into Italy and attacked Naples, thereby bringing the Franco-Spanish truce to an end. The English, by declaring war on June 7, 1557, compelled France to open a second front. Mary Tudor, queen of England and Philip II's wife, hoped that French

28. André Thevet, *Les Singularitez de la France Antarctique* (Anvers, 1558; new ed., ed. Paul Gaffarel, Paris, 1878).

29. *Ibid.*, 390–92, 395.

difficulties in Italy would allow the expansion of English control around Calais. Gathering an army in the Low Countries, Philip II sent it into northern France, where on August 2 the siege of the fortress town of Saint Quentin began. Six days later, the Scots joined the French in the war against England, providing additional enemies to Spanish shipping in the area of the English Channel and the North Sea and in the southern and western Atlantic. On August 10, Anne de Montmorency tried to relieve Saint Quentin but was defeated, so that the city finally had to surrender on August 27. Among the prisoners was the man who had directed the city's defense: Coligny, the admiral of France.[30]

With the outbreak of war between Spain and France, the truce of 1556 ceased to offer what little protection it had afforded to Spanish shipping in the Atlantic. Of particular concern to Spanish officials was a small fleet that had been sent to Puerto Rico under the command of Luís de Carvajal to pick up the silver brought into San Juan by ships of the Tierra Firme convoy of 1555, which had been hit by a hurricane while in the Bahama Channel.[31] In part to protect that fleet and in part to protect the Indies in general, Philip II ordered that all French officers and seamen captured in or on the way to the Indies, or even merely while lying in wait in the Azores for ships returning from the Americas, were to be thrown into the sea or hanged without mercy, for "thus it is suitable for the security of those places."[32] Frenchmen captured in Spanish territory were to go to the galleys. In addition, Spain sent warnings of the war to the Indies and made preparations to defend commerce against the fleet it had heard was fitting in France for an attack on the Caribbean according to a plan prepared by the "Portuguese clergyman"—perhaps Fray Godoy.[33] The Spaniards also hastened their preparation of two patrol fleets, one for European waters and the other for Santo Domingo.

From the fall of 1557 until the peace negotiations of the summer

30. Charles Merki argues that Coligny was already a "secret Calvinist" by 1555 (*L'Amiral de Coligny: La Maison de Chatillon et la Revolte protestante, 1519–1572* [Paris, 1909], 84–86). J. Shimizu, on the other hand, concludes that his conversion came later, probably after 1557, and that his support in 1554–1555 for his vice admiral of Brittany, Villagaignon, was politically motivated (*Conflict of Loyalties, Politics, and Religion in the Career of Gaspard de Coligny, Admiral of France, 1519–1572* [Geneva, 1970], 18, 25–29).

31. AGS, EDO 514, No. 37; Pierre Chaunu and Huguette Chaunu, *Seville et l'Atlantique* (8 vols. in 10; Paris, 1955–59), II, 530–35, 545.

32. SM to princess, Cambrei, August 10, 1557, AGS, EDO 514, No. 48. The draft of this order is AGS, EDO 515, No. 163.

33. AGS, EDO 514, No. 37.

and fall of 1558 and the first months of 1559, the war settled into a pattern of commerce raiding in the Atlantic and a few campaigns in Europe, including, in January, 1558, the duke of Guise's capture of Calais and Guisnes, the last English ports on the continent, and in June and July, 1558, the unsuccessful French invasion of Flanders.

As always during wartime, the Spaniards did their best to keep abreast of potential French threats to the commerce and settlements of the New World. In February, 1558, they received news that ships were fitting for Newfoundland at San Jean de Luz, on the coast of the Bay of Biscay. In June, word came from Flanders that a French fleet readying for the Indies had ceased its preparations. The advice to the regency government in Spain was to continue precautions, however, because the French might raid the Antilles and free the slaves as a way of getting their help in overthrowing Spanish control.[34]

The Spaniards went on the offensive in the Caribbean, although the result was a minimizing of losses rather than a significant capture of French raiders and smugglers. The patrol fleet planned in 1552 for use in the Antilles arrived on station at Santo Domingo in October, 1557, and soon was driving some French raiders and smugglers to seek less defended waters along the coasts of what are today Colombia and Panama. But the fleet had little success in capturing any French ships around Española and quickly ran into serious problems supplying itself. Before peace in Europe was concluded, Spain had ordered the fleet's disbandment. There was a decision to build a new fort at Havana, following—but also revising—plans taken from the archives, where they had apparently lain for some time. An engineer and masons were recruited at Seville. Money came from Mexico, but construction moved at a snail's pace after the groundbreaking on December 1, 1558. The militias continued poorly equipped even though the government sent a shipment of matchlocks, pikes, and gunpowder to Santo Domingo, Havana, Veracruz, Cartagena, Panama, and Nombre de Dios (on the Caribbean side of the isthmus) in 1557. Of these places, only Cartagena was attacked. In 1559, it fell with hardly a fight, in part because its governor and leading citizens were napping after lunch just as the French charged the outer defenses. Raids on smaller towns, plantations, and ranches continued, without meeting much resistance.[35]

At the same time that the Spaniards were beefing up their Carib-

34. AGS, EDO K1491, No. 64; AGS, EDO 517, Nos. 36, 90, 91.
35. Hoffman, *The Spanish Crown,* 90–103, 39–49.

bean defenses even if in limited and consequently ineffective ways, they seem to have decided to deal with the French strategic design that ostensibly sought to establish colonies on the flanks of the routes to and from the Caribbean. Extensive research in archives at Seville and Simancas has failed to locate the working papers in which the regency government set down plans such as those Solorzano and the "Portuguese clergyman" offered to the French. Nor have any documents surfaced that knit the various actions of 1557 into a coherent plan for meeting the French threat, either actual or potential. Yet more than happenstance must be behind timing that had the dispatch of the patrol squadron to Española occur just as weapons went to the militias and that authorized two concurrent major colonizing expeditions capable of occupying the strategic flanks of the Spanish empire. The patrol fleet had, it is true, been in the works since 1552, but the impetus to do something arose in the fall of 1556. Events in Italy probably were a consideration, but so too may have been the accumulating intelligence reports from France showing an active interest there in large-scale attacks on the Spanish empire. The decisions of 1557 to send colonies to the Brazilian and North American flanks of the empire look even more like the result of a well-thought-through analysis of the situation in which the Spaniards found themselves at the beginning of a new war with the French.

The Spaniards seem to have concluded that the Portuguese were unlikely to do anything about the French at Rio even after the death of João III, on June 11, 1557. Accordingly, they had the House of Trade make arrangements to send a private citizen to settle on the coast of Brazil and expel the French. Jaime Rasquin duly signed the contract on December 30, 1557, and the crown approved it on June 5, 1558. Rasquin was to settle as many as four places on the Brazilian coast using six hundred men, some of them married and accompanied by their wives and families. A range of skilled tradesmen, from miners to cattlemen, were to be among the settlers. But this expedition never reached Brazil. It ended up instead at Santo Domingo, where the men dispersed to other parts of the Spanish empire.[36]

The Spanish plan to occupy the Southeast had originated in Mexico

36. Rasquin's expedition awaits a narrator. For a summary of documents regarding it, see Archivo General de Indias, *O Arquivo das Indias e o Brasil: Documentos para a história do Brasil existente no Arquivo das Indias de Sevilha,* researched by João Cabral de Mello Neto (Rio de Janeiro, 1966), 134–41. Chaunu and Chaunu note Rasquin's departure from Spain (*Seville et l'Atlantique,* II, 576–78).

on the basis of concerns quite different from those having to do with the strategic geography of the Americas and a possible French challenge to Spanish interest in it. Nonetheless, approval of a modified form of the Mexican proposal in December, 1557, seems to have come only because such concerns supplemented the original, Mexican ones. The result was an expedition and the last diplomatic attempt to resolve the conflicting Spanish and French claims concerning exploration, colonization, and trade in the Americas.

VII

The Luna Expedition and European Diplomacy, 1557–1559

On December 29, 1557, the regency government at Valladolid issued an order for the settlement of a port on the northern coast of the Gulf of Mexico and the development of a string of settlements along a road from that port passing through Coosa to a settlement at the Point of Santa Elena, on the Atlantic coast.[1] The origin of this order had been a Mexican plan to develop missions along the Gulf coast, but as issued the order reflected lay interests in the interior of the Southeast and in the Atlantic coast which had grown out of Hernando de Soto's findings as well as Francisco Lopez de Gómara's revival of Ayllón's Chicora legend. Too, the order may have reflected the crown's interest, explicitly enunciated in 1559, in preventing the French or "any other foreign Kingdoms from entering there to settle or take possession of our land."[2]

The order marks the beginning of a new period of activity by the Spaniards in the Southeast. Initially they tried to establish a colony on the Gulf coast, but they shifted their activities to the Atlantic coast after diplomacy during 1559 failed to secure French agreement on the territorial limits of the Spanish empire.

The Mexican plan to develop missions along the Gulf coast arose from the missionary zeal of the Franciscan Andrés de Olmos and from the impression that the deaths of the survivors of the Padre Island shipwrecks of 1554 made on members of the mendicant orders and Spanish society in New Spain. Father Olmos began working among Indians on the fringes of the province of Pánuco, in northern Mexico, about 1544. From them he learned about tribes in the mountains to the north and west and, more vaguely, on the coast north of

1. Princess and the Council of the Indies to Viceroy Velasco, Valladolid, December 29, 1557, as quoted in audiencia to Tristan de Luna, Mexico City, March 30, 1559, in Priestley (ed.), *The Luna Papers*, I, 46–47. The Coosa road is noted *ibid.*, II, 259.
2. *Ibid.*, II, 15–17.

the mouth of the Pánuco River.[3] To this information about the area immediately around the site of Monterrey, Olmos seems to have added reports from men, such as Sotelo de Betancos, who had been sent in the early 1530s to search for Pánfilo de Narváez.[4] Wanting to spread the gospel to the villages and wandering groups of that region which were outside the sphere of Spanish control, Olmos asked his superior at Mexico City for additional missionaries. He received one companion. But helpful as the assistant was, he was not enough to enable Olmos to reach the Indians of the outlying areas. Olmos' frustrations grew. Then, providentially, a tragic event in 1554 provided him with an opportunity and an urgent necessity, as he saw it, to carry the gospel northward by peaceful means.

The tragedy of 1554 involved four ships sailing for Spain. Leaving San Juan de Ulua's roadstead late in the fall, they ran into a storm off the coast of Texas just east of Padre Island. Three of the four ships were driven ashore, but with relatively little loss of life. The survivors, thinking themselves closer to the Pánuco River than they really were, set off down the coast on foot. After a time, Indians attacked them. Because the Indians stripped the dead, those who got away concluded that their assailants were only after European clothing. Hence they stripped and continued on, with a rear guard trying to keep the unsatisfied Indians at bay. Little by little, exhaustion, ambushes, and river crossings took their toll. In the end, only two or three persons stumbled into the settlements on the Pánuco River. Among the dead were five Dominicans.[5]

Apparently deeply stirred by the martyrdom of his fellow clerics and perhaps deciding, as some of the mendicant clergy did, that it was a punishment for sins committed by the orders, and in any case seeing an opportunity to engage royal support for his main interest, Olmos put all the frustration and hope of his ministry in Pánuco into a letter he wrote to his king in late 1554 or early 1555. As he summarized it in 1556, he asked for royal support for wider mission efforts, especially on the frontier with the "Chichimeca" Indians, the seminomadic tribes who wandered in the interior basins of Mexico and who

3. Barcía, *Chronological History,* 24.

4. Sotelo de Betancos to king, Tamazsaltepeque, December 9, 1567, AGI, MEX 168.

5. For transcriptions and translations of all the relevant accounts of the voyage, the shipwreck, and the sixteenth-century salvage, see *Documentary Sources for the Wreck of the New Spain Fleet of 1554,* trans. David McDonald, prep. David McDonald and J. Barto Arnold III (Austin, Tex., 1979).

raided and were raided by the Spaniards, but also among the Indians who had killed the survivors of the 1554 wreck. Survivors of the storm had been killed, he claimed, because the Spaniards had slain at least fifty of the Indians from the north (but not necessarily from the same group that had assaulted the shipwreck survivors) when they came into Pánuco Province seeking food.[6] Violence had begotten violence; the gospel of peace was clearly needed.

Olmos' letter to the king must have been rhetorically powerful, because it elicited a royal reply supporting some initiative in the north but leaving the details up to the viceroy of Mexico. The results were unsatisfactory, as Olmos reported in a letter dated November 25, 1556. Olmos had asked the viceroy and audiencia for four things but had got almost nothing.[7]

First, he wanted a sufficient number of friars to work in four areas: Tampico, Tamaholipa (where he had baptized the chief), Tanchipa, and the valleys facing the "Chichimec" frontier. The superior of his order had said, however, that he had to content himself with the companion he had received earlier. The archbishop and other clergy had offered no additional help whatsoever, even though the archbishop had written the crown in 1555 that the Mexican church council of that year supported mission work in La Florida.[8] Olmos appealed again in his letter of November 25 for the king's help.

Olmos' second request was that three settlements be made "for the security of the north coast" on the Rivers Palmas (Soto La Marina) and Bravo (Rio Grande) and at Ochuse (probably Pensacola Bay). Spanish settlements there would provide haven for shipwrecked seamen and could serve as examples for the wandering tribes near each. Olmos thought that the patent advantages of Spanish agricultural civilization would draw the Indians into sedentary, Christian lives. The viceroy had deferred action, saying that it would be "very difficult" to settle three such places. Olmos again asked royal help, but in a way that suggested that he, unlike some laymen in New Spain, really did not favor the three coastal settlements, particularly the one at Ochuse.

On Olmos' third and fourth requests—for a reduction of tributes on

6. The letter of 1554 or 1555 is summarized in Andrés de Olmos' letter to the Council of the Indies from Mexico City dated November 25, 1556, AGI, MEX 280.

7. Andrés de Olmos to king, Mexico City, November 25, 1556, AGI, MEX 280, and Andrés de Olmos to the Council of the Indies, Mexico City, November 25, 1556, *ibid.*

8. The bishop of Cuba also endorsed missions in La Florida in a letter to the king dated April 20, 1556 (Lowery, *Spanish Settlements*, I, 354).

Indians in and near Pánuco Province[9] and for orders to the corregidors of Huasteca and Pánuco to force Spaniards to settle at Tampico—the viceroy had expressed a willingness to help. Olmos reported his confidence that suitable actions would be taken. He closed his letter of November 25 with a new plea for royal support of his mission plans.

Apparently leaving no stone unturned in his search for backing for his project, Olmos may have inspired a letter that the canon Pedro Hernández Canillas and the *alcalde mayor* of Pánuco, Rodrigo Ranjel, onetime secretary of Soto, wrote in April, 1557. Citing the king's letter to Olmos expressing a desire for the conversion of the Indians of Pánuco's frontiers, these men went on to recall Olmos' exemplary life, his holy desire and zeal for the conversion of souls, and his long labors in the field despite diminished physical capacity due to illness. They affirmed their belief that given additional companions, he would be able to do even more than he had done. Besides endorsing the appeal for missionaries, they supported the idea of the three coastal settlements. Unlike Olmos, however, Ranjel and Hernández Canillas declared that the Ochuse settlement was the one to be made in preference to the others, because it was the "best entrance" to La Florida. As an eyewitness, Ranjel attested to La Florida's bountiful resources. Settlement of La Florida, he and Canillas concluded, would be in God's service.[10]

Olmos' specific projects aside, the late 1540s and early 1550s were a period in which New Spain's interest in a return to La Florida grew. Viceroy Juan Hurtado de Mendoza's interest in the project in 1543, when the Soto veterans were returning and telling their stories of hardship in a land blessed with potential, was shared by others. In a letter of 1547 from Gerónimo Lopez to the king, there is a glowing paragraph about La Florida. It was, Lopez said, a big land, populated, and filled with many of the things of Spain, including vines, trees that give nuts like the chestnut, fields full of cattle (bison?), and forests of all sorts. Since the people were "very good and very able [*entendidas*]" and did not practice the sacrifices and idolatries of Mexico's natives, he went on, he believed they could be brought quickly to "know God." Mexico, he judged, would make an appropriate base for expedi-

9. The tributes had recently been reassessed and raised, and encomienda Indians had been reassigned, over the objections of many encomenderos (Diego Ramirez to king, Mestitlan, August 16, November 20, 1553, AGI, MEX 168).

10. Pedro Hernández Canillas and Rodrigo Ranjel to king, Tampico, April 15, 1557, AGI, MEX 168 (printed in translation, with a date of April 25, 1557, in *Documentary Sources*, trans. McDonald, prep. McDonald and Arnold, 241–42).

tions to La Florida because there were men there eager to return to it. Besides, in what may be an echo of the Münster cartography of North America, he averred that they might find a way to the Pacific Ocean and the riches of China and "all the world," so that the king would be the lord of "all the universe." That would serve the king, God, and the interests of men like himself, and it would give their children opportunities to serve the king and increase his kingdoms.[11]

Lopez' themes—of the similarity of the resources of La Florida to Spain's and of the usefulness of expeditions for the society of New Spain—are found as well in Francisco Cervantes de Salazar's *Life in the Imperial and Loyal City of Mexico in New Spain,* published at Mexico City in 1554.[12] At one point Cervantes de Salazar portrays an exchange between his interlocutors after a lengthy discourse on the resources of New Spain that concludes with Zuazo, the chief speaker, saying that only one thing is lacking for the perfect happiness of the province:

> ALFARO: What, I miss only wine and oil. ZUAZO: It is, of course, that Florida, lying distant only an easy and very short voyage by sea, and by land neither a long nor a difficult journey, should be conquered by the Spaniards and should acknowledge the Emperor, Cesar, as its lord. ALFARO: What advantage and profit would your province derive from this action? ZUAZO: Very much indeed, for whatever is produced by the other Spain in the Old World, from which merchandise is imported into ours with so much delay and difficulty, all this would be supplied by Florida, which produces much more abundantly and is contiguous to us. ALFARO: This will happen some day, I hope. ZUAZO: It will happen as soon as it seems best to the Emperor.[13]

Here, then, was a repetition of Ayllón's idea that the agricultural products of Old Spain, especially wine and olive oil, could be produced in La Florida. Cervantes de Salazar did not state his source for that idea. It could have been Peter Martyr's *Decades* in the 1530 edition or an edition of Ptolemy.

In a letter to the Council of the Indies dated May 4, 1553, Viceroy Velasco repeated the other theme sounded by Lopez: that La Florida could be an outlet for the energies of men in Mexico who wanted to return to it and for the children of the first generation of conquerors.

11. Gerónimo Lopez to king, Mexico City, March 1, 1547, AGI, MEX 96.

12. Francisco Cervantes de Salazar, *Life in the Imperial and Loyal City of Mexico in New Spain,* trans. Mimia Lee Barrett Shepard (Austin, Tex., 1953).

13. *Ibid.,* 79 (from fols. 288–288v of the original).

Noting the difficult economic conditions of the viceroyalty because of the great epidemic of 1545–1548 that had carried off much of the Indian population (modern estimates suggest up to 60 percent of the population of central Mexico), the concurrent loss of faith and optimism among the friars, the increasing incidence of vagrancy among Spaniards and others, and the restiveness and rebelliousness of black slaves, Velasco advocated a new conquest to draw off the idle and give direction to the restless. He recommended that if Spain did not approve a new conquest, it should prohibit immigration to New Spain.[14]

In short, from religious figures like Father Olmos and from various secular officials from the viceroy down, in the early 1550s the crown was receiving advice to sponsor some sort of expedition to the Gulf Coast of La Florida. The recommendation was for as many as three settlements, two in northern Mexico (at the Rivers Palmas and Bravo) and one in Florida (at Ochuse). The promised benefits were manifold, including winning souls for the faith and providing places of refuge for shipwreck victims and outlets for the restless, dispirited population of New Spain whose economic future and optimism had been dealt a sharp blow by the great epidemic of 1545–1548.

Aside from Olmos' letters of 1556, there are no documents prior to 1557 telling of the government's response to this advocacy. Still, a glimpse of the thinking at court over the winter of 1556–1557 is provided by a letter dated July 15, 1557, to Philip II (who was still in the Low Countries) from Dr. Pedro de Santander (who was at Seville). Santander was an inspector (*veedor*) about to go to New Spain to deal with the royal treasury, especially at Veracruz, the chief collection point for royal taxes on trade and hence second only to Mexico City as a source of revenue and a seat of tax evasion.[15]

Santander began by recounting a letter of January 3 about abuses in the treasury department of New Spain. He recalled how his knowledge of the irregularities led to his appointment, and he summarized a lengthy justification he had written earlier (in January?) for making war on the Indians in order to take their lands and expel them from the New World. In that paper he had cited Old and New Testament passages and the Papal Donation of 1493 to justify his position.

Santander observed that the peoples who lived in La Florida, in

14. Quoted by Jonathan I. Israel in *Race, Class, and Politics in Colonial Mexico, 1610–1670* (London, 1975), 13.

15. *DIE*, XXVI, 353–65.

particular, had killed many Spaniards and rejected the gospel. Among the dead, he listed Ayllón (killed by the Indians, he said), Ponce de Leon, Narváez, many of Soto's men, and Father Luís Cancer (killed in 1549 after the Scriptures had been "burned by the Indians"). Santander had seen Cancer and his men leave Veracruz and had seen Father Gregorio de Beteta and the others return. He also cited the killing of the shipwreck survivors of 1554 as a reason for the king to punish the Indians of La Florida: "barbarous nations" needed to fear the royal name and vengeance was due for the innocents killed.

Besides vengeance, Santander listed five reasons for a Florida settlement: to provide security for shipping, prevent vassals of another king from occupying the lands, to extend the Spanish colonial reach, to convert souls, and to furnish an outlet for the poor Spaniards of Spain, New Spain, and Peru who had no income. He concluded by likening the king to the shepherd who should divide his flock, to remove the devil from the New World and La Florida. La Florida was, he said, the "promised land that is and was possessed by idolatrous Amorites, Malachites, Moabites, Canaanites; it is the one that is promised by the Eternal Father to the faithful." The king might lawfully punish the evildoers and force them to believe, just as it is proper to force the ignorant to learn.

Santander's proposal for settlements called for achieving security for shipping by setting up lighthouses at the Bay of Ciruelo (*i.e.*, Miruelo, possibly Apalachee Bay or even Pensacola Bay), which gave access to the "abundant" province of Chuso (Coosa or Ochuse?), and at the Port of San Jorge (location unknown). By night, lanterns on a high mast and, by day, reflections from a spire "gilded" with tinned steel (*hoja de Milan*) would guide pilots and let them know where they could find help. In addition, Santander thought that a fleet of three galleys and two *zabras* (small ships with oars) should be built and based at Veracruz. Sailing only during daylight hours, it could patrol the coast as far as Havana in order to save shipwreck victims and recover bullion and other cargo. The crews could punish Indians who tried to harm the survivors of shipwrecks, and the fleet could supply the proposed interior colonies with goods. It could also furnish colonists from among the crews who had served their time and the rowers who had completed their sentences. Santander believed that the Tlascalan Indians of New Spain, exempt from tribute because of the help they gave the Spaniards in conquering Mexico, should be made to pay for the upkeep of the ships of the fleet, with other supplies coming from Pánuco Province.

The principal thrust of Santander's thinking was, however, the creation of settlements and the conversion of the natives. He rejected the need for more exploration, saying that enough was known and that if previous explorers had done what he was proposing, the land would now be settled. He expected to raise 1,500 men in New Spain, Pánuco, Jalisco, and Honduras, and to provide them with horses from various parts of New Spain. He would begin his settlements in the province of Achuse (given as Chuse in the transcription) by seeking out the best place in terms of soils, water, access, and clarity of the sky. There he would build a stockaded town into which he would put three hundred men. Filipina, as he would name the town, would give him a secure base, and because of it, little by little the nearby Indians would come to know God.

Once Filipina was established, Santander proposed to move inland to Tascaluza (Tuscaloosa) Province, which was on the River Despiche, as he called it, and very good and fertile. There he would build a second stockaded town, to be called Cesárea, on the same pattern as the first. He would leave the ill and less able soldiers there and replace them over time with men the galleys brought in. Once the nearby Indian towns had acceded to the king's dominion and the Christian faith, Santander proposed to move successively to the provinces of Talesi and Coza (Coosa). He would establish stockaded towns in each and repeat the process of placing the surrounding towns under Spanish domination. From Coosa he would move on to the coast on the "Gulf of Bermuda" in order to provide security for shipping but also because that province was rich, with many good pearls in the rivers. The last idea he clearly derived from Soto's finds at Cofitachequi.

To support his grand scheme, Santander made a variety of proposals. For attracting private soldiers, he wanted permission to distribute the Indians in encomiendas, reserving the principal and largest settlements for the king. The encomenderos would remit to the king 10 percent of the tribute (head tax) they collected from their Indians. The royal fifth—a 20-percent tax—on minerals would be imposed, and in due time the *alcabala* (sales tax) as well. The king's costs would be negligible, and the profit over time greater than from New Spain, where the costs of corregidors' salaries, pensions, and other charges levied on the tribute income from Indians directly under royal control left hardly ten million in profit for the crown from an income of over fifty million (in what unit of coin or account he does not say).

In concluding, Santander returned to moralizing arguments. He encouraged Philip II to take the opportunity to add much land and many souls to his kingdoms. He claimed that the addition would be greater than all the lands that the king possessed already, and richer too. God, Santander implied, had given Philip an opportunity that he ought not let slip. And in the end, the king did seize the opportunity, but he did not choose Santander to be the leader of the expedition.

Santander's letter is notable because it reveals that the Mexicans' Gulf Coast plan was turning into a larger design to occupy the better parts of the interior of the Southeast. Originally, Olmos had wanted missions on the Soto La Marina and the Rio Grande and along the coast of northern Mexico and southern Texas. He seems to have thrown in Ochuse later as a lure for lay support of his religious project. Ranjel and Cervantes de Salazar more clearly expressed the lay interest in creating a new colony inland from the Gulf coast, with Coosa as a major center. But none of these Mexican advocates of subduing the Southeast had proposed a coastal settlement on the Atlantic, and even Santander was vague about that part of the plan. His vagueness may have reflected, in part, a general ignorance of the geography of the Atlantic coast but it was more likely determined by Mexican priorities.

The royal order of December 29, 1557, completed the metamorphosis of Olmos' missionary scheme into a plan to build a chain of settlements linking, by way of Coosa and Cofitachequi, the Gulf-coast port of Ochuse with a port supposed to be at or near the Point of Santa Elena. In place of the vague reference to a road to the Atlantic from Coosa, the order specified the Point of Santa Elena as the site for the Atlantic terminus of the chain of settlements.[16]

A lack of documentation hinders definitive statements about why the royal order stipulated the Point of Santa Elena, but evidence already presented suggests that by 1557 the point had taken on symbolic significance beyond its actual location and geographical features. Thanks to Soto's men and Gómara, the point had become

16. Princess and the Council of the Indies to Viceroy Velasco, Valladolid, December 29, 1557, as quoted in audiencia to Tristan de Luna, Mexico City, March 30, 1559.

identified with Ayllón's Chicora and access to Cofitachequi, the pearl kingdom.[17] Gómara's book had made it the specific locus of Spain's territorial claim to North America. Its symbolic value thus can account not only for its inclusion in the plan of 1557 but also for the urgency of Philip II's order of 1559 that the point be occupied without further delay and for the persistent Spanish identification of it during 1564 as the location of René de Laudonnière's French settlement, which actually was well to the south.

The order of December, 1557, probably did not arrive in Mexico before mid-May, 1558. Viceroy Velasco dictated a reply on June 15 in which he told the crown what he had learned during the previous two years about La Florida and its settlement, outlined the steps he planned to take to implement the order, and raised the question whether corregidors, friars, and other Spanish administrators should be appointed to supervise the native villages that came under Spanish control. The difficulty was that the order of December, 1557, had granted a ten-year exemption from payment of tribute to all Indians who submitted to Spanish rule, yet tribute was the means for paying administrative officials in New Spain and other parts of the empire.[18] The viceroy requested resolution of the problem, at the same time that he went ahead with preparations for the Luna expedition.

Velasco proceeded with those on several fronts. To resolve the delicate issue of which religious order was to be in charge of the mission work, he called together the provincials of the three leading mendicant orders and asked them to decide. They seem to have reached agreement rather quickly because they had already discussed the question in connection with Father Olmos' plans of 1553–1556. They also probably had a feeling for what Spain wanted, because they sent representatives to court during those years. Their consensus was that

17. I have elsewhere suggested that the Mexican proposal included an Atlantic coast settlement at Dominican insistence and because of the revival of the Chicora legend in Gómara's book, but it seems to me now that although Gómara's account of Ayllón's expedition may have helped develop interest in the Atlantic coast, the main source of the interest was the Soto materials on Cofitachequi. The idea of a port downriver from that town grew from this base and then was directed to a specific location, the Point, or Cape, of Santa Elena, by what Gómara had to say. *Cf.* Paul E. Hoffman, "Legend, Religious Idealism, and Colonies: The Point of Santa Elena in History, 1552–1566," *South Carolina Magazine of History,* LXXXIV (1983), 62–63.

18. This letter has not been found, but is referred to in Viceroy Velasco's letter to the king from Mexico City dated September 21, 1559, AGI, MEX 280.

the Dominicans should have the field to themselves. Six friars would be chosen for their piety, knowledge, and skills in learning languages, with the royal treasury supplying their material needs.[19]

A second area of preparation involved finding out more about the geography of the area to be colonized. It was possible to talk to the Soto veterans still in Mexico City, but it was necessary to send out an exploring party as well. From conversations with the Soto veterans, Velasco concluded that he should start colonizing from the Gulf coast, putting off settlement of the Point of Santa Elena until later. As he explained to the crown on September 30, 1558, he was sending a scouting party to study the Gulf coast rather than the Atlantic coast

> because I understood from seamen who have knowledge of [the Atlantic] coast and from soldiers who were with Soto and walked about the land that it would be a better bet [*mas acertado*] to go the eighty leagues by land that there are from the district [*paraje*] of Havana to Santa Elena than by sea, not only because the road is longer [by sea but] because the land goes out [to the east] a lot and there are shallows on that coast upon which ships that go next to the land seeking a port run the risk of being lost. There is no certainty about where the port of Santa Elena is, except that the people who were with Soto say that they met a river that the Indians said was the river of the pearls and that they were three days' journey from the sea and that it is the one that enters the sea near the Point of Santa Elena. There is no certain knowledge whether there is a good port at this point. The seamen say that the one that is put on the maritime chart is not certain. If such a port is not found at the point, the settlement will have to be made at the closest port to it that has the qualities Your Majesty commands.[20]

All of this was to say that no one in Mexico knew much about the Atlantic coast and that there was an awareness there that the linking of Cofitachequi's river with Ayllón's port and Gómara's geography was too easy. Indeed, even the overland route to the Point of Santa Elena was uncertain. Velasco used the word *acertado* to describe taking the overland route. His adjective comes from a verb meaning to guess at or hit by chance, suggesting that he had his doubts about it.

The wording of Velasco's letter also suggests that the Mexican authorities, who had originally proposed settlements only on the Gulf coast, were in no hurry to expand the orbit of their activities to the Atlantic coast, whatever the royal will might be. The history of

19. AGI, MEX 19, No. 21, fol. 2. Regarding the earlier discussions and the sending of agents: AGI, MEX 68, Book, fols. 113–14.

20. AGI, MEX 19, No. 21, fol. 2.

the Luna expedition and Angel de Villafañe's report of 1561 indicate the same reluctance.

A scouting expedition under the command of Guido de Labazares left San Juan de Ulua with three ships on September 3, 1558, and returned on December 14. After stops at Tampico and on the Texas coast at 28½° north, Labazares had intended to sail along the upper Gulf coast, but a storm forced him to swing to sea. He missed the Mississippi Delta. His next landfall was at 29½° north on an east-west coast. That was probably near what is now Biloxi, because the water was shallow and there were islands some distance from the main coastline. Sailing east from there, Labazares found the entrance to a bay (Mobile Bay) that he named Filipina. He described it as having an entrance one and a half miles wide with, on one side, an island lying east-to-west that was seven leagues (about twenty-four nautical miles) long and, on the other, a "point of the mainland." He sailed a dozen leagues into the bay and estimated that it went another three or four leagues before it ended in the mouth of a great river. He noticed reddish bluffs around the bay, which were especially high on the eastern side. The bay was, he said, the "largest and most commodious in all that coast." But when he tried to sail farther east of it, head-winds and bad weather allowed him to advance a mere twenty leagues before he decided to turn back, on December 3. He dictated and signed his formal report on his voyage at Mexico City on February 1, 1559.[21]

During Labazares' absence, Velasco finished manning and supplying the expedition. He gathered four hundred soldiers, half footmen and half mounted, one hundred craftsmen and tradesmen, and a contingent of friars and secular clergy. These men were to travel on six large barges of a hundred toneladas each, with each able to carry forty horses, a hundred men, and four pieces of artillery. The ships had been chosen because they drew but four palmos of water, about half a fathom. The artillery was for use in forcing an entrance into the bays and rivers in La Florida, which Velasco had heard would be defended by large numbers of Indians in canoes.[22]

By early April, 1559, Tristan de Luna, the expedition's commander, and the majority of the men he was to command had gathered at Mexico City. True to earlier observations that there were a lot of

21. AGI, IG 738, No. 73a (Copy made in 1565 at Madrid). See also Lowery, *Spanish Settlements*, I, Appendix T, 473–74.

22. AGI, MEX 19, No. 21, fols. 1v–2.

restless young men in New Spain, the soldiers proved to be an unruly lot, especially those with some pretension to noble status. A curfew violation in mid-April led to the murder of a sheriff (*aguazil*) and to a riot by the companions of the men who were eventually arrested and jailed for the murder. The hanging of one of the men involved quieted things down. Thereafter, Velasco and several of the captains of the expedition worked with the audiencia to impose real but informal discipline. The audiencia complained, even so, that one of the chief troublemakers, Hortuno de Ibarra, evidently a rich merchant much in the viceroy's favor, was getting special treatment in jail, where he was being held for his part in the troubles.[23] The ultimate solution to the unruliness of the men was to move them to Veracruz during the last days of April and the early days of May, 1559. Velasco accompanied them as far as Tlaxcala to see that all went well.

Meanwhile the provincials of the three religious orders and the royal treasury officials wrote to the king expressing hopes for the success of the expedition and asking for royal funding for as long as four years. Hungry men and those needing estates made bad emissaries, the provincials observed. In the past, men of those sorts needing one bushel of corn had taken a hundred if they could and destroyed what they did not use. If the Indians resisted, the Europeans killed them. Royal permission to continue paying for the support of the men seemed especially urgent because the expedition was taking supplies for only seven or eight months. The provincials judged that the viceroy did not dare spend more money from the treasury without permission, because he had already spent a great deal, although with great care.[24] The treasury officials added for their part only the detail that all the preparations had been made without burden to the natives of New Spain and in such a way as to remove the immediate need to live off the land in La Florida. Many who were going on the expedition, they said, had spent up to three times what they received from the royal treasury in the grants in aid (*ayudas de costa*) that Velasco had given in the amounts of 100, 150, and 200 pesos according to the need and merit of the recipients.[25]

From Tlaxcala, Velasco wrote a letter to Philip II that suggests that he had begun to appreciate better the strategic importance of a settle-

23. AGI, MEX 68, Book, fols. 123v–125v.

24. Provincials of the three orders to king, Tlaxcala, May 4, 1559, AGI, MEX 280.

25. Royal officials to king, Mexico City, May 10, May 20, 1559, both AGI, MEX 323, the larger book of letters; Viceroy Velasco to king, September 1, 1559, AGI, MEX 280.

ment at the Point of Santa Elena. He said that having a town on the Florida coast 100 to 130 leagues from Havana and "in the middle of the Bahama Channel" would be useful because it would discourage corsairs from going to the Caribbean. The men and ships Spain based there would be able to attack the corsairs as they, like the Spaniards, exited the Caribbean through the channel.[26] Although Velasco's geography is confused—the Bahama Channel ends at the latitude of Cape Canaveral, not the 320 to 416 nautical miles north of Havana that he mentions—his main point expresses an idea that later writers would develop: that an Atlantic-coast settlement was an essential part of the defense of Spanish commerce because it protected the Bahama Channel. With the exception of the Council of the Indies' conclusion of 1540 that Jacques Cartier might be planning to occupy a port in peninsular Florida from which he could threaten Havana and Spanish commerce in the Bahama Channel, no Spanish writer had sounded this theme before in connection with La Florida's east coast. Conversion, riches, and the crown's territorial claim vis-à-vis other European sovereigns had all figured in earlier discussions. Now, in 1559, the military factor reappeared.

Velasco seems to have reached his strategic insight concerning an Atlantic settlement because the previous summer the French had attacked Puerto Caballos, in Honduras. In commenting on that in the fall of 1558, he had noted the proximity of the Honduran port to the trade route through the Yucatán Channel and the consequent danger to the Tierra Firme convoy and to Havana, the key to the Caribbean's commerce.[27] Now, in May, 1559, Velasco wrote that a French settlement at or near the Point of Santa Elena posed similar dangers to Spanish commerce. His recognition of Santa Elena's strategic importance was a small but important shift from his point of view of the previous year. Nonetheless, his primary concern was the settlement on the Gulf coast, not a settlement near the Point of Santa Elena.

Luna's fleet departed from the roadstead behind San Juan de Ulua Island on June 11, 1559. A little over a month later, Velasco received a reply to his letter of June 15, 1558, in which he requested guidance on what to do during the first ten years about paying the Spaniards who would preach in and administer the Indian towns of La Florida. The government's response was that he should do what he thought best.

26. Viceroy Velasco to king, Tlaxcala, May 15, 1559, AGI, MEX 1117 (Stetson).
27. AGI, MEX 19, No. 21, fols. 1v–2.

He answered that he had decided to have Luna appoint *alcaldes mayores* and corregidors from among the Spaniards who were mature and had the other qualities needed and to assign them salaries. Velasco stated his opinion that for at least three years the crown should be prepared to pay for supplying the Spaniards in Florida with foods from New Spain and the Antilles (mostly cattle) "unless the Indians willingly give it to support those officials." Furthermore, he suggested shortening the time during which the obedient Indians were exempt from tribute, so that both the Spaniards there already, as he hoped (on September 1, 1559, he had still not heard from Luna), and those who would go in the future might look toward a quick reward—an encomienda—for their services. The king had already agreed that after ten years the obedient Indians could be assigned to encomiendas whose incomes would support Spanish administrators and clergy selected by the viceroy of Mexico. The encomiendas, supervised by corregidors, as in New Spain, would be held for two lives. If those provisions were now coupled with a shorter time span during which the Indians did not pay tribute, it would serve, Velasco said, to attract many men to the conquest.

Velasco declared that his only intention in sending Luna to La Florida was to increase the patrimonies of Jesus Christ and the king. He had no other objectives, he vowed, and he had tried to guide the expedition with only those ends in mind. Writing somewhat later in September, the Dominican friars of Mexico City expressed the belief that the colony, begun with the Christian aims of peaceful conversion and Spanish settlement and guided by Christian hands in its preparations and on the ground, would surely prosper. The king's objectives in La Florida were also God's, they implied.[28]

Initial reports from Florida, arriving on September 9, 1559, suggested that the Divinity was pleased. The fleet had made a good crossing of the Gulf of Mexico and worked its way along the coast to Ychuse (Ochuse) or the Bahía Filipina de Santa María, as Luna now named Pensacola Bay. Colonists and some supplies were landed on August 15. The fleet had put ashore many of the horses at nearby Mobile Bay in late July, when it had put in there after missing the entrance to Ochuse as it sailed westward along the coast.[29] Luna's

28. Velasco to king, Mexico City, September 1, 1559; Fray Pedro de la Peña and others to king, Mexico City, September 22, 1559, AGI, MEX 280.

29. A history of the Luna expedition drawing on all the available sources is still to be written, although Herbert I. Priestley's *Tristan de Luna, Conquistador of the Old*

report, dated August 25, was full of enthusiasm for the new land and the enterprise.

In response to Luna's request for additional supplies, Velasco ordered the preparation of a small ship, the *San Antón,* also known as the *Francesillo,* and a galleon, *San Juan de Ulua.* This first of what were eventually four supply expeditions sailed from Mexico in early November.[30] About the same time that Velasco's provision ships left San Juan de Ulua, two frigates entered Havana harbor seeking foods to replace what the Luna fleet had lost when a tropical storm struck it at anchor in Ochuse Bay on September 19. Some of the ships had been driven ashore and destroyed along with their supplies, which had not been unloaded. At Havana, Governor Diego de Mazariegos provided three hundred head of cattle, casava bread, salted meat, over thirty horses and mules, and an additional ship to transport everything to the colony.[31]

The storm had transformed a promising beginning into a critical predicament made all the worse by the discovery that there were few Indians at Ochuse and little in the way of food to support the expedition until replacement goods arrived from Mexico and Cuba. Luna's and his subordinates' personalities soon exacerbated the problem by generating disputes over matters great and small. The bone-penetrating chill of the late fall and winter's rains added its misery to the hunger and dissension of the colonists.

Meanwhile, in Europe, diplomats worked on a Franco-Spanish peace treaty. Their failure to reconcile the two nations' claims and ambitions about overseas colonies meant one more complication for Luna's task.

While Velasco had been preparing the Luna expedition, Spanish and French diplomats were negotiating a general peace treaty. Their talks opened in September, 1558. Many of the details are of little concern here; it is enough to recall that the more difficult issues involved

South: A Study of Spanish Imperial Strategy (Glendale, Calif., 1936; rpr. Philadelphia, 1980) is a good longer account. There are short accounts in English in Lowery's *Spanish Settlements,* I, 355–76, and in Priestley (ed.), *The Luna Papers,* I, xxix–lxvii. Davila Padilla's *Historia de la Fundación,* 231–73, is a not entirely reliable account by a sixteenth-century Dominican which should be compared with the documents Priestley edited as well as with those cited below.

30. Viceroy Velasco to king, September 24, 1559, AGI, MEX 280; Viceroy Velasco to Goncalo Gayón, October 7, 19, 31, 1559, all AGI, SD 11, No. 50 bis, fols. 1–3. Record of preparations in AGI, CD 877, No. 1.

31. AGI, SD 115, fol. 47v.

Italy, Sardinia, and Calais and that the death of Mary I of England, on November 26, simplified matters temporarily by removing the English from the discussions. When they returned on February 12, 1559, their position on Calais threatened to prevent a general treaty, but the participants worked out a compromise of sorts by March 13.[32] Their agreement cleared the way for negotiating secondary questions, such as French activities in the Americas.

The Spanish position on the American empires united their own and Portuguese demands. The Portuguese wanted the French to acknowledge and to respect their "demarcation" and to agree to rules for the granting of letters of reprisal. The full details of the Portuguese demands are not available, so it is not clear exactly which demarcation they had in mind: that of Tordesillas or that of Alcaçovas or some combination of them. On September 8, 1558, Philip II agreed that his negotiators would present the Portuguese demands as his own. His decision was consistent with the policy his government in Spain was already following of looking out for Portuguese interests, as the Spaniards saw them, at a time when the minority of King Sebastian of Portugal deprived his country of strong leadership. The Jaime Rasquin expedition was one expression of the Spanish concern.

Spain's own demands, formulated at Brussels in September, 1558, centered on its preoccupation with the defense of commerce and colonies in the Atlantic and Caribbean. Philip II reminded his negotiators that in time of peace (*e.g.*, 1545–1552) as well as of war, armed French ships had gone to the New World and robbed Spanish ships and done "other damages." When confronted, the French in Europe had claimed they could not control the ship captains in question nor capture and punish them, yet the Spaniards knew that the captains commonly put into French ports and received supplies. Philip wanted this abuse discussed so that it could be stopped.

As to the larger question of the limits of the Spanish Indies, Philip II noted that that matter had been considered a number of times by his advisers and that neither he nor they were certain that it should be

32. A good overview of the negotiations: France, Treaties, etc., 1547–1559 (Henri II), *Traicté de paix fait a Chasteav-Cambresis l'an M.D.LIX, le III d'Avril, et ce qui se passa en la negociation pour ladite paix* . . . (Paris, 1637), 1–115 (with the treaties with England and Spain following to p. 160). Alphonse, Baron de Ruble, also discusses the negotiations, in *Le Traité de Cateau-Cambresis, 2 et 3 avril 1559* (Paris, 1889). Some of the Spanish documentation is found in the Archive General de Royaume, Brussels, Etat et de l'Audience 427[1], item A, fols. 42 ff. For the events of March, see AGS, EDO 518, Nos. 98, 99.

brought up and gone into in depth. He asked his negotiators for their ideas on what should be done. Antoine Perrenot Cardinal de Granvelle replied that when it seemed appropriate the negotiators would bring up the matter of the "navigation of the king of Portugal and the Spanish Indies" and that every effort would be made to secure what the Portuguese desired but not if doing so prevented, or even just delayed, a treaty. He was not optimistic, because he said, "I do not know what can be got; in truth, the reasons we have for this are more for persuading than for convincing."[33]

There the matter remained until December, 1558, when the absence of the English provided an opportunity to bring the negotiations to a rapid conclusion. In anticipation of that, Philip II wrote to his regent, the princess of Portugal, asking her to send him any documents and opinions that dealt with the Indies. She sent him copies of the opinions of the Council of the Indies and the Council of State.

The Council of the Indies wanted the French to recognize Spanish control of everything west of the Tordesillas line of demarcation. It wanted the French to be forbidden to sail west of the line on pain of death, and the French king to be obliged to enforce the prohibition on his own subjects and on any Spanish subjects who participated in violations of it by Frenchmen. It asked that all prizes taken from the Indies trade (*carrera*) at any place or time be fully restored and that the men who had captured them be punished. In particular, it thought that seizures made during the recent truce should be returned.

The Council of State, on the other hand, believed that the French should be restricted from sailing to specified places and that the Spaniards should bear the responsibility of punishing violators of the agreement. If the Spaniards were unable to punish a wrongdoer, there should be, it felt, provision for mutual Franco-Spanish action. But its opinion was that demanding French agreement to an absolute prohibition on voyages west of the Tordesillas line would be likely to cause trouble in the negotiations and should be avoided.[34]

That and other advice was on hand by mid-March, 1559, when Philip II wrote to his representatives to try to get a clause along the lines of a draft by the Portuguese ambassador (a document not found with his letter). If, however, it was necessary to work out something

33. AGS, EDO 517, No. 74; Granvelle, *Papiers d'état,* V, 285–86.

34. AGS, EDO 811, No. 103; AGS, EDO 519, No. 124; copies of *consultas,* AGI, IG 738, R. 3, Nos. 41, 41a. The full *consulta* of the Council of State is found in AGS, EDO 834, No. 186.

new, the king said, it should be done with great care so as to remove all objections (*inconvenientes*) and bases (*fundamentos*) the French might use in the future to excuse themselves. As an example of what he meant, Philip II noted that the French were making a point of the lands the Spaniards possessed but were omitting those they claimed (*las que avemos*) and had discovered but had not settled (*y tenemos descubiertas aunque no estan pobladas de Españoles*). Should getting into such matters cause difficulty, he said, it would be better not to discuss them but to leave things as they were.[35]

At some point in the two weeks between March 13 and March 28, the Spanish negotiators tried to obtain French agreement both on the territorial limits of the Spanish and the Portuguese empires and on the question of reprisals, a matter of great concern to the Portuguese. They failed to achieve a meeting of minds on either and decided to leave the matters for later discussions, especially the question of reprisals. Philip II ratified that decision on March 30.[36]

The treaty that was signed on April 3, 1559, contained no specific settlement of outstanding issues connected with the Iberian empires.[37] The treaty did contain a commerce clause that indirectly dealt with Spanish and Portuguese concerns:

> [The subjects of the Spanish and French crowns,] whosoever they may be, may, guarding the laws and customs of the countries, go to, come from, dwell in, frequent, commune with, and return to the lands of the one and the other in a mercantile fashion and as shall seem to their benefit, whether by sea or by land.[38]

Similar to the commerce clause of most of the earlier treaties between France and Spain, this one differed only in specifying that the subjects of the two powers were bound by the laws of each. In accepting this clause of the Treaty of 1559, the French agreed to be bound by Spain's navigation laws affecting trade with Spanish lands in the Americas. Unresolved were the issues of reprisals, the principal concern of the Portuguese, and of what constituted the limits of the Spanish and Portuguese empires.

35. Granvelle, *Papiers d'état,* V, 546.

36. *Ibid.,* V, 546, 564.

37. Anticipating Portuguese unhappiness with this turn of affairs, Philip II was quick to write to his ambassador at Lisbon to tell him that the Spanish had presented the Portuguese demands as their own and intended to pursue the matter further (AGS, EDO 519, No. 40).

38. Dumont (ed.), *Corps Universal Diplomatique,* V, Part 1, 35; and in France, *Traité de paix,* 123.

The restoration of normal diplomatic relations in June, 1559, offered a new opportunity to discuss those matters and to press the French government to prohibit its subjects from making voyages to the Iberian empires. The Portuguese ambassadors to Philip II's court and to the French court were both involved. The latter urged the French to agree to a proclamation forbidding sailing beyond a certain longitude and latitude, but the French rejected the idea because innocent seamen on ships blown into the area in question by a storm would have received treatment as corsairs.

The Spanish and Portuguese continued to talk among themselves about which longitude and latitude might be acceptable. For Philip II's consideration, they sent copies of a proposed sailing ban specifying coordinates and of another just naming the individual Spanish and Portuguese colonies that were to be off limits. He liked the Portuguese proposal, which apparently specified a latitude and longitude as well as named provinces, but he recognized that the French would not agree to that, so he authorized the duke of Alba, his acting ambassador at the French court—who was to conduct Elizabeth of Valois to Spain to become Philip II's wife—to seek French agreement to a slightly modified version of the other proposal.[39]

The proposal would have forbidden the French from sailing to lands held by the kings of Spain and Portugal or on the seas touching them without first obtaining permission under the laws that governed Spanish and Portuguese subjects. If Frenchmen were caught in those territories or on those seas, they were to be judged by the laws of the state in question, without the judgment's being grounds for a letter of reprisal or other legal action. If the French were in occupation of any part of the named possessions (*e.g.*, Brazil), they were to leave or be subject to forcible removal by the Spaniards or Portuguese. French port authorities were to try to prevent sailings that would violate the agreement. The Spanish provinces named were Peru, New Spain, the Antilles, and the Rio de la Plata. Brazil was the only Portuguese province named. Another version of the proposal dealt only with the Spanish crown and its possessions.[40] La Florida was omitted from the list of provinces because it was not known to be occupied by the Spaniards at the time the list was drawn up. At that time—June, 1559—Luna was just leaving New Spain.

39. Spain, Sovereigns, etc., 1556–1598 (Philip II), *Negociaciones con Francia, 1559–[1568]* (11 vols. to 1960; Madrid, 1950–), I, 37–44.
40. *Ibid.*, I, 39–43.

This proposal went to the cardinal of Lorraine, a member of the French royal council, shortly after it arrived in Paris. The reply of the council, which came within a few days, was that (*a*) the treaty over the Indies should be with Spain only, and if the Portuguese wanted a treaty, it would have to be separate; (*b*) the French would never accept a limit (*termino*) in heaven nor on the seas, nor would they agree to be generally forbidden from sailing to the Indies (by which they apparently meant all the world outside Europe, rather than just the Americas); (*c*) the French rejected the idea that any of their ships taken on the high seas would be a lawful prize in peacetime, and they intended to continue to risk themselves and their fortunes in sailing to the Indies; (*d*) the French were willing only to have the king issue a prohibition on sailing to or visiting lands actually "held and possessed" by Spain; and (*e*) if the Spaniards specified the lands the French had entered and occupied, they would reply whether or not they would leave them. Orally, they promised to forbid the sailing of French ships to the Spanish Indies, treaty or not, but they hinted that the general language of the commerce clause of the Treaty of Cateau-Cambresis gave them privileges they intended to use.

Spain's ambassador, Tomás Perrenot, Sieur de Chantonne, objected that if the French sailed to the Indies (*i.e.*, the Americas), they were bound to encounter Spanish ships, and if they wanted to acquire land there, they could not do so except on the same coasts as those the Spaniards held or had discovered. He mentioned that the Treaty of Tordesillas' division of the world showed that all the Americas were already held. He noted that the French would have trouble supporting a colony, and he protested that doing what the French seemed to be proposing would violate the peace treaty. He also said that without express orders from Philip II, he could not accept their counterproposal of a restraint against sailing to specifically named Spanish provinces that allowed them complete freedom on the high seas.[41]

Having raised objections, Chantonne forwarded the French reply to Spain, where Philip II gave it to his own council for discussion and recommendations. There the matter rested until late December, 1559. Meanwhile Chantonne reported that Jacques de Sores was arm-

41. *Ibid.*, I, 49, 74. A summary of the French reply: AGI, IG 425, Book 23, fols. 429–30.

ing but had promised to give bond that he was not going to any of the Spanish or Portuguese Indies. The ambassador also wondered on paper what had become of the reply from Spain to the French counterproposal.[42]

The reason for the delay was Philip II's effort to get the Portuguese to support the more inclusive prohibition, banning French voyages to the Portuguese and the Spanish Indies and to the seas around them and requiring the French to leave if they were there. He also wanted the Portuguese to protest the French colony at Guanabara Bay, because experience had shown that the French were not good neighbors. Philip II believed that a French settlement anywhere in the Americas would lead to invasions of the Spanish or Portuguese colonies and to the pretense that the French had conquered other areas even though they lay in the "conquest and demarcation" of Spain and Portugual.[43] It is unknown whether the Portuguese took up the issue with the French. Spanish records suggest that they did not do so until 1561, when the Portuguese were justifying the violence they had used to expel the French at Rio de Janeiro in March, 1560.

Philip II finally wrote to Chantonne on December 24, 1559. He approved of the reply Chantonne had made to the French in September and told him not to accept their offer unless they agreed to the Spanish demand, which he thought was "justified; we have the title and quiet, peaceful, and continuous possession."[44] Exactly what that meant is not clear, but Chantonne understood it to say that the French should agree to the proposal as formulated by the Spaniards.

When again presented with the proposal, the French royal council asked for a copy of what the duke of Alba had originally presented for their consideration and promised to study it and satisfy the Spaniards to the degree possible. Chantonne raised the question of Sores' voyage with Admiral Gaspard de Coligny, who assured him that Sores was going to Beny, in Ethiopia. The admiral asked that should the Spanish meet French ships on the seas, they not impute to the French thoughts that they had not thought—that they not assume that the French were sailing to raid Spanish ships and possessions. Chantonne answered that the way to avoid problems was to agree on a demarcation of the Spanish Indies by a set of latitudes and longitudes, but the admiral

42. Spain, *Negociaciones,* I, 86, 107.
43. AGI, IG 425, Book 23, fols. 429–430v.
44. Spain, *Negociaciones,* I, 128–29.

expressed displeasure at that idea. After this exchange at the Chateau of Blois early in January, 1560, the matter remained in suspension.[45]

The French were willing enough to agree that their ships should not sail in waters "under Your Majesty's fortresses," as Chantonne later reported regarding a Franco-Portuguese exchange of 1561, but they would not accept a definition of territorial waters that excluded them from the high seas or from sailing to and trying to colonize areas not occupied by Spaniards or Portuguese. Nor would they accept any restraints on their rights to seek reprisal for what they saw as unredressed injustices done their merchants by Iberian merchants. Their attitude here was no different from that of many merchants in the Low Countries, who objected to the peace treaty because it forbade reprisals against the English except under certain very limited conditions.[46]

Although apparently Philip II did not abandon hope immediately that the French might be brought around to a general prohibition, he took two steps that indicate that he did not expect that to happen. On December 29, 1559, he issued a peremptory order to Luna to see that a Spanish colony was placed on the Point of Santa Elena without further delay. Philip II said that he had learned that Frenchmen might attempt to colonize La Florida under cover of voyages to the cod fisheries. If effective occupation was to be the name of the diplomatic game, he intended to play it for that piece of North American real estate. Eleven months later, when all hope of an agreement with the French concerning American commerce and colonies had disappeared and when Spain's ambassador in France was reporting the sailing of French ships bound for trade in the Caribbean, Philip II issued orders to his governors in the Caribbean colonies to enforce the laws of the empire and seize any and all ships, especially French ships, that appeared in their areas without the proper Spanish licenses. The governors were to confiscate the ships and their goods and to send the crews to the House of Trade as prisoners.[47]

45. *Ibid.*, I, 157–58, 174–75.

46. *Ibid.*, III, 217; duchess of Parma to Philip II, August 21, 1559, in Margaretha of Parma, regent of the Netherlands, 1522–86, *Correspondance de Marguerite d'Autriche, duchesse de Parme, avec Philippe II*, ed. M. Gachard (3 vols.; Brussels, 1867–81), I, 18–20.

47. Priestley (ed.), *The Luna Papers*, II, 15–17; king to governor of Cuba, Toledo, November 27, 1560, in Diego de Encinas, *Cedulario Indiano* (4 vols.; rpr. facsimile ed., Madrid, 1945–46), I, 446; king to governor of Cartagena, Toledo, November 27, 1560, AGI, SF 987, Book 3, fol. 200.

It should be clear that neither the French nor the Spaniards agreed, in 1559–1560, to "no peace beyond the line."[48] Both wanted peace on the high seas. Where they differed was in defining which parts of the oceans were international waters. For the French, everything not "under the fortresses" of the Spaniards or Portuguese was open water. For the Spaniards, the closed zone included not only the entire Caribbean basin but also the sea approaches to and from it. When pressed, they had been willing to accept a definition of their possessions in terms of the largest units (the Antilles, New Spain, Peru, and the Río de la Plata) provided that that was coupled with language allowing them to seize, without reprisal, any French ship found in what they considered to be the territorial waters of those possessions or close enough to them so as to suggest that the French intended to violate the trade laws of the Spanish empire or attack a Spanish ship or settlement.

On the question of territorial possessions, the Spaniards showed great interest in getting the French out of Brazil, by peaceful means if possible. Brazil gave the French a base from which to try to take over other areas closer to the Spanish possessions but uninhabited by them or the Portuguese, although claimed under the papal donation and various discoveries. Unlike the Portuguese, the French would make bad neighbors, Philip II observed. He apparently chose to ignore the dispute his government was having with the Portuguese over areas that are today in southern Brazil but that the Spaniards then thought were in Paraguay, the center of their settlement in the Río de la Plata drainage basin.

The French, on the other hand, took the position that only effective occupation gave title to American real estate. They, too, wanted to share in the resources that this new world was making available. They had no reason to forgo colonial ventures that might cause the Spaniards discomfort then or later.

To put the territorial question another way, exclusively Iberian control of the territory of most of the New World was important to the

48. This phrase seems to have come into currency in the late 1580s and refers to the fact that the Spanish and Portuguese were intercepting as many foreign ships as they could in European and African waters south of the Tropic of Cancer. Since it was necessary to cross the tropic in order to voyage to the Americas using the common, southern routes, this policy amounted to closing off the western Atlantic. In effect, the Spanish and Portuguese had drawn a line at that latitude, with another at a longitude just to the west of the Canary Islands. South and west of those two lines—in practice only one, the Tropic of Cancer—any non-Iberian vessel was treated as hostile. See Garrett Mattingly, "No Peace Beyond What Line?" *Transactions of the Royal Historical Society* (London), 5th ser., XIII (1963), 145–62.

Spaniards because that safeguarded the main centers of their power and economic exploitation, against future attempts at conquest. What was most at risk in 1559–1560 was Brazil, but Philip II, like the Council of the Indies in 1540, recognized that the southeastern coast of North America could present the same long-term threat. That is why he ordered Luna to occupy the Point of Santa Elena, the place that legend and available information said was the only part of the southeastern North American coast worth having or capable of supporting a European settlement.

VIII

The Spaniards and the Atlantic Coast, 1560–1563

Tristan de Luna's expedition to the Gulf coast of La Florida was the first of four unsuccessful Spanish attempts to occupy the Southeast during the years 1559–1564. The other three were directed toward the Atlantic coast. Of these, two—those of Captains Martín Díaz, in 1560, and Angel de Villafañe, in 1561—were supposed to lead to a settlement at or near the Point of Santa Elena. The third, of Lucas Vázquez de Ayllón the Younger, in 1563, was probably intended to found a settlement at the Bahía de Santa María (Chesapeake Bay), which Antonio Velázquez had rediscovered in 1561.

Growing Spanish concern about French designs on the Southeast influenced all four ventures. Except for Luna's expedition, all resulted directly from the failure of diplomats in 1559–1560 to resolve rival French and Spanish claims concerning the rights to sail the seas and found colonies in the Americas. Díaz and Villafañe attempted to preempt French designs on the Southeast by occupying the Point of Santa Elena, the presumed gateway to the riches of the interior. Ayllón's purpose, like his destination, is less certain, but he seems to have been trying to establish a Spanish settlement to match the French post, Charlesfort, established in 1562—but on a part of the coast better able to sustain a European community. The failure of the French venture in 1563 and of Ayllón's expedition in 1564 set the stage for the Franco-Spanish confrontation of 1565.

The *San Juan de Ulua* and *San Antón* returned to Veracruz from Luna's colony at Ochuse (Pensacola) in early January, 1560. Viceroy Luís de Velasco immediately ordered the ships prepared for a new supply run in late March or early April under the command of Gonçalo Gayón, a pilot with some knowledge of the upper Gulf coast. Gayón had returned to New Spain even though Luna had thought at first to retain him at Ochuse so that he could pilot the supply ships up a river to Nanipacana de Santa Cruz, a half-deserted Indian town (probably on the Alabama River) to which Luna had moved his colony shortly after the loss of most of its supplies in September.[1]

Preparations went on steadily if slowly during the months from February to June. Eventually five ships sailed: the king's *San Juan de Ulua, San Antón, La Trinidad* (a *fragata*), and *Santiago* (a patache), and Gayón's own patache, *San Juan* (?). On board were a new factor named Luís Daça, Fray Gregorio de Beteta (Luís Cancer's companion of 1549), Captain Diego de Viedma with a company of soldiers, and a cargo of chickens, goats, sheep, horses, and large quantities of maize, ship biscuit, and other supplies. Departure from San Juan de Ulua seems to have occurred after July 1, a good three months past the date Velasco had decreed.

At about the same time, the party of 50 cavalrymen and 150 foot soldiers that Luna had sent north from Nanipacana to search for Coosa finally found it after suffering great hardship in crossing the long-needle pine barrens of southern Alabama. The troops remained at Coosa for three months, until October, 1560, when they were recalled to Polanco, as the Spanish settlement on Pensacola Bay was then known, as part of an effort then underway to remove Luna from his command. Until then the two to three hundred men who had made it to Coosa lived fairly well off the bounty that their hosts' labor and the fertility of the land made possible.[2]

At Nanipacana, the colonists fared poorly because there were few Indians and apparently little stored food. Accordingly, when the supply ships put into Ochuse (Pensacola) Bay the colonists deserted Nanipacana and returned to Polanco. Uncertain what had happened to the men sent inland, they buried a jug with a note sealed inside to tell them where the colony was.

The supply ships carried not only provisions that renewed hopes that the colony might yet establish itself, if with a considerable dependence on Mexico and Cuba for food, but also royal and viceregal orders that Luna was to send someone to settle at the Point of Santa Elena. That provided the first real opportunity for some of the would-be conquerors of the Southeast to leave and seems to have sown the

1. AGI, SD 11, No. 50 bis, fols. 5–6. Regarding location, see Lowery, *Spanish Settlements,* I, 361, 361*nn*1, 2.

2. AGI, SD 11, No. 50 bis, fols. 8, 10, 11 (passport of March 14 for Gayón to take twenty goats and sheep to Florida, fol. 11); expenses for the Luna fleet and its supply, January to July, 1560, AGI, CD 877, No. 1; Lowery, *Spanish Settlements,* I, 362–68.

seeds of serious discontent, which germinated the following fall and winter when supplies again ran low.

The king's order of December 18, 1559, had reached Mexico in March or April, 1560, as the second supply fleet was preparing to set out. Philip II wanted immediate occupation of the Point of Santa Elena because "notwithstanding that we are at peace with France we have learned that Frenchmen, under pretext of going to the Bacallaos [cod fishery] may possibly be desirous of going to that land of La Florida to settle in it and take possession of our lands."[3]

The urgency of the king's order was evident, as was the hint of displeasure if the Point of Santa Elena was not already occupied by a Spanish colony. Velasco responded in two ways. Since he already had appointed an agent, Hortuno de Ibarra, to go to Spain to discuss the encomiendas in Mexico, he now broadened Ibarra's assignment to include a report on the difficulties the La Florida colony was experiencing.

Velasco's second action was to send Philip II's order on to Luna. In a covering letter of his own, dated May 6, 1560, the viceroy added the Scots to the list of possible foreign occupiers, probably because of the alliance of Mary of Lorraine's Scots partisans with the French during the Scottish civil war of December, 1559, to July, 1560.[4] He assured Luna that he was writing to the king about the difficulties of moving the settlement, especially given the lack of horses. He told the commander of the expedition that once the horses came—with the second supply fleet—he was to go to Santa Elena himself or else send either Pedro de Acuña or Captain Baltasar de Sotelo there, provided the people who remained behind could be left "in safety" or "without much hazard." The transfer of some of the colonists to Santa Elena without further delay was necessary, Velasco said, because the king "is so insistent about it that he must have indications that foreigners desire to enter there."[5] Extensive research in the Spanish documentation has failed to find the basis upon which Philip II issued his order, aside, that is, from growing Spanish apprehension about the designs of the French and about the unlikelihood of restricting their activities by diplomatic means.

Luna decided that he could send a party to Santa Elena. He seems to have selected the *San Juan de Ulua* and two, possibly three, smaller

3. Priestley (ed.), *The Luna Papers,* II, 17.
4. Roncière, *Histoire de la marine,* IV, 25–29.
5. Priestley (ed.), *The Luna Papers,* I, 122–23.

ships to make the trip. He placed Captain Martín Díaz in command of sixty soldiers. Father Pedro de la Feria, the acting Dominican provincial prior to the arrival of Father Beteta, and two other Dominicans made up the religious presence in Díaz' fleet. The factor, the accountant, and the treasurer of the colony were also on board. Their presence indicates that discontent with Luna's leadership already existed. They were also with Díaz because of the need to acquire supplies at Havana for the expedition to Santa Elena and for Polanco. In addition, they may have been looking for a chance to advance their careers by being on an expedition that clearly had the king's attention.

The group heading for Santa Elena probably sailed from Polanco late in July or in the first days of August. On August 28, 1560, Governor Diego de Mazariegos, of Havana, reported that three men had just arrived—by what means he did not say—with the news that four ships had sailed from Polanco under command of Captain Díaz, had encountered bad weather, and would shortly enter Havana for supplies. He promised to aid them with two *fragata* loads of food. Later, in a letter dated April 22, 1561, Mazariegos related that only two ships reached Havana and that he had heard that a third had returned to Mexico. Apparently the ship that went back was the *San Juan de Ulua,* whose return on September 9 was reported to Viceroy Velasco by its pilot, Gayón. Captain Díaz seems to have been on it.[6] The fate of the fourth ship is unknown. The first attempt to occupy the Point of Santa Elena had failed.

In light of the apparently desperate conditions at Polanco despite the supplies sent in July, Velasco ordered the preparation of the caravel *San Marcos* to carry food to Florida. Gayón was named to pilot it, a service he requested so that he could return to Florida and reclaim his patache, which Luna had embargoed for the use of the Polanco colony. The *San Marcos* sailed about mid-September, 1560, with a cargo of maize and ship biscuit. It was back at San Juan de Ulua by mid-November.[7]

By the time the vessel returned from Polanco, it was clear that Luna would have to be replaced as governor, that more supplies would have to be sent to the colony, and that most of its people would have to be removed so that the Spaniards could occupy the Point of Santa Elena.

6. AGI, SD 115, fols. 79, 85; AGI, SD 11, No. 50 bis, fol. 9. See also Priestley (ed.), *The Luna Papers,* II, 250–53.

7. AGI, SD 11, No. 50 bis, fols. 7, 9; expenditures for the *San Marcos,* September, 1560, AGI, CD 877, No. 11.

Luna had been asking to be relieved even though Velasco had suggested that he would get the governorship of Cuba if he stayed on. As governor of Cuba, Luna would have been better able to coordinate supply to his colony. Pedro Menéndez de Avilés, then captain general of the New Spain convoy and the object of Velasco's personal favor, was briefly considered for Luna's position in La Florida but could not get out of his obligations as commander of the convoy and may not have wished to do so.[8] Velasco finally appointed Villafañe as the new governor of La Florida and specifically charged him to occupy the Point of Santa Elena.

At the time of his appointment as governor of La Florida, Villafañe was serving as *alcalde mayor* for Veracruz, an office to which Velasco had appointed him in 1560 because of his demonstrated skills in getting things done in politically difficult circumstances. As *alcalde mayor,* he had already helped to get the second supply fleet off to Polanco. He was thus familiar with the personalities and problems of the colony.[9]

The fleet that Villafañe took to sea in mid-March, 1561, consisted of the *San Juan de Ulua,* several *fragatas,* and the caravel *San Juan.* Gayón became chief pilot for the fleet, and other pilots who had participated in earlier voyages to Polanco joined the other ships. Supplies included biscuit, beans, salt pork, shoes, hats, parts for a portable forge, a seine (*chinchorro*), and ten pack mules. The fleet was to pick up horses in Cuba. Another caravel, the *Santa Catalina,* piloted by Alonso Goncalez de Arroche, a veteran of the first and second supply fleets, went to Campeche to load food. It was to rendezvous with the Villafañe fleet at Havana.[10]

When Villafañe reached Polanco in early April, he found its residents reduced to eating shellfish and grasses. They had already consumed all the leather they had. The supplies he brought, and the order to evacuate all but a small force, were welcome. Luna, relieved of his command, was ordered to Spain to answer the charges some of his

8. J. Ignacio Rubio Mañe, *Introducción al estudio de los Virreyes de Nueva España, 1535–1746* (4 vols; Mexico City, 1955–1982), II, 80. For Luna's biography, 1561–1573, see p. 81.

9. For Villafañe's biography, see Boyd Bowman, *Indice,* II, 179, entry 5933 (which places his birth in León, León Province); and Rubio Mañe, *Introducción al estudio de los Virreyes,* II, 76 (which places it in Valencia de Don Juan, León Province). See also AGI, MEX 168, fols. 4–4v.

10. Expenditures, January to March 13, 1561, AGI, CD 877, No. 1; AGI, SD 11, No. 50 bis, fol. 13.

former subordinates were making against his leadership. A captain and seventy or eighty men (estimates vary) were selected to remain at Polanco while the rest withdrew to Havana preparatory to sailing for the Point of Santa Elena. Father Domingo de Salazar remained as the chaplain of the garrison.[11]

Villafañe's two ships (*navíos*) and two *fragatas* arrived at Havana at the end of April with some 230 soldiers aboard. Governor Mazariegos later wrote to Philip II that he advised Villafañe not to let any of his men land lest they flee; the governor professed to lack the means to help round up any who did. Villafañe, however, allowed them to land. As he told Mazariegos, he had done them all a favor by removing them from La Florida and did not want to take anyone with him to the Point of Santa Elena who did not want to go. Those who did not want to make the trip had his permission to seek a living wherever they could. More than one hundred of the men took his offer at once, and of those who remained, others went AWOL before the fleet set sail on May 16. When the new bishop of Cuba, Dr. Bernaldino Villapando, arrived at Havana on June 5, he found about 150 of the La Florida soldiers still there. They had, he said, fared badly. He went on to observe that they had taken much clothing, many musical instruments, and other diversions with them to La Florida and had not had the stomach for work. That, he believed, accounted for many of the problems the colony had had. Sturdy peasants from the mountains of León should have been sent, he thought, instead of men from the Indies, especially from New Spain. By implication, he suggested that the peasants did not have the vices—chiefly a lack of discipline and an unwillingness to toil—that had helped bring the Luna colony to its end. Such vices and the circumstances in Havana caused some of the soldiers to create civil disturbances after Villafañe left.[12]

Prior to taking his departure from Havana, Villafañe wrote asking the king to order the authorities at Santo Domingo and Puerto Rico to supply him with foods. Apparently the earlier provisioning of Polanco and the need to stock the convoys, not to mention what Villafañe was taking with him and what was going to Polanco at about that same time, had drained western Cuba to the point that Villafañe and Mazariegos anticipated difficulties if Cuba alone was

11. AGI, MEX 105, R. 1, fols. 3–5; AGI, SD 115, fols. 91–91v.

12. AGI, SD 115, fols. 91–91v, 98; preliminary charges 80, 112, 206 in residencia of Diego de Mazariegos, Havana, 1565, AGI, JU 89, fols. 419v, 430v, 464v–465v.

the new colony's provider.[13] The need to seek stores in Campeche suggests, but does not prove, that even New Spain was having difficulty supplying the La Florida venture.

Information on Villafañe's voyage in search of a suitable site for a colony at or near the Point of Santa Elena comes from only four documents that have survived out of a larger number. Two of the surviving documents are letters by Mazariegos giving details of the expedition's departure and return, along with a few other observations—such as that depositions made at Havana by Villafañe and Gayón were less truthful than another made by one of the captains who had been on the trip. None of the three depositions is now known to exist. The other two documents that survive are an account of the voyage which the notary Francisco de Aguilar, who had accompanied Villafañe, put together at Monte Cristi, Española, on July 9, 1561, and a formal opinion about the nature of the coast that Villafañe and others swore to at Mexico City on March 3, 1562.[14]

Mazariegos estimated that Villafañe took seventy soldiers and their servants with him, or about a hundred men. Alonso Velázquez, the treasurer, went along. Gayón and Gaspar Jorge were pilots on the flagship. A crew of nine or ten manned one of the *fragatas,* of which Juan de Puerta was pilot; a crew of ten to twelve manned the other, of which Hernán Perez was pilot. The pilot and master of the caravel *San Juan* are not identified. Seven captains from the Luna colony also went along, with some of their men. An Englishman who had been captured at Campeche and who had been to the coast north of the Point of Santa Elena may also have been in the party.[15]

According to Aguilar's account of the voyage, once the four ships cleared the Bahama Channel they sailed north until they came to a river that the pilots declared was the Santa Elena, at 33° north, more or less. On May 27, Villafañe used one of the *fragatas* to explore the

13. AGI, SD 115, fol. 92v. Villafañe's letter and Mazariego's of June 29 were received at Seville on October 22, 1561 (AGI, CT 5185, Book 1 [1555–68], fol. 103). Villafañe's letter has not been found. Testimony in response to question 12 of Mazariego's defense during his residencia shows that food demands were heavy in 1561 (AGI, JU 90, No. 2, fol. 1231).

14. Diego de Mazariegos to crown, June 29, August 4, 1561, both AGI, SD 115, fols. 91–91v, 101 respectively; Francisco de Aguilar's certified account of the trip, Monte Cristi, July 9, 1561, AGI, PAT 19, R. 11, and AGI, IG 738, No. 73b; inquiry, Mexico City, March 3, 1562, AGI, PAT 19, No. 12.

15. For the Englishman, see Priestley (ed.), *The Luna Papers,* I, 192–93.

entrance and the river. Probably rowing the ship rather than sailing it—it was little more than a large row boat but did have a deck over a small, shallow hold—the party felt its way over the "many shallows" at the place that seemed deepest and without breakers. It found the depth to be barely a fathom at that point, and half a fathom in the breakers, sometimes less. The account says that the Spaniards looked over the bar and the river mouth, suggesting that they examined it from side to side. The Mexico City declaration adds that although the river was large and had a lot of water in it, no ship of over fifty toneladas could enter it, since there were scarcely six *palmos* (about half a meter or a fourth of a fathom) of water over the bar.

Once in the river, Aguilar says, the *fragata* went four or five leagues inland before the crew tried to land and take possession. That proved difficult, however, because of the heavy growth of trees and other vegetation along the river's edge. But once on firm ground, the party cut crosses on two trees and took the land in the name of Philip II. The men cut other trees to make a freestanding cross that they erected at the entrance to the river. They took possession of the land there, too. After that, the *fragata* crossed the bar and returned to the fleet.

The Aguilar narrative and the Mexico City deposition both declare that the Spaniards found no port at this point and that the land was not suitable for settlement because, in the words of the Mexico City document, it was "very low, sandy, and subject to flooding, and on the said river there [was] no town nor people nor good disposition of land for settling."

Mazariegos told a different story. He said that the expedition went to 32½° north and found a bay, where some Indians received Villafañe "in peace." If that is so, Villafañe entered a bay, Port Royal Sound, which would have been a suitable port. A decade later, Menéndez de Avilés estimated that the bay could accommodate the entire Indies Fleet (nine galleons and various *fragatas,* the galleons being of 250 toneladas capacity each)—indeed, that one of the convoys from the Caribbean (typically more than twenty larger ships) could use it. What is more, in modern times the principal natural entrance into Port Royal Sound has three to four fathoms even at low tide, ample clearance for any of Villafañe's ships.

If Villafañe was in Port Royal Sound, he could easily have gone four to five leagues, or 12.8 to 16.0 nautical miles, up the Broad River to a point where shoreline vegetation was rather thick, as it is along all the coastal rivers where clearing has not taken place. As for the rest of the description, it applies to Port Royal Sound and the Broad River as well as to any other river in the area. The area is low, sandy, and subject to flooding when there is locally heavy rain on the coast or inland over the watersheds of the rivers that come to the coast.

Without the other documents that Mazariegos mentioned, there is no way to know exactly which version of the voyage is true. It may be that Aguilar's recounting deceived by omission, by taking up the story at Villafañe's next stop, which may have been the Edisto River, which is closer to 33° north and has a shallower entrance than Port Royal Sound's. If that is so, a clue to the motive for the omission may lie in Villafañe's contention, recorded in Aguilar's account and the Mexico City document, that there was no suitable place for a settlement anywhere along the coast he examined. Had he admitted that there was a great, deep bay just to the north of the Point of Santa Elena, he would have had to offer justification for not trying to settle on its shore. By keeping quiet about the bay, he avoided the embarrassment of an explanation, especially inasmuch as the Mexican authorities had been telling Philip II for nearly three years that they did not think there was a port at the point. Villafañe's story, in short, was consistent with earlier Mexican opinion and with his need to carry out the king' explicit, urgent order without committing himself or any of his men to a venture in which neither they nor the Mexican authorities had much interest.

The rest of Villafañe's voyage involves no such contradictory evidence; at least Mazariego's version fails to say anything at variance with Aguilar's account and the Mexico City document. From Aguilar's "River of Santa Elena," the party sailed north along the coast until it had doubled a cape Villafañe labeled the Cape of San Román, at barely 34° north latitude. Once on the northeast side of that cape—generally agreed to be Cape Fear—Villafañe had his ships gather and anchor near the shore. The water was deep and the bottom clean. He then landed. The date was June 3.

Immediately behind the beach were lagoons. Water-collecting parties were ordered in from the ships, although there is no comment on whether they got their water from the lagoons or from shallow wells. While the watering parties did their work, Villafañe and some of his men went inland about a league (3.2 nautical miles?) until they came to the shore of a fine river (*gran río*) whose mouth they could not see because the land was flat and marshy. They took possession and marked three trees with crosses. After returning to the beach, the governor probably returned to his ship. Aguilar's narrative is silent about the next few days.

On June 8, using one of the *fragatas,* Villafañe entered the river that flowed out into the sea next to his Cape of San Román. He believed that the river was the Jordan. Once inside, he landed and took possession and made crosses on some trees. The land along the banks of the river was very thickly wooded and had many marshes and inlets.[16] He and his crew saw no human inhabitants, and the entrance was full of difficult shallows that ran, as they still do, a good distance into the sea. Although the river contained a higher volume of water than the "River of Santa Elena," the "Jordan" was no more suitable for settlement.

Upon leaving the supposed Jordan to go back to the ships, Villafañe saw one of them, the *San Juan,* under sail. Crossing the shallows that run southward from Cape Fear, Villafañe was able to reach the ship in open water and to learn that the storm rising around them had broken its anchor cables. He ordered the *San Juan*'s crew to sail close-hauled until the storm died down, and he had his *fragata* make for the other *San Juan,* the caravel he used as his flagship. The crew of the first *San Juan* had told him that when the storm blew up, his flagship had set sail in an effort to round the cape but had had to put back to the anchorage. That was where it was, having in the meanwhile picked up the anchors and cables the first *San Juan* had lost. Once aboard the caravel, Villafañe waited as long as he thought the loosed *San Juan* would need to make it back to the anchorage. When it failed to return, he ordered sail to be made.

Apparently his intention was to run up the coast to as high as 40°, making few stops himself. Accordingly, he sent the treasurer, Velázquez, in one of the *fragatas* to examine the Río de Canoas, said to be at 34½° north in Aguilar's document, and barely 35° in the Mexico City report. The latitude Aguilar mentioned seems more likely, because that would place Villafañe's men at New River Inlet, called Río de Atarazanas on the Vespucci map of 1526 but Río de Bajos in the Chaves materials. Diogo de Ribeiro bestowed the name Río de Canoas in his maps of 1527–1533.

Aguilar went on this side trip and reported that half a fathom of water, less in places, covered the bar at the river's entrance. Seeing that the land was low and that there were only dunes in sight, Villafañe put

16. The wording in Spanish is "la tierra en comarca del dho río es muy cerrada de montes, ciénagas, y esteros"; I have translated *esteros* to mean inlets, but it may instead refer to stands of mat-making grasses and reeds.

back to sea. The Mexico City deposition adds that the Río de Canoas was smaller than the rivers previously described. Between it and what Villafañe was calling the Río Jordán, the coast had a good, clean beach with deep water just offshore, so that ships could sail close to land without difficulty. The description matches conditions in Onslow Sound.

Continuing up the coast, the Spaniards identified what they saw on Saturday, June 14, as Cabo de Trafalgar. The cape they had reached was at 35° north, and it had shoals running seven or eight leagues seaward. The latitude is clearly an estimate; Villafañe and his pilots did not have the opportunity to land and take an accurate midday reading. In all likelihood they were at Cape Lookout, not Cape Hatteras, though it is Cape Hatteras that usually bore the name Cabo de Trafalgar.

According to Aguilar, at about ten that evening a storm blew up with great force, filling the sails of the *fragatas* until they looked like half moons coming up behind the flagship. When the gales first struck, the flagship seemed on the verge of being lost. From its stern the crew watched the *fragata* commanded by Puerta founder and heard the cries of its crew for God's mercy and for help, but between the storm and the blackness of the night, those on the *San Juan* could do nothing to save the ten or so men involved. The other *fragata* disappeared too, and when Aguilar wrote his report, he assumed it was lost.

Probably the next day, after the storm had let up and the *San Juan*'s crew realized that the second fragata was nowhere to be seen, Villafañe and his officers and remaining pilots held a council and decided that they could not continue the exploration without the auxiliary craft and without knowledge of a port in which they could take shelter from storms. The heavier weather typical of the higher latitudes would, they concluded, make exploration to the north even more of a risk. Hence, they set a course for the Antilles. The flagship made Monte Cristi twenty-five days later, on July 9, 1561. There Aguilar wrote up a summary of the voyage, to which he affixed his name and seal after listing various persons who were witnesses to the events in question.

From Monte Cristi, Villafañe sailed along the old Bahama Channel route to Havana, where he arrived on July 24. In describing his arrival and some details of the voyage, Mazariegos told the king that Villafañe was determined to await further orders from the viceroy in Mexico.[17] While waiting, the governor of La Florida wrote to the king and he, Gayón, and at least one of his captains made various depositions.

17. Gayón was then sent to Mexico (AGI, SD 11, No. 50 bis, fol. 12).

Villafañe did not leave Havana for three months and twenty days, that is, until about mid-November. During that period, his host grew tired of him and repeatedly urged him to go to Polanco or New Spain. Mazariegos noted that Villafañe treated his men badly, taking their food and arms and selling the supplies left from the expedition, apparently not to help them but out of other, undisclosed motives. Many of the men who had remained at Havana, or returned from the coast with Villafañe, fled during these months. In August, some were instrumental in helping the residents of Campeche recapture ships a French corsair had taken from that port, but the assistance they gave had little to do with the purpose they had volunteered for two years earlier. All the men who had been involved with Villafañe, not excluding Villafañe himself, showed by their actions the truth of Mazariegos' assessment in early August that "they would let themselves be quartered before returning to La Florida."[18]

Villafañe did eventually go to Mexico City, apparently none the worse for failing to have set up a colony on the Atlantic coast. In his next appearance in the records, Velasco called him in to give an opinion on the report, which had reached Philip II by way of Menéndez de Avilés, Mazariegos, and others, that the Southeast was a poor land and that, even if settled, it would be of "no benefit." The report went on to say that neither would the Point of Santa Elena be useful, "because that port has no entrance." In any case, it emphasized, there was no reason "to fear that the French will set foot on that land nor take possession of it."[19] Consequently, the recommendation was that the crown should spend no more money on the settlement at Santa Elena. On the other hand, above 38° north, there were ports reputed to reach three to four leagues into the land where settlement might be made if Spain served as a base. The crown had instructed Velasco to ask Villafañe and others what they thought about these facts.

The substance of the report that Villafañe and his captains made at Mexico City on March 3, 1562, has already been shown. They confirmed that all of the Florida coast that they had examined below 35° north was sandy, unpopulated, and unsuited for settlement:

> It seems to us that there is no land where settlement can be made nor a port suitable for it, nor native people who could be congregated nor joined to the

18. AGI, SD 115, fols. 103, 101 respectively.

19. The conclusion about the port had been stated by Viceroy Velasco in 1560. See Priestley (ed.), *The Luna Papers*, I, 192–93.

> Christian doctrine, as is Your Majesty's intention. Nor in all that we have seen is found gold or silver or a good disposition of land for settlement which would serve or benefit Your Majesty.[20]

They also agreed that Spain could send expeditions from across the Atlantic to explore the coast above 35° north, for the few men and ships needed were available at much less cost in Spain than in New Spain.

It was almost a decade before Philip II's government found out just how much the Mexican attempt to settle Florida had cost. The treasurer of New Spain, Hernándo de Portugal, eventually figured the total at 199,596 pesos de oro de minas, of which roughly 139,000 pesos had been paid at Mexico City and the rest at Veracruz. It had been an expensive failure, for which blame was placed on nearly everyone connected with the project. Perhaps Fray Alonso de Buyça summed the matter up best in his defense of Viceroy Velasco: "Don Luís de Velasco did and provided all that it is possible for a man [to do] in laying down rules and getting it under way and taking all the measures that any prudent governor and knowledgeable captain could have taken."[21] He was not to blame if the expedition landed in unknown, physically difficult territory without adequate supplies because of a misfortune at sea. Other great armies had done no better, as Philip II knew from personal experience and his acquaintance with military history. The fortunes of war were uncertain and the end result of human intentions was in the hands of God.

Once again, the Spaniards had examined the southeastern coast of North America and found it to be of no value to themselves or, they believed, anyone else. Yet reports about a voyage associated with the Villafañe expedition created a new, if weak, Spanish interest in the coast north of 35° north.

Philip II's order to Viceroy Velasco of September 23, 1561, was drawn up against a background not only of the data that Menéndez de Avilés and others furnished about the failure of the Luna expedition and of the general opinion in Mexico that the Atlantic coast, and specifically the Point of Santa Elena, were useless for settlement but also of the account that Antonio Velázquez, factor of the Florida expeditions under Villafañe, had sent of his voyage to the coast at 38° north.

20. AGI, PAT 19, No. 11, fol. 2.
21. Fray Alonso de Buyça to SM, Mexico City, February 6, 1564, AGI, MEX 280.

Velázquez' account, which had been sent on from Seville on September 9, 1561, spoke of a land north of Cabo de Trafalgar (Cape Hatteras) that held promise of being the new Andalucia that Ayllón had sought but not found in 1525–1526.

Velázquez' voyage, in fact, sparked renewed Spanish interest in the Atlantic coast of North America centered on the Bahía de Santa María (Chesapeake Bay). The French colonies Jean Ribault created served to divert that interest into a more immediate concern over expelling the French and holding the "useless" coast below Cape Hatteras. Yet the interest remained alive among a few Spaniards and, fused with the Verrazzano legend, was the basis for their guess as to where the English had set up their colony in 1585.

Velázquez was appointed factor to replace Daça in late 1560 or early 1561.[22] He may have been a relative of the expedition's treasurer, Alonso Velázquez, although that is not certain.

The caravel *Santa Catalina* had been sent to Campeche for food in February, 1561, when Villafañe was making his preparations in San Juan de Ulua for the fourth supply voyage to Polanco and his further voyage to the Point of Santa Elena. Apparently the trip to Campeche was under the ship's pilot, Goncalez de Arroche, who had taken other ships to Polanco on the first and second supply expeditions. But when the *Santa Catalina* returned to San Juan de Ulua prior to departing for Polanco, to which Villafañe had already gone, Juan de Torres was made its master.[23] Antonio Velázquez may have been aboard during both parts of the voyage.

After the arrival of the *Santa Catalina* at Polanco, Villafañe ordered Velázquez to remain there for a period of time and then to set out in the caravel for the Point of Santa Elena with supplies that Villafañe anticipated he would need for the new settlement. Velázquez set out as instructed, sailing by way of Havana. At Havana he repaired his ship, got what news he could of Villafañe's plans, and departed. It was probably late June.

Velázquez' recounting of his voyage has not been found, so not all the details are known. Letters and other documents that the House of Trade, at Seville, produced say that the ship cleared the Bahama

22. His earlier participation in the Luna and Villafañe expeditions is noted in Priestley (ed.), *The Luna Papers,* II, 250–53.

23. AGI, CT 5167, Book 1, fol. 110; expenditures, January to March, 1561, AGI, CD 877, No. 1, *passim.* The *Santa Catalina* had oars, which indicates that it was fairly small.

Channel without difficulty and rode the Gulf Stream northward. They also say that a storm—probably not the one that hit Villafañe's fleet on June 14—struck the ship as it sailed north and drove it beyond the appointed rendezvous with Villafañe to a stretch of the coast that later actions show was near the entrance to the Bahía de Santa María.

Once free of the storm, the *Santa Catalina* sailed to land, probably to allow the crew to renew its water supply, and Goncalez to take a latitude reading so that Velázquez, Torres, and Goncalez could decide where they were and what they should do next. Their point of landing is unknown, but apparently they either entered the bay or were near its mouth. At any rate, they encountered Indians who had previous experience of Europeans and were friendly. Two of them, one a principal person, the other his servant or at least of lesser position, decided to accompany Velázquez in his ship. Exactly how these Indians and the Spaniards achieved communication is not clear. The Spaniards had brought two Indians from New Spain along in the expectation that they could be trained as interpreters. But even if they knew Muskogean because of contact with some of the Indians Soto's men took to Mexico, it would have done no good, because the men from the Chesapeake spoke Algonquian.

The Spaniards decided that they would sail to Europe rather than try to return to the Antilles. They landed at Lagos, Portugal, in late August. Velázquez left the *Santa Catalina* there and went overland to Seville to report. He arrived on September 9, and his report was forwarded to Philip II with the House of Trade's letter of that date.[24]

Velázquez did not set out for court for nearly five weeks. He was waiting for the *Santa Catalina* to come from Lagos, so that he might account for its cargo and relieve himself of further legal responsibility for it. He also wanted to be able to show Philip II his guests from the new land. Evidently, bad weather delayed the ship's sailing, first from Lagos and then from Ayamonte, where it had put in for unknown reasons. It finally appeared at Seville on September 29.

Once the *Santa Catalina* arrived, Velázquez made preparations for his trip to court. Lacking funds for the journey or to care for his Indian guests, he applied to the House of Trade, which authorized fifty ducats for clothing for one of the Indians and for the expenses of the

24. AGI, CT 5167, Book 1, fol. 110; AGI, CT 5185, Book 1 (1558–66), fols. 125v–126, 118v.

journey. Both Indians were "naked," that is, dressed in few clothes and those probably inappropriate to the Spanish climate. The Indian selected to accompany Velázquez to court was a "principal person among them." His Indian name was Paquiquineo, but he was more generally known as Don Luís de Velasco, in honor of the viceroy of Mexico. His "servant," who is not named, remained at Seville, where the House of Trade was to see to his food and clothing until the king should order what to do with him and his master. The House of Trade took similar care of the two Indians who had been sent from New Spain to learn the "Florida" languages.[25]

Paquiquineo and Velázquez arrived at court in Madrid about October 24. In a message to the House of Trade, the king reported their arrival and approved the advance of funds to Velázquez. He authorized the House of Trade to sell the foods and other cargo on the *Santa Catalina* and either pay the crewmen what was owed them or make an advance of twenty ducats to each one against his salary so that the men would have expense money while waiting for work. The master and pilot were to get forty ducats each so that they could go to court to give information on the voyage. The royal orders had already been carried out with respect to the sale of the maize and beans and the fifty cotton *mantas* in the *Santa Catalina*'s cargo, which together had fetched 106,421 maravedis (291 ducats) at auction. The crew received advances, and the House of Trade prepared records for dispatch to Mexico, where the final accounting of crew salaries was to take place.[26]

Velázquez and Don Luís de Velasco remained at court until late February, 1562. Goncalez and Torres, on the other hand, returned to Seville in early December, apparently having given what information they could to officials at court. It seems that they needed to be on hand in Seville in case the *Santa Catalina* embarked on the voyage to Santo Domingo for which she was being prepared. Lope de Aguirre, a rebel from Peru, had successfully sailed the length of the Amazon and erupted into the Caribbean and raided the Venezuelan coast. When the first news of his action suggested that ships might be needed from Spain to help hunt him down, the *Santa Catalina* was designated for

25. AGI, CT 5167, Book 1, fols. 112–112v; approval of expense total of 265,640 maravedis, AGI, CD 286, No. 1, Datas, fol. 171v, entry 85.

26. AGI, CD 286, No. 1, Datas, fols. 171–171v, entry 85; cargo of 106,421 maravedis, October 30, 1561, *ibid.*, Cargos, fol. 100.

the task. The emergency passed, however, with the killing of Aguirre on October 27, 1561, and the king ordered the *Santa Catalina* sold because of its bad condition. The ship commanded 310 ducats at auction on February 21.[27]

The plan Philip II approved called for Don Luís and his companion to return to their homeland by way of New Spain. Accompanying them would be Father Beteta and another Dominican. The restless old man—who had accompanied Father Luís Cancer to Florida in 1549, had declined the bishopric of Cartagena de Indias, and had served with Villafañe in 1561—would finally get his chance to carry the gospel to the natives of North America. From New Spain, the quartet would sail in the newsboat that was to come back to Europe once the New Spain convoy of 1562 reached San Juan de Ulua. After leaving the missionary party at Don Luís' homeland, it would continue to Spain. Apparently the pilot of this ship was expected to get an accurate latitude reading for the place where the party landed. There seems to have been some uncertainty about that latitude in the testimony of Velázquez, Goncalez, and Torres.

Menéndez de Avilés, captain general of the New Spain convoy, was in charge of making the arrangements for the return of the Indians. Don Luís, the Indian servant, and Velázquez were to sail as passengers on Menéndez' flagship. The two Indians from New Spain who had been with Velázquez on the journey from Polanco were to return to Mexico as seamen on ships in the fleet. Trade goods and supplies were to accompany Don Luís as Spain's presents to his people, in a move calculated to ease the work of the Dominicans.[28]

By the time the party left Seville to join the fleet at San Lucar, on March 17, several minor changes had occurred in the arrangements. One of the Indians from New Spain, Alonso de Aguirre, had asked for and received permission to accompany Don Luís to his homeland. Apparently Aguirre had become fluent in Don Luís' native Algon-

27. AGI, IG 425, Book 24, fol. 67v (ordering 50 ducats given to Velázquez for his and Don Luís' expenses); payment of forty ducats to Gonzalez and Torres, December 16, 1561, AGI, CD 286, No. 1, Datas, fol. 127v, and payment for foods for sixty men for the anti-Aguirre voyage, AGI, CD 286, No. 1, Datas, fol. 185. See also careening expenses of the *Santa Catalina*, AGI, CD 294, No. 2, pliego 47, pp. 1–2; payment by Pablo Martín, February 21, 1562, AGI, CD 286, No. 1, Cargos, fol. 161.

28. AGI, CT 5185, Book 1 (1558–66), fols. 128–128v, 118v, 125v–126; payments totaling 58,874 maravedis, March 14, 1562, AGI, CD 286, No. 1, Datas, fols. 156v–157, entry 47 (25,496 maravedis were spent for the trade goods and presents). AGI, IG 425, Book 24, fol. 94v, records a payment to support Father Beteta and his companion.

quian and was devoted to him. Another change was that Father Beteta did not make the trip. Apparently worn out by many travels, he died at Toledo on the way south.[29]

The New Spain convoy of 1562 sailed from Cádiz at the end of May and arrived at San Juan de Ulua on August 10. If all had gone according to plan, Don Luís and his companions would have sailed with the newsboat that Menéndez de Avilés dispatched on August 30. But Don Luís and his servant became seriously ill shortly after reaching Mexico City, to which apparently they had been taken so that Viceroy Velasco could see them and arrangements could be made for missionaries to accompany them. They were so ill that the people around them despaired of the two men's lives, and they themselves were frightened enough to request baptism "many times" before they received that sacrament. After that, wrote Father Feria, provincial of the Dominicans of Mexico City, "our Lord was served to give them health." By then the newsboat had sailed.[30]

Seeing an opportunity to make Don Luís and his servant into lay missionaries, the Dominicans asked the viceroy for permission to keep them at the convent and teach them the Christian faith. The viceroy agreed to that. He further agreed that the king had ordered the return of the Indians to their homeland because they were pagans but that now that they were baptized it would be wrong to let them go back without sending along missionaries to keep them true to their vows. A lapse into their heathen ways would result in even greater condemnation of their souls than if they had remained pagans. Father Salazar and another Dominican agreed that they would go along when the right time came. Salazar was a veteran of the Luna expedition and knew a good deal about the languages of the southeastern Indians.

The right time for the mission seemed at hand in the fall of 1562. The viceroy agreed to make funds available and even mortgaged his own properties to obtain them. When, however, Menéndez de Avilés was approached about a ship, crew, and captain, he was unable to provide them. The Dominicans professed to believe that God had frustrated the plans for the mission in order that the king might better guide and direct the project. Meanwhile the archbishop of

29. AGI, CT 5185, Book 1 (1558–66), fols. 128–128v; Davila Padilla, *Historia de la Fundación,* 575.

30. AGI, CT 5185, Book 1 (1558–66), fol. 182; Fray Pedro de la Feria to SM, Mexico City, February 13, 1563, AGI, MEX 280.

Mexico prohibited Menéndez de Avilés from returning the Indians to their homeland. The converts were put at liberty and urged to return to Spain, but they preferred to remain in Mexico City with the Dominicans and under the care of the viceroy.

In a message to the king, the Dominican provincial suggested that the expedition returning these men to their homes "at the Point of Santa Elena" should consist of at least two Dominicans and forty to fifty men in one ship. The commander of the civilians should be Captain Antonio Velázquez, "a very honored man and a very good Christian" who had been in that land and knew something of the language. The provincial was referring to Velázquez' command of the *Santa Catalina* when it picked up Paquiquineo (Don Luís) and his servant. He suggested that Velázquez and his men remain as a garrison. Of course, he acknowledged, the king might designate whomever he wished or might delegate the responsibility of choosing the commander to the viceroy, who would likely name Velázquez.[31]

The Dominican's letter gives no indication whether he knew that Philip II had already decided to allow someone to follow up on Velázquez' "discovery" by setting up a small colony of Spanish farmers. What is known suggests that this colony would have been at the Bahía de Santa María and near the mission that Father Beteta had planned to create in Don Luís' home village. The contractor was Lucas Vázquez de Ayllón the Younger, son of the first adelantado of La Florida.

Ayllón the Younger last appeared in these pages when he petitioned for relief from the debts of his father-in-law, Miguel de Pasamonte, in 1547. His activities for the next six years are unknown, but in May, 1553, he was again at Madrid gathering testimony about himself and his father's work in La Florida as part of an effort to obtain some sort of favor from the king. His depositions focused on the legitimacy of his birth, the great expenditure his father had made, and the resulting poverty of that man's heirs.[32] Besides seeking reward for his father's services, Lucas may have been trying to combat the favoritism

31. Feria to SM, February 13, 1563, AGI, MEX 280.

32. Interrogatory, Madrid, May 15–17, 1553, AGI, SD 11, No. 43 bis. The original covering petition is not now with this document, which was incorporated into his 1561 petition concerning merits and services. His poverty was relative. In 1552, he and Diego Cavallero owned the sugar plantation La Xagua, on which they owed the king 4,338 pesos (AGI, CD 1051, Cargos [1552–60], fol. 30v).

his mother was probably already showing to his younger brother, Pedro Vázquez de Ayllón, who was rising to prominence at Santo Domingo. Pedro became a regidor there in 1554 and later married Juana de Pasamonte, a daughter of Esteban de Pasamonte and a sister to Isabel de Pasamonte, Lucas the Younger's first wife.[33]

During the eight years after 1553, Lucas the Younger again disappears from official documents. At some point during those years, probably prior to 1559, he married Beatriz Suarez de Galdo, daughter of a Captain Hernán Suarez and Doña Antonia Suarez de Galdo, residents of Seville. Suarez had been made a hidalgo (a member of the lowest rank of nobility) by Ferdinand the Catholic in 1511 as a reward for military services at Naples. The hidalgo held, among other properties, the Mesón de Alfalfa, in the parish of San Isidro of Seville, and some rural property near Utrera, a town in the vicinity of Seville. By 1565, a nephew, Pedro del Alcazar, was lord of the town of La Palma, treasurer of the mint at Seville, and a *viente-quatro* of Seville, one of the highest officers in that city's government.[34] Marriage to Beatriz Suarez de Galdo had linked Ayllón to the second rank of Seville's elite.

Once settled in Seville, Lucas engaged in commerce and may have received some revenue from his father's estate at Puerto Plata.[35] He might have remained quietly at home raising his daughters and attending to his commercial affairs had it not been for the appearance of Antonio Velázquez at Seville in September, 1561, with the news that he had visited land in the upper thirties north latitude.

By September 27, Lucas the Younger had heard of Velázquez' deed and had decided on a course of action. On that day he appeared before

33. See "Información," Santo Domingo, March 20, 1560, AGI, PAT 63, R. 24, which also lists Pedro's wife. Pedro's service on the cabildo is noted from signatures on a petition of March 5, 1554, to the king regarding the archbishop (noted in Colección Múñoz, Tomo 69, fol. 106v; citation from the catalog of that collection).

34. Order, March 28, 1565, that the notary Almonciar supply certified copies of various documents relating to the *hidalgía* of Captain Hernán Suarez, as requested by Hernán Suarez, his grandson, AP-SVQ, Oficio 9, 1565, Book 2, fols. 2025ff.; rental agreement between Antonia Suarez de Galdo and the licenciado Alonso de Almoroz, November 6, 1564, AP-SVQ, Oficio 9, 1564, Book 4 (?), fols. 755–756v; power of attorney from Antonia Suarez de Galdo to Rodrigo de la Torre of Utrera, to collect rents from Juan Hernández Saludo (?), after May 8, 1565, AP-SVQ, Oficio 9, 1565, Book 2, fols. 1444v–1445v. Pedro del Alcazar's relationship to the Suarez de Galdo sisters is noted in AP-SVQ, Oficio 9, 1565, Book 3, fols. 31, 684.

35. Power of attorney from Lucas Vázquez de Ayllón to his wife, Seville, August 4, 1563, AP-SVQ, Oficio 9, 1563, Book 4, fols. 831–36; power of attorney from Beatriz Suarez de Galdo to Fernando de Chaves, July 13, 1564, AP-SVQ, Oficio 9, 1564, Book 2, fol. 120.

the licenciado Pedro Rodriguez de Herrera, the lieutenant of the assistant of Seville, to request that the notary attached to that judicial officer's court take depositions for "perpetual memory" about certain matters covered in eleven questions to be put to the witnesses. The rather routine request was granted, and the notary, Juan de Escalona, went with Ayllón to the Monastery of San Pablo. There the notary placed Father Antonio de Cervantes under oath and recorded his replies to the eleven questions. The next day, he did the same with Alonso de Espinosa Cervantes, who was living in the parish of Santa Catalina. Both had been with Lucas the Elder on his trip to La Florida; they were probably the only members of the expedition whose testimony could be obtained in Spain at that late date. What they had to say supported Ayllón's claims, which now included the expenditure of 100,000 pesos and the contention that he alone was the surviving legitimate son and heir of his father.[36]

After receiving a certified copy of the depositions the notary had taken, Ayllón the Younger set off for court to press his right as heir to his father's contract, a right he apparently thought included the area of Velázquez' discovery. No papers exist concerning what he said and did at court, but the resulting document, his contract with the king signed at Madrid on February 28, 1562, survives.[37]

The contract began with a brief recapitulation of earlier unsuccessful efforts to settle and evangelize La Florida and of the recent decision to send the Indians of the region missionaries and other Christians who would lead them to the true faith. The contract went on to say that Ayllón the Younger had offered to carry out this decision by founding a colony and that the king had accepted his offer.

The terms agreed to were that Ayllón would take three caravels and 250 men, a hundred of them married. The company would include eight Dominican friars, a surgeon, and two barbers. The expedition would get a hundred horses and mares, a hundred young cattle, two hundred pigs, two hundred sheep, and some goats from Puerto Plata, which would serve as a staging base for sailing to North America and as a supply point for feeding the colony until it became self-sufficient. Ayllón was to found two towns of about seventy residents apiece, each equipped with a main building that would serve as a fort and storehouse. The first town had to be on the coast; the second might be

36. AGI, SD 11, No. 43 bis.
37. AGI, CT 3309, Florida Book, fols. 143–49.

inland. There were specific requirements for the town sites. A search for mines was permissible only after the settlers had established the towns and sown crops. Ayllón, in consultation with the royal officials and justices, could distribute lands but was forbidden to give away fields the Indians used. He was also to see to experimental plantings of sugarcane, cañafístola, vines, olives, and "other plants and trees and seeds of Castile" if the land was suitable; if it was not, the colonists were to cultivate it according to its possibilities.

If the Indians resisted the creation of the towns after being approached peacefully three times, the expedition could use force to set up and defend the towns. It was to employ trade and nonviolent means to persuade the Indians to reside in permanent settlements nearby so that they could supply the Spaniards with necessities, learn to live *políticamente,* become Christians, and accept Philip II's sovereignty. If Indian towns near the Spanish settlements expressed a desire for missionaries, Ayllón was to see that the Dominicans provided them. Once brought under Spanish rule, the Indians were to pay tribute, and that would be allocated among the Spanish settlers according to their rank and social quality after making certain that enough remained to pay the salaries of the officials in the province, provide for its defense, and leave something for the king's needs.

Ayllón was to sail from Spain within one year of the date of the agreement. Within six months of leaving Spain, he was to depart from Puerto Plata for La Florida, and one year after that, he had to have his two towns established. To ensure his compliance, the crown required him to post a bond of three thousand ducats, which he would forfeit if he did not meet the deadlines, although the king could cancel the contract without penalty if Ayllón was unable to gather the hundred married settlers. Once the expedition was ready, it could sail without waiting for the convoys within which all other shipping went under recently issued orders.

Regarding the rewards that would accrue to Ayllón for his service, the contract promised the titles of governor and captain general during his lifetime, with a salary of a thousand ducats a year drawn from the revenues of the province. He and a son or son-in-law to be named and approved before he sailed would enjoy during their lifetimes the title of adelantado and the office of *alcalde mayor* of the two towns. Ayllón and his heirs would enjoy a perpetual right to a fifth of all royal incomes in the province, figured after deducting expenses. Like his father, he could—without, however, prejudicing the rights of third parties—select a square of land fifteen leagues on a side for himself and his heirs to own forever. But he did not have the right of jurisdiction or any rights to mines there or elsewhere except those he might personally discover, and he would have to pay the same royal taxes that other miners paid. If the silk industry was established, Ayllón would enjoy an income of five hundred ducats a year from its profits. He was to enjoy the right to two fisheries he might select, if they were moderate in size. He could take eight Negro slaves to the Indies after paying only two ducats for each license instead of the normal fee of twenty ducats.

In common with the other settlers, Ayllón would enjoy a ten-year exemption from export duties on goods taken to the new province to sustain a family. Too, the province would have to pay only 10 percent on the products of mines during the ten years immediately following the founding of the first town.

The contract is especially notable for its underlying philosophy of peacefully converting the Indians through trade and preaching. The detailed provisions anticipate the Ordinances of Pacification and Colonization that were to be issued a decade later to codify how Spaniards were henceforth to carry out expansion of their empire in the Americas. The contract is also notable for the similarity of the rewards offered Lucas the Younger with those granted Lucas the Elder in his contract of 1523. The only omissions in 1562 concerned the provisions for the monopoly of trade and the repayment of the adelantado's expenses which were in the earlier contract. Equally notable is the intention, as in Soto's time, to use the Antilles as the point of supply until the North American colony was self-sustaining.

By way of implementation, on June 28, 1562, the titles of governor and captain general, with right of jurisdiction, and of adelantado of La Florida were issued.[38] By then, Ayllón was in Seville trying to obtain the money and settlers he needed. He seems to have remained at Seville into the fall conducting business in an apparent effort to raise capital.[39]

It was a bad time to be seeking large amounts of money. The mer-

38. *Ibid.*, fols. 149–51.

39. Power of attorney, June 13, 1562, AP-SVQ, Oficio 19, 1562, Book 2, fols. 719v–720v; data on Reyes from Book 1, fol. 1013, Book 2, fols. 597, 600, Book 3, fols. 56, 323, 341, 562, 602, 687, 712, 730, 801, 970, 975, 1018; debt acknowledgment by Lucas Vázquez de Ayllón to Captain Alonso Hernández de Ayala [1562 (?); dated as 1563], listed in AP-SVQ, Oficio 21, ABCDario, entry for 1562, Book 3, fol. 684 (the book itself has been lost).

chants involved in the American trade were just beginning to recover from the postwar depression and the royal bankruptcy of 1559. What is more, La Florida had a bad reputation that even the son of the dreamer of the Chicora legend could not overcome. Besides, informed persons knew, as Ayllón himself undoubtedly did, that the French might be trying to colonize in North America. That made a Spanish venture, especially one on the scale Ayllón had contracted for, all the more risky.

The first news of Ribault's voyage was from the Spanish ambassador in France, in a dispatch of December 15, 1561. He had learned that two or three merchant ships that had been fitting for Brazil had instead received orders to sail to a place on the North American coast between Cape Florida and Norembega. According to his information, a ship, *Dauphine,* commanded by Vicente Tiran and Grangean Bucier, had been there in 1539 and had brought back twenty-nine pounds of gold. A "Captain Ginribiul" (Jean Ribault) was to command the new expedition, which was to sail in January. The ambassador was able to supply the correct name of the commander and the incorrect information that six ships were involved when he next wrote to Philip II on January 13, 1562. Ten days later, he added that he had spoken to the queen mother, Catherine de Medicis, about the voyage and had had assurances that it was not intended to do any harm to Philip II's interests.[40]

Catherine de Medicis had, for her part, instructed France's ambassador at Madrid to try to persuade the Spaniards that Admiral Gaspard de Coligny was not an archvillain intent on breaking the peace but a trusted royal servant working to increase the peaceful commerce of France. That was her response to Spanish representations about France's Brazilian colony, but it applied as well to the new venture in North America, in which Coligny also had a hand.[41]

It is not clear whether all the Spanish ambassador's letters reached Madrid before the final touches were put on the plans to send Don Luís to his homeland and Ayllón the Younger to found two settlements there, but at least the first of the missives must have been on hand by mid-January and the rest by the time that Ayllón left Madrid for Seville. Too, he may have known of the French ambassador's repre-

40. Spain, *Negociaciones,* III, 172, 270, 294.

41. Catherine de Medicis, consort of Henry II, king of France, 1519–89, *Lettres de Catherine de Médicis,* ed. Hector de La Ferrière and Gustave Baguenault de Puchesse (11 vols.; Paris, 1880–1943), I, 613–14.

sentations to Philip II. In any case, Ayllón would have heard about Philip II's concerns of 1559 about a French move to occupy the Point of Santa Elena, about the French in Brazil, about the French attack on Campeche in August, 1561, and about at least some of the reports that French ships were fitting in the western ports for voyages to the Spanish and Portuguese empires in the Americas. The possibility of encountering an armed French party can thus hardly have been unknown to him.

Knowledge of French plans may help account for the slowness with which Ayllón carried out his contract. He could have drawn reassurance from the report of the Villafañe expedition that the Point of Santa Elena and the coast northward to Cabo de Trafalgar were useless for settlement, but he knew as well that the Bahía de Santa María, which Velázquez had visited, could not be so described. If that was where he intended to go, as seems likely from his contract's introductory statement, it might also be where the French meant to go. He had no way of knowing that the French had been ensnared by the revived form of the Chicora legend and had in mind discovering the location of Chicora and the Jordan River, which Ribault believed was near the Point of Santa Elena.

Whether because of financial difficulties or a prudent desire to know where the French had gone, Ayllón did not get his expedition to sea by February 28, 1563. Instead, he returned to court to seek funds, or privileges that could be converted into them, and an extension of the time within which he was required to set out. At court, he probably learned that Ribault had established a small fort with a twenty-man garrison at the Point of Santa Elena after leaving stone markers "at 29° and 30° north" (*sic;* 32° north). He may also have heard of three ships being fitted at Le Havre to reinforce the Florida fort and of the Portuguese pilot who had guided Ribault but who had fled from Le Havre when religious disturbances broke out. It is uncertain whether Ayllón also knew that the disturbances caused Ribault to take flight to England and so broke the thread of the design to reinforce Charlesfort. That does not seem to have become clear in Spain until late in 1563.[42] The important point is that the Spaniards were aware of the location and size of the French settlement and thus could avoid it. But the existence of the settlement made it imperative for Ayllón to act on his contract.

42. Spain, *Negociaciones,* V, 18–19, 51–52.

On March 6, 1563, Ayllón got the first of what eventually became three extensions. Because of delays he had encountered and "other important business dealings" he had, the king allowed him three months more to get his fleet ready to sail. That extension was modified by the second grant of a three-month extension beginning April 4. But the court turned down Ayllón's request for an outright grant of money or for three hundred slave licenses (worth about six thousand ducats) or their equivalent in a bill payable by the treasury of New Spain or by the treasury of Nombre de Dios (Panama).[43] The king did order the House of Trade to help Ayllón obtain the pilots and seamen that he needed but was having difficulty in finding. That assistance was particularly important because the government had just ordered enforcement of the long-standing rules requiring masters on ships in the Indies trade to be natives of Castile and either to pass an examination by the chief pilot or to have on board an examined pilot.[44] Understanding that this was all the help he would get, Ayllón returned to Seville by way of Badajoz, where he began the recruitment of his settlers.

He quickly ran into a legal obstacle. By law, every immigrant to the Indies had to have his religious orthodoxy, and that of his parents and grandparents as well, certified in his home village by reliable witnesses. No one could go to the New World who was Jewish or *converso* (converted from Jewish, but often only nominally, so as to escape persecution) or who had Jewish or *converso* ancestors or ancestors in trouble with the Inquisition for any reason. The intention was to catch, as well, persons fleeing debts, crimes, and marriages, and to make certain that only "old Christians" of good character came into contact with the Indians, who were thought particularly susceptible to being swept away by the vices of the Old World. The law also tried to keep restless, lawless, and otherwise disobedient persons out of the empire, where distance made the execution of justice difficult.

The surviving records for Ayllón's settlers show that by the end of May, 1563, only two married couples and eight single men had completed the inquiry the law required. The majority came from the province of Badajoz, where Ayllón may have had kin on the Bezerra

43. AGI, CT 3309, Florida Book, fols. 152–152v; petition (with note dated April 1, 1563, denying the request), AGI, SD 11, No. 43 bis, fol. 1.

44. AGI, CT 5167, Book 3, fols. 206v–207.

side of his family: at least some Bezerras with hometowns in that province show up later in the summer. Ayllón found other potential settlers in Seville, but they could not afford the cost and difficulty of returning to their hometowns for the inquiry. Therefore, in early June, after registering the contract and supporting orders in the books of the House of Trade, Ayllón asked permission from the Council of the Indies for the inquiries to take place in Seville, provided that the witnesses were natives of the village of the prospective immigrant. He also asked permission to use non-Castilian seamen because, he claimed correctly, there was a shortage of native-born. In 1558, Jaime Rasquin had obtained permission to use nonnative crew. Ayllón also sought an additional extension, since the time he had been granted would expire at the end of June. The Council of the Indies denied his request to use nonnative seamen but conceded him fifty more days and the right to have the inquiries conducted in Seville. Authorizing orders were issued on June 27 and presented to the House of Trade on July 5.[45]

While waiting for the government's permission to recruit settlers in Seville, Ayllón went ahead with preparations. On June 19, he conferred his power of attorney, as owner of the ships in question, on Vicente Frayle, master of the ship *Nuestra Señora de Esperanza,* alias *El Sedro,* and on Hernando Díaz Luzero, master of the ship *La Trinidad,* so that they could enter into an agreement with Juan García, merchant and resident of Seville, for the shipment of forty toneladas of merchandise (at twelve ducats apiece) to Santo Domingo. García apparently did not complete the transaction, probably because he was the Juan García who was part owner of the *San Pedro,* the third ship in Ayllón's fleet, about which there will be more later.[46]

In spite of what must have been the usual heat of late June and July, which Sevillanos call the healthy heat, the pace of preparations picked up after mid-July. A considerable number of prospective settlers concluded the process of their inquiries, and Ayllón began to shape the financial deals he needed for defraying the costs of the expedition. One way to gain revenue was to collect passage money in the amount of thirty or forty ducats from the emigrants. On July 24, he authorized a power of attorney for Geronimo Tellez, his alferez

45. AGI, PAT 19, R. 13; AGI, CT 5220, No. 45.

46. Power of attorney, Seville, June 19, 1563, and freight agreement marked "no paso," AP-SVQ, Oficio 17, 1563, Book for June–July, fols. 641–44.

general,[47] to receive potential settlers, to allot offices and to prescribe the duties appropriate to each office, to collect any monies he might be offered or given for any reason, and to sign whatever documents were necessary to the discharge of such functions.[48] How much Tellez obtained in this way is not known, but later events suggest that in addition to collecting passage money from legitimate emigrants who wanted to go to La Florida, he accepted payments, with Ayllón's acquiescence, from people who did not want to go to La Florida but wished instead to immigrate to the Indies and were willing to pay for the right to get as far as Santo Domingo.

Other parts of the financial arrangements that Ayllón worked out in July and August involved the ship *San Pedro* and its cargo. On July 20, he signed an agreement with the vessel's owners, Juan García and Gaspar Hernández, under which he designated it his third ship, to sail only as far as Santo Domingo. They paid him six hundred ducats and granted him twenty toneladas of cargo space at no charge. Ayllón agreed that if he did not sail by August 15, the contract would become null and he would have to return the money and pay any damages the owners suffered by waiting for him. In the end, they chose not to use that provision, perhaps because the ship's master, Lorenzo Yanes, already had a fair amount of cargo on board as well as a passenger who had paid for the use of half of the stern cabin, and because García himself shipped a quantity of goods and was a passenger. By the time Ayllón sailed, García and Hernández had been able to arrange prospectively profitable freight contracts for the *San Pablo*'s return voyage.[49]

47. An alferez was an ensign or the bearer of the flag of a military unit. The title given here suggests that Tellez was in charge of raising the soldiers; the power of attorney in question extended his authority to the entire recruitment process.

48. Testimony of Gerónimo Gallego, pilot, Francisco Cepero, Hernando de Miranda, and Alvaro de Valdés in reply to question 6 of an interrogatory for Pedro Menéndez de Avilés, 1567, AGI, JU 879, No. 3, Pieza 2, fols. 6v, 10v, 12, 15; power of attorney to Gerónimo Tellez, Seville, July 24 (?), 1563, AP-SVQ, Oficio 17, 1563, Book for August, first third, register 211.

49. Agreement between Ayllón, García, and Hernández, July 20, 1563, AP-SVQ, Oficio 17, 1563, Book for August, first third, register 210; company between Juan de Aravi and Pedro Álvares, August 30, 1563, AP-SVQ, Oficio 15, 1563, Book 2, fols. 343v–347, and power of attorney from Francisco de Estepa to Juan de Mediano, and another to Pedro de Tamayo, September 20, 1563, AP-SVQ, Oficio 17, 1563, Book for March, fols. 472–74; passage agreement with Inés de Alcoçer, August 31, 1563, AP-SVQ, Oficio 17, 1563, Book for September and October, fols. 285–86; agreement of Yanes, García, and Hernández, September 17, 1563, AP-SVQ, Oficio 17, 1563, Book for September and October, fols. 628–30; freight agreements between Gaspar Hernández and Gaspar de la Mondea, September 6, 1563, AP-SVQ, Oficio 16, 1563, Cuaderno for July and Sep-

For his part, Ayllón "sold" the use of his twenty toneladas to Juan de Mediano, a cleric (*racionero*) of the Santo Domingo Cathedral chapter who appears in the notarial records of Seville in 1562–1563 as a trader in cloth, hides, and sugar between that city and the island of Española. The so-called sale may have been Ayllón's way of making payment on his debts to Mediano. At least that was the reason for Ayllón's giving Mediano a power of attorney on September 18 to collect 269 hides in transit to Ayllón from Monte Cristi.[50]

Ayllón also got a little money for his venture by agreeing to take other people's slaves and goods to Santo Domingo as if they were his own. There are records of two instances of that fraud involving three slaves and six pipes of flour. Passage for one slave, her clergyman owner, and the flour yielded sixty-six ducats for the enterprise. Passage for the other two slaves may have canceled yet another debt.[51]

Besides engineering these financial arrangements and the clearing of his putative settlers through the immigration controls, Ayllón looked around for a pilot who would guide his ships to La Florida. Goncalez seems already to have returned to New Spain, and Gayón is not known to have been in Spain at the time. That is to say, the two pilots with the most recent knowledge of the Atlantic coast of the Southeast were unavailable. In the end, Ayllón hired Francisco Estroçagallo, a Catalan. For a hundred ducats paid in Seville and two hundred pesos of the money of Santo Domingo paid within twenty days of arrival there and for an additional two hundred paid when *Nuestra Señora de Esperanza* returned to the Antilles from La Florida, Estroçagallo agreed to pilot the ship to Santo Domingo and from

---

tember, and between Gaspar Hernández and Benito Baez, September 20, 1563, AP-SVQ, Oficio 17, 1563, Book for September and October, fols. 776–776v.

50. Debt acknowledgments signed by Mediano with Pedro Lopez, of Toledo, and others, June 15, 1562, AP-SVQ, Oficio 17, 1562, Book for March and June, fol. 97, with Antonio Selles and Cristobal del Rio, July 10, 1563, *ibid.*, 1563, Book beginning with August, register 1, and with Francisco de la Presa and others, and with Nicolao Gentil, July 29, 1563, *ibid.*, 1563, Book for March (?), fols. 1159–1160v; power of attorney from Ayllón to Mediano, September 18, 1563, *ibid.*, 1563, Book for September and October, fol. 723.

51. Obligation of Lucas Vázquez de Ayllón, August 17, 1563, AP-SVQ, Oficio 21, 1563, Book 2, fols. 925–925v; "Información" for Lopez Utiel, Seville, September 1, 1563, AP-SVQ, Oficio 9, 1563, Book 5, fols. 326–31; power of attorney from Lopez Utiel to Lazaro de Panyguerola, August 17, 1563, AP-SVQ, Oficio 21, 1563, Book 2, fol. 871v; acknowledgment, September 11, 1563, AP-SVQ, Oficio 17, 1563, Book for September and October, first third (approximately fols. 201–202); power of attorney, AP-SVQ, Oficio 17, 1563, Book for June and July, fol. 1016. Slaves were worth at least 151 ducats in the Indies according to information in AGI, CT 5185, Book 1 (1558–66), fol. 107, and AGI, IG 427, Book 30, fol. 117.

there to the port in La Florida that Ayllón had selected as the site for his attempt at settlement. If the expedition did not set sail from Santo Domingo in May, 1564, Estroçagallo was to be free of any further obligation and was to be paid four hundred pesos of the money of Santo Domingo. Furthermore, the pilot was obliged to spend only eight days in La Florida unloading and was guaranteed his wage as pilot for the voyage back to Spain whether the *Nuestra Señora de Esperanza* made the voyage or not.[52]

Ayllón also looked after personal matters and arranged for his family. On August 4, he granted full power of attorney to his wife, Beatriz, to handle not only his business affairs but also those resulting from her inheritance from her parents, instructing her, in particular, to try to obtain her portion of the division agreed among the heirs four years earlier.[53] Evidently Ayllón wanted that money also to support his expedition. In September, as the date of embarkation drew closer, Ayllón paid the remaining rent (for what period is not specified) on a house he was renting from the Colegio de Niños de la Doctrina Cristiana, in the parish of Santa Marina, "next to the *casa de la doctrina.*"[54] Ayllón's family was planning to live in the house until he sent for them to join him in La Florida.

Finally, on September 18, the notary Matheo de Almonacia was summoned to the house off Calle Real so that Ayllón could create two legal instruments. The first nominated the husband or husbands of his oldest daughter, Beatriz Vázquez de Ayllón, as his successor under the contract with the king. In the event of her death before him, the husband or husbands of his next daughter, Antonia Vázquez de Ayllón, were to carry the titles and have the rights that attached to his offices under the contract. If she also died before him, he reserved the right to name as his successor his other daughter or some other child whom God might give him. None of the three girls was of marriageable age, apparently, but he may have anticipated marriage for the oldest if he was successful in colonizing La Florida. The second legal paper consisted of a donation of part of his property to his oldest

52. Contract, August 17, 1563, AP-SVQ, Oficio 8, register 51, fols. 1377–78.

53. Power of attorney, August 4, 1563, AP-SVQ, Oficio 9, 1563, Book 4, fols. 831–36.

54. Receipt, September 13, 1563, AP-SVQ, Oficio 1, 1563, Book 2, fol. 613v; record of auction of rental of houses belonging to the Colegio de Niños de la Doctrina, March 21, 1563, AP-SVQ, Oficio 1, 1563, Book 1, fols. 796–798v. For a history of the Colegio de Niños, see Juan Ignacio Carmona García, *El sistema de hospitalidad pública en la Sevilla del Antiguo Régimen* (Seville, 1979), 51–52.

daughter. Under the law, she would inherit a third of his property. He now gave her the remainder of the fifth part of his goods as well.[55] In effect, he was making the sort of donation that setting up a *mayorazgo,* or entail, involved. His intention seems to have been to provide her with an estate that would give her good prospects of finding a rich, or at least well-connected, husband—one who would be of value to the family. Ayllón does not seem to have made a will; at least none has been found among the papers of the notaries with whom he did most of his business.

His preparations completed and his affairs in some degree of order, Ayllón bade farewell to his wife and daughters and went to San Lucar to join the ships and settlers that had been assembling there. Surviving immigration inquiries indicate that at least thirty-two persons were on the *Nuestra Señora de la Esperanza,* at least fifty were on *La Trinidad,* and at least seventeen were on the *San Pedro.* The 121 known emigrants included nine married couples without children and one woman (a widow?) with her son; the remaining 101 were single men.[56] After additional delays caused by a wait for royal dispatches, Ayllón sailed on Friday, October 8, 1563.[57]

The first of Ayllón's ships arrived at Santo Domingo on December 13. Apparently all was well through early February, but then trouble began. According to the licenciado Juan de Echagoyen of the audiencia of Santo Domingo, many of the people Ayllón had brought out had paid him for passage only as far as Santo Domingo. They were leaving for other parts of the Spanish empire. Some apparently decided that Ayllón had not lived up to whatever bargains Tellez had made in his name and sued Ayllón to recover their money. Whether to satisfy them or for some other reason, by early April Ayllón had been forced to sell one of his two ships. Echagoyen expressed suspicion that if the adelantado sailed at all it would be simply in pretense of complying with his contract. He also noted that the deal with Juan García for the voyage of the *San Pedro* was a matter of fraud that required some action.[58] Years later, Vasco Perez de Figueroa, one of Ayllón's cap-

55. Nomination and donation, September 18, 1563, AP-SVQ, Oficio 9, 1563, Book 5, fols. 455–456v.

56. Immigrant files Nos. 47 and 149, AGI, CT 5220.

57. For delays, see AGI, CT 5167, Book 3, fol. 220v, and AGI, CT 5185, Book 1 (1558–66), fols. 217v–218v, and AGI, CT 5167, Book 3, fol. 32.

58. AGI, SD 71, Book 1, fol. 235v; House of Trade to SM, April 20, 1564, AGI, IG 2002, fol. 220 (noting the arrival of ships sailing from Santo Domingo on February 7 and

tains, affirmed that the men had deserted and that he had tried to round them up, even removing some from between *pipas* in the holds of ships about to leave Santo Domingo's harbor.[59]

The next information on the expedition comes from New Spain. On June 8, 1564, the licenciado Jerónimo Valderrama reported from Mexico City that a few days earlier the *alcalde mayor* of Veracruz had informed him that more than thirty men, some married and with their wives, had arrived at Veracruz. Former members of Ayllón's expedition, they were hungry and seeking work. Even though they lacked licenses from the audiencia of Santo Domingo to go to New Spain, the officials at Veracruz decided to let them enter the province because of their destitution. Valderrama had heard that others from Ayllón's expedition had gone to Tierra Firme (Colombia and Panama). He gave it as his opinion that Ayllón's contract was nothing more than a way to get money from people who could not otherwise obtain colonial immigration permits from the king.[60]

The desertion, if that is what it was, of these people in May effectively killed Ayllón's project. With one ship and few remaining colonists, and with apparently a pile of debts and lawsuits against him, Ayllón had little prospect of setting up a colony. Moreover, he may have heard that the Dominican mission planned for Don Luís' homeland had not been started, depriving him of an expected preparation for his settlement. He apparently struggled with the problems a while longer in April, and possibly the following months, but then gave up. By August 10, 1564, Echagoyen could report that Ayllón had fled at night in a large bark. Suspecting he was bound for South America, the licenciado wrote to the officials of Tierra Firme and Peru to be on the watch for him.[61] Men still loyal to Ayllón, including Perez de Figueroa, sailed with the would-be adelantado.

Ayllón and his friends evaded Echagoyen's precautions by landing at Santa Marta. But the president of the audiencia of New Granada eventually learned of his presence there and ordered Governor Luís de

---

the news they brought, which included nothing about Ayllón); Juan de Echagoyen to SM, Santo Domingo, April 4, 1564, AGI, SD 71, Book 2 fols. 320v–332 (Stetson); testimony in replies to questions 3 and 6 of an interrogatory for Pedro Menéndez de Avilés, 1567, AGI, JU 879, No. 3, Pieza 2, fols. 6v, 10v, 12, 15.

59. AGI, PAT 160, R. 2, No. 7, fols. 1, 3v–4, 166v. This citation was provided by José Ignacio Avellaneda, a Colombian historian doing graduate work at the University of Florida.

60. AGI, MEX 68, Book, fol. 275.

61. AGI, SD 71, Book 2, fol. 352 (Stetson).

Manjarres to make an inquiry concerning Ayllón's alleged frauds in setting up the expedition and his flight to Santa Marta. Manjarres received the authority to arrest the adelantado if necessary.[62] Instead of making an arrest, however, Manjarres offered Ayllón the leadership (at his expense?) of the pacification of the Tairona Indians, who had risen against Spanish rule in 1555. In preparation, Ayllón led an ill-equipped expedition to the Upar River valley, evidently to enslave some of the Tupe Indians who lived there but perhaps also to obtain gold from placers. Probably while this expedition was in the field, Manjarres, in Santa Marta, and according to one witness, Ayllón, died.[63] It was the summer of 1565.

Echagoyen's and Valderama's judgment that Ayllón's whole contract was simply a stratagem for personal enrichment and that he had no intention of going to La Florida seems too harsh in view of the arrangements he made at Seville for his succession and in view of the various ways in which he raised money for the expedition. Some of the ways were fraudulent, but they suggest that he was a man desperately searching for cash to carry out a project that was close to his heart. Garcilaso de la Vega ("el Inca") suggested much the same in his comment that Ayllón the Younger died on Española of a broken heart while trying to carry out a project that had little prospect of completion to begin with and grew daily less likely to succeed.[64] Save for the inaccuracy about where Ayllón died, Garcilaso's statement may be a fit summing-up of the quixotic venture that Ayllón the Younger had undertaken. It is fair to suppose that the young woman in Seville had many occasions in the years after 1564 to curse La Florida and the legend that her husband's long-dead father had left as part of his legacy. Did she also reflect on the similarity of the behavior of father and son, who well past midlife abandoned young wives and children to pursue with inadequate means dreams of glory on the coast of North America?

Men with ampler means were even then entering the field, but like the Ayllóns, they were driven by dreams, one of which was the

62. Dr. Venero to SM, Bogotá, January 1, 1564 [*sic*; 1565], in *Fuentes documentales para la historia del Nuevo Reino de Granada desde la instalación de la Real Audiencia en Santa Fe,* ed. Juan Friede (8 vols. to 1988; Bogotá, 1975–), V, 125. This citation too was provided by José Ignacio Avellaneda.

63. AGI, PAT 160, R. 2, No. 7, fols. 8v, 167v. On the Tupes, see Trinidad Miranda Vazquez, *La gobernación de Santa Marta, 1570–1670* (Seville, 1976), 137; on the mines, see p. 69.

64. Garcilaso de la Vega, *The Florida of the Inca,* 13.

Chicora legend, a legend that had been created by Lucas the Elder and had trapped and ruined his son after Antonio Velázquez' rediscovery of the Bahía de Santa María in 1561. Another dream was a form of Verrazzano's geographic legend about North America, a legend that soon became linked in some Spanish, and later in English, minds with the great bay Velázquez had visited. The pursuit of these dreams by a new generation of explorers and colonizers occurred within a framework of international rivalry and hostility for control of North America's southeastern coast.

PART THREE

The Contest for Empire in the Southeast

IX

The Franco-Spanish Struggle, 1562–1565

Jean Ribault's voyage of 1562 marks the beginning of a twenty-year period of Franco-Spanish rivalry for the control of North America south of 40° north. For the first six years of that period, the struggle was intense and often violent. The Spaniards won but in doing so committed themselves to occupying the very coast that a generation earlier they had written off as worthless for the sort of settlement they customarily practiced.

Spain's victory over France in the contest to control the southeastern coast of North America soon established a pattern of interests that led to the virtual abandonment of Spanish efforts to explore and settle north of Cape Hatteras. A few voyages were planned (*e.g.*, Lucas Vázquez de Ayllón the Younger's) or carried out in the 1560s and early 1570s to follow up on Antonio Velázquez' discovery of 1561 and to try to learn the truth behind the conflicting geography contained in the French and Spanish maps and in the French and Spanish histories of the discoveries of the 1520s. But those efforts ended without resolution of the geographic uncertainty. The effect, however, was Spanish abandonment of the coast north of their settlement of Santa Elena.

Spanish and French failures to occupy the coast north of Santa Elena or effectively to disprove the Ayllón and Verrazzano legends associated with those latitudes made the area inviting to the English, who inherited all the earlier Spanish and French notions about the geography of the Southeast north of Cape Hatteras and south of 40° north. Consequently, their exploration and settlement during the 1580s focused where the supposed Verrazzano sea would provide a link to the Orient to the north of the latitudes of Andalucia and Ayllón's Chicora.

English settlement activity provided Spaniards who were interested in the Bahía de Santa María with one last chance to explore that bay and place a Spanish colony there. But dependence on government financing for such a venture, as well as other circumstances, prevented them from achieving their goals. The English ended in nominal possession of the one part of the southeastern coast where navigable rivers reached the better soils of the piedmont. It was thus they who opened up the possibility of extensive agricultural development capable of sustaining a larger population than could be supported by the sandy soils of the coastal zone where the Spaniards were settled.

The English did not follow up immediately on their settlements of the 1580s, but when after 1607 they did so, they developed a cash crop, tobacco, that led to the explosive growth of Virginia and eliminated the possibility of driving the English out of a region essential to the Spaniards if they were to retain any long-term control over the Southeast. The English had found a new Andalucia, although it did not give them the olive oil and wine of the old. But the way to the Orient that the Verrazzano legend claimed for those latitudes was nonexistent.

The Franco-Spanish rivalry is the subject of this and the two following chapters. The Anglo-Spanish contest for the Chesapeake Bay is the subject of Chapter XII. Wherever other authors cover parts of the history well, this account summarizes events, and the text and notes provide references to the fuller discussion.

The French voyages and colonization in La Florida during the period from 1562 to 1565 were at one time ascribed to the religious concerns of Gaspard de Coligny, the admiral of France.[1] It is better to understand them as part of a national policy that Henri II determined upon in the 1550s and that the Council of Affairs, an institution created to supervise the regency of Henri's son and heir, continued after his death.[2] Two pieces of evidence support that assessment. First, René Goulaine de Laudonnière says as much.[3] Second, the primary pur-

1. Jules, Comte Delaborde, *Gaspard de Coligny, Amiral de France* (3 vols.; Paris, 1879–82), II, 14–15, 325–26, and Walter Besant, *Gaspard de Coligny (Marquis de Chatillon), Admiral of France . . .* (New York, 1891), 123–24, and Arthur W. Whitehead, *Gaspard de Coligny, Admiral of France* (London, 1904), 319–25.

2. Claire Eliane Engel, *L'Amiral de Coligny* (Geneva, 1967), 185–93, and Shimizu, *Conflict of Loyalties*, 63–64. On the Council of Affairs, see Shimizu, *Conflict of Loyalties*, 56.

3. René Goulaine de Laudonnière, *L'Histoire notable de la Florida située es Indes Occidentales contenant les trois voyages faits en icelle par certains capitaines et pilotes françois . . .* (Paris, 1586), fol. 7v, as in Suzanne Lussagnet (ed.), *Les Français en Amérique pendant la deuxième moitié du XVIe siècle; Les Français en Floride* (Paris, 1958), 50. English translation of Laudonnière's work: *Three Voyages*, trans. Charles E. Bennett (Gainesville, Fla., 1975), 17. Hereafter, *Histoire notable* will be cited with folio

pose of Henri II's policy was to create French settlements on the flanks of the Spanish Caribbean which might provide goods the Spanish empire ordinarily supplied France and that could serve as bases for attacks on the Spanish in time of war. Ribault's colonies in North America fitted those criteria. As secondary benefits, the French national policy offered the prospect of uniting at least some of the nation's people across the deepening chasm of religion and of providing the Huguenots of the western ports with a possible long-term refuge at the same time that it gave them a livelihood and short-term outlets for their energies. The religious motives behind the policy were apparently not, however, primary.

Within the larger French design, Ribault's voyage of 1562 was a necessary preliminary because of the uncertainty of geographic knowledge about the coast. Besides the writings, already noted, of Francisco Lopez de Gómara, Giovanni Bautista Ramusio, and André Thevet, and the Münster cartography and Verrazzano's claim of an isthmus, Coligny had before him Le Testu's atlas of 1555. The depiction of the east coast of North America in that atlas followed the Spanish *padrón real* of the Chaves type. It did not show any arm of the Pacific reaching across North America to within a short distance of the Atlantic. Nor did it show the Santa Elena River extending into the continent to connect the Atlantic with a supposed arm of the Pacific.[4] Which version of North America was correct? Were Ayllón's reports of the riches of the upper thirties north latitude accurate? What of the twenty-nine pounds of gold that were said to have been discovered in 1539 somewhere on the Atlantic coast by Vicente Tiran and Grangean Bucier?[5] Relatively speaking, Coligny and Ribault had a wealth of information about the east coast of North America, but it was information that was contradictory on specific details even if full of promises of riches.

Ribault's job, as he reported it in his account of the 1562 voyage, was to

> discover and view a certain long coast of the West Indies, from the head of the land called La Florida, drawing towards the northern part until the head

---

and page numbers and *Three Voyages* with page numbers. A facsimile edition of the 1586 Paris *L'Histoire notable* was issued at Lyon in 1946. It too was consulted for this study.

4. Le Testu's North American map is reproduced in Cumming, Skelton, and Quinn (eds.), *Discovery of North America,* plate 163, p. 152.

5. Spain, *Negociaciones,* III, 172.

> of Britons, . . . 900 leagues or thereabout, to the end that we might certify you and make true report of the temperature, fertility, ports, havens, rivers, and generally of all the commodities that might be found and seen in that land and also to learn what people were there dwelling.[6]

With Ribault's "true report" at hand, Coligny and his associates could plan the trade that they hoped would enrich France and bring about the conversion of the natives to what Ribault termed "our faith."

Did Ribault also have orders to create a colony somewhere along the coast? On that question the evidence is less abundant and less convincing. Catherine de Medicis told the Spanish ambassador that Ribault was bound for a place on the North American coast but that it would not be "prejudicial" to Philip II's interests. The suggestion there was that Ribault was to leave a colony. On the other hand, Ribault's own account of his voyage implies that he placed a colony near Port Royal Sound as a result of circumstances on the voyage and of his decision as its commander to leave men in possession of the area he thought to be the most valuable of those he had seen. Two years later, the Spanish interrogators of Guillaume Rouffi, a French youth who stayed with the Indians when the Charlesfort garrison abandoned America, understood him to say that the Port Royal settlement was a first step in a plan to move toward the Bahama Channel for attacks on Spanish shipping there and in the Antilles.[7] That was, of course, a standard Spanish concern about any non-Spanish settlement on the east coast of North America, and the impression of the interrogators does not necessarily tell what Ribault's orders were.

On the whole, the evidence closest in date to the events suggests that Ribault's principal task was to explore the coast and determine which parts of the conflicting geographic information available in France were correct. He was probably not prohibited from leaving a

6. Jean Ribault, *The Whole and True Discouerye of Terra Florida: A Facsimile Reprint of the London Edition of 1563, Together with a Transcript of an English Version in the British Museum, with Notes by H. M. Biggar and a Biography by Jeannette Thurber Connor* (Deland, Fla., 1927), 53. Cited hereafter as Ribault, *Discovery.*

7. Spain, *Negociaciones,* III, 172, 294; Ribault, *Discovery,* 95–96; deposition of Rouffi, June 12, 1564, in Charles E. Bennett's *Laudonnière and Fort Caroline: History and Documents* (Gainesville, Fla., 1964), 118. Lowery notes the deposition as the principal motive for the voyages and colony (*Spanish Settlements,* II, 31). Johann Georg Kohl sees Ribault's voyage as a continuation of Verrazzano's explorations and suggests that the French crown did not authorize the colony but that it was rather the result of a Protestant plan known to the officers of the voyage (*A History of the Discovery of the East Coast of North America* [Portland, Maine, 1869], 421–23, Vol. I of Maine Historical Society, *Documentary History of the State of Maine,* 24 vols.).

colony, but probably any settlement was contingent on finding a suitable location. A site short of the Jordan River would not have seemed promising on the basis of what his countrymen knew before he sailed.

Ribault's fleet of three small ships sailed from Le Havre on February 18, 1562. He had 150 men, half of them soldiers. His pilot was an unnamed Portuguese, and among the gentlemen of his company was Laudonnière. Accounts of the voyage were published by Ribault in 1563 and by Laudonnière in 1586. In addition, the so-called Parreus Map is a contemporary tracing of the map William Cumming believes Nicholas Barré prepared from Ribault's logs.[8]

Ribault's course seems to have been not the usual one by way of the Canary Islands but a route farther north. That probably accounts for why he took two and a half months to make the crossing rather than the more typical six weeks. At any rate, he made landfall on the coast of peninsular Florida on April 30. He was at approximately the latitude of Saint Augustine. From there he began to coast northward. The boats the two larger ships of his fleet carried were used to explore the estuaries and the rivers behind the barrier islands from the River of May (Saint Johns River) to the South Edisto River. The exploration the boats conducted led to the discovery of the bays, rivers, and sounds behind the barrier islands of the Georgia and South Carolina coasts, and thus of what is now the inland waterway.

At the River of May, Ribault encountered Indians who proved friendly and allowed him to erect the first of two stone markers signifying his visit and French sovereignty. The placing of such markers—a practice the French perhaps borrowed from the Portuguese voyages along the west coast of Africa during the fifteenth century—suggests that Coligny anticipated the possible need of additional voyages to carry the exploration to Cape Breton. The Portuguese had used their stone markers both to claim the land and to identify the last point of each successive voyage of exploration. Ribault seems to have been following their example.

From the River of May, Ribault worked his way north inquiring after "Chicore" until he came to a bay he named Port Royal. Of all the estuaries visited until then, only this one had a channel deeper than

8. Ribault, *Discovery*, 58–98; Laudonnière, *L'Histoire notable*, fols. 7–21, pp. 50–67 (*Three Voyages*, 17–23); William P. Cumming, "The Parreus Map (1562) of French Florida," *Imago Mundi*, XVII (1963), 27–40. The Parreus map is in the Colección Navarette of the Museo Naval, Madrid.

one and a half fathoms at high tide. The eastern, "right-hand channel" at Port Royal Sound had four fathoms, enough to enable the larger ships to enter the sound without danger. The Broad River, which is the part of the sound seen dead ahead upon entering it, must have appeared very great indeed, although a closer look probably showed that it narrowed down quickly. Port Royal, the name Ribault gave the estuary, summed up his own appreciation of its possibilities, as did his observation that "all the ships in the worlde might be harbored" in it.[9]

After exploring a bit, he decided that "this is the River of Jordayne in myne oppynion, whereof so muche hathe byn spoken, which is verry faire, and the cuntrye good and of grete consequence, both for theire easye habitation and also for many other things which shuld be to long to wrytt." He did, however, note the "fairest and the greatest vynes with grapes" and the "yong trees" and sweet-smelling woods that made the estuary appear to be the "pleasantest and most comodious dwelling of all the worlde."[10] The apparently hospitable qualities of the land and his knowledge that settling in a new discovery was the best way to keep it caused him to tell his men things that led more than enough to volunteer as the first French garrison there. In the end, he selected thirty of the volunteers to install in a fortified house he named Charlesfort.

Neither Ribault nor Laudonnière says what else the commander told his men. Maybe it was enough to explain what "Chicore" was, to those who did not know: Ayllón's new Andalucia, rich in agricultural, sylvan, and mineral potential. The vision that the Chicora legend gave shape to, and that the richness of the woods in late May made persuasive, could have been sufficient once the French had established friendly relations with the Escamacu and Edisto Indians. If more was necessary, Ribault was in a position to appeal to the desire to serve the king and the admiral. With provisions for as many as eight months and trade goods for obtaining more from the Indians, the garrison had little to fear. Ribault promised to return the next spring with supplies and reinforcements. On June 11, he resumed his voyage of exploration.

Laudonnière says that, unlike Ribault, he doubted that this was the Jordan, and that in later conversations with the Indians he learned

9. Ribault, *Discovery*, 90–94, with quotation from p. 90.
10. *Ibid.*, 94–95.

that "Chiquola" was a great walled town farther north. It was rich in gold, silver, and pearls, he had heard, and the description reminded him of the story of the Spaniard from Santo Domingo who had captured slaves there in the time of Charles V.[11] Like Ribault, Laudonnière knew the basic story of Ayllón's Chicora.

Whether Laudonnière really disagreed with Ribault in 1562 and learned about "Chiquola" from conversations with the Indians is impossible to know. His account was published twenty-four years after the events and had the benefit of hindsight. Still, if he had seen Le Testu's maps or similar ones of Spanish origin, he must have known that the Jordan was well to the north of the Point of Santa Elena. Only Gómara's *Historia general* suggested otherwise. Ribault must have had the same facts at his disposal, yet he chose to interpret them differently. The explanation may lie partly in his personality, which Johann Kohl describes as sometimes "too enthusiastic and impulsive," partly in his need to justify leaving some of his crew when he may not have been under command to do so and when he had not carried out his orders to explore the coast to 50° north.[12]

Having left a garrison at Charlesfort, Ribault sailed up the coast a bit farther and then, in council with his pilots, masters, and gentlemen, decided that he could not go on to 50° north, because the weather was "troublesome and cloudy," his naval stores and foods were rapidly deteriorating, he lacked boatswains to guide the exploring parties and still have seamen on the ships, and the men in the fleet who had been farther north (presumably to the cod fisheries) said that the weather and sea conditions there were severe, with great "mists and fogs." Laudonnière added that Ribault had intended to go north until he fully and truly discovered the Jordan River but that he decided against the attempt when the first river he found north of Port Royal Sound—that is, the South Edisto—proved to have another shallow bar and when soundings showed that shoals reached out from the coast just as they had below Port Royal Sound. Ribault may simply have realized that exploring the coast northward would be a repeti-

11. Laudonnière, *L'Histoire notable,* fols. 15v–17, pp. 59–60 (*Three Voyages,* 29–30).

12. Kohl, *The Discovery of the East Coast,* 431. Ribault, *Discovery,* 95–96: "Wherefore (my Lorde) trusting you will not thinke yt amisse, considering the great good and comodyties that may be brought thence into France, if we leve a nombre of men there, that may fortifye and so provide themselves of thinges necessarye, for in all newe discovers yt is the chef and best thinge that may be done at the begining, to fortifye and people the country which is the true and chef possession."

tion of the troubles he faced from the River of May to Port Royal Sound. It had taken three weeks to make a run of less than three degrees of latitude. At that rate, reaching 50° north would have taken over five times as long, or about four months, far more time than the remaining supplies allowed. Anyway, returning to France for supplies and men for the next spring's exploration was a high priority. Ribault's fleet must have left the American coast behind about June 13. Laudonnière says that they landed in France on July 20.[13]

It is not known if Ribault returned to Le Havre or went directly to his home port of Dieppe. Wherever he landed, he quickly became embroiled in the defense of Dieppe, apparently fighting there until its surrender to French Catholic forces on October 20, 1562. He then fled to England with the English garrison that had been aiding in the defense of the city. In England, he set about extolling La Florida and trying to get English backing for a new venture. The English were interested, and by early 1563, Thomas Stukeley, a young Roman Catholic adventurer who enjoyed favor at Elizabeth I's court, had entered into an agreement with Ribault. When Ribault published his *Whole and True Discouerye of Terra Florida,* in May, 1563, he was able to obtain an audience with Elizabeth and the promise of one of her ships for the fleet. Stukeley promised two ships, Ribault was to put up one, and a fifth was to be chartered. The Spanish ambassador duly reported all this to Philip II.[14]

Meanwhile, in France, the interests behind the La Florida venture had been preparing three ships to carry men and supplies to reinforce the colony at Charlesfort. The preparations were well advanced when revolts broke out at Le Havre and the Portuguese pilot who had guided Ribault fled to Paris. There the Portuguese ambassador was said to have persuaded him to return to Portugal, although he probably did not do so. The Spanish ambassador in France reported these events and the details of Charlesfort and Ribault's voyage in letters dated during January, 1563.[15]

At roughly the same time that this news from Paris reached Madrid, the Spanish government learned that Wooden Foot (Pie de Palo), an infamous French commerce raider who had made his reputa-

13. Ribault, *Discovery,* 97–99; Laudonnière, *L'Histoire notable,* fol. 21v, p. 67 (*Three Voyages,* 38).

14. Ribault, *Discovery,* 8–11; copy of Quadra to Philip II, London, May 1, 1563, AGI, IG 2003.

15. Spain, *Negociaciones,* V, 18–19, 51–52, copies in AGI, IG 2003, fol. 523 (?), and AGI, IG 2004, fols. 277–277v.

tion in the wars of the 1550s, was using England as a base for a fleet of four to eight ships and intended to attack the returning convoys in the Azores. Apparently his squadron incorporated some of the ships that had been preparing at Le Havre for the La Florida voyage. Other reports spoke of a French-English plan to attack the Isthmus of Panama.[16]

In response, Philip II did three things. First, he warned Pedro Menéndez de Avilés, captain general of the Mexican convoy, and various governors in the Caribbean of the French and English naval preparations. Second, he ordered Menéndez and Governor Diego de Mazariegos of Cuba to find out more about the French settlement in La Florida. He instructed them to expel the French if they were at the Point of Santa Elena as reported. But he also told Menéndez not to delay his return to Spain on that account.[17] Third, Philip issued the orders that facilitated the readying of Vázquez de Ayllón the Younger's expedition.

The order to investigate the French settlement reached Mazariegos on October 6. Menéndez de Avilés had come and gone, as had most of the intra-Caribbean trading ships that had been in Havana during the summer. Mazariegos replied that when he tried to arrange for a ship and pilot, he was told that the season was too late for safe sailing along the coast at 32° north. Northers, the storms of winter, already would be setting in. The search for the French would have to wait, he decided, until the spring of 1564. He also wrote that no reports of a French colony in La Florida had reached Cuba except from Madrid. The ship that carried his letter, dated late November, 1563, to Spain had come from Veracruz with Goncalo Gayón as its pilot. The ship continued without Gayón, who remained in Havana so that Mazariegos could send him to the coast of La Florida in the spring.[18]

When the northern winter ended, Mazariegos did not go to La Florida in person to seek out the French. Instead, he commissioned Hernán Manrique de Rojas to command a single ship, the *fragata Nuestra Señora de la Concepción,* with Gayón as chief pilot. The *fragata* sailed from Havana on May 12, 1564.[19]

16. Report of the news that Domingo de Villota gave [*ca.* January 25, 1563], AGI, IG 2004, fol. 15.

17. Cedula, February 13, 1563, AGI, IG 427, Book 30, fols. 129v–132v.

18. AGI, SD 115, fols. 131–32; inquiry into merits and services of Gayón, Havana, July 13, 1564, AGI, SD 11, No. 50, question 6 and answers.

19. Instructions to Manrique de Rojas, Havana, May 10, 1564, copy in AGI, JU 90, No. 2, fols. 1159–62; report of Manrique de Rojas, Havana, July 9, 1564, AGI, SD 99, No. 34, trans. Lucy L. Wenhold, in "Manrique de Rojas' Report on French Settlement in Florida, 1564," *Florida Historical Quarterly,* XXXVIII (1959), 45–62.

Manrique de Rojas cleared the Bahama Channel in eight days, put in first at the Río de Corrientes (Ponce de Leon Inlet), and then sailed north to the Río de la Cruz, either Saint Augustine Inlet or Matanzas Inlet. Latitude readings, taken at noon on the twenty-second and again on the twenty-third, with a night reading on the twenty-second, all confirmed that the ship was at 29° north, the latitude where the first French pillar should have been found. There was none in sight, nor could the Spaniards find any Indians to ask about the French. But Manrique de Rojas and his men were not at 29° north if they were at the Río de la Cruz. They were at nearly 30° north (29°55′).

Departing the Río de la Cruz, Manrique de Rojas worked up the coast eight or nine leagues (twenty-five to twenty-eight nautical miles) to another river, whose latitude is given as 29½° north. The distance is right for the Saint Johns River, which is about thirty nautical miles north of Saint Augustine Inlet. On the twenty-sixth, he was at yet another river, said to be at 30° north. Woodbury Lowery believed that this was the Saint Johns River, but it was probably Saint Andrews Sound or Saint Simon Sound if Gayón's latitude readings were consistently one degree off. There Manrique de Rojas found an Indian town and learned that three ships had put in but then sailed on toward the north. European items seen in the village confirmed the visit of the ships.

Sailing on May 29, the Spanish party encountered a storm that drove them out to sea. When they regained the coast, the pilots said they were at 32° north. The description of the place is clearly, however, that of Guale, most likely Sapelo Sound, which is at roughly 31½° north. Once again inquiries revealed that Europeans had recently been in the area but had gone on north.

The Spaniards stayed at Guale until June 7, after which they worked their way up the coast by inlet hopping until, on the eleventh, they were at Saint Helena Sound. They encountered two Indians who told them that a ship with thirty-four European men had sailed not long before but that one European was still in the area. Manrique de Rojas at once sent him a wooden cross by means of an Indian messenger. A day later, Guillaume Rouffi appeared, dressed in Indian clothing.

Interrogated through a sailor who knew some French, Rouffi revealed that the French fort was to the south, on a river that branched off the one in which the Spaniards were anchored. He gave details of its latitude as computed by the French and their Portuguese pilot. He also recounted briefly the decision of the rest of Ribault's garrison to trust themselves to the sea rather than remain any longer in a strange land where starvation seemed likely.[20]

With Rouffi as guide, Manrique de Rojas went to Charlesfort and destroyed it. He and his men then went to the place where Ribault had placed his column. They rooted it out and took it back to the ship. Satisfied that the French had left and that the Spaniards had found at least one of their markers, Manrique de Rojas retraced his course to Havana. On July 9, 1564, he dictated the final part of his report.

Mazariegos decided to send Gayón to Spain with the report, the marble column, and Rouffi. Ever watchful for his own advancement, Gayón had the men who had been on the voyage answer a detailed interrogatory. That and Manrique de Rojas' account are the principal sources regarding the voyage. Curiously, Gayón's description of the coast misstates the depths of the ports, claiming that at high tide ships with a draft of three to five fathoms (eighteen to thirty feet) could enter any of the dozen or so ports that the Spaniards had visited. Rectifying the fraud of the Villafañe voyage, he acknowledged that the River of Santa Elena (Port Royal Sound) had as many as five fathoms of water over the bar at high tide.[21] The modern reader of the erroneous statements and the consistently incorrect latitudes Gayón recorded on the Manrique de Rojas expedition can only wonder at the heavily self-promoted reputation he had as an excellent pilot.

Even before Manrique de Rojas returned to Havana, the Spaniards had their first reports that a new French expedition was on its way to the Point of Santa Elena. In late May, French ships operating west of Havana under the command of Francisco Díaz Mimoso captured both a ship sailing from Honduras to Spain and a Cuban coastal trading ship. The Spaniards whom Díaz Mimoso briefly held reported the new French expedition.

Caribbean authorities were already familiar with Díaz Mimoso, because it was his two-ship squadron that in March, 1561, had captured four out of seven Spanish ships trying to work their way to the east around Saona Island in order to enter the Mona Channel and exit the Caribbean. That was one of the first French raids on Spanish

20. Laudonnière, *L'Histoire notable,* fols. 22–31v, pp. 67–80 (*Three Voyages,* 38–51).

21. Depositions for Gayón, Havana, July 13, 1564, AGI, SD 11, No. 50.

shipping after the signing of the peace treaties of 1559. The testimony of Spaniards whom Mimoso briefly held captive in 1561 clearly showed that Admiral Coligny had a half-interest in the venture, which had resulted in Spanish losses said to total twenty-five thousand pesos de oro. At least part of the later Spanish case against Coligny derived from these reports. Moreover, the French capture of the four ships led the Consulado of Seville to demand, and enabled it to obtain, the reinstitution of the convoy system, which had been abolished at the conclusion of the war.[22] Mimoso's reappearance in the Caribbean in the spring of 1564 was considered a bad sign. As the governor of Puerto Rico observed, the commander of the French ships was dangerous and knew every corner of that island as well as other parts of the Caribbean.[23]

The information that Mimoso's prisoners of 1564 had was that his three ships were part of a larger group of seven. According to one Spaniard who had had contact with Mimoso, the seven ships had gone to the Point of Santa Elena and set up a colony, and one ship had gone back to France for supplies and reinforcements, *before* Mimoso sailed to the Antilles with three ships, leaving three at the Point of Santa Elena. All other witnesses spoke, more accurately, of a plan for three French ships and a patache to go to Santa Elena while Mimoso cruised in the Caribbean. The Caribbean authorities relaying this news to the court agreed that the Point of Santa Elena was a place from which the French might strike at shipping in the Bahama Channel and that the Spaniards ought to take action to remove them while the colony was still weak.[24]

The accounts from the Caribbean confirmed dispatches to Madrid from the Spanish diplomatic service in 1563 and early 1564. In late 1563, the Spanish ambassador in France had written that Mimoso was fitting ships for new ventures, some in La Florida and in "other conquests" of the Spanish king. In March and June, 1564, he mentioned a fleet sailing for La Florida. The communication of March spoke of Jacques de Sores and four ships bound for La Florida, although the ambassador said that the destination sounded like what the English were said to be aiming for under Stukeley. The communication of June

22. AGI, IG 1562, Book for 1559–1562, fols. 15–29; AGI, JU 1160, No. 8, R. 1, and Hoffman, *The Spanish Crown*, 94–95.

23. Governor Caresa to king, Puerto Rico, July 2, 1564, in AGI, SD 155 (Stetson).

24. AGI, PAT 254, R. 38.

was quite specific that the destination was La Florida and that the queen mother, Madame Vandome, Cardinal de Bourbon, and Coligny were sending the ships. Rumor had Coligny saying that he wanted France to "reconnoiter an ideal [*idóneo*] site to which he could go to settle and [from which he could] conquer" the king of Spain's lands and "discover others." The ambassador's opinion, though, was that what the French were intent on was some robbery of shipping returning from the New World.[25]

The reports were nearly accurate concerning the number of ships Laudonnière had under his command and about his and Coligny's objective, which was to find an "ideal" spot for settlement, discovery, and action against the Spaniards. Trade too was an objective. One of Coligny's biographers quotes him as writing at about this time that he was "looking about to find new means whereby to traffic and make one's profit in foreign lands, and I hope so to manage that in a little while we may have the finest trade in Christendom."[26]

Other assertions, such as that Mimoso had been to the Point of Santa Elena before coming to the Antilles and that Sores was the commander of the La Florida squadron, were incorrect, but they did not seriously undermine the warning that the reports carried, namely, that the French had not abandoned their plans to occupy the area of the Point of Santa Elena, the site of Ribault's colony. Even officials in as remote a place as Campeche knew, or thought they knew, by late May, 1564, that that was where the French were establishing themselves. It is unlikely that, as one recent author has put it, "the actual intrusion of the Laudonnière expedition was obscured by the multitude of corsair reports which flooded continually to the Spanish Crown."[27] The Spaniards seem to have known that Laudonnière had sailed, even if they did not at first know his name or that he had not in fact gone to the Point of Santa Elena.

Laudonnière sailed from Le Havre on April 22, 1564. He had three ships and three hundred persons, including four women, various craftsmen and servants, and four of the survivors of the Charlesfort garrison's voyage back to Europe. Also on the voyage was the artist Jacques Le Moyne de Morgues. Twenty some years later, Laudonnière

25. Spain, *Negociaciones*, VI, 7, 154, 157–58, with quotation from p. 238.

26. Whitehead, *Gaspard de Coligny*, 336.

27. Dr. Diego Quexada to Philip II, Campeche, May 20, 1564, AGI, MEX 168; Lyon, *The Enterprise of Florida*, 36.

was to protest that he had explicit instructions from the queen mother that he was "to do no kind of wrong to the King of Spain's subjects, nor anything whereof he might conceive any jealousy."[28] That directive was consistent with the earlier command to Ribault to explore and find an "ideal" spot for settlement but ignored Philip II's claim to all of North America.

Laudonnière followed the traditional route by way of the Canary Islands and the Lesser Antilles. The fleet crossed the Atlantic in about two months and made landfall on the coast of peninsular Florida on June 22, not far from where Saint Augustine was to be founded the next year. Laudonnière explored that entrance and bay but decided to move on. His next landing was at the River of May (Saint Johns River), where the Indians received him with celebration and took him to see the column Ribault had erected, which they revered, and possibly worshiped. During the next few days, he explored the mouth of the River of May and sent a party inland. He learned where Saturiba, the local chief, had obtained a silver wedge that he gave to Laudonnière shortly after the landing. It came from a province several days' journey up the Saint Johns, probably Utina.[29] The information about the source of the silver, the evident abundance of maize, and the pleasantness of the woods and bluffs on the eastern side of the Saint Johns played key roles in what happened next.

Leaving the River of May, the French explored northward to another river, the Somme, according to Ribault's nomenclature, or the Saltilla, according to modern terminology. They were just south of Saint Simon's Sound, or they were in it, since they sounded the entrance and found it deep enough for the ships to enter. The river itself was not as deep as the River of May. Nor did the French see much evidence of Indian settlement.

Laudonnière at that juncture called a council of his officers to decide what to do. According to him, the options he laid out were turning south to the Cape of Florida, going on up the coast to Port Royal Sound or beyond, and returning to the River of May to await reinforcements and instructions from France. The first option, settlement on the Cape of Florida, was unattractive because the area was reportedly a marsh, unsuitable for settlement and hence of no profit to the king or the colonists. His opinion of Port Royal Sound was that

28. Laudonnière, *L'Histoire notable,* fol. 64v, p. 122 (*Three Voyages,* 99).
29. Lowery, *Spanish Settlements,* II, 56*n*4.

> we would not find it very comfortable or usable, at least if we were to believe the reports of those who had lived there for a long time [four of the soldiers of 1562 were with them]. Although the harbor there was one of the finest in the West Indies, the issue was not so much a question of the beauty of the location but more a question of the availability of things necessary to sustain daily life. In our first year, it would be much more important to live in a place with an abundant food supply than to be in a commodious and beautiful port.[30]

The River of May, on the other hand, gave promise of abundant food, as the first expedition as well as this one perceived, and of access to gold and silver.

The men who had been on the first voyage all spoke in favor of returning to the River of May and awaiting orders from France. The impression Laudonnière leaves is that only men who had not been to La Florida before favored complying with orders, which seem to have been to reoccupy Port Royal Sound and to continue exploration to find the Jordan River and Chicora and the truth about the geography of the Atlantic coast. But the veterans and Laudonnière overruled the men of that opinion. If that is what happened, a comment in an anonymous letter written in late July indicates that the officers reached a sort of compromise. The letter says that twenty-five leagues from Fort Caroline there was a river called the Jordan, which had excellent martens. According to the writer, the French hoped to go there in six weeks or so.[31] In other words, once they built the fort on the River of May, they planned to resume the exploration of the coast. The fleet returned to the River of May. They worked the ships over the bar and into the river.

Construction of the fort began at once and soon reached a stage that allowed Laudonnière to begin searching the Saint Johns for the source of the silver. His exploration and the settlement's trading yielded small amounts of gold and silver and some fifty small, fire-darkened pearls. An alligator was killed near the settlement and its hide and some medicinal wood samples included with mail in the manifest of the *Isabella* when it departed for France on July 28. One hundred fifty soldiers and fifty other persons remained at Fort Carolina.[32]

30. Laudonnière, *L'Histoire notable,* fols. 43–44, pp. 95–96 (*Three Voyages,* 68–69).

31. Copy of a letter from after July 18 but before July 22, 1564, in Bennett's *Laudonnière and Fort Caroline,* 68. The apparent ease with which the reinforcements under Captain Bourdet found Fort Caroline suggests that Laudonnière may have had instructions to build a camp on the River of May.

32. Lowery, *Spanish Settlements,* II, 76.

During the fall, the colonists fell to quarreling among themselves as well as intervening in Indian wars in the hopes of gaining friends and, possibly, access to the silver mine farther up the River of May that they thought they had heard the Indians refer to in conversation. The arrival of reinforcements on September 4 allowed the dispatch of a party that eventually spent six months exploring the interior of peninsular Florida. On the ship that had brought the reinforcements, Laudonnière sent home some of the less disciplined men. Other restless souls remained, however, and their mutinies had the effect of revealing the existence of the French colony to the Spaniards.

Three mutinies occurred among the French at Fort Caroline over the winter of 1564–1565. In the first, on September 20, thirteen men stole one of the barks and sailed south. Off eastern Cuba they captured a small coastal vessel larger than their own and raided a town. They then fell on hard times and eventually were captured near Havana. Shortly after the first desertion, two Flemish carpenters who had come with the September reinforcements stole the remaining boat. Laudonnière soon had other boats under construction. Two of those provided an opportunity for the third and largest mutiny. In late November, as the new barks were nearing completion, sixty-six men seized Laudonnière and others who resisted them. The mutineers extorted from him arms, passports, a pilot, and sailors. Dividing into two parties, they sailed on December 8, 1564.[33]

One bark, which lacked a pilot, spent the next two weeks in the Bahamas, eventually captured a Spanish coastal ship off Cape Saint Nicolas, and then sailed in the direction of Havana. The other bark, with the pilot, made directly for the coast of Cuba. There its crew captured a brigantine loaded with cassava biscuit. Most of the French got into the brigantine, which, accompanied by the bark, sailed to Jamaica, where the mutineers transferred to a caravel they captured. From there they went to Cape Tiburon, where, on January 16, 1565, they fought and captured a ship bound from Santo Domingo to Santiago de Cuba. In the fight, they killed Antón Núñez, secretary of the audiencia, who was on his way to Santiago on official business, as well as one of his servants. Putting back to Jamaica for supplies, the French fell into a trap laid by the governor there. The transcript of the

33. *Ibid.*, 79–81; Laudonnière, *L'Histoire notable*, fols. 60–66, pp. 116–24 (*Three Voyages*, 96–101).

interrogations of the men captured at Jamaica was soon on the way to Spain. Meanwhile, at Havana, Governor Mazariegos had captured eleven Frenchmen who had been in the first party of deserters. Using Rouffi as his interpreter, he interrogated them on December 22, 1564. On February 6, 1565, he sent the House of Trade three of the men and a record of what they and the others had told him.[34]

Back at Fort Caroline, conditions worsened during the winter. The French failed to maintain cordial relations with Saturiba or to profit from their overtures to Utina and other chiefs. Finally, in late January, 1565, Laudonnière sent Captain Thomas Vasseur and two boats to Port Royal Sound to find Audusta, as he called him, or Orista, as the Spaniards rendered his name (Edisto in English). That chief was delighted to be in contact again with the French. He sent them a load of maize and the news that Rouffi had been picked up—by the Spaniards, as Laudonnière later learned. Orista promised to supply more maize when his crop was in and offered the French a "large countryside" if they would come to live in his area.[35]

At the end of March, some of the men who had been in the party that had cruised between Cape Tiburon and Jamaica and who had escaped from the Jamaican trap in the bark the mutineers had taken from Fort Caroline in December, returned to the settlement and made peace with Laudonnière. By then the Indians had put in their spring plantings of maize and had dispersed into the woods to seek out roots, berries, and other late-winter food. The French managed to do fairly well until May, when their supplies ran extremely low. They had expected provisions from France in March, but those had not come.

Hunger led to desperation and a determination to build a boat large enough for the Atlantic crossing. Hunger also invited the Indians' exploitation of the French. Many demanded and got high prices, in European goods, for small amounts of food. Utina exacted help with his wars in exchange for food, but the French retaliated by capturing Utina. Eventually they returned him for a ransom consisting of a small amount of food. By early summer, the French found themselves

34. Deposition of Stefano de Rojomonte, Havana, January, 1565, AGI, PAT 19, R. 4, and Alberto Melenes, "Relación del suceso de la armada francesa" [March 1565], with Juan Rodriguez de Noriega to SM, Seville, March 29, 1565, AGI, IG 2004, fols. 287–289v, all translated in Bennett's *Laudonnière and Fort Caroline,* 97, 88. For general treatments, see Lyon, *The Enterprise of Florida,* 38–40, and Lowery, *Spanish Settlements,* I, 79–83.

35. Laudonnière, *L'Histoire notable,* fol. 75, p. 135 (*Three Voyages,* 113–14).

with little food and bad relations with all the neighboring Indian groups. Nor did the work on the boat proceed rapidly.[36]

John Hawkins arrived off the River of May on August 3. Martin Atinas, the leader of his landing party, was one of the survivors of Ribault's colony of 1562. He and the other men from that colony had been kept in England after English ships found them half dead at the end of their epic voyage across the Atlantic in a small open boat. Atinas had taken employ with Hawkins when the survivors from the colony, and Ribault as well, had been released in 1564. Laudonnière welcomed Hawkins. They soon got into discussions over the future of the French colony, with Hawkins offering to evacuate everyone to France. Laudonnière was uncertain, however, about the state of Franco-English relations and knew that the English had expressed considerable interest in a colony in La Florida in 1563–1564 and had held Ribault and others captive when they tried to leave for France after the Stukeley venture collapsed. Refusing the offer of evacuation, he asked if he might buy one of Hawkins' ships. The two men reached agreement on a price stated in artillery and powder, Laudonnière deciding to keep the silver from the Indians hidden lest the queen of England move to preempt the French claim in the hope of getting more. Hawkins also sold stores and fifty pairs of shoes and provided crews to take two Spanish prizes with loads of hides and sugar to France for sale. He left two Englishmen as hostages and was ready to sail a few days after he had arrived. Laudonnière completed his preparations to evacuate the colony over the next week. By August 15, the ships' departure awaited only good weather and a suitable conjunction of tides and winds.[37]

Favorable sailing conditions occurred on August 28. As two of the French ships were getting to sea, their lookouts spotted sails. An armed ship went to find out the nationality of the newcomers while the garrison stood to arms. The ship returned the next day with Jean Ribault and six longboats full of soldiers. By royal order from France, he relieved Laudonnière of his command.

During the next few days, Ribault brought three of his seven ships over the bar. The other four anchored off the coast. He landed colonists and stores and began work to restore the fort and build addi-

36. Laudonnière, *L'Histoire notable,* fols. 79v–91v, 93–93v, pp. 141–54, 157–58 (*Three Voyages,* 121–36, 140).

37. Laudonnière, *L'Histoire notable,* fols. 94v–97v, pp. 158–63 (*Three Voyages,* 141–46).

tional housing. Indian chiefs came to visit Ribault and to receive gifts. Then in the late afternoon of Tuesday, September 4, soldiers who had been walking on the beach near the mouth of the River of May reported that six ships had come up the coast from the South and were making for Ribault's four. A storm obscured the view from land for a number of hours, but when it cleared, Ribault saw that his ships had slipped their anchor cables and were sailing south, with the other ships following.[38] The Spaniards had arrived to challenge the French colony.

The story of the Spanish response to Ribault's colony has been told many times, most recently and fully by Eugene Lyon in his award-winning *The Enterprise of Florida: Pedro Menéndez de Avilés and the Spanish Conquest of 1565–1568.* Only the barest of details are necessary here.

Vázquez de Ayllón the Younger was already at Santo Domingo when the first news of the Laudonnière expedition reached Spain. The breakup of Ayllón's expedition did not become known until at least late September, 1564. On the other hand, Gayón, the French column, and Manrique de Rojas' report on his expedition to the Point of Santa Elena were in Seville by September 24, 1564.[39] Later in the fall, Spain received news of John Hawkins' second expedition, which some informants said was bound for La Florida as well as the Caribbean.

Therefore it is probable that discussions took place that fall about the apparent continued French and English interest in the Point of Santa Elena and about what the Spaniards should do concerning it in view of Vázquez de Ayllón's failure, but so far no documentation of such discussions has come to light. It is also possible that officials in Seville and Madrid judged the evidence of imminent French and English expeditions to La Florida to be weak or planted to hide preparations for raids on Spanish shipping, as the Spanish ambassador in Paris believed. If that was so, the silence of the documents is not puzzling.

With the coming of the year 1565, the Spanish ambassador in France sent word that ships were being prepared in the French chan-

38. Laudonnière, *L'Histoire notable,* fols. 99–100, 104v–105, pp. 165–67, 171–73 (*Three Voyages,* 149–51, 157–58).

39. AGI, IG 2002, fol. 188.

nel ports, some thought to go to La Florida though in his opinion really to attack Spanish commerce.[40]

This information probably got to Madrid about mid-February. Not many days before, on January 24, 1565, the Council of the Indies had rendered its final judgment on the appeal of Menéndez de Avilés of its sentences in a case involving his conduct as captain general of the convoy of 1562–1563. In the final judgment, he was found guilty of six of the original fourteen charges, fined a thousand ducats, and exiled from office in the American empire for one year. He had earlier received a fine of a hundred pesos de oro for smuggling two bars of unregistered silver. Offsetting the fines, however, were revenues awarded to him in his dispute with the Consulado of Seville over the expenses of ships of his that his own order had pressed into duty as escorts for the convoy. A few additional matters in these cases were resolved in the sentences that the council issued on February 3, 1565.[41] On the whole, Menéndez came through with only minor penalties. Still, the council made the point that even he was not exempt from the law and that future captains general of the convoys would be held to account.

With the conclusion of the suits and criminal proceedings, Menéndez de Avilés needed to find a way to restore himself to royal favor and to rebuild his fortunes and reputation. In the eighteen months that he had been in and out of various jails during the case and its appeals, he had lost two of his three ships, and his son, Juan, had disappeared at sea while trying to bring a convoy to Spain in the late summer. Menéndez de Avilés' pride and pretensions had been laid low. Providentially, an opportunity for him to regain his position and fortune presented itself. Sometime in February, Philip II asked him to summarize what was known about La Florida, to assess the French threat to occupy part of it, and to suggest what could be done to prevent that.[42]

In reply, Menéndez repeated the by then well known news of Díaz Mimoso's plans as he had heard them and the rumors that the English too were intending to go to the coast of La Florida. (The story about

40. Spain, *Negociaciones*, VII, 76.

41. Lyon, *The Enterprise of Florida*, 26–37 *passim*, 41.

42. "Memorial de Pero Menéndez de Avilés respecto a las medidas que sería conveniente tomar para la segura posesión de la Florida y evitar que los franceses e ingleses pudieran causar perturbación en aquellos dominios" [February, 1565 (?)], AGI, PAT 19; and in Eugenio Ruidiaz y Caravía's *La Florida: Su conquista y colonización por Pedro Menéndez de Avilés* (2 vols.; Madrid, 1893), II, 320–26.

the English was an echo of the Ribault-Stukeley venture of 1563 and of talk about Hawkins' possible plans for 1564–1565.) Menéndez added the recently received information that five English galleons—Hawkins' fleet—had put into Ferrol, Galicia, in December. That seemed to confirm that some sort of Anglo-French activity was under way in La Florida.

Settlement in La Florida by Spain's enemies presented three possible dangers, Menéndez wrote. Spain's foes, once settled, could use galleys or other light warships to attack the convoys and other shipping coming from the Caribbean by way of the Bahama Channel. Second, the activities of Jacques de Sores, which Menéndez placed in 1553, showed that there was a danger to Spanish possession of the Antilles. According to him, Sores had freed slaves when he attacked Margarita, Cabo de la Vela, La Burburata, Santa Marta, Cartagena, Santiago de Cuba, and Havana, and with their help he and fifty-three men had been able to capture all of those places. He was convinced, he said, that the "design of those who went to settle in La Florida is to be lords of those islands and impede the commerce of the Indies." Third, a danger arose from the possibility that the French or English in La Florida would gain control of the arm of the sea that Menéndez, as early as 1554, had heard lay five hundred leagues north of Mexico and connected with Newfoundland and the Pacific Ocean. From that body of water they could have commerce with the Orient and also threaten the mines of New Spain.

Menéndez deemed it essential to prevent reinforcement of any settlement that might have taken root in La Florida during the previous summer. Should the enemy be reinforced, Menéndez said, he would establish himself so strongly with the Indians that the Spaniards would have trouble winning them over later even if they expelled the French. The reason for this, he thought, was that the French and English were "Lutherans" and they and the Indians shared "almost one law." Furthermore, with the French dominant in Newfoundland, to which they sent two thousand ships a year (a clear exaggeration of their fishing activities!), they were well placed to support a colony in the new area, especially since it was close to France and England and could grow, so he had heard, sugarcane and cattle, from which the French could derive hides and wool, both in short supply at home.

If there were no enemies to drive out, Menéndez said, five hundred men sailing in one or two galleons and a number of small ships—

chalupas and zabras, all with oars—could create Spanish settlements at two or three places between the Point of Santa Elena and Newfoundland. With supplies for a year, the expedition would cost about eighty thousand ducats or somewhat more. Among the five hundred should be a hundred craftsmen with their tools and with weapons, twelve friars, four Jesuits, and twelve *niños de la doctrina* (orphans trained to teach the catechism). The commander should go directly to the Point of Santa Elena and from there explore northward. He should investigate every entrance and port and scout the land around it to a depth of four or five leagues. Ports he found to possess suitable hinterlands should be settled with as many persons as possible.

Such an expedition could best be mounted from Spain, Menéndez thought. Goods cost too much in the Indies, and ships of the right sort were not available there. Further, raising such an expedition in the Indies would occasion delays, he felt, with the resulting danger that the enemy might become established.

Menéndez' memorandum is remarkable for a number of its ideas. First, it follows a recommendation of the Villafañe group in Mexico City in 1562. It will be recalled that the recommendation then was for exploration of the coast northward from 35° north by expeditions from Spain. Menéndez changed the beginning point to the Point of Santa Elena, whose importance to Philip II's conception of North America he probably knew better than the Mexicans did. Second, like the Mexicans and most Spaniards after Vázquez de Ayllón the Elder, Menéndez seemed to write off the coast below the Point of Santa Elena. On the other hand, his stress on cattle and sugar production in areas north of 32° north suggests that he believed in the idea of comparable climates at comparable latitudes; cattle and sugar were among the products of Andalucia.

Third, Menéndez' memorandum contains the first clear evidence that he believed in Giovanni da Verrazzano's concept of North America. He based his belief on the testimony a Frenchman offered about having ascended a river—likely the Saint Lawrence—four hundred leagues and then portaged a fourth of a league to another "arm of the sea," on which he and some companions traveled three hundred leagues to large Indian settlements. Viceroy Luís de Velasco was said to have reported the same man's testimony but to have stated the distances as two hundred leagues for each "arm." Later, Menéndez would enlarge on this theory of North American geography, but even in March, 1565, he could write to the general of the Jesuits, Francisco de Borgia, saying that La Florida was near New Spain, Tartary and China, and the Spice Islands, being either a continent joined to the first two or separated from them by an arm of the sea along which it would be possible to communicate between them and La Florida.[43]

Also of note is the memorandum's inclusion of the idea that control of the Antilles and La Florida would give an enemy control over commerce in the Caribbean. That idea, like others, seems not to have been original with Menéndez, but it was later developed by him into a strategy for dealing with the problem of illegal traders and commerce raiders.[44]

Menéndez seems to have had his facts wrong in several instances. Sores sailed in 1555 and seems to have had no significant help from slaves or free persons of color in any of his attacks. In addition, it will be recalled, Menéndez exaggerated the number of French fishing ships sailing to Newfoundland and inaccurately related the French voyage on the Saint Lawrence.

Such inaccuracies aside, the memorandum summarizes the geographic conceptions Menéndez and others held at the time and shows that the Spaniards were not certain there was a French or Anglo-French colony on the Atlantic coast of North America. It also makes plain that they still thought the Point of Santa Elena was an important place, with potential for settlement. And it makes manifest that the Spaniards were aware, thanks to Villafañe and Antonio Velázquez, that good land and good ports might lie north of Santa Elena. The question was whether Philip II wanted to invest eighty thousand ducats in a new scouting and settlement expedition or whether he could persuade someone, like Menéndez de Avilés, to undertake it without royal support. It was possible to persuade Menéndez, in part because there were rumors that his son, Juan, might have been shipwrecked in North America.

After some bargaining, Menéndez de Avilés signed a contract with Dr. Juan Vázquez de Arce, acting for Philip II, on March 15, 1565. In general outline, it provided for an expedition similar in size and equipment to what Menéndez had described in his memorandum. During the year beginning May 31, 1565, Menéndez was to explore the Atlantic face of North America and select a site for his first

43. Zubillaga, *Monumenta Antiquae Floridae,* 1–2. For Velasco's report, see Antonio Sotelo de Betanzos to SM, Mexico City, June 5, 1566, AGI, MEX 168.

44. Paul E. Hoffman, "The Narrow Waters Strategies of Pedro Menéndez," *Florida Historical Quarterly,* XLV (1966), 12–17, and Hoffman, *The Spanish Crown,* 129–31.

settlement. By the end of three years, he was to have five hundred settlers—including a hundred farmers and two hundred married men—established in at least two towns, each adequately fortified to protect the residents against Indian and European attack. In addition, he was to see that as many as five hundred slaves were imported, primarily for the sugar works he thought feasible for the region. As for the Indians, the contract fails to say whether Menéndez could grant encomiendas but simply enjoins good treatment and refers to the laws of the empire. Those laws allowed grants of encomiendas for up to three lives. Apparently the expectation was that missions would draw the Indians into obedience to the Spaniards; only when that occurred would a decision be made about encomiendas. Like earlier contracts for La Florida, this one presupposed that the Spaniards would establish their own communities in North America and then through missions, example, and trade draw the Indians under their control rather than conquer them by military force, as they had done elsewhere in the Americas.

To help meet the expenses of the expedition, Philip II offered a fifteen-thousand-ducat bonus if the fleet sailed by May 31. Certain privileges involving trade outside the convoy system were probably the most valuable part of the contract for Menéndez and potential financiers of his expedition. On a personal level, he received various titles and the right to select a square of land twenty-five leagues on a side. Comparison with the privileges of earlier Florida explorers and adelantados underscores that Menéndez' contract was not much different from theirs in these matters.[45]

Menéndez was on his way to Asturias to enlist relatives and capital when Governor Mazariegos' letter of February 8, 1565, arrived in Seville, together with three of the Frenchmen captured off Havana. Forwarded from Seville on March 26, the letter and its news that the French had settled "at the Point of Santa Elena" arrived in Madrid on March 30.[46]

This news changed the dimensions of Menéndez' task and led to his immediate recall to court and the revision of his contract, to

45. Lyon, *The Enterprise of Florida,* 52–53, 54–55, Appendix 2.

46. House of Trade to king, March 26, 1565, AGI, CT 5167 (Stetson). Mazariegos' letter of February 8 has not been found, but its content is summarized in another letter from him to the king, April 7, 1565, AGI, SD 115, fols. 139–139v. The latitude Mazariegos gives, 28½° north, and the deposition of Stefano de Rojomonte at Havana in January, 1565 (AGI, PAT 19, R. 4 [or 14 (?)]), make it clear that the French were not at the point but well to the south of it.

provide for royal troops. The Frenchmen from Havana said that the colonists expected reinforcements of several hundred men that spring, and their statements fitted with the diplomatic report that a new expedition was under preparation in the channel ports. What is more, although Mazariegos and the House of Trade referred to the site of the French settlement as the Point of Santa Elena, the latitude given in depositions at Havana and Seville made it clear that the French were in fact much closer to the mouth of the Bahama Channel, at a cited latitude of 29½° north. Any doubt on the question of location was put to rest by Robert Meleneche's deposition in Seville, which clearly stated that the French were not at the Point of Santa Elena, where their settlement in 1562 had been. Juan Rodriguez de Noriega, the interrogator, commented that "that Frenchman said that the entire [location of the 1564 settlement] is flooded because it is much too low, but that it is a healthful region. I certainly think that the Cape of Santa Elena, where they settled first, is much better and [has] more favorable surroundings [for settlement] because it is not so flooded, although he said that where they settled [in 1562], they found no freshwater river such as [the Saint Johns]."[47]

Additional reports of French reinforcements caused the Spanish ambassador in France to send an agent to the channel ports to find out what was going on. The agent eventually returned with details of the Ribault reinforcement and its sailing. He learned of other expeditions making up; as a result, Philip II ordered an expedition under Sancho de Archiniega to reinforce Menéndez and provide troops to garrison the Antilles against an anticipated French attack in 1566 or 1567.[48]

Menéndez made it to sea on June 29. Owing to a series of mischances, including a tropical storm that scattered and damaged his fleet, he arrived on the coast of Florida on August 28 with only five ships—four from his fleet and one picked up at Puerto Rico—and about eight hundred men, five hundred of them soldiers with varying degrees of skill in using their weapons. The contingents of men and the animals and supplies Philip II had ordered Santo Domingo and Cuba to furnish were not available. Thus Menéndez de Avilés met the French on approximately equal terms, with about five hundred sol-

47. "Relación del suceso de la armada frances . . . " [March, 1565], enclosed with Juan Rodriguez de Noriega to SM, Seville, March 29, 1565, AGI, IG 2004, fols. 287–289v (translation corrected by the present author from that in Bennett's *Laudonnière and Fort Caroline*, 93).

48. Lyon, *The Enterprise of Florida*, 59–60, 109, 147.

diers, two hundred seamen, and perhaps a hundred other persons on each side. The French under Ribault had the advantage of faster ships than those Menéndez commanded, but the weather and Menéndez' luck and determination overcame that advantage.

Menéndez' luck came into play first. Most of the soldiers in Ribault's fleet were caught ashore on September 4, when the Spaniards approached the larger French ships off the mouth of the River of May. Without soldiers on board, the French ships could not give battle. When the French soldiers were again aboard Ribault's ships, his attack on the Spanish fleet at anchor off Saint Augustine Bar was frustrated by a sudden change of weather, a storm that blew Ribault to sea and eventually down the coast to wreck near Cape Canaveral. That storm led Menéndez to send his great galleon, *San Pelayo*, to sea, where it eventually disappeared, apparently hijacked to Denmark by some English prisoners he had picked up in Puerto Rico. The same storm provided the adelantado with cover for his march overland from Saint Augustine to attack and capture Fort Caroline. On that occasion, his determination carried the day for the Spanish cause.

The rest of the confrontation between the Spaniards and the French on the coast of Florida in the fall of 1565, including the massacre of the French at Matanzas Inlet, was a sort of anticlimax. By mid-November, 1565, Menéndez de Avilés had completely destroyed the French in Florida, sparing only a few Catholics and musicians.[49] Forty or so others managed to escape from Fort Caroline and make it back to a France newly torn by religious strife. In the test of power and international claims, the Spaniards had won.

49. *Ibid.*, 71–129. Writers then and since have debated the justice of Menéndez' execution of his prisoners. The official Spanish position was that they were pirates as well as heretics, and as such merited no mercy. Indeed, it had been standard practice in times of peace to execute seamen engaged in attacks on Spanish ships and possessions after putting them to a summary trial, regardless of what legal title they claimed under letters of reprisal. The execution of the French in Florida had been recommended by Juan Rodriguez de Noriega as early as the end of March, 1565 (AGI, IG 2004, fols. 289–289v). In justifying the action to the French, Philip II had his ambassador say that Ribault was a pirate sent by Admiral Coligny, and a heretic, and that Menéndez had lacked supplies and ships to send them to France (Spain, *Negociación*, VIII, 246–50). It is clear, however, that the Spaniards were uneasy about what they had done, because they knew, although they denied it, that Ribault had a commission from the king of France. As royal agents, Ribault and his men were not pirates outside the protection of the law, even Spanish law.

X

Theories, Hopes, and Realities: Spanish Florida, 1565–1572

The founding of Saint Augustine and the capture of Fort Caroline established Spanish sovereignty in La Florida under the doctrine of effective occupation. Although the extension and consolidation of the occupation by Spain after 1565 took nearly a decade, by the time Pedro Menéndez de Avilés left La Florida in 1572, the results of his labors, and of his failures, were clear. Menéndez' interest in the Bahía de Santa María and the supposed way to the Orient had withered and then disappeared altogether with the destruction in 1571 of the mission he had allowed the Jesuits to found in 1570 at Don Luís de Velasco's land on the shore of the bay. Captain Juan Pardo's efforts to pioneer a land route to the mines of northern Mexico and to establish Spanish control over the Indians of the interior of the Southeast had failed, although Pardo did find Xapira's "terrestrial gems": quartz crystals. The numerous garrisons and missions Menéndez set up in southern Florida during 1565 and 1566 had all been withdrawn in the face of, or had fallen victim to, Indian hostility to uninvited guests. Only Saint Augustine and Santa Elena remained as Spanish settlements. Located on the "useless" coast, they required institutionalized support from the royal treasuries of Tierra Firme and New Spain. Although Menéndez had not abandoned his plans to establish Spanish farmers and his own landed estate at and inland from Santa Elena, by 1572 he had exhausted his own and his supporters' resources and had fallen back on exploitation of his offices in the royal Indies Fleet and in Cuba and of the Florida payroll (*situado*) in order to make a living and gather resources to invest in the colonization of La Florida. The hard realities of the limited resources of the coastal environment had gradually destroyed the grand schemes that Menéndez had built on the basis of the Chicora and Verrazzano legends. He did not have the opportunity between 1572 and his death in 1574 to apply the hard-won lessons of 1565–1572 to building a colonial empire in the

Southeast in a way that would have prevented later French and English trading and colonization along the coast.

Among what was captured at Fort Caroline on the dreary, rain-drenched September morning of its fall were Laudonnière's and some of Ribault's books and papers. The Spaniards promptly burned the religious books.[1] The remaining books and papers probably contained at least some geographical information about the Southeast, including what the French had learned, or thought they had learned, from their conversations with the Indians. That, at least, is the inference one can draw from Menéndez de Avilés' letters to Philip II of October 15 and December 25, 1565.[2] In them he displays a far more detailed knowledge of the supposed cross-Florida route and of the supposed arm of the sea to the west of the Bahía de Santa María than he had nine months earlier. Only a part of his new information is likely to have come from the prisoners he took at Fort Caroline. They would have known of the previous winter's explorations and would have acquired some of the general ideas about the geography of North America that the anonymous letter writer of the fall of 1564 displayed, but they are unlikely to have commanded the sort of detail Menéndez put into the letters in question.

The letters of October 15 and December 25 constitute a summary of what Menéndez believed about the geography and potential of North America, of what he hoped to achieve, and of the order in which he aimed to create an empire in the Southeast. Both letters, but especially that of October 15, are also cleverly constructed pleas for money, bidding the king to bear his part in occupying the Southeast and claiming its promise. Descriptions of the strategic importance and economic potential of the region alternate with discussions of the means that turning the region's promise into reality would require and that Menéndez largely lacked because of both the scattering of his fleet during the midpassage storm and the loss of many of the supplies he had counted on using to fulfill his part of the contract.

1. Menéndez to crown [November, 1569 (?)], in Archivo del Instituto de Valencia de Don Juan, Envio 25, H, No. 162 (noting the capture of some of Ribault's papers at Fort Caroline [information courtesy of Eugene Lyon]). Bartolomé Barrientos notes that the Spaniards found six boxes of bound books, "all of them heretical" (*Pedro Menéndez de Avilés, Founder of Florida,* trans. Anthony Kerrigan [Gainesville, Fla., 1965], 55 [translation], 57 [Spanish text]).

2. Pedro Menéndez de Avilés to Philip II, Saint Augustine, October 15, 1565, Havana, December 25, 1565, January 30, 1566, in Ruidiaz, *La Florida,* II, 84–105, 127–41, 142–54 respectively. Cited hereafter as "Menéndez, October 15, p. . . ."

Menéndez began the letter of October 15 before he knew of Ribault's shipwreck and before he moved to intercept Ribault on his march up the coast toward Fort Caroline. After an account of his victory, he explained that he had garrisoned Saint Augustine and San Mateo (as the Spaniards renamed the French Fort Caroline) with three hundred soldiers each and was planning to go to Havana to gather the rest of his expedition and seek supplies for the men he was leaving in Florida. He then intended to take five hundred soldiers and a hundred seamen in small boats, including the two he had captured from the French, and head north to the Point of Santa Elena and the Bahía de Santa María. At Santa Elena, he planned to select the best of the three ports, build a fort, and leave a three-hundred-man garrison. With the other two hundred soldiers, he meant to pass up the coast to the Bahía de Santa María, at 37° north. That was the land of Don Luís ("el indio que esta en Mexico"). There he expected to build a second fort and leave the two hundred men.

The Bahía de Santa María (the Chesapeake Bay) was, he wrote, the "key to the defense [*fortificación*] of these lands."[3] North of the bay, settlement should not take place, he thought, because eighty leagues inland and north there was a mountain range at whose western foot was an arm of the sea going to Newfoundland that was navigable for the entire distance of six hundred leagues. Half a league beyond the southwestern end of that arm of the sea was another "arm of salt water" that ran west-northwestward to, many believed, the Pacific Ocean. In his December 25 letter, he added that this arm of the sea was over five hundred leagues long, beginning at 42° north and stretching northwestward to 48° north. The western outlet, he concluded, could not be more than a hundred leagues from the Pacific Ocean, or even China itself.[4] The Indians who lived near the body of water that ran southwestward from Newfoundland killed many of the "cows of New Spain [*i.e.*, bison] that Francisco Vázquez Coronado found on those plains" and carried their hides to Newfoundland to trade with the French. In the last two years, Menéndez affirmed, French ships from La Rochele had carried over two thousand of the

3. Menéndez, October 15, p. 94.

4. Menéndez, December 25, p. 131, January 30, p. 151. His description sounds as if he had a copy of the Münster printed map in front of him, for it shows those latitudes. In his letter of January 30, 1566, he said that he had discussed the supposed strait with Father Andrés de Urdaneta, long a vocal believer in its existence. He promised to tell Philip II more about how it might be explored once he returned to Spain the following winter.

hides to Europe. The French, by using their ships' boats, could easily ascend the arm of the sea from Newfoundland and so reach the land of Don Luís. Besides, the foot of the mountains where that waterway ended was but four hundred leagues from the mines of San Martín and New Galicia. All the French would need to do to gain the mines would be to place their "frontiers" at the foot of the mountains and win control over the Bahama Channel. That done, they could conquer the mines of New Spain at their leisure.

On the other hand, if Philip II controlled that area, he could become master of Newfoundland by using galleys to patrol along that arm of the sea and collect tribute from all who wished to fish. In addition, he would control a possible way to the Orient that came out on the Pacific "near China," and so provide a means for "illumining" the people there, that is, for bringing them the Christian gospel, as well as a means for giving the Spaniards access to the trade of the Moluccas (the Spice Islands).[5]

From the strategic importance of the Bahía de Santa María, Menéndez turned to the problems he faced in carrying out his design: men and supplies. Although Philip II had authorized him to take five hundred soldiers paid by the crown when he left Seville, considerations of time had made him sail with only three hundred and supplies for a year. Many of the provisions had gone bad or he had had to throw them overboard to lighten the ships during the hurricane that struck the fleet in the Atlantic. Because he had only enough to last five months more, he asked Philip II to send out the other two hundred soldiers, with supplies. He assured the king that, against his own account, he was ordering Pedro del Castillo, his agent and one of his financial backers at Cádiz, to send three hundred soldiers and a year's food for them and the eight hundred other persons he claimed were with him in Florida and Havana. Once the three hundred men he had requested arrived—and that would be in April, 1566—he would have brought more than a thousand people to Florida, he pointed out, instead of the five hundred his contract committed him to.

That thought led Menéndez to the next part of his design: his plan to place a settlement of two hundred persons on the Bay of Juan Ponce, whence contact would be possible with Coosa as well as the garrisons already established. Contact, he said in the letter of December 25 and another of January 30, would be easy because it was fifty leagues by land

5. Menéndez, October 15, pp. 94–95.

across the peninsula and because the River of San Mateo (the Saint Johns) ran across Florida to near the Bay of Juan Ponce, if not to it.[6] He had picked up the idea about the River of San Mateo from the French at Fort Caroline and, possibly, verified it by conversations with Indians from northeast Florida.

He went on to assert that once the Spaniards settled the Bay of Juan Ponce, they could open the road to the mines of northern New Spain. Apparently believing that the Sierra Madre Oriental—the eastern range of mountains that defines the central Mexican Plateau and becomes the front range of the Rockies—runs northeastward to become the mountains he knew were north of Coosa, he told his king that the road from Zacatecas to the ports of Florida was but three hundred leagues, or about 940 nautical miles, a mere hundred leagues farther than to San Juan de Ulua. He confidently predicted that within a few years the miners would prefer to ship overland to the Atlantic coastal ports rather than risk the sea voyage through the Gulf of Mexico.

Next, he extolled the agricultural potential of the Southeast, noting the possibilities for sugar, vines, cattle, hemp, naval stores and boards, salt, wheat, rice, pearls (from the rivers near Santa Elena), and silk, as well as "all sorts of fruits."

Having whetted the king's appetite, as he must have hoped, Menéndez turned to the problem of money, specifically the thirty thousand ducats he claimed he needed to finance the three hundred men and the supplies he was ordering from Cádiz. In an apparent reference to the settlement of the lawsuits of 1563–1564, he suggested that Philip II could help him meet his costs by ordering payment for certain freights and other items due him.

On October 10, the drafting of Menéndez' letter was interrupted at this point by news that Fort San Mateo had burned, with all the supplies in it, and that Jean Ribault had arrived at Matanzas Inlet with 150 men. When Menéndez resumed his letter, he told Philip II that he had killed Ribault and some seventy of his men. (Most of the rest had fled south.) Only about 150 Frenchmen remained at large, and Menéndez supposed that his Indian friends and a lack of supplies would soon destroy them. According to Menéndez, if the forty or so who escaped from Fort Caroline in two boats reached France, they would at least not be able to tell of Ribault's fate. It was Menéndez'

6. Menéndez, December 25, p. 133, January 30, p. 143.

opinion that the killing should be kept secret as long as possible so that the French, thinking Ribault safely established, would not bother to reinforce him.

Menéndez then explained that with the flight of the French he had an even better opportunity to entrench Spanish power on the Atlantic coast—if the king only saw that he got the men and supplies he needed. He promised that in the future La Florida would sustain itself at little cost and return large revenues to the royal treasury. Indeed, it would "be worth more to Spain than New Spain or even Peru." On that note, he closed the letter and sent it off to Spain in the hands of Diego Flores de Valdés, a trusted lieutenant. Menéndez then set out for Havana, pausing along the way to capture a last group of Ribault's men and set up a garrison among the Ais Indians who lived near Saint Lucy Inlet.[7]

Menéndez' remarkable letter shows that he, like his predecessors, succumbed to the verdant charm of the Atlantic coast and to the legend of a new Andalucia that Ayllón the Elder had woven and to which Hernando de Soto's expedition had contributed by finding the pearl kingdom and Coosa. To that Spanish legend, Menéndez added what Antonio Velázquez and Don Luís had recounted about the area of the Bahía de Santa María. And he mixed the legendary geography of Giovanni da Verrazzano with an authentic report from a Frenchman who had ascended the Saint Lawrence River to a portage that gave access to what he took to be another branch of the oceans, but that was one of the Great Lakes. Menéndez had a heady, if partially mistaken, vision of the geography and potential of North America, especially of the Southeast.

His letter suggests that he had in mind to seize the real economic prizes for himself while leaving the king to support garrisons in strategic but possibly unprofitable spots. His letter thus foreshadows his unwillingness to try to colonize the Bahía de Santa María with large numbers of people. Menéndez was to have three hundred men sent on his account, the number he planned to put at Santa Elena. Two hundred soldiers, the number he was to leave at the Bahía de Santa María, were to be sent on the king's account. The numbers, and what is known of later events, suggest that even this early, Menéndez was aiming to put *his* men at what he, and all his contemporaries except possibly Antonio Velázquez and Ayllón the Younger, regarded as the real prize: the

7. Menéndez, December 25, p. 133.

Point of Santa Elena. From there he would have access to the pearls of Cofitachequi and a way inland to Coosa. Moreover, he knew that of the three ports near the point (he apparently counted the Savannah River or at least Calibogue Sound as the first of the three), one (the middle one, Port Royal Sound) had depths of six fathoms, making it the best along the entire coast south of the Bahía de Santa María. The king would be left to supply garrisons at the strategic forts on the Bahama Channel (Saint Augustine and San Mateo) and at the Bahía de Santa María. The channel forts were on a part of the coast long thought useless and incapable of supporting colonies; the potentials of the bay area seem not to have been well delineated and consequently were not appreciated by Menéndez. In any case, the Bahía de Santa María was in an area of potential international conflict. Thus it was suitable for the king to bear the costs.

Less clear in the October letter was how many of the men going to the Bay of Juan Ponce were to be the adelantado's and how many the king's, but by implication, they were all to be Menéndez'. His December letter explicitly says that, and shows that his plan was to put settler-farmers there along with some missionaries.[8] Philip II's three hundred soldiers in La Florida were tied down in garrison duty at Saint Augustine and San Mateo. The arrangement was consistent with Menéndez' goal of grabbing the richer pickings, among which a route from the Bay of Juan Ponce across Florida and access to Coosa clearly figured.

Menéndez arrived at Havana on November 13, 1565. The adelantado remained there until mid-February, 1566, except for a brief voyage eastward along the northern coast of Cuba, from November 30 to possibly December 10, in search of his lieutenant Esteban de las Alas and corsairs whose capture would yield booty. What he learned and what happened during his sojourn in Cuba worked changes in his plans and further prefigured the extent of his ultimate achievements.

What he learned falls under three headings. First, it became apparent that a major part of the supplies he and his associates and backers had provided for the conquest had been lost, as had many of the supplies the king had sent. Ships that went seeking his great galleon, *San Pelayo,* found no trace of it in the Antilles. It had been carrying a large quantity of goods; some belonged to the king but most belonged

8. Lyon, *The Enterprise of Florida,* 129–30. The later history of this garrison is told on pp. 139–41, 150. Only 75 of the original 250 men survived.

to Menéndez de Avilés. In addition, provisions coming from Asturias as part of his private venture sank in a storm north of Cuba. And a supply and reinforcement expedition from Santo Domingo ended wrecked off northern Cuba. Two captures that his lieutenants Esteban de las Alas and Pedro Menéndez Marqués made in the Antilles and a third that the *Santa Catalina,* the flagship of the New Spain convoy of 1565, made near Havana did not compensate for the losses, although they were worth at least eighteen thousand ducats, which Menéndez planned to apply to the purchase of some replacement goods.[9]

Second, Menéndez received news during his stay at Havana that Philip II was sending a fleet with as many as 1,500 men, and supplies for them for a year. Reports from the Caribbean, France, and England in the spring and summer of 1565 had suggested that a large force was preparing to reinforce France's presence in La Florida and to attack the Antilles, as Menéndez had predicted in his memorandum of February, 1565, and as he had stated on the basis of prisoner interrogations in his letters of October 15 and December 5.[10] Learning of Philip II's fleet from dispatches that he intercepted on their way to the audiencia of Santo Domingo and officials in Cuba, Menéndez did not know at first what the king had in mind, but it was clear that many of the men would be needed at the garrisons he had already established in Florida as well as at those he hoped to create in the spring of 1566. Too, the coming of the fleet meant that in the spring of 1566 he would have to devote his energies to preparing the La Florida posts to accommodate the new men, to receiving them, and then to doing whatever the king might order. Menéndez decided that the expedition of

9. *Ibid.,* 132–33, 138.

10. Diego de Mazariegos to SM, Havana, April 7, 1565, AGI, SD 115, fols. 139–139v (which reported that French deserters from Fort Caroline said that ships had been sent to France to bring five hundred more men [Ribault's fleet?]); Guzmán de Silva to SM, London, June 25, 1565, in Great Britain, Public Records Office, *Calendar of Letters and State Papers Relating to English Affairs Preserved Principally in the Archives of Simancas, Elizabeth, 1558–1603,* ed. Martin A. S. Hume (4 vols.; 1892–96; rpr. Nendeln, 1971), I, 442 (reporting eight French ships with twelve hundred men off the English coast). The eight ships were from the expedition of Peyrot de Monluc, which eventually numbered twenty-three French and English ships and attacked Funchal, Madeira, on October 3, 1566. Monluc's death from a wound he suffered in the attack caused the expedition to break up. Its objectives were not disclosed at the time but seem to have been African rather than American. Still, the expedition and the impossibility of discovering its objectives alarmed the Spaniards (Roncière, *Histoire de la marine,* IV, 83–90).

Sancho de Archiniega, when it came, would be both a help with and a diversion from his own plans.

Third, Menéndez obtained information during his time in Havana which had to do with the supposed strait in North America. As it happened, ships from Miguel Lopez Legazpi's expedition had successfully returned from the Philippine Islands to New Spain by the northern great-circle route. Among the members of that expedition who passed through Havana on their way to Spain to report on what the voyage had achieved was Father Andrés de Urdaneta, an Augustinian. Recognized as *the* Spanish authority on the geography of the Pacific Ocean, Urdaneta was the perfect man for Menéndez to consult about the supposed geography of North America.[11]

Some idea of what the friar told the adelantado can be gleaned from the comments one of Urdaneta's companions from the expedition made years later. He recalled that Urdaneta had said that the Strait of Anian was "narrow" and at the latitude of 51° north.[12] Urdaneta's characterization of the strait certainly did not match the understanding Menéndez had of it. His "arm of the sea"—based quite clearly on the cartographic tradition from Verrazzano—was broad and came out to the Pacific Ocean at 48° north.

Whatever Urdaneta told Menéndez, it was like a cold shower to his enthusiasm. Whereas in October and December, Menéndez had evinced great interest in the Bahía de Santa María and had expressed concern that the French might occupy an area of such strategic importance before he could, at the end of January he spoke of the bay with something approaching indifference. In his letter to Philip II of January

11. Urdaneta had first gone to the Far East in 1525 with Loaysa's expedition. He had remained in the Moluccas until 1536, when he returned to Europe by way of Lisbon. His reports of 1537 helped clarify the question of Spanish rights under the papal donation. When he arrived in New Spain, he was enlisted to assist Pedro de Alvarado in an expedition to explore further and possibly to conquer the islands of the western Pacific. After Alvarado's death, in 1541, the expedition dissolved, however. Urdaneta decided in 1553 to take the habit of Saint Augustine and lived as a friar until the king sought his participation in the Legazpi expedition of 1559. Although he was authorized to return to the Philippines in 1567, he died in Spain on June 3, 1568, at the age of seventy (*DIU*, II, 98–99*n*2). Urdaneta's reputation is attested by a letter dated May 29 and June 1, 1565, to Philip II from those who remained in the Philippines: "Aver alumbrado, asi en lo espiritual como en lo temporal, en todo lo que en este viaje se ha ofrecido, por no venir en el armada persona que nos diese lumbre, sino fue la suya" (*DII*, XIII, 529).

12. Fray Andrés de Aguirre to archbishop of Mexico [Mexico City (?), 1583 (?)], in *DII*, XIII, 546.

30, 1566, he said, "If I can, I will send a captain with the Indian [Don Luís de Velasco] to the Bahía de Santa María so that [the captain] can see this arm of the sea with [his own] eyes, so that Your Majesty may provide what is most suitable to your royal service in this matter."[13] Menéndez himself no longer planned to go to the bay or establish a garrison there during the coming spring and summer. He had already, in his more enthusiastic moments the previous spring and fall, sent for Don Luís.[14] It remained to be seen if he would have a ship and men to spare to follow up on his first step toward the Bahía de Santa María.

The more significant events of his stay at Havana had to do with his reaction to the supply situation he discovered upon his arrival. His immediate course was to send deputies to other parts of the Caribbean to organize shipments of meat and maize, to arrange loans, and to sell the plunder his lieutenants had taken. Some of what he did would have been inevitable even if the shipments from Spain had arrived intact, but much was dictated by the situation and involved opening up or drawing upon lines of credit that he might not otherwise have tapped so early in his venture. For example, he might not have put himself in debt to Juan de Hinestrosa, at Havana, had he had supplies.[15] He compromised the long-term financing of his venture even as he arranged the short-term means of supply. But those means of supply were important: without them, the La Florida garrisons might well have had to abandon their ground during the spring of 1566.

The sale of booty brought Menéndez into conflict with the governor of Cuba and led in the long run to a diverting of Menéndez' energies, although one less damaging than another that also grew from the idea of using prizes as a way of financing the Florida venture. The governor of Cuba, Diego Pardo Osorio, did not share Menéndez' enthusiasm for, nor believe his propaganda about, La Florida. Worse, Pardo Osorio seized the *Santa Catalina*'s prize when it entered port.

13. Pedro Menéndez de Avilés to SM, Havana, January 30, 1566, in Ruidiaz, *La Florida*, II, 151.

14. Pedro Menéndez de Avilés to SM, Seville, May 18, 1565 (requesting an order that Don Luís and "certain friars" who had been in Florida be sent to Havana), Pedro Menéndez de Avilés to SM, Matanzas, December 5, 1565, in Ruidiaz, *La Florida*, II, 65, 105–125 respectively; audiencia to SM, Mexico, March 28, 1566, AGI, MEX 68, Book, fols. 225v–226. The audiencia acknowledged receipt of a request from Menéndez that had come with a ship that docked on January 7, 1566; the audiencia's letter said that four Dominicans would accompany the convoy when it sailed in the spring.

15. These activities are ably described by Lyon in *The Enterprise of Florida*, 134–35, 138–39.

In challenging the governor's action, Menéndez maintained that the *Santa Catalina* was under his command by virtue of a royal order that her crew cooperate with him against the French. But Pardo Osorio refused to give up a haul worth twelve thousand ducats, and the suit that followed quickly developed into a clash of personalities and jurisdictions. Intensified by further quarrels over jurisdiction in 1567, the rancor between the men led Menéndez to mount a successful campaign to secure Pardo Osorio's dismissal.[16]

It occurred to Menéndez that a long-term source of funds for his enterprise might be found in the capture of Portuguese smugglers and French commerce raiders. Thus, on December 5, he proposed that he be granted a license to deploy a fleet to patrol the Caribbean. He envisioned that the prizes would rebuild his fortune, as would the thousand slave licenses he requested as compensation for his service.[17]

Having set a supply system in motion and begun toward a long-term solution to his financial problems, Menéndez returned to the explorations his contract required. Consistent with his announced intentions and his Caribbean orientation, he sailed in February, 1566, for the Florida Keys and the lower west coast of the peninsula. An exploration of the Tortugas–Key West area during his voyage showed that the water between some of the keys was deep enough to allow convoys bound from Veracruz to Havana to pass that way. Menéndez spent most of his time on the voyage of 1566, however, in entering into an alliance with a local lord known as Carlos. As the Spaniards eventually discovered, that man dominated southern Florida through military power and marriage alliances. Menéndez was drawn to Carlos' area—probably Calosachache Bay—because the local lord held survivors of Spanish shipwrecks as captives, lived on a major bay and river that might be the western end of the supposed all-water route across Florida, and had gold and silver salvaged from the shipwrecks.

16. *Ibid.*, 133–34, 158–59, 173, 176, 178–79, 191–92. Not everyone was pleased with the naming of Menéndez de Avilés to replace Osorio. Diego Lopez Durán opposed Menéndez' appointment as governor on the grounds that "his being governor will result in the consumption of this land by his taking from it the men, harvests, and herds in order to make [a prosperous place] in that [land] that Your Majesty gives him in Florida for his inheritance" (Diego Lopez Durán to SM, Havana, January 26, 1565 [*sic;* 1566], AGI, SD 115, fol. 163).

17. Pedro Menéndez de Avilés to SM, Matanzas, December 5, 1565, AGI, SD 115, and AGI, SD 168 (Stetson).

Gonzalo Solís de Merás, uncle of Menéndez' wife, María de Solís, and the author of one of two contemporary accounts of this part of the Florida adventure—at which he may have been present—says that Menéndez himself did not trade for any salvage but allowed his men to do so.[18] In that way, the men were rewarded for their labors.

From Carlos' chiefdom, Menéndez sailed to Saint Augustine, where he spent March, 1566, distributing essentials and trying to quiet mutinous soldiers. Once he got the situation more or less under control, he set out for Guale and the Point of Santa Elena.

Word from the Indians during the previous fall had suggested that Frenchmen might be at Guale. Menéndez found only one "Frenchman," a Spaniard who had fled his native Cordoba, married in France, and gone to Brazil—and eventually to Florida with Ribault. Menéndez also found that the Guale, who lived on the bluff-edged shores of Sapelo Sound and the inland sides of the barrier islands north and south of it, were at war with the Cusabo Indians, who lived along the rivers flowing into Port Royal and Saint Helena sounds and into the Atlantic Ocean north of the latter. Attempting to establish hegemony over both groups, Menéndez offered to arrange a peace treaty and an exchange of prisoners in return for an acknowledgment of Spanish rule and permission to leave persons who could begin to learn the local language and teach Christianity. The Guale accepted.

Sailing from Guale about April 7 or 8, Menéndez entered Port Royal Sound a day later. By the end of the month, he had established peace between the Guale and Cusabo and had laid out a fort on the southeastern end of what is today Parris Island. Alas, a principal backer from Austurias, was named to command a sixty-man garrison that Menéndez charged with completing the fort and maintaining the Spanish presence at this key to the riches of the Southeast.

Menéndez left Santa Elena on May 7. Pausing only briefly at Guale to allow a small group of Spaniards to disembark to instruct the Indians in Christianity and to maintain control, he returned to Saint Augustine. There he found such unrest that he was forced to allow the departure of Captain Juan de San Vicente and more than a hundred soldiers for the Antilles, or wherever else they might choose to go. According to Solís de Merás, the effective strength of Menéndez' forces was thus reduced to 150 men at Saint Augustine and San

18. Gonzalo Solís de Merás, *Pedro Menéndez de Avilés: Memorial,* trans. Jeannette Thurber Connor; facsimile reproduction intro. Lyle N. McAlister (Gainesville, Fla., 1964), 138–52.

Mateo, 60 at Santa Elena, and 5 at Guale. Supplies were also critically short.[19]

To obtain necessities and to further the alliance with Carlos' Indians, Menéndez departed from Saint Augustine and went to Havana and then to see Carlos. Returning to Havana, Menéndez gathered supplies and sailed to Saint Augustine. When he arrived, he was greeted by salvos from the artillery of the ships in Archiniega's fleet, which had arrived June 29. The fleet had not brought all the supplies that the 1,100 soldiers it carried would need, but they were supposed to be on the way in an *urca, Pantecras,* that was to follow the fleet. That ship was also to bring two Jesuits to begin the mission work Menéndez planned as a complement to his settlements.[20]

In the mail that came with Archiniega were orders that his ships were to be discharged as soon as they unloaded men and supplies. The masters, especially of two larger ships that, unable to cross the bar at Saint Augustine, had anchored off the coast, were especially anxious to return to Europe before the danger of tropical storms increased. Use of these ships for further exploration was clearly out of the question.

A council of war had already decided that Captain Pardo's company of some two hundred men—nominally three hundred—should move to Santa Elena to reinforce its garrison, which a mutiny that spring had reduced in size. Pardo sailed on July 6 in the ships that had had to anchor off the bar.[21] Menéndez divided the remaining troops into a group he intended to take to the Antilles to garrison ports there against an expected French attack in the spring of 1567 and into groups he was going to garrison at San Mateo and Saint Augustine and on the west coast of Florida. He did not mention the Bahía de Santa María in his letters of this period.

Leaving Archiniega and his officers to unload their ships and build

19. For the numbers of men in the different posts, see *ibid.,* 152–86, esp. 164, 176, 181. On p. 188, Menéndez is quoted as saying that 110 men were at Santa Elena. That, however, is incorrect. According to "Listas de gente de guerra . . . 1566–67," AGI, CD 941, twenty were left at Guale.

20. SM to Pedro Menéndez de Avilés, Madrid, September 1565, in Ruidiaz, *La Florida,* II, 360–62. For the background and fitting of this fleet, see Lyon, *The Enterprise of Florida,* 142–47, 162, 164. There are detailed accounts of its preparation, and that of the *Pantecras,* in AGI, CD 294, No. 2b, AGI, CD 304, No. 1, and AGI, CD 306, No. 2. Menéndez' reception with artillery salutes is suggested by a note that he was so saluted on a later occasion. See account of powder used by *Nuestra Señora de la Ayuda,* September 14, 1566, AGI, CT 2929, No. 2, 1566 [Doc. 2]. Barrientos (*Pedro Menéndez,* 112–13) gives the incorrect date of June 10 for his return to Saint Augustine.

21. Requirement, Saint Augustine, July 5, 1566, AGI, SD 11, No. 50, D, fol. 11.

a new fort and housing for the augmented garrison, Menéndez went to San Mateo with reinforcements. From there he ascended the Saint Johns River until Indians stopped him near Lake George.[22] They prevented him from discovering whether the supposed all-water cross-peninsular route was a reality. An approach from the west, by way of Carlos' lands, became even more important.

From San Mateo, Menéndez sailed to Santa Elena to inspect the arrangements that Alas and Pardo had made. Finding tension between the commanders and wanting to push ahead with his plans for the development of La Florida, Menéndez ordered Pardo to take 150 of his men and march inland along the supposed route to New Spain. He was to fortify selected positions along the road and return in the spring of 1567 to relate his findings. Pardo's expedition relieved the garrison at Santa Elena of a number of months because his people were expected to live at least partially off the land, that is to say, off the local Indian population.[23]

Returning to San Mateo, on his way to Saint Augustine, Menéndez found that Don Luís, the Indian from Bahía de Santa María, had come from Mexico with two Dominican friars, Fathers Pablo de San Pedro and Juan de Acuña. Because he had ample men and needed to send a dispatch boat to Spain, the adelantado decided, according to what he wrote Philip II, to follow through on his revised plans for the exploration of the Bahía de Santa María by sending a captain to discover the truth about the geography of the area.

On August 1, 1566, Menéndez named Ensign Pedro de Coronas captain and commander of a force of fifteen soldiers and three officials who were to accompany the Dominicans and Don Luís to the Indian's homeland. He named Domingo Fernández pilot and master of *La Trinidad.* Coronas, an Asturian who had given distinguished service in the attack on Fort Caroline, had served with Menéndez in earlier fleets. Clearly, he enjoyed the adelantado's confidence. Fernández was considered one of the two most knowledgeable pilots for the east coast of North America. The other was Goncalo Gayón, Hernán Manrique de Rojas' pilot. Fernández' instructions called for him to spend up to a month exploring the coast and delivering Coro-

22. Solís de Merás, *Memorial,* 201–208.

23. *Ibid.,* 209–11. There are no copies of Menéndez' orders to Pardo for this expedition, but their general nature can be gathered from what Pardo did, as told in the *relación* of Francisco Martinez, July 11, 1567, AGI, PAT 19, R. 22, No. 2. For a full discussion of the expeditions, see DePratter, Hudson, and Smith, "The Route of Juan Pardo's *Exploration,*" 125–58.

nas and his company to Don Luís' land, referred to as the Tierra de Santiago. After that, he was to sail to Spain to deliver the mail.[24]

La Trinidad departed from San Mateo on August 2, put into Saint Augustine for an undisclosed purpose on August 3, and then sailed northward. By August 14, it had reached 37°30′ north, the approximate latitude of Don Luís' homeland. *La Trinidad* anchored near the mouth of a river, identified by Louis-André Vigneras as Chincoteague Bay, Maryland, just to the north of the entrance to Chesapeake Bay. As Fernández was preparing to sound the entrance, a storm or strong northwesterly wind blew up and drove the ship out to sea. Four days later, when the wind had calmed somewhat, Fernández set a course to the west. On August 24, the party approached the coast at 36° north, according to the record of the voyage, but probably at 36°30′ north. Again the men found a river, and this time they successfully entered and explored it. Named the San Bartolomé, it proved to have no human inhabitants and to be totally unfamiliar to Don Luís. It was probably Currituck Sound, in North Carolina.[25]

On August 28, the Spaniards sailed northward along the coast to the river they had tried to enter twenty days earlier. But as they were about to anchor, a violent storm arose that again drove them out to sea. There, on September 6, they held a council, at which the Dominicans and Coronas requested a return to Saint Augustine. Fernández, however, decided that the foul weather must extend to Florida and that his orders to sail on to Spain precluded a return to the peninsula. He therefore turned his bow to the east. On October 23, 1566, *La Trinidad* made port at Cádiz.[26] The first attempted reconnaissance of the Bahía de Santa María had failed.

Writing in 1567 in praise of Menéndez de Avilés, Solís de Merás blamed the failure of the expedition on the Dominicans, saying, "As it appeared to them that they could no longer endure such a difficult life [they had been in Peru and Mexico], they secretly drew some of the soldiers into a conspiracy, for there was no need of much effort to

24. Louis-André Vigneras, "A Spanish Discovery of North Carolina in 1566," *North Carolina Historical Review,* XLVI (1969), 403–404, and AGI, PAT 257, No. 3, R. 4. Solís de Merás gave the number of persons in the party as thirty (*Memorial,* 208), but Menéndez said that twenty soldiers, two friars, and Don Luís were sent (Letter to SM from Havana, October 20, 1566, AGI, SD 115, fol. 167). The list of persons who went that is found in AGI, PAT 257, No. 3, R. 4, fols. 3–4, totals twenty, including the two friars, two officers, a notary, and fifteen soldiers.

25. Vigneras, "A Spanish Discovery," 406.

26. *Ibid.,* 407. The friars and Don Luís received some funds from the House of Trade on November 1, 1566 (AGI, CD 299, Datas, pliego 3, p. 1).

accomplish this, and won over the pilot; and being in accord, and taking testimony to the effect that on account of a storm they had been unable to go to the Bahía de Santa María, they went to Seville, defaming the country."[27] The division of the expedition's supplies on August 27 and 28, while the ship was at the San Bartolomé River, is ambiguous evidence that might be read to support Solís de Merás' charge by suggesting that the decision to abandon the voyage occurred prior to the second storm. The Dominicans took their shares of the goods. Yet Menéndez' seeming ambivalence about exploring the Bahía de Santa María may also be partially to blame, because it doubtless suggested that a merely formal effort at landing the missionary party would be acceptable to him. Moreover, if one believes the Jesuits, Menéndez did not want any order but their own in La Florida and may have indicated as much at the time. Menéndez' hostility may have given the Dominicans a reason to seek an excuse to leave the field.[28]

Back at Saint Augustine, Menéndez spent the balance of the summer and the early fall of 1566 making ready for his expedition to the Antilles. Just before setting out, he again put pen to paper in a long review of what he had achieved and expected to achieve in both the Antilles and La Florida. In the course of his letter, he came back to the question of the supposed waterway to China, tying exploration for it to a proposal that the king build a fleet of a dozen frigates to patrol the coasts of North America. Menéndez' doubts as to the waterway's existence were clear. He said that if the king agreed to fund the fleet, the secret of the passage to China, *if any* (my emphasis), would be discovered within two years more easily and cheaply than by the other possible methods of discovery.[29]

His specific proposal was to build a dozen twenty-bench *fragatas* of about a hundred toneladas each. With the king's approval, he would

27. Solís de Merás, *Memorial,* 209.

28. AGI, PAT 257, No. 3, R. 4, fols. 5v–7. From the depth of a personal disillusionment with mission work in Florida, the Jesuit father Juan Baptista de Segura wrote the order's general, Francisco Borgia, that the Dominicans had abandoned Florida because, like him, they had concluded that it would bear little spiritual fruit, but he seems to have had no direct knowledge of their motives (Letter, Santa Elena, December 18, 1569, in Zubillaga, *Monumenta Antiquae Floridae,* 408; for Menéndez' preference for the Jesuits, see pp. 38, 209, 214–15).

29. Menéndez to SM, Saint Augustine, October 20, 1566, in AGI, SD 115, fol. 169. In a letter to the Jesuit father Avellaneda of the same date, Menéndez displayed no doubt about the waterway, saying that there was a "gran relación" of it, as there was of large numbers of Indians in the interior (Zubillaga, *Monumenta Antiquae Floridae,* 98).

draw rowers from among foreign seamen rounded up in the Caribbean and criminals sent from Spain and Mexico. Spain would have to send artillery, as well as two thousand soldiers and appropriate supplies, all against the royal account. With that force, Menéndez planned to patrol the coast, intercepting the two thousand or so French ships that, by his estimate, visited the cod fisheries annually and the other thousand ships of other nations that, again by his estimate, also went there. He told the king he would either destroy the foreign ships or levy a toll on them for fishing in Spanish waters. When not engaged in patrols, the *fragatas* would explore the continent further, in the south during the winter and in the north during the summer. In the south, they would look for the cross-Florida route that Menéndez was convinced existed. The fleet's crews would grow their own food, reducing the volume of provisions that the king needed to ship each year.

The *fragatas'* northern base would be built at 38° north. A port there, Menéndez said, which fifteen to twenty French ships visited each year for fishing and fur trading, was the best "there is in all [of the Indies]."[30] Just north of it was where the passage to China was supposed to be. A river from the port at 38° north reputedly led to the arm of the sea that ran southwestward from Newfoundland—where it began at 60°—to within a half league of another arm of the sea that went, it was thought, toward China and entered the Pacific Ocean at 50° north. Menéndez placed the portage from one arm of the sea to the other at 42° north.

In many respects, the geography here is the same as in Menéndez' letter of a year earlier, but with some refinements as to the latitude of key points and the addition of the river connecting the Atlantic coast with the Saint Lawrence Valley. Evidently Menéndez' talk with Urdaneta had filled in such details. In particular, the adelantado now said that the western mouth of the strait was at 50° north, whereas earlier he had thought it was at 48° north. Urdaneta, it will be recalled, apparently believed that the outlet was at 51° north.

What was the origin of the idea that a river connected a port at 38° north with the arm of the sea running southwestward from the cod fisheries (*i.e.,* with the Saint Lawrence River)? There are only speculative answers. If the latitude Menéndez gave for the northern port is exact, he may have been thinking of the Potomac River's entrance

30. Pedro Menéndez de Avilés to SM, Saint Augustine, October 20, 1566, AGI, SD 115, fol. 170.

into Chesapeake Bay or of the Delaware River's into Delaware Bay. He could have learned of the Potomac only from Don Luís, and then without benefit of a latitude. No known Spanish or other European voyager had been far enough up the Chesapeake Bay yet to see the Potomac. It may also be that the river was the Susquehanna, perhaps vaguely known to Don Luís.[31] The Susquehanna connects the head of Chesapeake Bay to the Saint Lawrence Valley by way of various other rivers. If Menéndez was referring to the Delaware River and the Delaware Bay, his knowledge probably went back to the story told by an Englishman in New Spain in the 1550s (see p. 123 above). Still another possibility is that the notion of the river came from Urdaneta's familiarity with maps in the Verrazzano tradition that show such a river—although most of them placed its Atlantic end at the Point of Santa Elena. An example is the so-called Harlien map, *circa* 1544. In any case, the river offered a much easier way to the half-league portage than the eighty-league march over the mountains that Menéndez had previously known of. That is probably behind his comment that the discovery of a waterway to China could be made more easily and cheaply with the *fragatas* than by other methods—that is, with the *fragatas* ascending this river.

Having disburdened himself of his proposals and hopes, Menéndez set sail for the Antilles, where he inspected forts and installed temporary garrisons. At Havana, he made further arrangements for the supply of his settlements,[32] until in the spring of 1567, he again returned to La Florida. His first call was at Carlos' port, where a garrison under Captain Francisco Reinoso had been stationed since the previous fall. Menéndez had originally hoped that the river near Carlos' town ran up to Lake Miami (*i.e.*, Lake Okeechobee), whence a connection by water to Chief Mayaca's territory would carry the voyager to the San Mateo River (the Saint Johns). The Indians told him, however, that the connection was farther north, at Tocobaga (generally accepted to be the Safety Harbor Site on Old Tampa Bay). Tocobaga also happened to be an enemy kingdom. Offered the opportunity to guide the Spaniards

31. James F. Pendergast to author, personal communication concerning a study he has in progress.

32. His activities in the Antilles are described in Solís de Merás' *Memorial,* 213–23, 229, and in Pedro de Valdés to SM, Havana, January 19, 1567, AGI, SD 155, No. 187. Lyon is especially good on the supply arrangements Menéndez made (*The Enterprise of Florida,* 172–79).

to Tocobaga, Carlos accepted. He evidently thought that his new Spanish allies would aid him in destroying his enemies.

At Tocobaga, Menéndez established another garrison but failed to explore in search of the water route to Mayaca's lands. The Tocobagans told him that there were many hostile Indians on that route, and Menéndez apparently decided that he lacked the forces to explore it.

After visits to Carlos' region again and to Tequesta (Miami), at both of which sites he left a small garrison and a Jesuit missionary, Menéndez sailed for San Mateo, Saint Augustine, and Santa Elena. After making dispositions for the government of each during his absence in Spain, he sailed for Seville on May 18, 1567.[33]

At Santa Elena, Menéndez had received Captain Pardo's report of the journey inland, the first indication he had of the vast distance that really lay between the east coast of North America and the mines of northern Mexico. The adelantado probably also learned of Sergeant Hernando Moyano de Morales' fights with the Chisca Indians on the upper Nolichucky River (or on the Watauga River; scholars differ). Ordering Pardo to remain at Santa Elena over the summer in case the French attacked it, Menéndez also directed him to return to the exploration in September, 1567. On that journey he was to take care to see that each chief along the route swore obedience to Philip II and the adelantado in the presence of a notary and agreed to pay tribute in maize, salt, or deerskins. Pardo was to establish a chain of forts in addition to the one he had built at Joada, rather in the fashion of the successful conquest of Yucatán a generation earlier. But he was to return to Santa Elena by May, 1568, again to fortify its garrison against possible French attack, Menéndez expected that over the winter Pardo would penetrate to the mines of Santa Barbara and included in his orders provisions for that eventuality.[34]

So far as is known, Menéndez gave no orders for the further exploration of the Bahía de Santa María, the only part of his grand design that he did nothing to advance in the spring of 1567. He could have visited

33. Lyon, *The Enterprise of Florida,* 180–81.

34. DePratter, Hudson, and Smith discuss the recent scholarship on Pardo's routes, in "The Route of Juan Pardo's Exploration," 125–28, esp. *nn*6–10. They give their reconstructions of the routes on pp. 129–58. Charles Hudson has also published a monographic study of the routes, with translations by the present writer of key documents (*The Juan Pardo Expeditions* [Washington, D.C., 1990]). Robert S. Chamberlain describes the techniques used in Yucatán, in *The Conquest and Colonization of Yucatán, 1517–1550* (Washington, D.C., 1948), 204.

the bay on his way to Spain but did not. That was curious, since he had every reason to expect his agents to have discovered more about its geography. His behavior leads one to think that Eugene Lyon may be correct in the suggestion that Menéndez knew of the failure of Coronas' expedition to Don Luís' land by the time he visited Santa Elena in May, 1567.[35] Yet his failure to follow up on the expedition is also consistent with his apparent disenchantment with the Verrazzano geography after he talked with Urdaneta, and it fits his earlier apparent intention to ensure that the exploration and garrisoning of the area be at the king's expense. Coronas was sent only, one suspects, because Don Luís and his Dominican sponsors and a ship were at hand. Their presence deprived the adelantado of any reason to put off the exploration by a "captain," as proposed in his letter of January, 1566.

Menéndez' return to Spain in the summer of 1567 marked the beginning of a four-year period during which the colony's future was reshaped along lines that proved permanent, whatever Menéndez' intentions were in his more sanguine moments during that period or afterward. The reasons the reshaping became necessary were evident at the time he returned to Spain. For one thing, he had exhausted his finances. Knowledge in Spain of the scant natural resources of the coastal zone was having a negative impact on investment and the desire to settle in La Florida. Also widely known was the Indians' resistance to the wholesale transformation of their ancient ways of life. Philip II had other uses for the energies and the inextinguishable practical self-confidence of Menéndez de Avilés, and only limited funds to commit to new enterprises. Clearly not a fool even though he sometimes wrote as if his readers might be, Menéndez seems to have recognized that the conquest could not go forward along the lines he had optimistically sketched in his lengthy letters of 1565–1566. He probably no longer wholly accepted the geographical ideas and the descriptions of natural resources he had written during the previous two years.

Basking in his triumphal return to the royal court, Menéndez turned to the pragmatic matter of who would pay for the development of the colony. That was in part a question of who would pay for what

35. Lyon, *The Enterprise of Florida*, 182. On the other hand, no letter is known from the fall of 1566 or the first months of 1567 informing Menéndez of the failure of the expedition.

he had so far achieved. The king had put perhaps 200,000 ducats into the colony's support, although a major part (130,000 ducats) of that was in order to cover the expenses of the expedition under Archiniega, which had purposes not exclusive to La Florida. Lyon has shown that Menéndez and his associates probably spent 75,000 ducats during the first two years of the venture and that Menéndez had clearly reached the limits of his money and his credit.[36] His meanspirited, bitter reaction to the suit of Jacobo Pierres, a Flemish artilleryman on the expedition of 1565 who dared to claim his wages and the payment he had been forced, he said, to make to the adelantado before they sailed from Spain, was a mark of Menéndez' financial desperation.[37] Menéndez, moreover, had not yet sent any of the married people he was required to settle in La Florida under his contract.

To retrieve his financial situation and to gain the means to continue the colony, Menéndez claimed expenses with the king's soldiers that he asked Philip II to repay and obtained royal orders to garnishee the wages of soldiers who had served in Florida and owed him, he said, for supplies he had provided. Although not all his claims were accepted in 1567 or later, some were. Too, he was rewarded with other economic privileges, such as the governorship of Cuba and a *commendador*ship in the military order of Santiago, which would recompense him for his expenses, whatever they might be. He received payment on some of his claims from the convoy of 1563. What is more, his new prestige with the king and his new offices (see p. 253 below) seem to have revived his credit. By late 1567, he had the means to continue with his enterprise in La Florida.

Philip II, for his part, contributed to the survival of the colony by providing supplies for the royal troops still there.[38] The royal support of the garrisons beyond the initial year contemplated in 1565 opened the way for Menéndez eventually to saddle the royal treasury with the expense of provisioning and paying the majority of the Spaniards in La Florida. Under that arrangement, Menéndez' own funds could go for the support of his family and a few retainers and settler-farmers and for investment in commercial ventures capable of milking a profit from the stocking of the garrisons.

Menéndez had, besides, to contend with the widespread, highly

36. *Ibid.*, 183–85, 188–94.

37. Case of Jacobo Pierres against Pedro Menéndez de Avilés, Madrid, April 4, 1568, Justicia 1166, No. 5, R. 2.

38. Lyon, *The Enterprise of Florida*, 190–94.

negative reputation that La Florida had gained. Persons who had returned to Spain from the province before him had described a physical and human reality that was far from Ayllón's new Andalucia and from the picture Menéndez himself had painted. Various letters the Jesuits in Spain wrote to one another and their general, Francisco de Borgia, in the spring of 1567 counseled sending no more from their order to the province until it was pacified, if then, and informed the general that the Indians were rude savages, not people living *en policía,* as Menéndez' propaganda had said. They described how Spaniards could not leave their forts except in large armed parties. Menéndez had acknowledged some of the problems in his own letters to the order, but he had minimized the worst in the colony's situation.[39]

Equally damaging to the colony's reputation were the letters of officials in the Antilles. Concerned with their own defenses and aware of the difficulties the colony was having, they suggested that the whole undertaking was a waste of money since "it is impossible to guard, or pretend to guard, all the coast of La Florida, nor all of the sea."[40]

To rebut adverse comments about La Florida, Menéndez had to stress the glorious deed of driving out the French, the resources that lay *inland,* the prospects for development and mission work, and the bad character and ignoble purposes of the returnees who were spreading tales of woe about the coastal zone. He had set the tone as early as October, 1566, when he described most of the men who had come with Archiniega as *bellacos* (vile) and *chusma* (a term for the oarsmen in galleys, or a mob, but having the force of the English *scum*). Solís de Merás asserted, in support, that many had joined the expedition only as a way to get to the Indies and had no stomach for the hardships of the first months. Persons who believed the detractors had not taken "note that all who said these things had only gone along the sea-shore, through swamps and sandy stretches, guarding the forts and making

39. Father Bartolomé Bustamante to Francisco Borgia, Alcalá, May 31, 1567, Father Jerónimo Ruiz del Portillo to Francisco Borgia, Seville, June 26, 1567, Pedro Menéndez de Avilés to Avellaneda, Saint Augustine, October 15, 1566, in Zubillaga, *Monumenta Antiquae Floridae,* 168, 183, 90–96 respectively; Lyon, *The Enterprise of Florida,* 196.

40. Audiencia of Santo Domingo to SM, June 16, 1566, AGI, SD 71, Book 2, fols. 410–410v. For the view of a former ensign with Menéndez who claimed he had been jailed because he presumed to write to the king about the problems in Florida, see Hernán Perez to SM, Santo Domingo, Nov. 28, 1567, *ibid.,* Book 1, fol. 367.

war against the Lutherans; and that there was not one of them who had gone one league inland in Florida."[41]

All this only partially overcame, however, the uninviting impression of La Florida that informed persons got from the accounts of the returnees. Critics on the Council of the Indies, who had long accepted that La Florida was inhabited by savages and lacked resources, were silenced for the moment by Menéndez' triumph and propaganda, but not convinced.[42] The Jesuits continued to seek an opportunity to abandon the La Florida mission without provoking Menéndez' ire.[43]

As to the colony's future, the summer and fall of 1567 proved decisive. Whatever Menéndez' plans when he sailed to Spain in the spring of that year, when he arrived at court he found that Philip II had decided he should be commander of the fleet preparing to carry the king to Flanders. Philip II intended to go there to meet the demands of his northern subjects for his presence and to hear various grievances they had because of his reformation of the administration of the Spanish provinces in that part of Europe and the Catholic church in them.[44]

Although that plan was abandoned, Philip II persisted in his apparent aim of removing Menéndez from the direct management of La Florida. He did so by granting two of the requests Menéndez had presented in order to remedy the supply problem of La Florida: he gave the adelantado control over Cuba, and he gave him a source of income by allowing him the take from patrols against illegal traders and commerce raiders. He thus solved several problems and satisfied Menéndez' vanity. On October 24, 1567, over the objections of the *procurador* for Havana, Menéndez was named governor of Cuba without prejudice to his rights in La Florida and with the prerogative of serving in absentia through deputies. On November 3, 1567, he was

41. Anonymous account of visit of Menéndez to Jesuit College of Seville, December 16, 1567, in Zubillaga, *Monumenta Antiquae Floridae,* 216–17; Menéndez to SM, Saint Augustine, October 20, 1566, AGI, SD 115, fol. 172; Solís de Merás, *Memorial,* 163. Solís de Merás' and Barrientos' accounts of Menéndez' conquest set the general tone of praise for great deeds in the face of considerable difficulties.

42. Menéndez' own assessment as given in anonymous account of visit of Menéndez to Jesuit College of Seville, December 16, 1567, in Zubillaga, *Monumenta Antiquae Floridae,* 214.

43. Zubillaga, *Monumenta Antiguae Floridae,* 168ff.

44. Pedro Menéndez de Avilés to Father Juan Baptista de Segura, Madrid, September 11, 1567, in Zubillaga, *Monumenta Antiquae Floridae,* 201. For the background of this fleet, see [Noel] Geoffrey Parker, *The Dutch Revolt* (Ithaca, N.Y., 1977), 85–90, 99–105; for the situation in 1567, see especially p. 105.

named captain general of a new fleet of a dozen "galleyed galleons" to be built in Vizcaya for the purpose of patrolling the Caribbean and protecting its commerce, even on the transatlantic run.[45] The later appointment, more than the earlier, would take the adelantado away from La Florida.

Looking toward the possibilities of gain and faced with the duties of his new offices and the realities of his limited personal finances, Menéndez reckoned with the geographical and human resources of La Florida when he formulated his plans for the immediate future of his colony. With a candor not evident in his letters to his sovereign, he laid out his ideas for the Jesuits when he visited their house in Seville in December, 1567. Since the Indians lived in estuarine areas especially blessed with fish, Menéndez intended, he said, to put his settlers—four hundred married couples—to work on some islands in the coastal rivers which the Indians did not occupy, or "wherever seemed best."[46] Although he did not say so to the Jesuits, the island locations of the settlements not only met his obligation under royal policy to treat the Indians "justly" but also provided protection for his colonists from the natives and gave the settlers quick and easy access to the oceanic supply lines that would be essential for the short-term survival of the colony. In addition, the occupation of strategic ports was, after all, the *raison-d'état* behind his original contract with the king, and efforts in that direction would give the king's treasury reasons to stay engaged in the enterprise.

Looking farther into the future, Menéndez said that eventually he hoped to build two towns on the overland route to New Spain. Citizen-soldiers would settle them, and they would become the sites for Jesuit colleges, to educate the sons of Indian chiefs as Christians. He said nothing about exploration in search of the supposed waterway to China, even though the French ambassador reported at about that time that Philip II was much interested in this project and that Menéndez would be returning to La Florida to pursue it.[47] The Spaniards may have

45. Title as governor of Cuba, October 24, 1567, AGI, SD 115, and Lyon, *The Enterprise of Florida,* 191–92; Durán to SM, Havana, January 26, 1565 [*sic;* 1566], AGI, SD 115, fol. 163v; title as captain general, November 3, 1567, in Pedro Menéndez de Avilés, "Letters of Pedro Menéndez de Avilés and Other Documents Relating to His Career, 1555–1574," trans. Edward W. Lawson (2 vols.; typescript copy at P. K. Yonge Library of Florida History, University of Florida), II, 133.

46. Zubillaga, *Monumenta Antiquae Floridae,* 216.

47. Raimond de Beccarie de Pavie, Baron de Fourquevaux, *Dépeches de m. de Fourguevaux, ambassaduer du roi Charles IX en Espagne, 1565–1572,* ed. L'Abbé

deceived the ambassador in order to hide the purpose of the new royal fleet, during a period when they were particularly concerned about French objectives in the Americas.

Menéndez' words to the Jesuits of Seville in late 1567 proved to be an accurate foretelling of the next few years, although Menéndez may not have intended everything to turn out as it did. Over the winter, the Spaniards abandoned some of the remaining mission presidios in southern and western Florida, and the Indians who had been their unwilling hosts destroyed the rest (Table 2). A Jesuit, Juan de Rogel, placed part of the blame on the Spanish soldiers but concluded that the Indians were savages addicted to their devils and thus unworthy of further Jesuit efforts. Pardo's forts in the interior were destroyed in attacks by the Indians, although a few of the troops returned to the coast with women from the interior. The Frenchman Dominique de Gourgues and Saturiba's Indians attacked and demolished two outlying blockhouses of the fort at San Mateo, causing the garrison of that fort to withdraw to Saint Augustine. The action by Gourgues, a Catholic nobleman, taken to avenge the death of Jean Ribault and his men, gives yet another indication that the La Florida project was in fact a national, not just a sectarian, project.[48] The Spaniards briefly reoccupied San Mateo but abandoned it by 1570.

By the time the first settlers reached Santa Elena in the fall of 1568, it and Saint Augustine, San Mateo, and the mission at San Pedro de Tacatacuru (Cumberland Island, Georgia) were all that remained of the posts Menéndez had created during his first year in La Florida. As Menéndez had said in Seville, his settlements would be on islands in the bays and rivers of the coast. Santa Elena was such an island, and Saint Augustine was nearly one, surrounded as it was by water on three sides.

Even though some of the bad news about how things were going in La Florida became available before the Indies Fleet sailed on its maiden voyage, in October, 1568, Menéndez must have had every reason during the winter of 1567 and the spring and summer of 1568 for renewed optimism about his enterprise. He had gained offices that commanded extensive resources, and he had somewhat improved his

---

Douais (3 vols.; Paris, 1896–1904), I, 358 (and noted by Lowery in *Spanish Settlements*, II, 371).

48. Pedro Menéndez Marqués to SM, Havana, March 28, 1568, AGI, SD 115, fols. 205–208; Juan de Rogel to Francisco Borgia, Havana, July 25, 1568, in Zubillaga, *Monumenta Antiquae Floridae*, 321–27; Lyon, *The Enterprise of Florida*, 198–201.

Table 2. Florida Military and Mission Posts Established and Abandoned, 1565–1574

Place	*Date Established*	*Size of Party at Founding*	*Date Abandoned*
San Mateo	September 20, 1565	?	April 25, 1568
Aís	November 2 or 3, 1565	200 Spaniards and 50 Frenchmen	December, 1565
Santa Lucía	December 13, 1565	More than 100 men	March 18 (?), 1566
"Carlos" (San Antonio de Padua)	After October 15, 1566	23 men and friars; 50 men added in March, 1567	June 15, 1569
Tocabaga	March, 1567	30 soldiers	January, 1568
Tequesta (Miami)	April, 1567	30 soldiers and 1 Jesuit	Late March, 1568
San Pedro de Tacatacuru	1569	50 soldiers in August, 1570	*Ca.* 1573 (?)
Guale	August 17, 1566	20 men	November 18 (?), 1566
Santa Elena	April 15 (?), 1566	?	August 16, 1587
Inland From Santa Elena			
Orista	After September 1, 1567	?	By April, 1568
Canos	After September 1, 1567	?	By April, 1568
Guatari	After September 1, 1567	?	By April, 1568
Joara (Juada)	After September 1, 1567	18 soldiers	By April, 1568
Cavehi (Cawchi)	After September 1, 1567	31 soldiers	By April, 1568
Chiaha	January 1, 1567 (?)	39 soldiers	By April, 1568

Source: Paul E. Hoffman, *The Spanish Crown and the Defense of the Caribbean, 1535–1585: Precedent, Patrimonialism, and Royal Parsimony* (Baton Rouge, 1980), 142–43; reproduced by permission of Louisiana State University Press.

personal finances. Philip II had continued to favor him and his business affairs—for example, by rebuking the House of Trade when, on the pretext that his contract had expired, it tried to prevent his settlers from sailing, and by extending the term during which he might use the shipping licenses the contract of 1565 had granted.

Equally important, Philip II seems to have resolved the tension between the crown's interest in maintaining garrisons in strategic ports in La Florida and Menéndez' interest in, and obligation to, create civilian settlements at places of his own choosing. Philip II agreed to provide financial support for 150 soldiers from the resources of the new Indies Fleet. His decision relieved Menéndez of the cost of defending the settlers he was sending and opened the way for persons associated with him to engage in private trading with the soldiers, since he had the responsibility of organizing the provisioning of the royal troops as well as of his own settlers. A further incitement to optimism was that the Jesuit father Rogel was writing from Havana of the goodness of the land at Guale and Santa Elena and of his hopes that there, in contrast to the experience in southern Florida, the harvest of souls would be great.[49]

But reality soon intruded on the hopefulness of Rogel and Menéndez. The Indians continued to show hostility to the demands of the Jesuits, they resisted the payment of more than token tribute, and the Spaniards confronted very real difficulties in providing food, supplies, and livestock to the two settlements. Rogel discovered that the Indians of the estuarine environments of the coastal zone moved about during the year, adapting to local and seasonal scarcity and abundance. Their unfixed pattern of life made his mission work difficult, especially when they dispersed from their villages into kin groups that hunted and gathered in the forests. The officials of the Indies Fleet did not always do what Menéndez commanded, nor could his lieutenants in Havana and other supply points in the Antilles always succeed in obtaining what he needed on the terms he offered. The farmer-settlers quickly discovered that the island of Santa Elena had poor soil and that as much as two-thirds of its area flooded over during the conjunctions of the full moon and spring tides. Too, the men had to fell the forest cover. Insects and wild animals attacked their crops and what little livestock the adelantado provided.[50] By the summer of 1570, the

49. Lyon, *The Enterprise of Florida,* 206–207; crown to officials of the Indies Fleet, July 15, 1568, in sobrecedula, June 17, 1570, AGI, CD 548; Rogel to Borgia, Havana, July 25, 1568, in Zubillaga, *Monumenta Antiquae Floridae,* 327.

50. Juan de Rogel to Juan de Hinestrosa, Santa Elena, December 11, 1569, Juan de Rogel to Pedro Menéndez de Avilés, Havana, December 9, 1570, in Zubillaga,

survival of what Menéndez had begun in La Florida was in doubt. Moreover, the fact that he was in charge of the provisioning of both the soldiers and the colonists exposed both him and his agents to the temptation of misappropriating royal supplies. Their corruption raised a whole new set of issues that critics of the venture in La Florida could use against it.

Menéndez and his lieutenants tried to breast their difficulties and to muffle the complaints that started to go to the king in 1569 by practicing intimidation and physical coercion. Persons who, like Antón Rezio, a resident of Havana, refused for a while to grant credit escaped verbal abuse and threats only by reluctantly giving what Menéndez' people demanded. The adelantado's men apparently intercepted letters from La Florida, and they denied the Jesuits the freedom of movement between the La Florida settlements and Havana that the missionaries believed they were entitled to. Pedro Menéndez Marqués, a nephew of Menéndez de Avilés and chief lieutenant in La Florida at the time, dealt with an audit of the colony's books by Andrés de Equino without flinching: he shipped Diego de Valle to Yucatán in 1569, to languish in jail there until 1571. Valle was a notary who had tired of certifying the truth of false statements. His testimony and private papers, which Menéndez Marqués seized before deporting him, would have contradicted the claim that the records Equino needed for his audit had been lost in a fire in the fort at Saint Augustine. In the spring of 1570, some of the soldiers were quartered in Indian villages, while demands for increases in tribute payments went to others. The settlers found themselves billed for the imported livestock that, supposedly, had been part of the support the adelantado was giving them.[51]

Coercion was ineffective, however, against Dr. Alonso de Cáceres

---

Monumenta Antiquae Floridae, 398–404, 471–79 respectively. See also Larson, *Aboriginal Subsistence,* Chapters 1–4; Pedro Menéndez de Avilés to crown, n.p., [November, 1570 (?); Eugene Lyon dates this to November, 1569], in Instituto de Valencia de Don Juan, Envio 25, H, No. 162 (citation supplied by Lyon); Antón Rezio to SM, Havana, June 24, 1569, AGI, SD 115, fol. 235; "La Florida, lo que es" [1569], AGI, PAT 19, R. 33. For Menéndez' promises, see Eugene Lyon, *Santa Elena: A Brief History of the Colony, 1566–1587* (Columbia, S.C., 1984), 3.

51. Rezio to SM, Havana, June 24, 1569, AGI, SD 115, fol. 235; Father Juan Baptista de Segura to Francisco Borgia, Santa Elena, December 18, 1569, in Zubillaga, *Monumenta Antiquae Floridae,* 408; Father Antonio de Sedeño to Francisco Borgia, Guale, March 6, 1570, in Zubillaga, *Monumenta Antiquae Floridae,* 422 ("por tener entendido que las cartas no se llevan con fidelidad"); confession of Diego de Valle, Madrid, May 17, 1572, AGI, JU 1160, No. 13; Lyon, *Santa Elena,* 5, and *n*17.

and the Jesuits in Rome. Dr. Cáceres had come to the New World to investigate charges made in 1567 that La Florida was a waste of the king's money and that Menéndez was not doing a good job. Although Cáceres never went to La Florida but was content to gather information at Havana, his report was highly unfavorable. Not only did he go into many of the abuses in Menéndez' administration and speak frankly of the poor quality of the land, he also put sharply the question whether La Florida should be settled at all. He discovered that far from increasing the royal patrimony, the colonies were costing money. Nor were they advancing the cause of the faith. There were few Indians to convert, and even the Spaniards in La Florida were losing their faith for want of a priest. Besides, the two remaining forts were incapable of preventing the French from using the many ports of La Florida as bases from which to attack shipping. As for a French settlement in the region, Cáceres saw that it would suffer even greater supply problems than the Spanish colonies had experienced and could easily be laid waste by forces from the Antilles if the occasion arose. Cáceres suggested that if settlement continued, it should be completely under royal control, with a government separate from that of Cuba and subject to frequent audits and inspections. He felt that Spanish colonization and development of La Florida should not continue but that if it did, it should not be as a mixed private and royal venture.[52]

Intent on keeping the colony going in order to preserve his seignorial rights and future under the grant of the marquisate of Oristan even though he lacked the means further to develop La Florida,[53] and thwarted by the long-standing failure of the crown to equip and provision its troops adequately or to pay for the supplies he and his agents claimed they had procured for the soldiers, Menéndez determined to force the issue of La Florida's future. In June, 1570, he ordered the withdrawal from Florida of all soldiers except the 150 the king had agreed to support. Among those who left were many of the men Menéndez had taken with him in 1565 and a number of his relatives and friends from Asturias. Their arrival at Seville in October, 1570, resulted not only in investigations but also in a meeting of representatives of the Council of the Indies and the war and treasury councils

52. Dr. Caceres to king [1569 (?)], in AGI, PAT 19, R. 33.

53. Father Segura to Borgia, Santa Elena, December 18, 1569, in Zubillaga, *Monumenta Antiquae Floridae,* 407; AGI, JU 1001, No. 2; Gundisalvus de Esquivel to Francisco Borgia, Madrid, October 21, 1570, in Zubillaga, *Monumenta Antiquae Floridae,* 455.

in mid-October, 1570, to resolve the future of the North American province. In La Florida, the soldiers who remained threatened to mutiny and abandon the colony but agreed to stay until relief might come in the spring of 1571.[54]

The outcome of the meeting in October was the regularization of royal support for the garrisons in La Florida. In addition, Menéndez worked to ensure that he did not lose his rights under the contract of 1565. A royal order of November 15, 1570, provided a payroll (*situado*) of approximately 23,400 ducats a year for the garrisons, including 1,800 ducats for munitions and 1,500 ducats for bonuses that Menéndez could pay to those who enjoyed his favor or performed special duties. The royal treasury of Tierra Firme, at the Isthmus of Panama, was to pay this money upon receiving certification of the number of men serving in La Florida. The court entrusted the bookkeeping to the officials of the treasury of the Indies Fleet, but Menéndez' deputies in La Florida played a major role in administration and so prolonged the period when the adelantado's affairs were joined with those of the royal treasury. Menéndez wanted a royal payroll because it guaranteed both investors and settlers that the colonies would not have to face the enemy with only their own resources.[55]

Menéndez secured additional farmer-settlers during his stay in Spain and decided to send his family, including his wife and a daughter and son-in-law, Don Diego de Velasco, grandson of the constable of Castile and a nobleman, to Santa Elena to take up residence. Menéndez may have anticipated that sometime in the future he would be relieved of command of the Indies Fleet and thus become free to live in Santa Elena and pursue the development of the colony. In the meanwhile, the presence of his family would ensure that his seignorial rights were not vacated by nonuse and would serve to reassure the Jesuits, for example, that they would have enough food.

Menéndez, his family, and the new contingent of settlers sailed with the Indies Fleet in the spring of 1571 and arrived at Santa Elena in mid-July. Besides carrying needed materials, the ship brought an epidemic disease, which Lyon thinks to have been typhus. Almost the entire town fell ill.[56] Menéndez notified Philip II that he intended

54. Pedro Menéndez Marqués to SM, Havana, February 15, 1571, AGI, SD 115, fol. 247.

55. Menéndez de Avilés to crown, n.p. [October, 1570 (?); November, 1569 (?)], in Instituto de Valencia de Don Juan, Envio 25, H, No. 162. Copy of text of the royal order is incorporated in accounts of Tierra Firme, AGI, CD 1454, fols. 117v–19.

56. Lyon, *Santa Elena*, 6. María de Solís' will, written before she undertook this journey, is in Archivo de Protocolos, Oviedo, Legajo 57, Cuaderno 1, Alonso de Heredia,

to remain in residence at Santa Elena until the fall, when he expected to take two *fragatas* he was constructing to the Antilles to join his fleet's admiral, Juan de Cardona, on patrols against the corsairs. The six galleons of the Indies Fleet which he had brought to Havana in early July had proceeded on to overtake and escort the New Spain convoy, which had already left Havana by the time they arrived. Cardona had another of the fleet's nine galleons; two others had stayed in Cádiz to serve as escorts for the Tierra Firme convoy in the late summer of 1571.[57]

The Jesuits had also been taking stock. By the end of 1569, the fathers in La Florida and Cuba had concluded that, contrary to Rogel's optimistic assurances of 1568, little spiritual fruit would mature even at Guale or Santa Elena, because of the small size of the Indian villages—typically with fewer than twenty households, they estimated—as well as the distance between them, the topography that made travel difficult, and the resistance of the Indians to instruction and to changes in their cultural patterns. There were, too, the bad effects of the Spanish soldiers' conduct: the soldiers' exactions angered the Indians, and their vices called the name of Christian into disrepute in spite of the examples the fathers themselves tried to set.[58]

Prepared to abandon La Florida as soon as they could, the Jesuits nonetheless agreed to a plan by their local vice-provincial, Father Juan de Segura. He wanted to lead a mission to Don Luís' land as a final test of La Florida's potential for missions. Father Antonio Sedeño was openly skeptical that that area would be any more fruitful, for not only had Don Luís said that there were only thirty thousand persons in an area of 500 by 250 leagues but "it is in la Florida."[59] Segura and some others persuaded themselves that Don Luís would assist them and that the absence of Spanish soldiers would avert the

notary. Menéndez' view of his family as a sort of guarantee to the Jesuits is suggested in his letter to Borgia from Seville dated January 10, 1571, in Zubillaga, *Monumenta Antiquae Floridae,* 481–82.

57. Pedro Menéndez de Avilés to House of Trade, San Fanejos, May 15, 1571, AGI, CT 5101; Pedro Menéndez de Avilés to king, San Lucar, May 16, 1571, AGI, IG 1094; Pedro Menéndez de Avilés to king, Santa Elena, July 22, 1571, AGI, SD 231 (Stetson).

58. Francisco Villareal to Francisco Borgia, Tupiqui, La Florida, March 5, 1570, Father Antonio de Sedeño to Francisco Borgia, Guale, May 14, 1570, Rogel to Borgia, Havana, July 25, 1568, in Zubillaga, *Monumenta Antiquae Floridae,* 419–20, 430, 317–18 respectively. For Borgia's announcement of 1571 that no additional Jesuits would be sent to Florida, see p. 490 of that collection.

59. Father Sedeño to Borgia, Guale, May 14, 1570, in Zubillaga, *Monumenta Antiquae Floridae,* 430.

problems the Jesuits were having in the south. Once again there was Spanish interest in the coast north of 35° north.

How and when Don Luís came to be in Havana are unclear. Luís Jerónimo de Oré said that after returning to Spain in 1566, Don Luís eventually went to live with and acquire schooling from the Jesuits in Seville. Learning of the slight progress that their mission to La Florida had made by 1569, he offered to help the Jesuits if they undertook to spread the gospel in Jacán. On the other hand, Juan de la Carrera said that Don Luís returned to Havana in search of Menéndez de Avilés. Apparently Don Luís traveled with the group of Jesuits sent out in 1570.[60] Once in Havana and in contact with the order, he persuaded Father Segura that he would serve the vice-provincial as Timothy had served the apostle Paul. Menéndez apparently approved of the mission Don Luís had in mind, but whether his support was more than formal is a matter of dispute.[61]

Thanks to financial assistance from Hinestrosa, who besides being one of Menéndez' associates at Havana was a supporter of the Jesuit order, those setting off secured a ship and supplies, and employed Vicente Gonzalez as their pilot. Sailing by way of Santa Elena, the party reached the Bahía de Santa María and landed the missionaries on September 10, 1570. Clifford M. Lewis and Albert J. Loomie place the landing point on the James River a few miles east of the later site of Jamestown. From there the missionaries transported the few supplies and trunks of vestments, ornaments, and clothing overland to a site on the north bank of Kings Creek just above where it enters the York River. Once that activity was well under way, Gonzalez sailed for the south, promising to return with supplies the following spring.[62]

Just before Gonzalez sailed, Fathers Luís de Quirós and Segura

60. Luís Gerónimo de Oré, "Relation," 1617, in Clifford M. Lewis and Albert J. Loomie, *The Spanish Jesuit Mission in Virginia, 1570–1572* (Chapel Hill, N.C., 1953), 180; Juan de la Carrera, "Relation," 1600, *ibid.*, 123. The return to Havana of the other Jesuits is noted *ibid.*, 75.

61. Lewis and Loomie reprint the opinion of Francisco Sacchini, in *Historiae Societatis Iesu, pars Tertia, sive Borgia* (Rome, 1649), that Menéndez "both approved and encouraged" the Segura mission "although after the event he wanted to appear otherwise" (*The Spanish Mission*, 222). Carrera also suggested some enthusiasm (p. 123). See, however, p. 26*n*58, where Menéndez' enthusiasm is questioned. Lowery's treatment suggests that the project was wholly the work of the Jesuits (*Spanish Settlements*, II, 360), but he used later Jesuit histories, not the documentation Zubillaga made available a generation after Lowery wrote.

62. Lewis and Loomie, *The Spanish Mission*, 26–41, and plate V, p. 40.

wrote a letter to Hinestrosa that makes it plain that Menéndez' ideas about the geography of North America were still a factor in what was happening and that gathering information toward their proof or disproof was a secondary mission of the Jesuits. The fathers recalled that their goals were the "conversion of these people and the service of Our Lord and His Majesty and [finding] the way [*entrada*] to the mountains and China."[63] They mentioned that inland Indians they had met along the lower course of the James River said that the mountains were three to four days' journey away, two of which one could accomplish on the river, and that a day or two beyond the mountains was the "other sea." They would need a *chalupa*, or whale boat, before they could learn more, they said (by rowing upriver?); the Indians were so poor that they lacked canoes that could be used for that purpose. The fathers promised that they would make further inquiries and send news when there was opportunity. Meanwhile, they asked for supplies "with all speed" and set down the method by which the supply ship should signal its presence. They also asked that no Spaniard bringing materials be allowed to trade on his own; an incident of barter had already undermined the willingness of the Indians to aid the fathers without receiving trade goods in return.[64]

Left alone, the party of Jesuits and catechistical boys, assisted by the Indians, built huts to house the Europeans during the winter and to use as a church. As the pleasant days of late summer gave way to the passage of wet cold fronts and the color of fall in the hardwood forests, the Jesuits realized that Don Luís was no longer coming to see them and that the Indians' charity had dried up, superseded by a demand for European goods in exchange for food. According to the later hagiographers, Segura early imposed a strict spiritual discipline, which soon aimed openly at preparing the fathers, lay brothers, and boys for martyrdom.

When a supply ship expected in mid-January, 1571, failed to appear, the Jesuits made another attempt to invoke Don Luís' aid. Receiving the delegation with friendly words, the Indian promised to follow the group back to the mission. Along the way, on February 4, he killed two; he and his comrades found the third member of the party hiding in the woods the next day and killed him. Arriving at the mission on

63. Luís de Quirós and Juan Baptista de Segura to Juan de Hinestrosa, Bay of Jacán, September 12, 1570, *ibid.*, 86.

64. *Ibid.*, 87–88.

the morning of February 9, Don Luís and his men asked for, and were given, axes to cut wood for the Jesuits. With these weapons to supplement their own, the Indians killed all the remaining missionaries except Alonso de los Olmos, a boy who happened to be away at the time, whom the chief of the village he was in saved from death.[65] If the Jesuits gained any new geographical knowledge, it died with them.

In the spring of 1571 and many months late—the exact chronology is unknown—a ship sailed with supplies from Havana. Putting into the Bahía de Santa María, Gonzalez, its pilot, looked for the signs agreed upon. Not seeing them but observing men in Jesuit garb on the shore, Gonzalez approached warily. Canoes full of warriors met him. In the brief fight that followed, the Spaniards captured two Indians. One Indian jumped overboard on the journey south to Santa Elena and Havana. He easily struck out for shore, since the ship was running just off the coast. The other Indian, who was interrogated in Havana, apparently did not tell all that had happened, or could not be fully understood, but the Jesuits and Hinestrosa comprehended enough to be sure that whatever had occurred was serious.

The Jesuits in Havana prepared a second load of supplies and placed it under the care of Father Juan de Carrera. Gonzalez was again the pilot. When that ship arrived at Santa Elena in September 1571, Menéndez de Avilés detained it. The colony needed supplies, and it was late in the season for sailing in the open Atlantic. Menéndez sent Gonzalez back to Havana, where Father Rogel had testimony taken about what the adelantado had done and, then, for a third time, gathered supplies and sent them forward. Once again, when Gonzalez reached Santa Elena—it was now December—Menéndez seized the cargo and prohibited the voyage farther north.[66] Menéndez must have concluded that the Jesuits were dead.

In February, he set out for Havana. After visiting Saint Augustine, he set sail down the coast, taking advantage of the countercurrent just offshore. It was a dangerous course even in good weather. Not far north of Cape Canaveral, a storm struck and drove the ship ashore. Miraculously, no one drowned, and the crew saved some of the supplies. After beating off Indian attacks, the cold, rain-soaked travelers marched north until they found friendly Indians who took them to

65. *Ibid.*, 43–46.
66. *Ibid.*, 50–51.

Saint Augustine by paddling canoes up the bays and rivers behind the barrier islands. The party arrived at Saint Augustine in time to help man the defenses when an English ship appeared off the bar in early March. Then once again, Menéndez set out for Havana. This time he made it.[67]

When the adelantado got to Havana, the Jesuits demanded of him that something be done to search for their brothers. Menéndez agreed that upon returning from the Antilles he would go to Santa Elena and then to the Bahía de Santa María. As good as his word, he left Saint Augustine on July 30, 1572, with several of the Indies Fleet's *fragatas*. Entering the Bahía de Santa María in mid-August, he sent Gonzalez to capture one of Don Luís' uncles, a village chief in the area where the Jesuits had landed in 1570. With that Indian and others as hostages, the Spaniards sent a demand inland for the boy Alonso de los Olmos. He arrived and quickly told the whole story. The Indian messengers bore a new demand back to their people: that they surrender Don Luís and the other guilty Indians to the Spaniards within five days. Otherwise, the Spaniards threatened to execute the hostages. When the Indians did not meet the Spanish deadline, the Spaniards hanged from the ships' spars some of the captives who they determined were among those who had killed the Jesuits. Although Rogel requested exploration of the bay in search of the bodies and the relics of the missionaries which the Indians were said to possess, Menéndez refused because of the lateness of the season. He promised, however, that he would return the next year to seek the bodies.[68] He did send Diego de Velasco, his son-in-law, though, with a hundred-man party to explore and give Menéndez' thanks to the chief who had saved Alonso de los Olmos' life. The scant information available on that exploration suggests that it was on the York Peninsula, and not very extensive.[69]

Having avenged the deaths of the Jesuits, Menéndez set sail for Spain, never to return. The Jesuits who had accompanied him to the

67. The voyage is described in graphic detail by Father Sedeño in his letter to Father Polanco from Santa Elena, February 8, 1572, in Zubillaga, *Monumenta Antiquae Floridae*, 497–504. Other recountings: Sancho Pardo Osorio to king, Havana, May 25, 1572, Pedro Menéndez Marqués to king, Havana, May 29, 1572, both AGI, CT 5105.

68. Lewis and Loomie, *The Spanish Mission*, 52–54; account by Rogel, *ibid.*, 117.

69. Oré, "Relation," *ibid.*, 184. Lewis and Loomie's discussion of the Carrera account of this expedition concludes that Velasco went to Strachey's Kecoughtan, not up the bay as is sometimes said (p. 141*n*18). Rogel's letter to Borgia of August 28, 1572, did not mention that exploration and stressed Menéndez' haste to conclude the business and return to Spain—indicating a brief exploration at most (pp. 107–12).

Bahía de Santa María returned to Havana, their work in La Florida at an end.[70]

Father Rogel's judgment on Jacan was that

> there are more people in this land than in any of the others I have seen so far along the explored coast. It seems to me that the natives are more settled than in other regions, . . . and I am confident that should Spaniards settle here, so that the natives have reason to fear should they wish to do us harm, we could preach the Holy Gospel more easily than in any place we have had. . . . If this [task] should fall to me, I would consider myself most fortunate. I fear that there will be the same difficulty among these [people] in making conversions as there has been in the places where we have been. If there is to be any fruit, it will have to be over a period of time, wearing them away like a drip on a rock.[71]

Once again, the attempt to achieve visionary European ends on the Atlantic Coast of North America had run up against the hard realities of the environment and the people who lived in it. Yet, once again too the resources of the coast declared a potential that might make them worth pursuing under certain conditions. Even as Rogel wrote, a new round of colonial rivalry to control those resources was getting under way.

70. Lewis and Loomie, *The Spanish Mission*, 55. Concerning Menéndez' trip to Spain: Hernand Grajayz to House of Trade, Angra, October 22, 1572, Pedro Menéndez de Avilés to House of Trade, San Lucar, November 18, 1572, both AGI, CT 5105.

71. Juan de Rogel to Francisco Borgia, Jacán, August 28, 1572, in Lewis and Loomie, *The Spanish Mission*, 106, 111. I have corrected the translation on p. 111 against the Spanish text on p. 106.

XI

Transition in Spanish Florida, and New French and English Initiatives, 1572–1583

The year 1572 marked the beginning of the penultimate chapter in the story of Europeans' pursuit in the American Southeast and during the sixteenth century of the new Andalucia and the way to the Orient that the legends arising from the explorations of the 1520s promised. Pedro Menéndez de Avilés journeyed to Spain, never to return to La Florida. That same year, there was a revival of French interest in exploration and colonization in the Southeast. The consequences of those unrelated events worked themselves out during the next decade.

By 1583, the Spanish presence in La Florida was only two garrisons wholly dependent on the royal treasury. Menéndez de Avilés' seignorial colony had vanished, along with private initiatives to extend the geographical scope of Spanish control. The French, after temporarily, and by accident, establishing a presence among the Indians of the coast between Guale and Santa Elena in the years 1577–1580, had largely abandoned the Spanish coast. Further north, English and French explorers spent the late 1570s and early 1580s searching for favorable sites for colonies from which they might, among other things, seek out the Northwest Passage, especially by the middle route: the Saint Lawrence Valley. Their search prepared the way for the final sixteenth-century round of colonial rivalry in the Southeast (see Chapter XII).

An important accompaniment of the search for the Northwest Passage during the years 1572–1583 was a new interest in the various facts and fantasies about the resources and geography of North America which were to be found in Spanish and French books and maps.

When Menéndez de Avilés reached Spain in the early summer of 1572, he claimed to be so poor that he had to borrow money from the House of Trade to outfit himself and pay his way to court. There he received orders to proceed to Santander to take command of a fleet that was preparing to carry reinforcements to certain Spanish garrisons then under siege in the Low Countries, in particular to Middleburg. The fleet was to sail in the spring of 1573, allowing Menéndez to return to La Florida the following spring. As events turned out, the spring of 1573 brought news of Spanish successes against the Dutch rebels and the Spanish court postponed sending the relief force until so late into the summer of 1574 that Menéndez was reluctant to sail and began to find reasons why he should not until the following spring, if then.[1] He died at Santander on September 17, 1574, still waiting for the right combination of weather and orders.

While he was at court over the winter of 1572–1573, he secured a number of royal orders intended to further his enterprise in La Florida. On February 23, 1573, he received an extension of the area in which he could colonize. The court now defined La Florida as beginning at the Pánuco River in northern Mexico. The audiencia of Mexico objected, to no avail.[2] Menéndez' rationale seems to have been that he needed to control the western end of the land route he expected to develop from the mines of northern Mexico to Santa Elena. He may also have been influenced by the legendary promise of dense Indian populations inland from the Gulf of Mexico's coast. Certainly the outline of plans which he presented before the Jesuits in December, 1567, suggests the influence of that legend.[3] In any event, the new grant, involving as it did an area of proven access to silver mines and native labor, was expected to attract new capital to the enterprise of La Florida.

Complementing the Pánuco grant were an order of March 3, 1573, authorizing the recruitment of fifty families from Asturias to go as farmers and craftsmen to populate Menéndez' colonies and orders of April 8 continuing his privilege of sending ships to La Florida outside the convoy system.[4] Taken together, the grant and orders amounted to a renewal of Menéndez' enterprise and gave him something to offer prospective investors. The degree to which he was able to turn the advantages the court conceded him into financial leverage is not yet known, but he did begin to recruit the settler families. His last letter to his nephew, Pedro Menéndez Marqués, said that familie from Santander and the Rio de Miño, in Portugal, were congregating at

1. Hoffman, "The Narrow Waters Strategies," 15–16.

2. Lyon, *Santa Elena*, 22*n*35. The details of this grant were clarified in cedulas of June 1 and August 20, 1574.

3. Zubillaga, *Monumenta Antiquae Floridae*, 216–17.

4. AGI, SD 2528 (Stetson).

Bayona in anticipation of the adelantado's return to La Florida in the spring of 1575. He instructed Menéndez Marqués, in La Florida, to gather as much as he could of the money owed the uncle and to come to Spain with the funds, so that they could support the new colonists and so that the nephew would be at hand to take the emigrating families to La Florida should Menéndez de Avilés encounter delay yet again. The adelantado was evidently concerned about enough of a delay that his Pánuco grant might lapse.[5]

His carefully laid plans came to nothing when he died. His son-in-law Hernando de Miranda secured power of attorney from his wife, Catalina, and went to court—from Asturias where they were living—to claim his rights as adelantado.[6] In La Florida, news of Menéndez de Avilés' death arrived on April 30, 1575. The two Franciscans who were working as missionaries at Santa Elena and Guale and who had finally won some converts among the Indians at both places the previous fall, immediately left the province.[7] Miranda, meanwhile, made preparations to go to La Florida to take up his wife's inheritance and to exploit it for his personal benefit. At the same time, Philip II ordered an audit of the La Florida treasury records and of Menéndez de Avilés' term of office.[8]

Miranda proved to be unfit to direct a colony controlled by contentious men and women related to one another by blood and marriage, motivated by dreams of the wealth they could amass by exploiting the labor of Indians and poor Spaniards and by squeezing the royal payroll, and surrounded by Indians who were at best acquiescent to the Spanish presence and demands for tribute. Within weeks of his arrival at Santa Elena in the spring of 1576, he and his brother-in-law, Diego de Velasco, who had been lieutenant governor, became embroiled in controversies that landed Velasco in jail. Velasco was charged with misappropriating the bonus money the payroll included for rewarding merit and special work in the garrison (*e.g.*, that of artillerymen). The twenty remaining settlers demanded either release from La Florida or the delivery of

5. Ruidiaz, *La Florida,* II, 288–92.

6. Letters of Hernando de Miranda, December 20, 1574, to April 26, 1575, AGI, JU 817, No. 5, Pieza 3.

7. Zubillaga, *Monumenta Antiquae Floridae,* 533–34.

8. *Consulta* of the Council of the Indies, October 4, 1575, AGI, IG 738, No. 144, and notarized record made in Havana on January 13, 1577, of Baltasar de Castillo y Ahedo's presentation of his commission of January 4, 1576, and other documents establishing his authority to make the visitation, AGI, SD 80 (Stetson); Lyon, *Santa Elena,* 9.

livestock and the access to good soils that Menéndez de Avilés had promised them. Miranda gave them no satisfaction, so they complained to Philip II. Miranda himself soon struck a series of deals with Pedro Menéndez de Avilés the Younger, who was the dead adelantado's nephew and the royal treasurer as well as an agent for various of the dead adelantado's merchant associates. Miranda also seems to have ordered that the tribute from the Indians be increased, or at least collected on schedule irrespective of conditions in the Indian economy. And he ordered an unnecessarily fierce revenge on the Guale for their murder of their Christian chief, commenting offhandedly that one or two dead Indians were of no concern to him. Miranda then sailed to Havana to see what profit he could milk from the payroll that was coming from New Spain that spring.[9]

Upon returning to Saint Augustine, Miranda sent Menéndez de Avilés the Younger and the other treasury officials to Santa Elena to pay the garrison. At Sapelo Sound, the Guale ambushed and killed them. About the same time, the Indians at Escamacu rebelled. Sergeant Hernando Moyano de Morales and his squad of twenty-one men had gone to the village to get food and had taken the evening meal from the Indians' pots. All but one of the Spaniards paid with their lives as they slept that night. The rebellion soon spread to other villages from Guale to Edisto. Parties of braves moved onto Santa Elena Island, driving the Spaniards back into their fort.[10]

Hernando de Miranda had meantime arrived at Santa Elena, as had his brother Gutierre de Miranda. Gutierre had come to take his wife and household to Havana, preparatory to removing them to Spain. He claimed that he attempted to strengthen the physical defenses of the town and to get his brother to organize his men to resist the Indians. Hernando maintained that that is just what he did, but other witnesses to the events declared that he had shown cowardice, even allowing the women of the town to carry him off to the ships once evacuation to Saint Augustine had been decided upon. In that version of the events, Miranda the coward abandoned a defensible position. Eugene Lyon argues that the decision to abandon Santa Elena was a community decision by people who had lost their homes to Indian torches and their spirit to years of relative privation.[11] But whoever

9. Lyon, *Santa Elena,* 9–10.

10. *Ibid.,* 10.

11. Case of Gutierre de Miranda against fiscal and Hernando de Miranda, Madrid, September 2, 1578, AGI, JU 1002, No. 5; Lyon, *Santa Elena,* 11.

made the decision, the result was the same: the evacuation of Santa Elena and its looting and burning by the Indians.

The evacuees touched first at Saint Augustine, where Hernando placed Gutierre in charge as lieutenant governor. Hernando then set sail for Spain, with the announced purpose of obtaining help from the government so that the Indian rebellion could be suppressed. A storm drove Miranda's ship to Puerto Rico, with the result that news of the loss of Santa Elena preceded him to Spain by some months. The court never allowed him to return to La Florida.[12] Others of the evacuees managed to get to Havana and even to Mexico City.

The quasi-seignorial government of La Florida and the possibility of a marquisate of Oristan were at an end. The king took over the administration of the colony. Lawyers shouldered the family's effort to extract something of worth from Menéndez de Avilés' privileges in La Florida. In the end, a cash settlement extinguished all the privileges under the contract of 1565. Only the title of *adelantado de la Florida* remained as a hereditary right.[13]

Efforts to deal with the situation in La Florida began almost as soon as the loss of Santa Elena became known. At La Yaguana, in Española, Captain Diego de la Rivera and the officers of the royal Indies Fleet met and decided to send Captain Alvaro de Valdés and a launch to look into conditions at Santa Elena, to enable them to decide on other appropriate steps. From Havana, the *visitador* Baltasar de Castillo wrote to the Council of the Indies with the news. The council on March 20, 1577, recommended to Philip II the appointment of Menéndez Marqués as governor. The king accepted the council's advice to send Menéndez Marqués with as many men as Seville could muster on short notice.[14] The old adelantado's nephew sailed for Florida with fifty-five soldiers and a small quantity of supplies. He arrived at Saint Augustine on July 1, a few days after the last flour in the storeroom had been distributed to the troops, according to Gutierre de Miranda.[15]

12. Audiencia to SM, Santo Domingo, January 8, 1577, AGI, SD 50, R. 5; petition of Catalina de Borbon, Mexico City, March 24, 1577, AGI, PAT 75, R. 4. AGI, EC 154–A, contains additional details of the evacuation and of Miranda's behavior, according to Lyon (*Santa Elena*, 23*n*43).

13. See AGI, EC 1024–A.

14. Diego de la Rivera to SM, La Yaguana, January 22, 1577, AGI, SD 79, No. 104; *consulta* of the Council of the Indies, March 20, 1577, AGI, IG 739, No. 15.

15. Jeannette Thurber Connor (ed.), *Colonial Records of Spanish Florida* (2 vols.; Deland, Fla., 1925–30), II, 27; I, 265. On the supply situation, see question 15 and

Obedient to an order with which he disagreed, Menéndez Marqués prepared a prefabricated fort, or part of one, to take to Santa Elena. He did this out of concern that Indian hostility would make it impossible to send working parties into the forests to cut timber for such a building. He readied cut and hewn boards and beams so that the Spaniards could establish themselves in a secure stronghouse from which to sally to attack the Indians.

Menéndez Marqués' plan to sail to Santa Elena in early September, 1578, was set back by a tropical storm that blew all his ships aground in Saint Augustine harbor. He managed to refloat them, however, and made the trip to Santa Elena in October. Although he lost some of the timbers when the ship carrying them sank along the way, the new fort, called San Marcos, rose quickly on the edge of the marsh about three hundred feet south of the ruins of Fort San Felipe. The Spaniards were in their stockade before the Indians could decide on a plan of attack.[16] Still, danger from the tribes remained acute for some months. That danger was heightened in Spanish minds by the discovery that a French ship, *Le Prince,* had wrecked at Port Royal and that some of its crew were at large among the Indians (see p. 278 below).[17]

With the new fort well along, Menéndez Marqués wrote Philip II concerning the need for a three-hundred-man garrison divided between the forts at Santa Elena and Saint Augustine. He had 153 men, 83 at Santa Elena and 70 at Saint Augustine, enough to defend them against the Indians but not against a European force. He asked for an additional 150 men, as well as supplies and two *fragatas* to haul cargo back and forth between the forts and the Antilles. The colony should continue to be an appendage of the governorship of Cuba, he went on to say, as it had been under Menéndez de Avilés. If the additional men and materials were impossible, he recommended abandoning the province and leaving its patrol to two galleys and a *galeota* that might be stationed in the Antilles.[18] Evidently he had heard of the discus-

---

replies in "Depositions for Gutierre de Miranda," Saint Augustine, July 13, 1577, AGI, JU 1002, No. 5.

16. Connor, *Colonial Records,* I, 266–67.

17. *Ibid.,* II, 26.

18. Pedro Menéndez Marqués to SM, Santa Elena, October 12, 1577, summarized in *consulta* of the Council of the Indies, March 12, 1578, AGI, IG 739, No. 58. For the debate about whether the Florida governorship should be independent of or dependent on Cuba, see Delgado's report on the Junta de Guerra, February 15 (?), 1578, AGI, IG 1094.

sions in Spain in 1576–1577 about whether to send Mediterranean galleys to Santo Domingo and Cartagena de Indias.[19] In other letters also of late 1577, he suggested consolidating the garrisons at Saint Augustine. Notably absent from his letters was a discussion of the potential of La Florida or of ways to expand the Spanish presence. A rather practical man, he was concerned with the immediate problem of reestablishing Spanish control over the existing settlements and their hinterlands.

Madrid's response to his request was unusually swift. Orders to gather men and materials and to provide ships for them went to the House of Trade on March 16, four days after Captain Rodrigo de Junco, the chosen envoy of Menéndez Marqués, had met with the Council of the Indies to present the governor's requests. An order for funding followed on March 27, as an exception to the general suspension of spending for La Florida ordered on July 24, 1577. The royal Indies Fleet provided transport in the form of a *fragata* and a galleon that was being retired from active duty. The vessels got to sea with the Indies Fleet on July 1–5 and dropped anchor off the Saint Augustine Bar on September 27.[20]

A storm drove the galleon ashore, causing it to lose some of its passengers and crew and most of its cargo. Still, the garrison of Saint Augustine welcomed the relief force. Menéndez Marqués had lacked the manpower to do more than negotiate with the Guale to receive satisfaction for the deaths of the treasury officials in 1576, and with the Cusabo, without success, to obtain the French still at large among them. Reinforced, he undertook a campaign against the Guale in the spring of 1579, during which he burned nineteen of their villages and destroyed whatever stored maize he could find. In August, he turned his attention to the Cusabo. After twice sending a squad of soldiers to discuss peace and having his overtures refused in a shower of arrows, he attacked Orista, driving its defenders into the forests. He next attacked Coçapoy, an important village long hostile to the Spaniards and said to

19. Hoffman, *The Spanish Crown,* 181–84, 188–92.

20. *Consulta* of the Council of the Indies, March 12, 1578, AGI, IG 739, No. 58; king to House of Trade, San Lorenzo, March 24, March 27, 1578, both AGI, CT 5013; *consulta* of the Council of the Indies, April 17, 1578, AGI, IG 739, No. 65; Chaunu and Chaunu, *Seville et l'Atlantique,* III, 250; petition and orders for a visitation of the ships *Santiago el Menor* and *El Espiritu Santo,* Saint Augustine, September 27, 1578, AGI, CD 462, No. 9, fols. 8–9. Other materials on this supply fleet and its losses are in the same account.

be harboring forty Frenchmen. Only half that number were found, and three of them fought to the death rather than surrender. The seventeen who surrendered were hanged at Santa Elena.

After the raids, Menéndez Marqués had little trouble persuading the various Indian groups to resume their vassalage to the Spanish king and to surrender the Frenchmen among them. His ironfisted policy also prevented the uprising of Indians around Saint Augustine.[21]

An enlargement of the payroll (*situado*) to take account of the new troop strength was worked out during the years 1578 to 1580, and the crown sent additional troops in 1580 to replace the men lost in the wreck of 1578.[22] Thus underwritten by the king and his treasury, the two towns of Saint Augustine and Santa Elena entered upon a five-year period of relative prosperity as the orchards and truck gardens bore fruit and peaceful, if uneasy, relations with the Indians along the coast yielded tribute and trade in maize, deerskins, salt, and sarsaparilla roots.[23] Although questions about the need for the garrison colonies continued to be raised from time to time, notably by Juan Mendes in a bitter if insightful letter of 1584, Madrid took no decisions to change the status quo.[24] The French and English were again exploring the North American continent. Some of their ships even appeared along the southeastern coast, as almost every mail from Florida informed the Council of the Indies. The royal will needed no profounder rationale for sustaining the Spanish presence in La Florida.

The English and French explorations of the mid-1570s and early 1580s concentrated on finding the supposed Northwest Passage.

21. Connor, *Colonial Records,* II, 224, 248–50, 252–56, 282–84. Mary Ross gives a rather romanticized and not entirely accurate account of these events ("French Intrusions and Indian Uprisings in Georgia and South Carolina, 1577–1580," *Georgia Historical Quarterly,* VII [1923], 258–66).

22. AGI, IG 739, No. 118, and AGI, CD 944. No. 8, and AGI, SD 2528, fols. 112v–114v.

23. Eugene Lyon, "St. Augustine 1580: The Living Community," *El Escribano,* XIV (1977), 20–33; Lyon, *Santa Elena,* 13–14; entries recording payment of *almojarifazgo* on Florida sarsaparilla, 1583–84, AGI, CD 1089, No. 2, R. 1, R. 2.

24. Juan Mendes to SM, April 6, 1584, AGI, SD 231 (Stetson). In essence, Mendes said that Menéndez de Avilés had chosen bad sites because he was a seaman ignorant of the soils needed for farming and more interested in trade than in developing a successful colony. Mendes maintained that Menéndez' successors continued in his path because they profited from the royal payroll. The Jesuit reports (see Chapter X above) suggest that Menéndez intended the coastal settlements as staging bases from which to penetrate to the good soils of the piedmont, but if so, he did not live to carry out his design. In any case, there is much truth in what Mendes said, as the Castillo y Ahedo *visita* and the various lawsuits by Menéndez de Avilés against the crown prove.

Three possibilities seemed to exist. The first, which carried one the farthest north, was to seek a passage between Newfoundland and Greenland. Martin Frobisher explored that possibility in 1576–1578. Frobisher's voyages lie outside the scope of this study.

The second possibility was to ascend the Saint Lawrence River to the portage that Cartier's men had spoken of. Of varying width in the several versions of the legend, this portage was thought to lead to the arm of the Pacific Ocean that Verrazzano had said crossed North America to near the east coast. The possibility of the Saint Lawrence portage interested the French explorer the Marquis de La Roche and the English explorer Sir Humphrey Gilbert, among others.

The third possibility was to use one of the rivers or bays at the middle latitudes (about 37° to 40° north) that French maps in the tradition of Verrazzano showed connecting to, or reaching inland near, the same arm of the Pacific Ocean that supposedly extended close to the east coast and the Saint Lawrence River. The third possibility brought into play the Chicora legend and its promise of a new Andalucia. Gilbert and, after his death, Sir Walter Raleigh took an interest in the possibility of a passage at the middle latitudes, and the English colonies at Roanoke Island, in North Carolina, were the result. The French may also have had an interest in this possibility during the 1570s, although the extant documentation allows their interest to be only inferred.

The interrelationships between the French and English voyages of this period have not received much attention, since historians have usually written from nationalistic perspectives. Yet it is evident that there was a sharing of information and a rivalry between explorers seeking to establish claims and colonies. For example, both Richard Eden and Richard Hakluyt the Younger consulted leading French experts on navigation and discovery, in particular André Thevet. Hakluyt encouraged, subsidized, and in some cases served as editor for the publication at Paris of accounts of French and Spanish explorations, and he put together his own compilation of accounts of the English voyages. What he had a hand in bringing out stimulated not only English but also French interest in the Americas.[25] Other personal contacts must have occurred, but they await their historian.

25. Eva G. R. Taylor, *Tudor Geography, 1485–1583* (London, 1930), 37; George B. Parks, *Richard Hakluyt and the English Voyages*, ed. James A. Williamson (New York, 1930), 99–122; Roncière, *Histoire de la marine*, IV, 312–13.

Similarly, a tracking of the flow from one country to the other of news of proposed and actual voyages and a record of the responses of other persons have not been available to the present study. Much of what follows is, therefore, a juxtaposing of events whose relationships remain unknown or uncertain.

The origins of the new round of Anglo-French interest in North America are not completely clear from surviving documents. Apparently French interest revived first, with English activity delayed until after 1574 by Elizabeth I's foreign policy of not antagonizing the Spaniards. Once North America captured England's attention, however, that nation rapidly developed a coherent approach that focused on colonization at the points long identified as most promising: Norembega, in Maine, and the upper thirties north latitude, Raleigh's Virginia. French initiatives, in comparison, suffered from an increasing lack of coordination and seem to have turned toward trade rather than colonization.

Although the details are sketchy, it is known that in 1571–1572 a diverse group of the powerful revived Gaspard de Coligny's general design of using colonial activities as an outlet for the Huguenots, as a way of possibly uniting Frenchmen regardless of religion, and as a means to attack Spanish power. One of Coligny's biographers credits him with a scheme according to which a series of diversionary raids in the Caribbean was to be part of the war with the Spaniards that he hoped to provoke. Philippe Strozzi, the queen mother's cousin, is given credit by his biographer for a comparable plan, which the Spaniards expected to involve no fewer than twenty-eight ships and an estimated six thousand men. Eight ships are known to have sailed in the spring of 1572. Among them were Guillaume Le Testu's ships, which went to the Isthmus of Panama, where Francis Drake found and joined them for his famous raid on the *tren* of mules carrying silver across the isthmus. Other French crews raided Spanish targets throughout the Caribbean. Discussions seem to have gone on in France that spring about following up the raiding and information-gathering voyages with the seizure of Spanish towns or the founding of colonies, including one in La Florida, but the Saint Bartholomew's Day Massacre, on August 24, 1572, and the fourth French war of religion (1572–1573) that grew out of it brought the discussions to an end.[26] The available documentation does not clarify whether the

26. DelaBorde, *Coligny*, III, 323–24; Hermann Taffin, Sieur de Torsay, *La Vie, Mort, et Tombeau de Haut et Puissant Seigneur Phillippe de Strozzi* . . . (1582; rpr. Paris,

proponents of the La Florida colony hoped to use it as a way station toward the Verrazzano sea or simply as a base from which to raid the Spanish Caribbean and to trade with the North American Indians. If it had been properly located at Santa Elena or a port north of it, the colony could have served all three purposes.

Even less is known about the second revival of French colonial ambition during 1575–1576. It appears, however, that individual entrepreneurs and groups of investors fitted exploring and raiding expeditions that they intended to lay the groundwork for ventures of larger scope. For example, Guillaume Le Fèvre backed the Parmentier brothers' voyage to Sumatra in 1576.[27] Nicolas Strozzi's ill-fated voyage of 1576–77 to the Caribbean and La Florida was another example of entrepreneurial activity (see pp. 278–79 below). Too, by about 1575 there may have been the loose Franco-English coordination of a plan of attack on the Spaniards. Colonies on the east coast of North America probably figured in French and English intentions; certainly that was the case in the 1580s. By 1577, the ever-suspicious Bernardino de Mendoza, Philip II's ambassador in England, thought that a coordinated campaign had been agreed upon.[28]

In England, 1576 was the year that Sir Humphrey Gilbert published his *Discourse for a discoverie of a new passage to Cataia.* Gilbert's book was the first of a half dozen books about China and the search for the Northwest Passage which appeared in the years 1576–1578. It was in 1576 that Frobisher set out on the first of three voyages to the area between Newfoundland and Greenland in search of the Northwest Passage.[29] Frobisher failed to find the passage and got sidetracked into the mining of iron pyrite (fool's gold), but Gilbert's book, together with similar information supplied by Dr. John Dee in later years, provided the basis for most later English hopes of discovering the passage in the far north. Publication of Gilbert's book also seems to have marked the renewal of his interest in exploration and possible colonization, which led, within two years, to his patent as a sort of

---

1608), 434–35, and Roncière, *Histoire de la marine,* IV, 122–31; Duc de Nevers to Duc D'Anjou, May 20, 1572, noted in Roncière's *Histoire de la marine,* 133.

27. Roncière, *Histoire de la marine,* IV, 201*n*3.

28. *DIE,* XCI, 243–44; and in David B. Quinn (ed.), *The Voyages and Colonising Enterprises of Sir Humphrey Gilbert* (2 vols.; London, 1940), I, 187.

29. Humphrey Gilbert, *A discourse for a discovery of a new passage to Cataia* (London, 1576), in Quinn (ed.), *The Voyages of Gilbert,* I, 129–66; Taylor, *Tudor Geography,* 181–85, Appendix I, "Catalogue of English Geographical or Kindred Works . . . to 1583"; Morison, *European Discovery of America,* 500–554.

lord proprietor of all of North America not occupied by other Christians. Voyages of exploration followed (see pp. 283, 288 below).

No other event alarmed the Spaniards as much as Nicolas Strozzi's voyage, the result of which seemed to be a direct challenge to their possession of the Point of Santa Elena. Possibly a brother of Philippe Strozzi, Nicolas Strozzi sailed in *Le Prince* in the spring of 1576. During that summer its crew raided a number of settlements in the Caribbean. In January, 1577, it anchored off the Saint Augustine Bar for a few days, evidently trying to see if it could enter. Finding too little depth of water over the bar, and perhaps in fear of being driven aground by a storm, its crew set sail toward the north.[30] While trying to enter Port Royal Sound, the ship was wrecked. The Spaniards found its stern when they went to rebuild Santa Elena.[31]

There is little doubt that *Le Prince*'s presence off the La Florida coast was part of a larger design resembling the French colonial ventures of the early 1560s, but it seems unlikely that Strozzi's purpose was to seek a "base on the mainland," as Mary Ross and David B. Quinn have suggested.[32] Had he intended to build a fort as a first move toward reasserting French control over the area of Santa Elena, he would have taken care not to arrive in La Florida in the middle of the winter after spending the summer raiding and trading in the Caribbean. Most likely Strozzi's purpose, aside from making money by raiding the Spanish Caribbean, was to gather information, on his way home, about the Spanish presence in La Florida—he had probably heard of the abandonment of Santa Elena—and to test the temper of the Indians toward a French return. Ross's and Quinn's evaluation of his aim does, however, reflect what the Spaniards seem to have thought.

Whatever Strozzi's objective, his shipwreck at Port Royal Sound led him and his crew to construct a triangular fort of earth and fagots, with corner bastions. They erected five buildings inside the enclosure, which was about 130 feet on a side (sixty-six paces). The Spaniards found one piece of bronze artillery weighing 1200 pounds. An early report said that 280 men had been in *Le Prince*'s crew, of whom the Indians killed two hundred when they attacked the fort in

30. Connor notes *Le Prince*'s activities in the Antilles, in *Colonial Records,* I, 268–69. The ship's appearance off Saint Augustine received comment in "Depositions for Gutierre de Miranda," Saint Augustine, July 13, 1577, AGI, JU 1002, No. 5.

31. Connor, *Colonial Records,* II, 26.

32. Ross, "French Intrusions," 251, and Quinn, *England and the Discovery of America,* 269.

the period prior to the Spaniards' return to Santa Elena. The numbers may be exaggerated, but other witnesses attested the fact of the massacre, one of whom spoke of finding a great many bones of dead Frenchmen in the fort the returning Spaniards discovered in the spring of 1578. The surviving Frenchmen—initially estimated as eighty or a hundred—had been taken to Indian villages. Over the next two years, the Spaniards got hold of about thirty Frenchmen, the remaining survivors of *Le Prince*'s crew. Except for a barber-surgeon, an artilleryman, and a few boys, all were hanged.[33]

Apparently Strozzi sent his ship's launch for help. At least the Spaniards thought that he did, because they considered the French ships that appeared off the coast during the winter of 1577 and the spring of 1578 to be seeking the lost crew of *Le Prince*. The first of those ships loomed off Santa Elena at sundown one day in October, 1577. The vessel, which did not enter the bay, was driven to sea by an evening storm. Then on May 12, 1578, two ships anchored off Saint Augustine but later sailed north. A Spanish reconnaissance mission found that their crews had not attempted to land south of Santa Elena.[34] Whether the ships were really searching for Strozzi there is no way of knowing; the Spaniards at Saint Augustine thought that they were, but why they thought so they did not state.

The motives of the French who were sailing near the coast of La Florida in 1577 and 1578 apart, those that came in 1580 were clearly intent on finding Strozzi and, it seems, renewing trade contacts with the Indians in preparation for a move against the Spaniards at Saint Augustine and Santa Elena.

The Spaniards discovered the objectives of the French when, on July 18, 1580, a postsiesta (3 P.M.) meeting at Saint Augustine of the governor and his officers was interrupted by an Indian from the San Mateo area who brought news that a French ship had anchored in the river there. When the Spaniards learned that the ship's crew had offered to trade with the Indians and had inquired about the number and situation of the Spaniards at Saint Augustine, they mounted an expedition at once. After a bloody fight amid the shoals at the mouth of the river on July 20, in which eighteen Spaniards and fifty-four

33. Connor, *Colonial Records*, II, 78–82, 26, 224, 252–56, 282–84, 112. The connection between Strozzi's voyage and earlier French attention to the southeastern coast seemed to be shown by the fact that among those executed was one Felix, who had been with Ribault in 1565 and been held prisoner by the Spaniards until he and some comrades stole a boat in 1569 and made their escape.

34. *Ibid.*, II, 78–82. The date of the first ship's appearance is not clearly stated.

Frenchmen died, the Spaniards learned from their prisoners that the French *galeaceta* of eighty to ninety toneladas had been commanded by a Captain Gil, a native of Corsica. After raiding and trading in the Caribbean, he had come to La Florida to trade and to try to locate *Le Prince.* A larger ship that did not enter the San Mateo River had accompanied his *galeaceta,* and that went on up the coast after the sea battle, reportedly reaching San Pedro (Cumberland Island) on July 22. The sponsor of Gil's voyage was Nicolas Strozzi's brother.[35]

Gil's was not the only rescue and trading mission that the French had set in motion for the summer of 1580. Within a week of the battle at the bar of the San Mateo River, two French ships entered Gualequini (Saint Simons Sound) and established friendly relations with the Indians. Learning of the fates of both Strozzi and Gil, the Frenchmen informed their hosts that they would return the next spring with five ships. They asked that the Gualequini organize a rebellion by the other coastal Indians, the Guale and the Cusabo, and promised that after the French and Indian force had driven the Spaniards from Santa Elena, the French would join with the Gualequini to attack the Guale, who had turned Strozzi over to Menéndez Marqués, and the Cusabo, who had attacked Strozzi's fort and killed many of his men. In that way, both the French and the Gualequini would settle their scores with their enemies. Whether the French thought of then moving into Santa Elena, to which they had a claim based on Ribault's voyage of 1562, they did not say.[36] This French expedition may have been led by a Captain Champion, of Le Havre, who, according to one account, brought an "old Indian War standard" from La Florida in 1580.[37]

On July 28, at about the time that these events were taking place in Gualequini, five ships were reported off the bar at Guale, but they did not enter because of rough seas. Ten days later, on August 7, three ships approached Zapala, one of which sounded the bar and entered. Three weeks after that, on August 28, there was a sighting of two other ships at Zapala. Again, one sounded the bar and entered, spending some days exploring the rivers and bays. But no ships came near Santa Elena.[38]

Spanish documents do not allow a determination of how many

35. *Ibid.*, II, 318–23. See also Ross, "French Intrusions," 270–73.
36. Ross, "French Intrusions," 275, 277–79.
37. Roncière, *Histoire de la marine,* IV, 311.
38. Connor, *Colonial Records,* II, 323; Ross, "French Intrusions," 276.

groups of ships were involved in all this. Perhaps there were just two groups: one with two ships either associated with Gil's vessel or acting independently of it but, like it, looking for Strozzi, and another with five ships that a storm separated after they stood off Guale on July 28, some of them putting in an appearance at Zapala on different dates in August. Ross believes that each ship seen was from a different voyage. If true, that would mean that many of the French trading and raiding expeditions to the Caribbean in 1580 were on alert to stop along the southeastern coast in an attempt to locate Strozzi. Given his apparent familial connection, that is not unlikely, but it remains to be demonstrated from French sources.

There is no doubt that once the Spaniards learned of the apparent conspiracy of the French and Gualequini in September, 1580, they moved rapidly to break it up, but not before as many as a thousand Indians again had Santa Elena under siege, if its commander's numbers are to be believed. The movement of reinforcements to Santa Elena and some diplomacy by Captain Vicente Gonzalez cut short the uprising. By the end of 1580, the area around Santa Elena again enjoyed an uneasy peace.[39]

The French do not seem to have returned to the southeastern coast until January, 1582, when the Indians began to tell of a fort the French had built at Cayagua (Charleston harbor). Gonzalez, Menéndez Marqués' chief pilot, went to scout the bay in late February but found no evidence of a French presence. He did, however, establish friendly relations with the local chiefs, even carrying one to Saint Augustine to meet with Menéndez Marqués.[40] No French ships were reported on the southeastern coast for the rest of the 1580s.

If the wreck of *Le Prince* at Santa Elena seems to have been accidental, the voyages of the Marquis de La Roche and of Sir Humphrey Gilbert in 1578 reflected an aim to colonize at or near the middle route to the Orient (the Saint Lawrence–Norembega route). Once again, the French were the first to prepare a plan and an expedition.

The Marquis de La Roche was a Breton gentleman who had been Catherine de Medicis' page. In January, 1578, he received an appointment as viceroy of the "new lands." With funds supplied in part by François de Bourbon, ships from some of his friends from Brittany,

39. Ross, "French Intrusions," 279–81.

40. Paul E. Hoffman, "New Light on Vicente Gonzalez's 1588 Voyage in Search of Raleigh's English Colonies," *North Carolina Historical Review*, LXIII (1986), 204.

and a sailing guide a Basque pilot had drawn up, he intended to sail to Canada and establish a colony. His success would entrench French claims to the area—endangered by English interest in it—and advance Catherine de Medicis' case for compensation from Spain for not pressing her right to the Portuguese throne. The plan to send Philippe Strozzi to Brazil was also part of the policy of using colonial ventures to secure Catherine's dynastic interests in Europe.[41]

La Roche set sail in June, 1578, but the English cut his voyage short when they intercepted him in the English Channel and imprisoned him, purportedly for his support in 1575 of James Fitz-Gerald, a pretender to the earldom of Ulster. In fact, the English seem to have been acting in defense of Sir Humphrey Gilbert's interests.[42]

The plans Gilbert had in 1578 are not known with certainty. His patent of June 11, 1578, granted him the right to explore and colonize any land between Florida and Labrador not occupied by another Christian prince.[43] The Spanish ambassador, Mendoza, wrote that according to William Stukeley, Gilbert intended to go to the island of Santa Genela, in the Middle East. Gilbert supposedly had a Chaldean (a Babylonian) to accompany him. In a subsequent letter, Mendoza felt able to say that Gilbert's pilot was going to be Simon Fernandes, a reputed expert on the North American coast. The French ambassador recorded that Gilbert had told him he was going to the "southern region" at the same latitude and climate as France and England, below 45°, or at most 50°, "from the equinox, going towards the other Pole."[44] The announced objective reminded the ambassador of stories he had heard at La Rochelle that called that land rich in precious metals and fertile and said that it contained approaches to a passage across North America. He was reminded that is, of the Chicora legend as it fused with the Verrazzano-Cartier geography of North America.

Gilbert's true objective was probably Canada, or possibly New England (Norembega), where he could set up a colony from which to

41. Roncière, *Histoire de la marine,* IV, 167–71, 200, 308. *Cf.* Charles G. M. B. de La Roncière, "Colonies éphémères," in Gabriel Hanotaux and Alfred Martineau, *L'Amérique* (Paris, 1929), 38, Vol. I of Hanotaux and Martineau, *Histoire des colonies françaises et de l'expansion de la France dans le monde,* which gives a different date for La Roche's appointment.

42. Quinn, *The Voyages of Gilbert,* I, 38, esp. *n*5.

43. *Ibid.,* I, 188–94.

44. *DIE,* XCI, 230, 243–44, and Quinn, *The Voyages of Gilbert,* I, 187; Quinn, *The Voyages of Gilbert,* I, 195–96. Regarding the meaning of this rather garbled indication of latitude, see Quinn, *The Voyages of Gilbert,* I, 38, but *cf.* Morison, *European Discovery of America,* 568–69.

mount raids on Spanish shipping at the cod fisheries and in the Caribbean. He apparently had little interest in the Northwest Passage.[45] Gilbert's Canadian objective is evident in his "Discourse How Her Majesty May Annoy the King of Spain," of November 6, 1577, and in Dr. Dee's diary, which says that a Mr. Raynolds, of Bridewell, took leave of him on August 5, 1578, going to join Gilbert for a voyage to "Hocheleya" (Hochelaga being the Indian name for the site of Montreal).[46]

In any case, Gilbert failed to achieve any result from his voyage of 1578. He started so late, September 26, that winter storms were already blowing on the Atlantic that forced his fleet back into Dartmouth. When he sailed again on November 19, it was with three fewer ships. They had followed Henry Knollys on a cruise in search of Spanish and other captures. Gilbert himself apparently ended up doing the same, eventually putting into Ireland to resupply and finally limping home to England in February, 1579.[47]

During the half dozen years between Gilbert's failed expedition of 1578 and the outbreak of the Anglo-Spanish war in 1585—when Philip II seized English shipping in Iberian ports—the idea that there was a way to the Orient through the Saint Lawrence River was strengthened in the thinking of persons interested in North America, whether Spanish, French, or English. A number of voyages were undertaken to strengthen claims to the area around the Gulf of Saint Lawrence and to prepare the way for possible colonies, but the first colonization occurred later.

The notion of a Northwest Passage across North America remained alive and reinforced itself among Spaniards during these years. The continued acceptance of this idea is clear in Menéndez Marqués' letter to Philip II of May 15, 1580. The governor of La Florida, who had learned that Drake was at large in the Pacific Ocean, felt certain that he would have to return to Europe by way of the "back of Florida," because the "cold is at the same latitude [as the Straits of Magellan]" and he had heard that the English intended to "enter there," that is, at

45. Quinn, *The Voyages of Gilbert,* I, 31–34, 38–39, 45–46, 69.

46. John Dee, *The Private Diary of Dr. John Dee . . . ,* ed. James O. Halliwell (London, 1842), 4. Gilbert's "Discourse" is printed in Quinn's *The Voyages of Gilbert,* I, 170–75.

47. Morison, *European Discovery of America,* 568–69; Quinn, *The Voyages of Gilbert,* I, 40–44.

the western entrance of the passage.[48] The Council of the Indies agreed that that was a possible route for Drake's return. A second example of the continued acceptance of the idea of a transcontinental Northwest Passage was the report that Spanish prisoners Drake captured at Saint Augustine in 1586 had told their English captors about the two arms of the sea and the portage between them that lay just over the mountains from the Bahía de Santa María.

The possibility that the Saint Lawrence River might be part of the passage was underscored by a document that Father Martín de Rada left among his papers in New Spain. Rada's document, which was forwarded to Spain in 1580, compiled the information he had acquired during many years in New Spain. From Juan de Ribas, of San Sebastian, he had learned of Cartier's explorations of the Saint Lawrence Valley. From an unnamed Portuguese who had been on an expedition to the same area, Ribas had learned the course from Cape Breton into the Saint Lawrence. All his informants believed that the river was a strait reaching to China. At present nothing is known about the use the Spaniards made of this information in the 1580s.[49]

Among the French and English, the early 1580s saw the publication of a number of books that provided information about the Saint Lawrence area and Jacques Cartier's voyages. Intended as propaganda in support of schemes of colonization both in that area and as far south as Norembega (at the Penobscot River, in Maine), one of them contained information about Chicora and another pointed to a possible southern route, at or below 40° north, to the trans-American passage.

The first of these books to appear was Giovanni Florio's English translation in 1580 of Cartier's narrative of his first two voyages to Canada.[50] That volume had previously been available only in Gioranni Bautista Ramusio's Italian version of the late 1550s. The information Cartier gave was the best available on the Saint Lawrence Gulf and River.

Far broader in scope, and in importance to both French and English

48. Connor, *Colonial Records,* II, 306–307. For Drake's interest in the western end of the passage, see Parks, *Richard Hakluyt,* 108–109.

49. "Copia de un papel que se hallo entre los que tenía Fray Martín de Rada, sobre el estrecho que se decía haber en tierranova," 1580, AGI, IG 1528, and AGI, PAT 19, R. 33. The copy in IG 1528 is in a bundle that also contains a report on Hudson's voyage, from 1611.

50. Jacques Cartier, *A shorte and briefe narration of the two Nauigations . . . to Newe Fravnce,* trans. Iohn Florio (London, 1580).

voyages, was *Les Trois Mondes,* by Lancelot Voisin, Sieur de La Popelinière. Published in Paris in 1582, La Popelinière's book opened with a call for Frenchmen to interest themselves in overseas discoveries and colonization. Book One dealt with the Old World, including the Portuguese voyages to Asia. Book Two covered the Spanish discovery and conquest of America and French activities in La Florida. Using Francisco Lopez de Gómara as his source, La Popelinière recounted the Spanish expeditions to La Florida before 1560, devoting about a third of a column to Chicora, more than to any other North American location. He then passed to French voyages to the cod fisheries in 1504, Giovanni de Verrazzano's voyage of 1524, Jean Ribault's voyage of 1562, and in more detail, Dominique de Gourgues' revenge of 1568. Interspersed, and more fully developed in a section that followed, were comments on Spain's assertion of titles, especially in connection with North America. La Popelinière rejected them all, even suggesting that the English had the best claim to La Florida because of Sebastian (*sic*) Cabot's discovery of 1496, "if seeing a country first is enough to give one a right over a country." In the end, he argued that only permission from the Indians and effective occupation conveyed title. He thus established a case for French resumption of colonization in La Florida. In Book Three, he gave an account of French colonization in Brazil, Amerigo Vespucci's voyages to Brazil, the Portuguese presence there, Magellan's voyage, and the Treaty of Tordesillas. Other chapters of Book Three recounted Spanish voyages to the Far East.[51]

La Popelinière's work appeared in support of Catherine de Medicis' renewed campaign to win compensation in virtue of her claim to be an heir to the Portuguese throne. Early in 1582, she had Philippe Strozzi named viceroy in anticipation of a new French venture in Brazil. Voyages since 1579 had prepared the way. It may be that the French voyages to the southeastern coast in 1580 and 1582 (see pp. 279–81 below) were also reconnaissances preparatory to the new colonial initiatives that La Popelinière justified by denying the Spanish titles and showing the priority of French expeditions and settlements. Strozzi's death during the summer of 1582 in the Azores, which he was defending on behalf of Don Antônio, the pretender to the Por-

51. Lancelot Voisin, Sieur de La Popelinière, *Les Trois Mondes* (Paris, 1580). The material on Chicora is in Book II, fol. 25v. The quotation is from Book II, fol. 42.

tuguese throne then held by Philip II of Spain, put on end to the Brazilian part of the scheme. The North American aspects of the project await study.[52]

The third book to appear, also in 1582, that contained information about eastern North America was Richard Hakluyt the Younger's *Divers Voyages, touching the discouerie of America, and the Ilands adiacent unto the same, made first of all by our Englishmen, and afterwards by the Frenchmen and Britons: And certaine notes of advertisements for observations, necessarie for such as shall heereafter make the like attempt . . .* Designed as rhetorical support for Gilbert's new endeavors but also, apparently, to answer the question of what was known about North America, this volume followed the story from the Cabot voyages and the mythical Zeno expedition, both in the fifteenth century, through Verrazzano's explorations, to Ribault's first voyage. It concluded with a list of American products and with essays by the elder Hakluyt on what explorers should look for and on how colonization ought to be carried out. Hakluyt thus covered everything from the evidence for the supposed Northwest Passage to the resources of the southeastern coast and provided as good a practical guide for the colonizer as was available.[53]

In his discussion of the eight reasons for believing that a passage existed through North America, Hakluyt noted that Verrazzano's map showed such a passage. That is probably the map Verrazzano gave Henry VIII that Hakluyt mentioned on other occasions. He also marshaled the testimony of various Indian sources and European explorers and chroniclers, including Lopez de Gómara, who told of explorations from Mexico in the 1520s. To complete the case for a passage, Hakluyt reproduced the map of Michael Lok, which shows Verrazzano's sea cutting across North America at about 40° north, and apparently open water north of Baffin Island (Map 8). Thus, like La Popelinière, Hakluyt introduced materials about the southern or "Chicora" way to the supposed passage to Asia.

52. Roncière, "Colonies éphémères," 38, and Roncière, *Histoire de la marine,* IV, 167–71, 200.

53. Parks, *Richard Hakluyt,* 68–74. Quinn says of the *Divers Voyages* that it was intended to "make available what was known about eastern North America in order to assist more direct propaganda in support of the Gilbert ventures" (David B. Quinn [ed.], *The Hakluyt Handbook* [2 vols.; London, 1974], I, 274). Richard Hakluyt's *Divers Voyages* was published at London by Thomas Woodcocke in 1582 and was reprinted as *Divers Voyages Touching the Discovery of America and the Islands Adjacent* (London, 1850).

In the same year and in 1583, additional if less comprehensive information about the Saint Lawrence area was put on record in the works of Parmenius, Christopher Carleill, and Sir George Peckham.[54] Except for Carleill, who had his own plans, the writers were touting for Gilbert. A second edition of *Les Trois Mondes* was licensed, although apparently not printed. Even so, the authorization of the edition indicated wide public interest.

Equally significant, when Adrian Gilbert, Sir Francis Walsingham, who was secretary of state, and Dr. Dee conferred about the Northwest Passage early in 1583, Dee presented a manuscript map he had made that showed all four variations on the supposed passage across or around North America (Map 10). On the map are the presumed open-water route at 60° north and the Saint Lawrence route, which is shown reaching to the Gulf of California, with tributaries of the Saint Lawrence River running to Verrazzano's sea and the Atlantic by way of Norembega. Farther south the map displays the portage that had been alleged at 40° north, and even farther south a route by way of the "Jordan River" (the River of Santa Elena), a lake, and a portage to Verrazzano's sea. Clearly Dee and others had gleaned every shred of cartographic and literary information they could about North America. The younger Hakluyt had already provided a list of products, including some drawn from Peter Martyr's account of Chicora's Andalucia-like yield. The writers and mapmakers had set the stage for new English exploration along the east coast of North America.[55]

One feature of the cartography of Lok and Dee helps explain the project of Gilbert and Peckham in 1583. The maps of both drafters show a river flowing from the Saint Lawrence Valley to the Atlantic. On Lok's map, it is identified with Norembega. If that representation had been correct, it would have meant that colonists at Norembega

54. Stephanus Budaeus Parmenius, *De Navigatione . . . Humfredi Gilberti* (London, 1582), in David B. Quinn and Neil M. Cheshire (trans. and eds.), *The New Found Land of Stephen Parmenius* (Toronto, 1972), 74–105; Christopher Carleill, *A Breef and Sommarie Discourse upon the entended Voyages to the Hethermoste Partes of America* (London, 1583) in Quinn (ed.), *New American World,* III, 27–34 (and in Quinn [ed.], *The Voyages of Gilbert,* II, 351–64), and George Peckham, *A True Reporte of the Late Discoueries . . . of the Newfound Landes by . . . Sir Humfrey Gilbert Knight* (London, 1583).

55. Parks aptly describes this state of affairs: "[The conference] proves how much of a geographical dossier had been built in England for at least fifteen years before 1582 for Gilbert's use and largely by his means. All the local sources . . . had apparently been tapped. All the continental authorities in so far as they were to be located in print had likewise been gone over" (*Richard Hakluyt,* 80–81).

had access not only to the large Indian town of that name—and the gold that the "great captain" was said to have found there—but also to the fisheries of Newfoundland by way of an inland route. Cartier's description of Canada promised abundant sylvan resources and opportunities for the fur trade. In Dee's rendering, the river between the Saint Lawrence Valley and the Atlantic gives access to the passage to the Pacific. Thus Norembega, in the Dee cartography especially, presented all the opportunities that Menéndez de Avilés had fancied in connection with the Bahía de Santa María, without the impediment of the eighty-league portage over the mountains to the passage to China. It is not surprising that Gilbert would make Norembega his first objective or that Peckham would remain interested in a colony there even after Gilbert's death at sea.

Action to follow up on the growing body of information and belief about the geography and resources of North America was slow in developing. Because the details are of importance here only insofar as they bear on the English effort in Virginia, the story can be told briefly.

Occupied with Irish affairs and perhaps embarrassed by his expedition of 1578, Gilbert did no more than send Fernandes on a voyage in 1580 about which little more is known than its length of three to four months. Irene A. Wright believes that he may have gone to the southern part of Gilbert's patent area, that is, the modern Carolinas, but Quinn shows that he most likely went to the north, to scout the coast from Newfoundland to Norembega.[56]

When Gilbert returned to his colonial projects in 1582, his interest focused on Norembega. He intended to go to Newfoundland, establish his control under his letters patent of 1578, and then scout southward along the coast to that place of promise. He would leave a colony over the winter, and Peckham and other Catholic gentry would organize additional colonists to come in the spring. The Spanish ambassador, Mendoza, had heard as well that Elizabeth I meant to give Gilbert a large army to lodge at Norembega once he had established a settlement there.[57]

As in 1578, Gilbert failed to get to sea opportunely. Originally scheduled to sail in May, he departed only in September and once

56. Irene A. Wright (trans. and ed.), *Further English Voyages to Spanish America, 1583–1594* (London, 1951), xxii; Quinn, (ed.), *The Voyages of Gilbert,* I, 50.

57. Quinn, *England and the Discovery of America,* 267–68. On the lack of evidence for Gilbert's interest in the Northwest Passage at this time, see Quinn (ed.), *The Voyages of Gilbert,* I, 69.

again encountered unfavorable weather. As a result, he returned to port and postponed his voyage from 1582 until June 11, 1583. When he arrived at Newfoundland early in August, he proclaimed his lordship. The wreck of one of his ships later on, with the loss of most of his maps and papers, however, seems to have caused a change in his plans. He abandoned Newfoundland and the thought of a voyage on to Norembega, with the promise that the next year he would return with two expeditions, one to the north *and a second to the south.* Sailing home in a partially decked ship, Gilbert was lost at sea on September 9, when a following wave swamped his vessel.[58]

Gilbert had largely placed his plan for a settlement at Norembega in the hands of Peckham and other Catholic gentry even before he sailed in 1583, and Peckham maintained his interest after Gilbert's death in the face of pressure from Ambassador Mendoza and, perhaps, his own confessor. Though Mendoza had told Peckham that what he envisioned amounted to religious treason, Peckham's own view was that colonization between 30° and 60° north was "honest and profitable" and even a religious duty. England, he believed, had excellent claims, reaching back to the twelfth century and the voyage Madoc reputedly made. The land was rich, and large estates would flourish. Yet in the end, Peckham's project lapsed for want of support and, perhaps, because Raleigh, who received his half brother's privileges in 1584 by new letters patent, did not find the project of interest.[59]

Meanwhile the French under the direction of the Cardinal de Bourbon and others, had spent 1583 exploring both Norembega's river and the Saint Lawrence. Etienne Bellinger, of Rouen, visited Norembega, where he secured a valuable cargo of furs, and Michel Frotet de La Bardelière sailed up the Saint Lawrence a considerable distance during August.[60]

But the attempt to build on this successful exploration met with no better result than did Gilbert's voyages of 1578 and 1582. The Marquis de La Roche once again attempted to found a colony in the Saint Lawrence and Norembega area. On this occasion, in 1584, some of his ships sank before he was well clear of Europe.[61] Later French sailings

58. Quinn (ed.), *The Voyages of Gilbert,* I, 83–89, and Quinn, *England and the Discovery of America,* 377–79. Morison asserts that the ship was swamped by a following wave (*European Discovery of America,* 577).

59. Quinn (ed.), *The Voyages of Gilbert,* I, 71–76, 90–93; Quinn, *England and the Discovery of America,* 379–80 (quoting from Peckham's *A True Reporte*).

60. Roncière, *Histoire de la marine,* IV, 311–12.

61. *Ibid.*

to Canada were to concentrate on the known resources of the Saint Lawrence River valley and to relegate Norembega to service as an occasional trading stop.

With the failure of the several French and English expeditions of the 1570s and early 1580s to find sites for colonies or to establish colonies when they found sites—colonies that might serve as bases for the exploration of the putative Saint Lawrence River route to the Orient—the interest of explorers began to turn toward the southernmost of the three possible routes, if the conjectured way from the River of Santa Elena to the Verrazzano sea is excluded. The southern route was thought to lie at or below 40° north. During these years, the English, in particular, started to pay attention to the possibility of a passage there, and Gilbert, by the time of his death in 1583, was making the plans to go to that area which his cousin Raleigh carried out and followed up with the establishment of the Roanoke Island colonies.

The southern regions held the prospect not only of a way to the Orient but also of all the advantages of a new Andalucia whose products of field and forest might complement those of the Saint Lawrence area and provide England with a self-sufficient empire. Those potentials, elaborated upon in Carleill's *A Breef and Sommarie Discourse upon the entended Voyages to the Hethermoste Partes of America,* of 1583, and in Richard Hakluyt the Younger's "Discourse of Western Planting," of 1584, became especially attractive as the clouds of war with Spain grew darker over England. The Roanoke Island colonies were tests of those potentials.

XII

The English Test the Legends, 1583–1590

If the Saint Lawrence Valley area proved inhospitable and a graveyard of dreams during the 1570s, there remained the idea of a more southerly way to the passage to the Orient. Placed at or below 40° north, the southern way was credited with the additional advantage of a latitude offering the agricultural and sylvan potentials asserted for Chicora.

One can trace the gradual emergence of English interest in a southern route in the plans and propaganda of the 1570s and early 1580s. Direct action in pursuit of that interest began with Philip Amadas and Arthur Barlowe's voyage of 1584 and ended with Sir Richard Grenville's and Sir Walter Raleigh's Roanoke colonies and with the Spanish search for them in the context of ideas Vicente Gonzalez supplied on the basis both of Pedro Menéndez de Avilés' knowledge and his own experiences at Bahía de Santa María in the 1570s.

English attention to the presumed southern route to the Orient probably owed much to the fact that the French appeared during the 1570s to be attracted once more to the lower part of the North American coast. French activities in those years were along the same lines as in the 1560s and, like the voyages of Jean Ribault and René Goulaine de Laudonnière, were probably heavily influenced by the Chicora legend, which had widened its influence with the publication in French of Francisco Lopez de Gómara's book in 1569, 1577, and 1578.[1] The experiences of the 1560s, however, likely allowed French planners to recognize the error in Gómara's too southerly implied location for Chicora. At least Laudonnière had seen the mistake when he wrote his *L'Histoire notable de la Florida,* which was published in 1586.[2]

1. Francisco Lopez de Gómara, *Histoire generalle des Indes Occidentales et terres neuues, qui iusques a present ont esté decouuertee,* trans. Martin Fumée (Paris, 1569). Two different printers issued this work in 1569. It was reprinted in 1577, 1578, 1584, 1587, 1597, and 1605.

2. Laudonnière, *L'Histoire notable,* fols. 15v–17, pp. 59–60 (*Three Voyages,* 29–30).

Informed Englishmen like Hakluyt may have seen it by the early 1580s.

The publication of Richard Hakluyt the Younger's *Diveres Voyages* in 1582, with Michael Lok's map, and of *Les Trois Mondes*, by Lancelot Voisin, Sieur de La Popelinière, in 1583, further focused thought on the southern option in the search for a way to the Orient. La Popelinière's work also underlined the agricultural and mineral promise of Chicora.

Dr. John Dee's map of 1582, though not a public document, shows that Englishmen interested in western voyages had gathered together all the available information about the possible routes for the passage to the Orient. In the case of some of the possibilities that Dee depicted, such as that of a connection between the River Jordan, shown at the Point of Santa Elena, and Verrazzano's sea, one can discover the probable original in the Harlien Mappemonde, a manuscript map of the 1540s. In the case of other possibilities, such as that of the Saint Lawrence route, the ideas come from Jacques Cartier's voyages. In the case of still other possibilities, his source is unknown. The inclusion in Dee's map, as in Lok's, of the southern route shows that information about the lower part of North America was available in England by 1582, even if some of the key books containing it had not yet been reprinted or translated there, as they were later to be under the direction of Hakluyt the Younger.

Christopher Carleill's pamphlet *A Breef and Sommarie Discourse . . .*, of 1583, gives further evidence that the potential of a southern colony was well understood in England. After reviewing the dangers facing England's foreign trade, Carleill argued that a colony at 40° north or thereabout would give his countrymen a location from which to exploit the fish, timber, and furs of the northern part of the continent. Below 40° north, they could develop a wine industry, he thought, and produce olive oil. They could get wax and honey from the Indians, and salt works were a possibility. Eventually, he suggested, other products that England imported from "Dutchland, Italie, France, and Spaine" might come from the southern part of the continent, reducing dependence on producers who might become enemies and on sea routes that passed potential enemies' shores. The colony would also be an outlet for English textiles and other manufactures that the native population might buy. Furthermore,

> if there bee any possible meanes to finde a sea passage or other freshe water course, whiche may serve in some reasonable and convenient sorte, to

> transport our marchandize into the East Indian Sea, through any of these Northerly partes of America, it shalbe sonest and moste assuredly performed by these who shall inhabite and first grow into familiaritie with the Inlande people.[3]

Whether for immediate returns on trade, longer-term prospects, or the possibility of a way to the Orient, a colony at about 40° north was, in Carleill's judgment, the answer to England's need.

In Richard Hakluyt the Younger's "Discourse of Western Planting," of 1584, the long list of possible products from an American colony also ran strongly to imports from Andalucia, such as olive oil, wine, and certain dyestuffs. Like Carleill, Hakluyt discussed the passage to the Orient as a possible benefit from the proposed colony.[4] The "Discourse" was the last in the line of promotional tracts preceding actual colonization.

In view of these materials, which must be but the tip of an iceberg of others that once existed, it is not surprising that Sir Humphrey Gilbert could announce in 1583 that he would head out on more southerly voyages in 1584; nor is it surprising that, when Gilbert died, his half brother, Raleigh, undertook the expeditions and followed up with a colony at a latitude that promised access to the southern, or Chesapeake Bay, passage to the Orient and the potential riches of a new Andalucia.[5]

Once Raleigh had secured his letters patent of March 16, 1584,

3. Carleill, *A Breef and Sommarie Discourse,* in Quinn (ed.), *New American World,* III, 30 (and in Quinn [ed.], *The Voyages of Gilbert,* 358). For a discussion of Carleill's reasons for preparing this pamphlet, see *The Voyages of Gilbert,* I, 76–81.

4. For a discussion of resources, see Richard Hakluyt, "A Discourse of Western Planting, 1584," in Richard Hakluyt, *The Original Writings and Correspondence of the Two Richard Hakluyts,* ed. Eva G. R. Taylor (2 vols.; London, 1935), II, 223–26, 232–33, 317. On the strait, see pp. 254, 283–89, esp. 287.

5. David B. Quinn theorizes that Raleigh was interested in the southern part of North America because (*a*) Gilbert's original grant of all of North America not occupied by another Christian prince's subjects had been reduced by Gilbert's concession of his interests north of 50° north to Dr. Dee, who passed them on to Adrian Gilbert (confirmed by a patent of February 6, 1584); (*b*) Newfoundland and its fishery were considered either the queen's dominion or the property of Sir John Gilbert, Humphrey's heir; and (*c*) the Peckham project for Norembega was still alive (*Set Fair for Roanoke: Voyages and Colonies, 1584–1606* [Chapel Hill, N.C., 1985], 9). Quinn also suggests that the selection of Roanoke was due to the influence of Simon Fernandes, who claimed to have expert knowledge of the coast which he had gained prior to 1584 ("A Portuguese Pilot in the English Service," in *England and the Discovery of America,* 254). It is my contention that the Chicora legend and the legend surrounding Verrazzano's false sea were as important, if not more important, in determining where Raleigh chose to begin his work of exploration and colonization.

making him Gilbert's heir, he immediately sent out a scouting expedition under the command of Amadas and Barlowe. Their pilot was Simon Fernandes.

Sailing in April, Amadas and Barlowe used the Canary Islands–Antilles route. Once clear of the Straits of Florida, they proceeded directly north on a course that has always been taken to indicate that they knew where they were going, at least in general terms. On July 2, they smelled the land, and on July 4, they made landfall, probably to the east of Cape Fear. From that point they coasted northeastward, seeking inlets. They found the first at Hatarask (now filled in and part of modern Bodie Island). Entering Pamlico Sound with some difficulty because of the shallowness of the estuaries, they began a period of exploration and contacts with the Indians who lived along the sound's shores and on Roanoke Island.

Barlowe's published account of what he found was worthy of Ayllón or Verrazzano:

> We viewed the land about us, being whereas we first landed very sandy and low towards the water side, but so full of grapes as the very beating and surge of the sea overflowed them. . . . I think in all the world the like abundance is not to be found. . . . This island hath many goodly woods and full of deer, conies, hares, and fowl, even in the midst of summer in incredible abundance. The woods are . . . the highest and reddest cedars in the world, . . . pines, cypress, sassafras, the lentisk or the tree that beareth the mastic, the tree that beareth the rind of black cinnamon, . . . and many other of excellent smell and quality.[6]

Barlowe perceived the area as one of abundance, whose inhabitants were friendly toward the English even if sometimes at war among themselves. Not a farmer, he did not assess the quality of the soils or the extent of the ground capable of supporting agriculture. Like his predecessors who had been new upon the coast, he assumed that the plenty he saw was limitless, and he did not inquire why the Indian villages were widely scattered and had moderate populations of a few hundred at most.

Roanoke Island, with its one Indian settlement, particularly impressed him and the other Englishmen, who saw it as suitable for a colony. The island was large and heavily wooded. Indian old fields apparently dotted it, especially at the northern end where the Indians

6. Arthur Barlowe, "Discourse of the First Voyage," in David B. Quinn (ed.), *Roanoke Voyages, 1584–1590* (2 vols.; London, 1955), I, 94–95.

lived. Their crop was just coming in when the English visited, which must have given additional but misleading evidence of abundance. The English had exceptionally cordial relations with the local chief, Granganimeo. Offsetting the ostensibly favorable conditions, though, was the difficulty that shallow entrances through the Outer Banks caused for getting to the island. But it seems that that difficulty in time came to be viewed as an advantage, a defense against the Spaniards.

After no more than a month of explorations, Barlowe's party returned to England, arriving about mid-September, 1584. It was accompanied by Manteo and Wanchese, men from different, sometimes hostile villages. Manteo soon became Thomas Harriot's chief informant about Algonquian and eventually a source about the prospects of the region.

David B. Quinn has presented evidence that while Barlowe was engaged at Pamlico and Roanoke sounds, Amadas sailed northward along the Outer Banks looking for other entrances and acquainting himself with the details of the coastline. Apparently Amadas and Simon Fernandes entered Chesapeake Bay, where they may have encountered Indians who attacked and killed some of the crew. From there they appear to have sailed toward Bermuda and then the Azores in search of Spanish ships. Failing to find any, they returned to England sometime after Barlowe had come back.[7]

If Amadas and Fernandes did explore the Chesapeake Bay, their report would have strengthened the position of those urging creation of the first settlement at Roanoke Island. Large and deep as it was, the Chesapeake Bay harbored hostile Indians, and any approach to it would have required extreme care. The account Barlowe wrote of his experiences was quickly copied, and it circulated to interested persons. Amadas signed it, but appended nothing about his own activities. The stage was set for the colony that Grenville would take to North America in the spring of 1585.

Grenville departed from England on April 9, 1585, with seven small ships and as many as six hundred men. In his voyage through the Antilles, where he obtained animals and samples of plants from sometimes willing Spaniards, he made no secret of his general destination and intentions. On June 26, the forward vessels of his fleet, reduced by a storm encountered off Portugal but augmented by prizes taken in

7. Quinn, *Set Fair for Roanoke,* 42–43.

the Antilles, entered Wococon Inlet. During the next two weeks, other ships of the original fleet straggled in, and Grenville decided to leave a hundred men at Roanoke Island under the command of Ralph Lane.[8]

The details of the founding of this first English colony and of the settlement's relations with the Indians have recently come in for extensive scholarly and popular discussion in connection with the four hundredth anniversary of the Roanoke Island settlements.[9] For the purposes of the present study, three parts of the story merit attention.

First, during the fall and winter of 1585–1586, Lane, John White, Thomas Harriot, and others systematically explored and mapped a major part of the area. One party conducted a survey of the sounds behind the Outer Banks but sighted no deep entrance or harbor. Hence, they realized that a Roanoke Island colony would continue to depend on the smallest ships and the ones of shallowest draft. On the other hand, the party sent to the south side of Chesapeake Bay found good, deepwater anchorages. The third party went a four days' row up the Roanoke River, to perhaps near modern Plymouth, North Carolina.

White's map was the fruit of these voyages. Remarkably accurate, it in engraved form remained the standard representation of the area of the Outer Banks for a century. Included in the lower left of the manuscript version of the map was the depiction of a route from the River of Santa Elena to a large body of water, either Verrazzano's sea or the lake that Dr. Dee's map showed lying between the Santa Elena and Verrazzano's sea. Thus did legend get coupled with accurate, on-the-ground cartography. Printed versions of the map, however, did not include that feature.

The second part of the story to recall is that the English did not discover exploitable resources capable of making the Roanoke colony profitable. The tropical plants from the Antilles probably did not survive the voyage to Roanoke, but even if some did, the relative cold

8. *Ibid.*, 55–66.

9. Besides Quinn's *Set Fair for Roanoke*, the following items have been published: David N. Durant, *Raleigh's Lost Colony* (New York, 1981): David Stick, *Roanoke Island, The Beginnings of English America* (Chapel Hill, N.C., 1983); Karen O. Kupperman, *Roanoke: The Abandoned Colony* (Totowa, N.J., 1984); Paul Hulton (ed.), *America, 1585: The Complete Drawings of John White* (Chapel Hill, N.C, 1984). The America's Four Hundredth Anniversary Committee of the state of North Carolina has also issued a set of poster-leaflets and a series of pamphlets on various aspects of the Roanoke colonies' history and on Indian life and culture.

of a North Carolina winter and the unsuitability of the soils of Roanoke Island must have killed them. Even crops native to the European temperate latitudes do not seem to have done well, primarily because the English did not cultivate them, relying instead on Indian labor, rather like the Spaniards elsewhere in the New World. The Indians had a few dyestuffs but nothing the English judged to be of commercial value. An attempt to reach the copper mines, and what were possibly gold mines, reputedly lying up the Roanoke River failed well short of its objective. It must have become obvious by June, 1586, that the areas of good soil on Roanoke Island and along the margins of rivers feeding into the sounds were limited. Even with willing Indian labor, which had virtually disappeared by then, cultivation of this ground would not support more than a few hundred Europeans, well short of the force that Raleigh had projected. From an economic standpoint, it was evident that Roanoke Island would not do in the long run as a seat of colonial activity.

The third part of the story of interest here is that Lane and most of the other Englishmen squandered the initial friendliness of the Indians by arrogant, and eventually violent, demands for food and labor. The crisis came, as it had come for the French at Fort Caroline, in May and June. The English found themselves short of food because their supply ships did not arrive, as promised, by Easter (April 3, 1586 o.s.). Unable to get enough food from their increasingly uneasy hosts, in the end they resorted to violence to prevent what they saw as an imminent concerted Indian attack on the colony. They thus ensured that their further presence at Roanoke would be an armed one.

Sir Francis Drake, who appeared off the colony on June 8/18, brought relief. Lane seems by then to have determined to abandon the settlement but only after he had made some discovery that would justify the year's expense and so let him escape responsibility for failure. The Chesapeake Bay seemed to hold the greatest likelihood of allowing such a discovery. Lane therefore got Drake to agree to provide supplies and a shallow-draft ship so that he could continue the exploration of Chesapeake Bay he had begun the previous winter. Drake would carry the disillusioned and unfit to England, with Lane and his party following once they had finished with the bay.[10]

The plans they had settled upon changed when a storm blew up on June 13/23 and drove Drake's fleet to sea. When the ships reas-

10. Quinn, *Set Fair for Roanoke,* 134–38.

sembled after three days, the vessel they had been preparing for Lane's use was among the missing. Since no other ship of suitable draft was available, Lane and Drake agreed on June 17/27 to withdraw the colony, and on June 18/28, the fleet sailed for England. Within a matter of days, the supply ship that Raleigh had fitted arrived. Late in sailing from England, and perhaps delayed en route, it found no one. Its captain returned it to England.

During the time that these developments were occurring at Roanoke, Grenville was once again at sea, this time with a complement of five ships and about four hundred men. He seems to have intended either to reinforce the Roanoke Island colony by setting up a new village on the mainland—and seizing Indian lands—or to go to Chesapeake Bay. When he arrived at Roanoke in mid-July, he found no one, although a Spanish pilot who was on this voyage as a captive later said that the bodies of an Englishman and an Indian were hanging from a gallows. After perhaps two weeks of exploring the sounds, Grenville determined to return the major part of his force to England. By then he had captured an Indian who knew enough English to indicate that the first colonists had left with Drake. Not wanting to abandon the enterprise completely, Grenville left fifteen volunteers at the Roanoke Island site until he or some other representative of Raleigh might return. He then sailed for Bermuda and the Azores in search of Spanish ships. The Indians eventually attacked the men he left. Those of the English who escaped death in the assault fled in a small boat that was probably lost at sea.[11]

The conclusion that Lane and his backers drew from the first experiences with the reality, as against the legends, of North America in the mid-thirties north latitude was that

> the discovery of a good mine . . . or a passage to the South Sea, or some way to it, and nothing else can bring this country in request to be inhabited by our nation. And with the discovery of any of the two above showed, it will be the most sweet and healthfulest climate, and therewithal the most fertile soil, being manured, in the world. And then will sassafras and many other good roots and gums there found make good merchandise and lading for shipping, which otherwise of themselves will not be worth the fetching.[12]

11. *Ibid.*, 143–47.

12. Ralph Lane, "Discourse on the First Colony," in Quinn (ed.), *Roanoke Voyages*, I, 273 (quoted by Quinn in *Set Fair for Roanoke*, 147).

Pedro Díaz, the Spanish pilot Grenville captured in 1585 and took with him to Roanoke in 1586, later summarized English motives in essentially similar terms, saying,

> The reason why the English have settled here is . . . because on the mainland there is much gold, and so that they may pass from the North to the South Sea, which they say and understand is nearby.[13]

In sum, the conclusion was that the future of Virginia lay in the exploration of the mainland for mines and the passage to the Orient, not in developing an agricultural settlement on a small island in a shallow sound, even if it was at 36° north, the latitude of Andalucia. Future reconnoitering would be from the shores of the Chesapeake Bay. Lane's plans for the summer of 1586 suggested as much, and Raleigh's for the spring of 1587 made it altogether clear. The Chicora legend, in its larger form, was all but dead among the English. Gold and the legendary passage to China occupied their interest after 1586. Only much later, and slowly, did the possibility of an agricultural colony regain its appeal.

The Spaniards knew about Raleigh's colonial plans in February, 1585, but it was the middle of 1586 before they thought they knew where the colony was. As Bernardino de Mendoza, Philip II's ambassador to England—who had been expelled in 1584—reported from Paris, Raleigh's plan was to sail for Norembega. News from Lisbon later that spring gave Grenville's destination as "Naranvel," a land between La Florida and Newfoundland. Grenville's passage through the Antilles gave rise to the speculation that he was bound for La Florida or an island in the Bahama Channel. That conjecture caused the governor of Florida, Pedro Menéndez Marqués, sufficient concern that he went back from Havana to Saint Augustine and postponed his return to Spain, planned for the summer of 1585. All he could learn in La Florida was that the English had sailed up the coast beyond the limit of his network of Indian reporters.[14]

13. Wright (trans. and ed.), *Further English Voyages,* 239 (and in Quinn [ed.], *Roanoke Voyages,* 791; quoted by Quinn [ed.], in *Set Fair for Roanoke,* 145).

14. Mendoza, in Quinn (ed.), *Roanoke Voyages,* II, 728–29; memorandum regarding English corsairs in letter of Don Alvaro de Bazán to House of Trade (?), Lisbon, April 30, 1585, AGI, CT 5101; Antilles reports, in Wright (trans. and ed.), *Further English Voyages,* 9–12, 15–16 (and in Quinn [ed.], *Roanoke Voyages,* 733–38); Diego Fernández de Quiñones to king, Havana, January 18, 1586, AGI, SD 126 (Stetson).

In Spain, the opinion seemed to be that the English had indeed gone to La Florida to settle but intended to do so well to the north of Spain's colonies and thus were no immediate threat to them. Even in November, when the Council of the Indies had confirmation that the English had settled in La Florida, it used its information only to hasten consideration of and action on Menéndez Marqués' long-standing requests for replacement soldiers and supplies for La Florida.[15]

A more precise estimation of where the English had settled developed in La Florida and the Antilles early in 1586. Menéndez Marqués concluded that the English had gone to a headland (*cabo*) on the coast where there was said to be a passage to the southern sea. In Jamaica, a man put ashore by one of Grenville's ships revealed that the English were going to a headland at 36° north on their charts but at 38.5° north on a Spanish map he was shown. The same Englishman accurately described the sounds behind the Outer Banks and mentioned the supposed passage to the southern sea. At Havana, the king's officials decided that the English had gone to the Bahía de Santa María, and Menéndez Marqués came to accept that view during the spring.[16] Alonso Suarez de Toledo, who had been to the Bahía de Santa María in 1572, described it as having a "good climate, thickly populated country, with great plantings and stores of maize on the cob in great closed houses, vast meadows, the Indians [illegible] and without arms, wild fruits like those of our Spain."[17] In short, from their own knowledge of the land perhaps more than from what they had been able to learn from the English, the Spaniards in La Florida and the Antilles formed the belief that the foreigners had gone to the one place on the coast that seemed especially desirable for further exploration and settlement. The information obtained in Jamaica was interpreted as supporting the correctness of this opinion rather than appreciated as fact that could guide the Spaniards to where the English actually were.

The Spaniards formulated their ideas against the background of Drake's attack on Saint Augustine, during which he stripped the

15. Deposition of Enrique Lopez, Fayal [November 18, 1585 (?)], in Wright (trans. and ed.), *Further English Voyages*, 12–15; *consulta* of the Council of the Indies, December 14, 1585, AGI, IG 1866, No. 2. The supplies did not arrive at Saint Augustine until after Drake had attacked and burned it.

16. Pedro Menéndez Marqués to Gutierre de Miranda, Saint Augustine, February 8, 1586, AGI, SD 231, No. 64, fol. 15; the licenciado Francisco Marqués de Villalobos to king, Jamaica, June 27, 1586, in Wright (trans. and ed.), *Further English Voyages*, 175.

17. Alonso Suarez de Toledo to king, Havana, June 27, 1586, *ibid.*, 172–73.

settlement of ironwork, doors, and other items of value to a colony. Apparently intending to drive the Spaniards from Santa Elena rather than Saint Augustine, he had attacked the latter only because one of his pilots had pointed out that they were opposite it.

Menéndez Marqués' defense of Saint Augustine had been largely pro forma, and he evidently felt he needed to tender some explanation. Too, since Drake had supposedly threatened to return to Saint Augustine in 1587 to seize it for use as a base against the Spanish convoys and Antilles, the town needed supplies of all sorts in order to regain its defensibility. Menéndez Marqués had reason to send an agent to Spain, and he chose Captain Gonzalez, who reached Spain early in September.[18] The Council of the Indies met shortly thereafter and suggested consolidating the La Florida garrisons into a single fort at the head of the Florida Keys. It said nothing about the English colony.

At Madrid, in response to an invitation to discuss La Florida's needs, Gonzalez offered his thoughts on where the English had settled: at a port with a mouth two leagues (6.4 nautical miles) wide that was thirty leagues long and five or six leagues wide. Mountains were nearby, where the Indians obtained gold and Captain Juan Pardo's men had found diamonds. The land was rich in various sorts of agricultural products, and New Mexico was but a five days' journey once one had crossed the mountains. The English, Gonzalez hypothesized, had settled on a river north of this port, a river that the Indians said ran to the southern sea.

The Council of the Indies quickly drew Gonzalez' remarks to Philip II's attention, noting that if he was correct, the port of which he spoke might be suitable for a Spanish settlement that could help pay the expenses of La Florida's garrisons. Philip II relayed the substance of Gonzalez' comments in an order of November 27, 1586, addressed to Menéndez Marqués, instructing him to investigate the truth of what the captain had laid out as quickly as possible and to determine the location of the corsair settlement.[19]

Gonzalez handed Menéndez Marqués the king's order when he got back to Saint Augustine in May, 1587. With the rebuilding of Saint

18. *Ibid.*, 184–86, 188–89, 190–91.

19. *Consulta*, October 24, 1586, AGI, IG 741, No. 125; king to Pedro Menéndez Marqués, Madrid, November 27, 1586, AGI, IG 541, fols. 7v–8 (Stetson). Hoffman discusses Gonzalez' declaration, in "New Light on Vicente Gonzalez's 1588 Voyage," 209–216.

Augustine then well along and no reports of an English fleet preparing to attack the Caribbean, Menéndez Marqués decided to carry out the order in person. Using two ships and accompanied by Gonzalez, he sailed northward, stopping at Santa Elena and a number of other, unspecified, ports as he went. He found, he later reported, that there was "no memory" of the English. His attempt to enter Chesapeake Bay failed because a storm blew him to sea when he tried to round Cape Henry. Forced to sail for the Bahamas, he ended his voyage at Havana on June 19. Writing a few days later, he said that he would try again the following spring and asked permission to sail as far as Newfoundland. He had found that his charts were inaccurate and recognized the need to gather better information.[20] He may also have wanted to raid the English fishery at Newfoundland in retaliation for Bernard Drake's devastating attack of 1585 on the Spanish and Portuguese fishing fleets in those waters.[21]

At Havana, Menéndez Marqués met with the major general (*maestre de campo*) Juan de Tejeda, the man who had final authority on whether to consolidate the two La Florida garrisons and, if so, where to locate the resulting defense. They agreed to dismantle Santa Elena and return its soldiers and civilians to Saint Augustine to strengthen it against the attack that Menéndez Marqués believed the English would deliver in 1588. When he returned to La Florida, he implemented the decision they had reached, withdrawing the Spanish settlement at Santa Elena during August, 1587. What Sir Francis Drake had failed to accomplish directly, he accomplished indirectly, through his threat to return and seize Saint Augustine for use as a base against the convoys.[22]

Unknown to Menéndez Marqués, Englishmen under the command of White were also at sea that June, on their way to Chesapeake Bay by way of Roanoke Island. When they made Roanoke, Fernandes, the chief pilot, refused to take the ships farther, claiming that the season was late, by which he apparently meant that it was getting late to go on a privateering cruise, his objective once he left the colonists. White "weakly acquiesced" in that judgment, to quote Quinn. The settlers rebuilt Roanoke, but apparently only as a temporary stopping place until they could make arrangements to move fifty miles into

20. Wright (trans. and ed.), *Further English Voyages*, 232–33.

21. Morison briefly describes Drake's raid, in *European Discovery of America*, 472–73.

22. Lyon, *Santa Elena*, 15–16.

the mainland. Quinn suggests that they had already decided to locate the city of Raleigh among the Chesapeake Indians, along the Elizabeth River. The colonists had apparently wanted to approach their site by going up the Elizabeth from the Chesapeake Bay but now intended to do so from Roanoke. They also decided, and eventually persuaded White, that he should return to England for supplies and, because of his command of the coastal geography, lead the relief ships to Chesapeake Bay. Reluctantly, he sailed for England on August 28/September 7, 1587.[23]

Three years elapsed before he returned to Roanoke Island, and by then the colony had vanished. Recent scholarship suggests that the settlers successfully made the move to the Chesapeake Indians' area and that some of the English lived with those Indians as late as 1606, the year that Powhatan had both the Englishmen who were there and the Chesapeake Indians killed so that he would have no rivals in dealing with the English then moving into Jamestown.[24] Spain knew none of the history of the third English colony until 1589, except for the English intention to move to the Chesapeake Bay, which it was aware of in the spring of 1587. Even in 1589, it knew only part of the history.

With the coming of May, 1588, Menéndez Marqués again prepared to seek out the settlement that the king's order mandated him to investigate. Not having received Philip II's permission to explore the coast as far as the cod fisheries and then return to Spain, nor any instructions beyond the original, Menéndez Marqués sent Gonzalez in a single ship to scout the coast to 39° north and to take careful latitudes and soundings, especially at the Bahía de Santa María. If possible, Gonzalez was to contact Don Luís de Velasco, the Indian who had figured in the tragedy of the Jesuit mission. Gonzales sailed from Saint Augustine about May 30.[25]

He seems to have gone directly to Chesapeake Bay. Entering it early in June, he carefully explored the western side to the mouth of the Susquehanna River and then less systematically worked down the eastern shore before recrossing to the west and leaving the bay. He had

23. Quinn, *Set Fair for Roanoke*, 275–94, with quotation from p. 279.

24. *Ibid.*, 295–377. See also David B. Quinn, *The Lost Colonists: Their Fortune and Probable Fate* (Raleigh, N.C., 1984).

25. Instructions to Vicente Gonzalez, Saint Augustine, May 24, 1588, copy in merits-and-services petition of Vicente Gonzalez, Madrid, September 27, 1593, AGI, PAT 260 (Stetson).

little contact with the Indians and saw no evidence of an English presence. Apparently satisfied that he had carried out his assignment, he was sailing south along the Outer Banks when a storm arose that threatened to drive him to sea. Not wanting to be forced to the Antilles, he struck sail and had his ship rowed into one of the inlets among the banks, where he encountered his first evidence of the English. He apparently did not see the Roanoke Island settlement; at least there is no mention of it in the surviving accounts of his voyage. But that the English had been there was beyond doubt. When the weather cleared, he sailed for Saint Augustine with that important finding.[26]

During the same summer, officials at Havana got confirmation that the English were settled at the Bahía de Santa María. George Carey had captured Alonso Ruiz, a seaman, off Matanzas, Cuba, in June, 1587. Carey had put into the Bahía de Santa María on his way home to England, and Ruiz had seen "signs of horned cattle and a branded mule" but no settlers,[27] as he told the officials at Havana after working his way back from England by way of the Antilles.

This intelligence, and the lack of word from Menéndez Marqués about the success of Gonzalez' voyage, prompted Philip II to order the governor to scout the coast personally and then to return to Spain with what he had been able to learn about the location of any foreign settlements. When a new governor arrived in the spring of 1589, Menéndez Marqués, Gonzalez, and Juan Menéndez Marqués, Pedro's cousin, sailed for Spain with the information Gonzalez had acquired. They were aware that Díaz was on his way to Spain at the same time to recount his experiences as a captive of Grenville from 1585 until his escape in 1588 owing to a seizure by French privateers. An experienced pilot who had been to Roanoke twice in Grenville's service, Díaz could give a detailed account of the English effort and of the location of the settlement, to the south of the Bahía de Santa María.[28]

At long last, from Gonzalez' on-the-ground discovery and Díaz' testimony, the Spaniards knew exactly where the English had settled.

26. The only account of the voyage is found in Luís Jerónimo de Oré's *Relación histórica de la Florida* (1612; rpr. Madrid, 1931–33), translated by Maynard Geiger as *The Martyrs of Florida* (New York, 1936). The translation appears in Quinn (ed.), *Roanoke Voyages,* 772–75; and in Lewis and Loomie's *The Spanish Jesuit Mission,* 185–88 (Spanish, pp. 175–78).

27. Wright (trans. and ed.), *Further English Voyages,* 233–35 (and in Quinn [ed.], *Roanoke Voyages,* 781–84).

28. Díaz' report is in Wright (trans. and ed.), *Further English Voyages,* 237–41 (and in Quinn [ed.], *Roanoke Voyages,* 786–95). Wright's translation is not entirely accurate.

They also knew that a colony had been left at Roanoke in 1587 but had not been resupplied in 1588 because the French had captured the ships carrying supplies—and Díaz. The stage was set for action against the English colony and for a Spanish move to seize the Bahía de Santa María and, with it, access to the supposed passage to the Orient and the gold and diamond mines in the mountains behind the coast.

Menéndez Marqués reached Seville on July 5, 1589. It is not known when he reached Madrid. According to the mistaken story of the seventeenth-century Franciscan chronicler Luís Jerónimo de Oré, major discussions followed as the Spaniards tried to decide how to deal with the English colony, which they feared would be a base for commerce raiders against the Antilles. The result of the deliberations, according to Oré, was a plan to send Pedro Menéndez Marqués back to Florida with reinforcements and supplies. Sailing by way of Havana, where he was to add the Havana galleys to his fleet, he was, on making Saint Augustine, to exchange the new soldiers for the veterans of the garrison there and then proceed to Roanoke Island to drive the English from their settlement. Afterward, he was to go to the Bahía de Santa María to establish a fort with a three-hundred-man garrison that could explore the backcountry in search of the mines and the way to the Orient. On Oré's telling, only a sudden urgent need to bring Philip II's revenues from Tierra Firme in 1590 prevented action on this plan. Menéndez Marqués had to command the two *galizabras* that fetched the royal revenues.[29]

In fact, there is no sign of a discussion of an expedition against the Roanoke Island settlement in the documents in the Archive of the Indies or the Archivo General de Simancas. Apparently the English colony was of low enough priority by the summer of 1589 that it did not merit extended, recorded discussion. What actually happened is that in April, 1590, Philip II and his closest advisers realized that the convoy due to sail to Tierra Firme that spring would not be able to return safely that fall, because of its lateness in getting under way and its poor armament. Inasmuch as the king's credit was at stake, they decided to have two *galizabras* make a quick run for a million pesos, enough to tide the government over until they could bring the rest of the funds in greater safety early in 1591. They were conscious that,

29. Oré, as found in Quinn (ed.), *Roanoke Voyages*, 814, and Juan Menéndez Marqués' deposition of 1606, *ibid.*, 817. Quinn's discussion of this supposed plan is on p. 775.

small and swift but lightly armed, the *galizabras* would be no match for any fleet the English might have lying in wait once the vessels' route and timetable were evident. Hence, Philip II and his advisers developed a double deception to hide the purpose of the *galizabras'* voyage. On the one hand, the commander of the convoy to Tierra Firme received instructions to hasten his preparations for sailing so that his convoy could make the round trip. The *galizabras* were prepared as part of that convoy. On the other hand, the king's advisers sent Pedro Menéndez Marqués to Seville to assume command of the *galizabras* under the public order to take them to La Florida because there was "news of English corsairs."[30] These public orders were what Oré recorded as fact. Only after the ships were at sea did Menéndez Marqués steer for the Isthmus of Panama and did the commander of the convoy open his sealed orders calling for him to winter at Havana.

Menéndez Marqués made the trip to Tierra Firme in near-record time. He left Cartagena, in Colombia, for Spain between July 3 and July 7, entered Havana on the twentieth, and departed on the twenty-third. He was at Viana, Portugual, by the end of August.[31]

By the end of August, 1590, new reports circulated in the Antilles and in Spain that the English might be planning a major fleet action for 1591 and that their colony in North America might be a part of the action. The report that a "governor" for the colony was on one of the English ships that came near Havana in the summer of 1590 seemed to confirm the threat. In fact, White was on one of the privateers. Another report, accurate as to White's intentions if not in its details, said that the English were going to North America to try to rescue two hundred men who had been shipwrecked there.[32]

Exactly when these reports from the Antilles reached Madrid in the fall of 1590 is not certain, but the degree of Spanish interest in the English menace and in the Chesapeake Bay area and its reputed mineral and geographical resources is obvious in a note written on a Council of the Indies *consulta* of November 8, 1590. The *consulta* advised Philip II of talk that Sir Francis Drake was arming twenty galleons for an attack on Havana and said that it was in the air that

30. *Pareceres* of Antonio de Guevarra, Pedro Menéndez Marqués, *et al.*, April 9–14, 1590, AGS, GA 302, Nos. 190–95, with quotation from No. 195.

31. Chaunu and Chaunu, *Seville et l'Atlantique,* III, 450, 464.

32. Wright (trans. and ed.), *Further English Voyages,* 253–54, 256; Diego Menéndez Marqués to SM, Puerto Rico, May 13, 1590, AGI, IG 1877, No. 82.

English corsairs had wintered at their settlement in La Florida. Later events proved that this note, although not intended as such, was the epitaph for Spanish belief in the sixteenth-century forms of the legends of the 1520s as well as for Spain's official interest in extending its colonies toward the north, to the latitudes of the Chesapeake Bay and Andalucia. The note says,

> In regards the English who have settled in Florida, when it can be done, expelling them from there will be looked at in all the respects that ought to be considered.[33]

33. *Consulta,* November 8, 1590, AGI, IG 741 (Stetson).

Epilogue

John White's failure of 1590 to find the third Roanoke Island colony and the postponement that fall of further Spanish consideration of action against that colony marked the end of efforts during the sixteenth century to find out the truth about the Chicora and Verrazzano legends by carrying out exploration and colonization in the American Southeast. The year 1590 also marked the end of the period that saw publication of source materials that, on the one hand, turned the light of experience on the Chicora legend, causing it to fade, and on the other, gave some additional hope that there existed a passage across much of the North American continent. After 1590, the legends lingered on in the minds of a generation of men who had learned them during the years 1560–1590, but they did not galvanize new actions.

Because the Chicora legend dealt with agricultural and sylvan potentials that were tested in the coastal zone itself, it, of the two legends, suffered the more rapid erosion as experience with the coast enlarged and won exposure in print. As the present study shows, the Spaniards learned early that the Chicora legend was largely fiction. It regained currency among them only in the 1550s and 1560s because it became linked with Soto's Cofitachequi, an inland province, with the Point of Santa Elena, and with French imperial designs. Spaniards' experiences at Santa Elena during the 1560s and 1570s disabused all but the most irrepressibly optimistic of any notion of great agricultural, sylvan, commercial, or mineral wealth along the coast at that point. The few Spaniards who visited the Chesapeake Bay in 1570–1572 recognized that its shores held the promise of agricultural, sylvan, and trade benefits, but they were unable to overcome the negative image of the coast that had formed after Ayllón's failure, which had contrasted sharply with the Chicora legend's boasts. Moreover, a Vicente Gonzalez lacked the financial resources and sociopolitical clout to gain more than a hearing for his message that the Chesapeake Bay was a site where a colony of Europeans could flourish. Too, the coupling of the bay with the Verrazzano legend in the writings of Pedro Menéndez de Avilés and his intellectual heirs such as Gonzalez probably increased the official skepticism of any plan to use the bay as a point of colonization and exploration. Official Spanish cartography showed North America as a wide continent, with no arm of the western sea reaching toward the Atlantic Ocean.

The French experience with the coast at Port Royal Sound was of short duration—about eight months—in 1562–1563 but long enough so that when René Goulaine de Laudonnière returned to La Florida in 1564 he and his captains determined to build their first camp well to the south, among the Timucuan Indians of the Saint Johns River. The Timucua seemed to have abundant food resources as well as access to salvaged precious metals. The Indian societies around Port Royal Sound had neither. The French planned further explorations in and around, and possibly north of, Port Royal Sound because they still thought that Chicora was real even if they knew that it was not at Port Royal Sound, as Jean Ribault had wanted to believe in 1562. Menéndez de Avilés and his soldiers destroyed the French at Fort Caroline before they could carry out their intentions. Laudonnière, however, escaped and wrote down a history of the French in La Florida.

Thanks to the interest of Richard Hakluyt the Younger, Laudonnière's manuscript was published in Paris in 1586 and in English translation in London in 1587. Although Laudonnière meant the book to promote the Roanoke Island settlements and further French imperial ventures against the Spaniards, the volume made it clear that Francisco Lopez de Gómara's geography was wrong. Chicora was not near the Point of Santa Elena, as Ribault had thought, but farther to the north.[1] To reinforce the point, Laudonnière inserted the Le Moyne map that showed Chicora well above Santa Elena and up a broad river or bay (Map 11). How he reached his conclusion about the location he does not say, but it is likely that having seen the reality of the coast, even in its most verdant summer garb, he had doubts—as he says, retrospectively—and went back to Lopez de Gómara and the Spanish maps that showed the "tierra de Ayllón" at the high thirties north latitude, rather higher than the Point of Santa Elena. However he reached his conclusion, its publication in 1586–1587 ended any idea that Chicora was near Santa Elena, thus setting to rest that particular form of the Chicora legend.

1. Laudonnière, *L'Histoire notable,* fols. 15v–17, pp. 59–60 (*Three Voyages,* 29–30).

Laudonnière's *L'Histoire notable de la Florida* did not directly attack the substance of the Chicora legend: the promise of a new Andalucia at the same latitude as the old. Recognition of the unfounded aspects of that promise could come only by taking into account other experiences on the southeastern coast, like those the French had through their voyages of the 1570s and early 1580s and the English were acquiring in the Roanoke voyages. Still, Laudonnière's book was an important corrective to the form the Chicora legend had assumed outside Spain during the 1560s. It was especially useful since Hakluyt also sponsored the publication in 1587 at Paris of the full text in Latin of Peter Martyr's *Decades,* the book that had started the Chicora legend on its extra-Iberian career.

The first report of the English experience at Roanoke Island in realistic terms, as contrasted to Arthur Barlowe's idyllic account, came in 1588 with the publication of Thomas Harriot's *Briefe and True Report.* A careful observer of plant and animal life but dependent on unreliable "German" mineral "experts," Harriot described the resources of Raleigh's Virginia under four broad headings: commodities of market value, native foods, building materials, and military, political, and religious opportunities that Indian society and culture offered for the establishment of an English colony. Except for some of the minerals (alum, protosulphate of zinc, potassium nitrate, and edible clays), and the silver hoped for in the rivers farther inland, the resources Harriot enumerated were those that actually existed, not those in other places which might be found but had not been.[2] His picture, especially of food resources, was one of abundance provided that the English ate native fare and did not insist on "their olde accustomed daintie food" prior to the establishment of English crops.[3] The better soils of the interior, only glimpsed during searches up the rivers, promised excellent harvests, he thought, once they could be farmed. As for the Indians, they would present no obstacle to English settlement, Harriot assured the reader, because the English weapons and discipline were superior and a partial solar eclipse, a comet, a mysterious disease that struck only Indians who were unfriendly to the English, and belief in the transmigration of souls had convinced many Indians that the Englishmen were beings to fear. Harriot piously voiced the hope that the Indians' fear might in time

2. Thomas Harriot, "A Briefe and True Report," as found in Quinn (ed.), *Roanoke Voyages,* I, 317–87. Quinn's notes on the minerals are found on pp. 327, 331–33.

3. *Ibid.,* 323, 383, with quotation from p. 323.

produce love and conversion to Christianity, but his main point was that "by carefulnesse of our selues neede nothing at all to be feared" of the Indians.[4]

Only once did Harriot stray from writing of what was, to speculate on what might be. In his conclusions he said, "What hope there is els to be gathered of the nature of the climate, being answerable to the Iland of Iapan, the land of China, Persia, Iury, the Ilandes of Cyprus and Candy, the South parts of Greece, Italy, and Spaine, and of many other notable and famous countries, because I meane not to be tedious, I leave to your owne consideration."[5] Here he reverted to the general notion of similar climates and resources at similar latitudes, the root of the Chicora legend. But he gave southern Spain—Andalucia—only passing mention in a long list of places at the same latitude as, or higher latitudes than, Raleigh's Virginia.

Whatever Harriot may have known of Ayllón's Chicora, he did not see it at Roanoke Island nor try to persuade his reader that it might be somewhere nearby. Roanoke was a reality for him to render accurately, however much he overlaid the reality with the design of an English colony. The reissue of his work in 1590 with Theodore de Bry's engravings of some of White's drawings helped take it still further from being a promotional tract to being a book from which later generations would draw "knowledge about American facts and customs." Harriot and White presented the facts and customs with "attitudes of wondering discovery."[6] For the English and all readers of the book outside England, the Chicora legend of a new Andalucia along the coast of North America at the high thirties north latitude had died in the face of an extraordinarily careful observation and recording of reality. The reality was exciting and promising for colonial development, but it was not Ayllón's Chicora or even what Hakluyt had suggested existed in his "Discourse of Western Planting." Olive trees, for example, are not an entry in Harriot's list of plant resources.

As for the Verrazzano legend, it hung on as a vague promise well into the seventeenth century. Information that the English gathered in the late 1580s seemed to confirm the existence of a passage to the Pacific. Richard Hakluyt the Younger heard the story of such a passage from a French seaman who had been up the Saint Lawrence River as far as modern Montreal. Spanish prisoners taken at Saint Augustine spoke

4. *Ibid.*, 382.
5. *Ibid.*, 383.
6. Franklin, *Discoverers, Explorers, and Settlers*, 111.

of it. Hakluyt had no way to know that belief in its existence was common in Spanish Florida, deriving from Menéndez de Avilés' time but resting on no better sources than those he had access to in France. Too, the publication of Antonio de Espejo's *Historia* at Madrid in 1586 told of the Spanish discovery of silver in New Mexico, on the southern shore of the supposed passage. The great geographer Ortelius incorporated the passage into a map of the far western parts of North America. Though Hakluyt influenced the construction of that map, its configuration of North America helped convince him that the Saint Lawrence route would quickly bring the explorer to near New Mexico. As he wrote in his dedication of Laudonnière's *L'Histoire notable de la Florida,* in 1587, "For my part I am fully persuaded by Ortelius' late reformation of Culvacan and the gulf of California, that the land on the back part of Virginia extendeth nothing so far westward as is put down in the Maps of those parts."[7] Curiously, however, he wrote this sentence with reference to John Davis' recent explorations in search of the Northwest Passage at high latitudes rather than with reference to the Saint Lawrence River version of the Verrazzano legend.

Versions of maps showing the passage continued to be published after 1590. Either as the Strait of Anian or as a vaguely defined passage from the Great Lakes area, a passage across North America continued a strong idea into the seventeenth century. The specifically Verrazzanan concept seems to have disappeared with time and better knowledge of the Great Lakes and the breadth of North America. Still, as late as the 1680s, Robert Cavalier, Sieur de La Salle, could find backers for attempts to learn whether it was possible to reach New Mexico by way of the Ohio and Mississippi rivers. Even after he showed that that route led to the Gulf of Mexico, the idea of a passage survived in the notion of the Strait of Anian, which was not finally laid to rest until the end of the eighteenth century, when Spanish and English explorers mapped the west coast of North America above Baja California.

For exploration and the attempted colonization of the Southeast, however, the Chicora legend and the legend of Verrazzano's sea ceased to play leading roles in men's thoughts by 1590. Spaniards, Frenchmen, and Englishmen had all accepted the two legends, but they had also all discarded them as they had experience with the southeastern coast of North America. The general reaction to the

7. Parks, *Richard Hakluyt,* 108–109.

reality of the coast was negative because of the exaggerated hopes the legends had raised and because of the great difficulty of living well on the limited resource base of the coastal zone. Juan Lopez de Velasco, the Spanish cosmographer, expressed this judgment as well as any contemporary when in 1574 he wrote,

> Even though all of this coast has been sailed along and almost discovered and it is known that it is peopled by natives in many places, [and] that the land appears good and disposed for harvests, all the people who have been seen until now are barbarians, miserable and very poor and without any sort of *policía* or manner of living, and all the land is very cold and not cultivated. For these [reasons] and because no indication of gold or silver nor even, almost, other metals have been found up until now, [the coast] is little requisitioned by any nation. Thus although the English and French, with the covetousness that they have always shown to introduce themselves into any part of the Indies, have coasted it several times and there is news of towns that they have founded on it, it is understood that up to the present none of the settlements that they have founded in any part of it has endured.[8]

Yet a few men of each nation learned enough about the coast and the interior to see that great prosperity might yet be if people were prepared to deal with the land on its own terms and not as a new example of a familiar place. Survivors of Ayllón's, Soto's, Menéndez de Avilés', and Raleigh's colonies held that point of view, it should be clear. The future belonged to another generation of such men, men who approached the interior through the Chesapeake Bay's greater riparian resources. The way for that generation was prepared by the sixteenth-century explorers who created or accepted and acted upon the legends associated with Ayllón and Verrazzano.

8. Juan Lopez de Velasco, *Geografía y descripción universal de las Indias* (Madrid, 1894), 170.

Appendix:
Alonso de Chaves' Rutter and the Locations of Ayllón's Explorations and Colonies

The locations of Ayllón's colonies have been the subjects of controversy in the scholarly literature. This controversy reflects the various statements found in sixteenth-century sources, the gradual addition of manuscript material to investigations of the topic, and varying degrees of scholars' knowledge about the actual geography of the southeastern coast of North America. Until the present study, no author has used Alonso de Chaves' rutter, a document that clears up the uncertainties created by the other sources.

The first indicators of the location of Ayllón's activities were the manuscript maps of Juan Vespucci in 1526 (Map 3) and of Diogo de Ribeiro in 1527–1533. These and later, printed maps, such as the so-called Ramusio map of 1534, show a stretch of coast in the thirties north latitude, with legends ranging from a simple "Land of Ayllón" to brief summaries of his colonial activity and the resources of the area (see Chapter IV for the legend from the Rome Ribeiro of 1529, the most informative of the legends). Some maps show the Jordan River and the River of Santa Elena, but none of them derived from the Spanish *padrón real* indicates that Chicora was on the Jordan or where San Miguel de Gualdape lay in relation to the River of Santa Elena or the Point of Santa Elena, which was just to the south of the river.

Nineteenth- and twentieth-century scholars who have used these maps have done so primarily in inquiries concerning the sequence of names along the coast; their research has focused especially on determining the sources from which particular cartographers drew their information rather than on learning the specific location of Ayllón's or anyone else's colonies.[1] Attempts to employ the coastal outlines to

1. For example, Stokes, *The Iconography of Manhattan Island,* II, chart following p. 40, and William F. Ganong, *Critical Maps in the Early Cartography and Place Nomenclature of the Atlantic Coast of Canada,* ed. Theodore E. Layng (Toronto, 1964), 140–41, and Swanton, *Early History of the Creek Indians,* 51.

locate particular places have generally been viewed as exercises in futility.

Books published prior to 1560 were more specific about the locations of Ayllón's activities but offered information that, on the one hand, reflected Ayllón's deceptions, and on the other, seemed to contradict things he had already said. Martyr's *Decades* in the 1530 edition contained Ayllón's remark that his discovery of 1521 and Chicora were "at the same degrees and identical parallels as Vandalian Spain, vulgarly called Andalucia."[2] Andalucia is centered on latitude 37° north, as any seaman or cartographer familiar with its ports would know. Francisco Lopez de Gómara, on the other hand, published a statement in 1552 that said Chicora and Gualdape, the site of Ayllón's final colony of 1526, were a "land now called Cape Santa Elena and the Jordan River," which he located at 32° north, the latitude of the Cape of Santa Elena.[3] The "gentleman of Elvas"' account of Soto's expedition, published in 1557, stated that Ayllón had been at a port two days distant from Cofitachequi. That was a variation on the idea of many who survived the expedition that Ayllón had been on the River of Santa Elena.[4] Gómara apparently based his statement on this idea, although his wording allowed for the possibility that the adelantado had been to two places rather than one.

Jean Ribault chose to believe that Chicora was at or near the Point of Santa Elena (see Chapter IX), but in later years the French came to understand that Chicora and the Jordan River were well to the north of the Point of Santa Elena. René Goulaine de Laudonnière's account, published in 1586, clarified Gómara's geography by clearly separating Chicora and the Jordan River from the Point of Santa Elena. By way of reinforcement of that point, the Le Moyne map published in 1591 showed Chicora beside the Jordan River—which looks remarkably like Winyah Bay—and definitely north of the Point of Santa Elena (Map 11).[5]

The official Spanish history of the early years of the Spanish empire in the Americas, Antonio de Herrera y Tordesillas' *Historia general,* published between 1601 and 1617, repeated both Martyr's informa-

2. Anghiera, *Decadas,* II, 595–96.
3. Lopez de Gómara, *Historia general,* II, 66–67.
4. Gentleman of Elvas, *True Relation,* II, 95–96.
5. Laudonnière, *L'Histoire notable,* fols. 10v–20v, esp. 16–16v, pp. 53–66, esp. 59–61 (*Three Voyages,* 22–36, esp. 29–30); Jacques Le Moyne de Morgues, *Brevis narratio eorum guae in Florida Americae* (Frankfurt, 1591), in Hulton, *The Work of Jacques Le Moyne,* II, plate 92.

tion and Gómara's assertions. Early in his work he noted that Ayllón had a contract to settle at 35°–37° north, but later he said that Ayllón sailed to the Point of Santa Elena, a hundred leagues north of Florida, and discovered there a town called Orista, which he and his settlers called Chicora "because the Castilians never fail to corrupt words a little." Near there was another place called Guale, that "they called Gualdape." The Jordan River "is found in this area."[6] Herrera thus showed Ayllón to have contracted to settle in one place but to have settled in another, farther south.

The text of Ayllón's contract of 1523 was first published in 1825 by Martín Fernández de Navarrete and was reprinted in the *Colección de documentos inéditos* after 1864.[7] The text of the contract adds nothing to what Martyr and Herrera said aside from providing verification that Ayllón had contracted to settle between 35° and 37° north.

Navarrete went beyond the simple publication of the text of Ayllón's contract to offer an opinion about where he had actually settled. Using manuscript sources copied from the Archive of the Indies and, for the first time, Goncalo Fernández de Oviedo's complete manuscript *Historia general* (held by the Royal Academy of History in Madrid), Navarrete nonetheless followed Herrera in locating the discovery of 1521 in the vicinity of the Cabo de Santa Elena. Port Royal Sound, he judged, had to be the Jordan River, even though some of the authorities he knew said it was the Santee River at 33° north. Following Oviedo, Navarrete placed the initial landing of 1526 at 33°40′ north (another Jordan River) and then had Ayllón's men sailing *north* to discover the site of Gualdape at a river next to Cape Lookout.[8]

No more information about where Ayllón was active became commonly available until the publication in the 1850s of the complete text of Oviedo's *Historia general.* In Book 21, Chapter 9, Oviedo provided latitudes for the Cabo de Santa Elena (33° north), the Cabo de San Román (33½° north), and the Jordan River (33⅔° north), and distances between them and other named features along the coast.[9] While shedding light on the location of key geographical features, Oviedo's text introduced a confusion, because it placed the Cabo de

6. Herrera, *Historia general,* VII, 103, 310.

7. Martín Fernández de Navarrete (ed.), *Colección de los viages y descubrimientos que hicieron por mar los Españoles desde fines del siglo XV* (5 vols.; Madrid, 1825), III, 166–73; *DII,* XIV, 506, and *DII,* XXII, 82.

8. Fernández de Navarrete (ed.), *Colección,* III, 84, 86–87.

9. Oviedo, *Historia general,* II, 144, III, 628 (Jordan River).

San Román *before,* or south of, the Jordan River; that was an error that was to lend support to the thesis that the Cape Fear River or another in that vicinity was the Jordan River. Whatever map Oviedo was copying would have been of the Ribeiro-Chaves type and would have shown the Jordan River to be south of the Cabo de San Román.

Oviedo's text provided an additional datum not found in any earlier text: the admission, on the one hand, that the location of Gualdape was unshown on any sailing chart, and the affirmation, on the other, that it lay forty to forty-five leagues away "toward the western coast" from the Jordan River, that is, toward the southwest.[10] To that he added a brief description of the *gran río* where the Spaniards built the town of San Miguel de Gualdape and some information on resources and the proximity of at least one Indian community.

The publication of Oviedo's *Historia* did not result in an immediate improvement in the literature about Ayllón. For example, Johann Kohl, who published in 1869, followed Navarrete in having Ayllón land near the Cabo de Santa Helena in 1521 and sail northward in 1526. Kohl's Jordan was, however, near Saint Helena Sound. He concluded that Gualdape was on the Cape Fear River. Kohl did make clever use of the Ribeiro map of 1529 to flesh out the outlines of the voyage of 1525, which he was one of the first to recognize as the second of Ayllón's three.[11]

Corroboration of some of the details in Herrera's version of Ayllón's story occurred about this same time in the publication of parts of the Matienzo-Ayllón suit of 1526. Found in the Archive of the Indies, Justicia 3, No. 3, this document includes the formal act by which the Spaniards took possession of the new discovery in 1521 and recorded their latitude as 33½° north. The formal act of possession and Pedro de Quejo's testimony were not, however, published at this time.[12] Nonetheless, perhaps from a copy in Buckingham Smith's collection, those parts of the suit were known to James C. Brevoort and Henry C. Murphy, who wrote about Verrazzano in 1874 and 1875. Henry Harrisse also used the Justicia materials. Harrisse agreed with

10. *Ibid.*, III, 630 (not on any chart), 628 (40–45 leagues toward the western coast).

11. Kohl, *The Discovery of the East Coast,* 247, 396–401; Henry Harrisse, *The Discovery of North America* (1892; rpr. Amsterdam, 1961), 209, 213.

12. For a transcription of Matienzo's petition and of Ayllón's interrogatory and replies of March 5, 1526, from a copy in AGI, PAT, see *DII,* XXXIV, 563–67, and *DII,* XXXV, 547–62.

Kohl as to the location of Gualdape but placed the landing of 1521 at Winyah Bay on the basis of the Justicia act of possession.[13]

Of all the late-nineteenth-century writers, John Gilmary Shea made the most extensive use of the Justicia materials. He apparently obtained a copy of most of the lawsuit and based a large part of his narrative about Ayllón on it. But Shea misread the testimony about the name the Spaniards bestowed on the *land,* thinking that they had applied that name, San Juan Bautista, to the *river* on whose bank the formal act of possession took place. In fact, the text gave no name for the river. It noted the latitude of the act of possession (33°30′ north), but Shea in his discussion of sources dismissed all modern attempts to locate the San Juan Bautista, because, according to him, Ayllón's contract said that the river was at 35° (it did not explicitly say that) and this contradiction ensured that "conjecture is idle" over the location of the discovery of 1521.[14]

Having disposed of the first voyage, Shea introduced from manuscript sources the testimony of Father Antonio de Cervantes and Alonso de Espinosa Cervantes to date Ayllón's departure from "Puerto de la Plata." That was the first use of this testimony. Shea then repeated Navarrete's notion that the expedition of 1526 reached a river at 33°40′ that it called the Jordan. Shea made no effort to name the modern river that that might be but in a note said that it would be the Wateree if the latitude was correct. Deserted by Francisco ("el Chicorano"), Ayllón "resolved to seek a more fertile district. That he sailed northward there can be little doubt."[15] Shea went on to assert that Francisco Fernández de Ecija stated that the English colony of 1609, Jamestown, was located at Guandape, a place he found Espinosa Cervantes to mention in his account of the expedition of 1526. On that evidence, Shea had Ayllón founding San Miguel at the site of Jamestown.

Woodbury Lowery followed Shea in using not only Oviedo and the other chroniclers but also the Justicia 3 materials. He did not seem to have seen the testimony of Cervantes and Espinosa Cervantes, and he

13. James Carson Brevoort, *Verrazzano the Navigator: or, Notes on Giovanni da Verrazzano and on a Planisphere of 1529 Illustrating His American Voyage of 1824* (New York: 1874), 70, and Henry C. Murphy, *The Voyage of Verrazzano: A Chapter in the Early History of Maritime Discovery in America* (New York, 1875–76), 123. The present writer was unable to examine these books but Harrisse notes their use of the lawsuit of 1526 (*The Discovery of North America,* 206).

14. Shea, "Ancient Florida," 239, with quotation from p. 285.

15. *Ibid.,* 240–41, 285–86.

took the Justicia materials (the act of possession) at face value in his text but agreed with Shea in a note that the landing place of the expedition of 1521 could not be determined. He placed the landing in 1526 near the Cape Fear River, like Shea, but correctly read Oviedo on the direction of travel, which was west, not north. San Miguel de Gualdape accordingly ended up at the Peedee River, near modern Georgetown.[16]

When John Swanton examined the sources in preparing his *Early History of the Creek Indians and Their Neighbors*, he noticed that the act of possession named the land, not the river, and so concluded that the Jordan River was the same as the river discovered in 1521. He accepted the act of possession's latitude but decided that the river had to be the Santee River rather than Winyah Bay. He also reasoned that Ayllón went there again in 1526 and then moved his colonists south to the Point of Santa Elena, where the Savannah River provided the "great river" that Oviedo mentioned in connection with Gualdape. Swanton's league was a short one, about 2.5 miles.[17]

In 1956, Paul Quattlebaum addressed the story of Ayllón and his colonies in his book *The Land Called Chicora*. An engineer by training and a resident of Georgetown, South Carolina, Quattlebaum sought out Shea's copies of the manuscripts dealing with Ayllón as well as the by then standard sources. Accepting a landing at Winyah Bay in 1521, Quattlebaum followed Navarrete to the extent of having the expedition of 1526 land at the Cape Fear River, which it named the Jordan. Paying attention to Oviedo, Quattlebaum noted that Ayllón's party then moved southwest to the site of Gualdape. That is, Quattlebaum, like Swanton, rejected the thesis of Navarrete and Shea about a movement north to the Chesapeake Bay. Quattlebaum believed, however, that the party moved along the beach between Cape Fear and the entrance to Winyah Bay, with the ships just offshore. He thus placed the settlement Gualdape on the shore of Winyah Bay, not farther south. Quattlebaum's league was 1.5 nautical miles, a value derived from Columbus' usage.[18]

All previous studies of the locations of Ayllón's colonies have relied in varying degrees on the published texts of Ayllón's contract and of the chroniclers of the sixteenth century, especially Oviedo, and on the manuscript sources connected with the lawsuit of 1526 in Justi-

16. Lowery, *Spanish Settlements*, I, 155, 165, 448–51.
17. Swanton, *Early History of the Creek Indians*, 35, 41.
18. Quattlebaum, *The Land Called Chicora*, 10–11, 21–23, 126–29.

cia 3 and the testimony of Cervantes and Espinosa Cervantes in 1561. That is a rich but limited range of sources, to which Juan Vespucci's map of 1526 adds information drawn from Quejo's rutter of 1525, a document noted in letters of 1525 but no longer extant in its original form. The interpretations that have grown from those sources are almost as varied as the sources themselves, although over time scholars have come to accept that the discovery of 1521 occurred in the area of the Santee River and Winyah Bay and that the colony of 1526 moved southwest from its initial base. Disagreement continues about where that base was and where San Miguel de Gualdape was.

In the preparation of the present study, use has been made of Chaves' rutter, a source I. N. P. Stokes knew and partially published, but in a form that was difficult to interpret. In 1977, the full text of Chaves' fourth book was published in Spain, making an important source available to scholarship.

Chaves compiled his work as part of an effort to obtain the position of *cosmógrafo mayor* of the House of Trade of Seville. Ribeiro died in 1533, and Chaves was among those who petitioned for his position. The manuscript in question carries the date of 1537, but internal evidence suggests that Chaves may have put together much of it at least as early as 1533.[19] In its totality, it is a point-to-point survey of the Americas, the stuff that one could construct a map from or that one could employ as sailing directions if one were a mariner. There is every reason to believe that it is a collection of sailing directions (rutters) prepared by seamen under the House of Trade's standing rules and by explorers specifically commissioned to survey various coasts. Quejo was such an explorer in 1525.[20]

Table 3 is a translation of the Spanish text covering the coast of North America from the Río de Corrientes (Ponce de Leon Inlet, Florida) to the Cabo de Arenas (Ocean City, Maryland?). Each line bears the same number used in the Spanish edition except that the section on the Costa del Norte has had numbers added, beginning with 37. In addition, computed distances in nautical miles and the modern latitudes of the points in question are supplied.

This tabulation of names, latitudes, distances from and to, and brief descriptions should be simple to plot on an equal-distance map

19. Chaves, *Espejo de navegantes,* 21.

20. Declaration of Ayllón, March 31, 1526, AGI, JU 3, No. 3, fol. 7; king to Lucas Vázquez de Ayllón, Toledo, December 1, 1525, AGI, IG 420, Book 10, fols. 190–190v.

once a single point in the sequence is identified and the correct equivalent of the league established. If that identification and equivalence are correct, all the points should fall at or near modern rivers and "capes," with due allowance for the changing nature of the sandy coast in question.

A number of estimates exist for the length of the maritime league, which is the most probable league for Chaves to have used. Roland Chardon has shown that a value of 3.1998 nautical miles or four Roman miles is correct for the maritime league of the late fifteenth and early sixteenth centuries.[21] That value has been used to prepare the conversions shown in Table 3.

The task was to begin plotting from a known point or points. A quick examination of Chaves' materials shows that he used two points. Cabo de la Cruz is one. It is the bulge on Amelia Island just south of Saint Augustine Inlet, a "cape" that lies at almost exactly 29½° north.[22]

The second point of reference is the Cabo de San Román. Chaves was quite explicit as to the relationships between that cape and the Jordan River. In his note on line 32 he said that "this cape has some shoals in front of it that reach into the sea some three leagues. On the west side there is an inlet [or small bay; *ensenada*], and it has the Jordan River." He added that the Jordan River is a "great river" and is "called the River of Ayllón because he died here." He gave its distance from the cape as four leagues, putting it about thirteen nautical miles west of the Cabo de San Román.

The physical description and the distance from the cape to the river, as well as the presence of a bay on the western side of the cape, fit the area of the South Santee River, Winyah Bay, and North Island almost exactly. Furthermore, the coastal description of 1605 agrees on the distances and the extent of the sand bars off the point of North Island, although it does not use Chaves' nomenclature.[23] No other "cape" along the coast south of Cape Hatteras fits Chaves' materials.

Chaves' statement that the Jordan River was the river where Ayllón

21. Roland Chardon, "The Linear League in North America," *Annals of the Association of American Geographers*, LXX (1980), 140–42, 151.

22. Andrés Gonzalez Rutter, 1609, AGI, PAT 19, No. 31. In the sixteenth century, the term *cape* referred to any place where there was a projecting angle in the coast, where a trend changed abruptly. It did not necessarily mean a major geographical feature, as it would today. Quejo may have exaggerated the importance of his discoveries, however, by making relatively small projections, more accurately described as points, into "capes."

23. *Ibid.*, "Señas del Río Jordán."

died is not correct, as Oviedo's account clearly shows. How Chaves got the wrong idea is unknown, but he may have mistakenly thought that the Jordan, the site of Chicora, was the only place Ayllón went in 1526. That seems hard to believe if he was working with reports of the voyages south from the Jordan River in 1526, but they may have been simple point-to-point records of the explorations that preceded the actual move of the colonists and so would not have logged the fact of the move.

Chaves' statement may help explain the impression of Soto's men that at Cofitachequi they were at the river where Ayllón had been. They were on the Wateree River, a tributary of the Santee. How they transformed the Jordan into the Santa Elena is unknown, although it is likely that the Point and River of Santa Elena were better-known geographical features than the Jordan River, which, for example, gets only one mention in Chaves' table, whereas other points are mentioned a number of times (see also Chapter VIII, for what the Mexicans of 1560 did not know about the southeast coast).

The puzzles of Chaves' historical statement aside, the weight of his evidence—description, latitude, and the plotted results (Table 3 and Maps 4 and 6)—establish that the Cabo de San Román and the Jordan River should be taken to be North Island and the South Santee River. The Cabo de San Román, the second point from which Chaves plotted his data, has as certain an identification as the first, Cabo de la Cruz.

An attempt to locate the rest of Chaves' points using the distances and reference points he gave discloses that Cabo Grueso and Cabo de Santa Elena cannot be plotted without conflicts between the distances given in line 25c (which places Cabo Grueso at Tybee Island and is compatible with the distances given in lines 26a and 26b) and in lines 28b and 29a, which place Cabo Grueso twenty leagues southwest of Cabo de Santa Elena, plotted at Tybee Island using line 29b, a distance of thirty-six leagues from the Cabo de San Román. Since the distances in lines 30a and 30b total thirty-eight leagues between the Cabo de San Román and Cabo de Santa Elena, and line 31a taken with line 31b, and line 32a, both give distances of thirty-four leagues, it is clear that the Cape of Santa Elena should be at or near Tybee Island, at 32° north, where Gómara placed it. Chaves' latitude, as against his plotted distances, puts the cape twenty minutes or twenty nautical miles farther north, roughly at the bulge of Hilton Head Island. But twenty nautical miles is not the same as twenty leagues.

Table 3. Chaves' Rutter of the Coast of La Florida, South to North

Place	Chaves' Latitude	Modern Latitude	Distance: Leagues	Distance: Nautical Miles
24. Río de Corrientes	28 1/2°	29°5′		
a. NW of Cabo Cañaveral			20[a]	64.0
b. S of Cabo de la Cruz			15	48.0
25. Cabo de la Cruz	29 1/3°	29°52′		
a. NNW of Cabo Cañaveral			32[a]	102.4
b. NW 1/4 W of Bahama Islands			50	160.0
c. S 1/4 SE of Cabo Grueso			40	128.0
26. Mar Baja	30 3/4°	31°8′		
a. N of Cabo de la Cruz			24	76.8
b. SSW of Cabo Grueso			20	64.0
"A sort of small bay [*ancón*] and has some shallows in it."				
27. Río Seco	31 1/4°	31°33′		
a. N 1/4 NE of Cabo de la Cruz			34	108.8
b. SW of Cabo de Santa Elena			28	89.6
28. Cabo Grueso	31 2/3°	31°56′		
a. N of Cabo Cañaveral			70	224.0
b. SW of Cabo de Santa Elena [*sic*]			20	64.0
29. Cabo de Santa Elena	32 1/3°	See text		
a. NE of Cabo Grueso [*sic*]			20	64.0
b. SW 1/4 W of Cabo San Román			36	115.2
"This cape has the River of Santa Elena on its northeast side and a large cove [*ensenada grande*] on its western side."				
30. Río de Santa Elena	32 2/3°	32°20′		
a. N of Cabo de Santa Elena			8[a]	25.6
b. WSW of Cabo de San Román			30	96.0
31. Río Jordán	33 1/2°	33°7′		
a. NE of Cabo de Santa Elena			30	96.0
b. W of Cabo San Román			4	13.0
"This river is large [*grande*]; this river is called the River of Ayllón because he died here."				

(*continued*)

Table 3. (*continued*)

Place	Chaves' Latitude	Modern Latitude	Distance Leagues	Nautical Miles
32. Cabo de San Román	33 1/2°	33°17′		
a. NE 1/4 E of Cabo de Santa Elena			34	108.8
b. WSW of Cabo de Trafalgar			80	256.0
"This cape has before it some shallows that enter the sea about three leagues [9.6 nautical miles], and on its western side it has an inlet [*ensenada*] and it has the Jordan River."				
33. Río de Canoas[b]	34 1/2°	33°53′		
a. NE of Cabo de San Román			22	70.4
b. W 1/4 SW of Cabo de Trafalgar			60[a]	192.0
34. Río de Bajos	35°	34°33′		
a. NE 1/4 E of Cabo de San Román			—	—
b. W 1/4 SW of Cabo de Trafalgar			36	115.2
35. Río del Principe	35 1/2°	34°55′		
a. NE 1/4 E of Cabo de San Román			70[a]	224.0
b. W of Cabo de Trafalgar			14	44.8
36. Cabo de Trafalgar	35 1/2°	35°13′		
a. E of Río del Principe			14	44.8
b. NNE of Cabo de San Román			80	256.0
c. SW of Cabo de San Juan			38	121.6
"This cape is the one that sticks out the most on all this coast and is the best known. The east coast of La Florida ends here, and the coast of the North begins. This cape has some shoals in front of it."				
37. Bahía de Santa María				
a. N of Cabo de Trafalgar			20	64.0
"The waters flow to the north-northeast."				
38. Cabo de San Juan				
a. ENE of Bahía de Santa María			20	64.0
"The waters flow to the north-northeast."				
39. Cabo de Arenas				
a. NE 1/4 N of Cabo de San Juan			25	80.0
"The waters flow strongly to the northeast."				

[a]Evidently estimated rather than derived from dead reckoning. The value given by Chaves is wrong.

[b]All the latitudes Chaves gives from the Río de Canoas through the Río del Principe are shifted back one line from their correct location. Thus the latitude given for the Río de Canoas is really that for the Río de Bajos.

Because it is known that Quejo surveyed the coast in 1525 and that Ayllón sent out one or more scouting parties in 1526 to run southwestward along the coast from his Jordan River in search of a suitable site for the colony, it seems likely that the conflict reflects Chaves' attempt to *collate* reports from these voyages (no other Spanish voyages are known for this coast before 1539) *using the names.* The result is confusion that can be untangled through the referencing system he supplies.

Study of Chaves' materials suggests that he had as many as four sources before him. The A-source references northward from Cabo de la Cruz to Cabo Grueso and includes lines 24b, 25c, 26a, 26b, and 27a.

The B-source references places north of the Cabo de San Román, using the Cabo de San Román and Cabo de Trafalgar as reference points (lines 32b, 33–38). A marking-out of its distances shows no conflicts, although the system of just two reference points ceases north of Cabo de Trafalgar, with line 37a making reference to the Cabo de Trafalgar and line 38a to the Cabo de San Juan, which becomes the referent for the Cabo de Arenas. The points plotted using the B-source fit nicely with those estimated from the Vespucci map of 1526, suggesting that the B-source—as well as one of the other sources to be discussed—is the record of Quejo's voyage of 1525 (Table 4 and Map 12).

The remaining entries in Chaves' table seem to break into three sets. The C-source embraces lines 27b, 28b, 29a, and 29b and represents a voyage south along the coast from the Cabo de San Román, to the Cabo de Santa Elena, to a Cabo Grueso, to a Río Seco. These points, when mapped, match the estimated positions of the named features on the Vespucci map if the Cabo de San Román is taken to be his Cabo de San Nicolás. Other names have been changed as well. Vespucci's and Quejo's Río de la Cruz has now become the Cabo de Santa Elena; the Cabo Grueso of this series falls at the Mar Baja of the A-source but is unnamed on the Vespucci map; Vespucci's Cabo de Santa Elena is here named the Río Seco, which can also be integrated with the D- and the E-source by tracking south of their Cabo de Santa Elena in accordance with line 27b.

The D-source lays out a series of interconnected points running south from the Cabo de San Román to the Cabo de Santa Elena and embracing lines 30a, 30b, and 31b.

The E-source fixes the set of points covered by lines 31a and 32a. It

Table 4. Distance Estimates from Vespucci Map of 1526, South to North

	Degrees of Latitude	*Leagues, at 17.5 Leagues per Degree*	*Chaves' Leagues*
From Cabo de Santa Elena to Río de la Cruz	1.5	26.25	20.0[a]
From Río de la Cruz to Río Jordán	1.9	33.25	32.0[b]
From Río Jordán to Cabo de San Nicolás	0.25	4.4	4.0[c]
From Río Jordán to Río de Arecifes	1.8	32.5	26.0[d]
From Río de Arecifes to Río de Atarazanas	1.1	19.25	—
From Río de Atarazanas to Cabo de Trafalgar	1.6	28.1	36.0[e]
From Cabo de Trafalgar to Bahía de Santa María	2.3–2.5	40.25–43.8	40.0[f]
From Bahía de Santa María to Cabo de Arenas	1.5	26.25	25.0[g]

[a]Distance 26b, from Mar Baja to Cabo Grueso.
[b]Distance 31a, from Cabo de Santa Elena to Río Jordán.
[c]Distance 31b, from Río Jordán to Cabo de San Román.
[d]Chaves does not give this distance but it can be found by adding distances 31b and 33a, for the course from Río Jordán to Cabo de San Román to Río de Canoas.
[e]Distance 34a, from Río de Bajos to Cabo de Trafalgar.
[f]Distance to Cabo de San Juan (Cape Charles), distance 37a taken with distance 38a, rather than to the Bahía de Santa María shown in Chaves.
[g]Distance 39a, from Cabo de San Juan to Cabo de Arenas.

covers the distances between the Cabo de San Román, the Río Jordán, and the Cabo de Santa Elena.

Both the D- and the E-source can be extended southward using line 27b. That extension might be appropriate as a way of plotting the supposed voyages of the two scouting parties sent out in 1526, assuming, that is, that Quejo made a voyage in 1526 corresponding to the set of points in the A-source. That assumption, which is one the present study makes, seems highly probable. The existence of two other scouting parties is less likely, although the testimony of Cervantes and Espinosa Cervantes in 1561 seems to indicate that at least two scouting parties (Quejo's and another?) were sent.

In sum, the B- and the C-source are probably the report that Quejo sent of his voyage of 1525, whereas the A-, the D-, and the E-source seem to have originated in 1526 as part of Ayllón's efforts to find an alternative to the Jordan River area.

Conclusion: The Location of San Miguel de Gualdape

Until additional information on Ayllón's voyages turns up, Chaves' materials would seem to dispel the problems left by Oviedo's text and by the statements of Gómara and others, all of whom knew that Ayllón had gone south from the Jordan to at least the Cabo de Santa Elena. How much farther south can now be ascertained.

Chaves shows that the A-source voyager put into Sapelo Sound (his Río Seco, in line 27a) in 1526. That sound also happens to be forty to forty-five leagues (at 3.1998 nautical miles to a league) to the southwest of the Jordan River (the South Santee River). In the 1560s and later, Sapelo Sound was the home of the Guale Indians. Uniquely along that part of the coast, so far as is now known, the sound had a fairly dense Indian population. As the present study has made plain, such a population was essential for the sort of colony Ayllón envisioned. Chaves tells us where Gualdape was.

Confirmation of sorts of the conclusion that San Miguel de Gualdape was built on or close to the shores of Sapelo Sound comes from Herrera. He stated that Gualdape was really Guale, although he added that Orista was Chicora, and that clearly was not the case. I do not place much faith in Herrera, because he is so often wrong in his details, but he does offer the connection between Guale and Gualdape. Perhaps someday the site will be found by archaeological means and the question of its location can be settled for all time.

Bibliography

Archival Sources

Archivo General de Indias, Seville

Patronato 18, 19, 21, 29, 63, 75, 150, 160, 174, 254, 257, 260, 267, 295
Contaduría 286, 294, 299, 306, 462, 548, 877, 941, 944, 1050, 1089, 1454
Contratación 2929, 3309, 4675B, 5009, 5013, 5090 (?), 5101, 5103, 5105, 5167, 5185, 5220, 5776
Justicia 3, 13, 42, 48, 50, 89, 90, 817, 879, 1001, 1002, 1160, 1166
Escribania de Cámara 1024A
Santo Domingo 11, 49, 50, 71, 77, 79, 80, 99, 115, 126, 127, 155, 168, 224, 231, 2528
Mexico 19, 68, 96, 105, 168, 280, 323, 1117
Guadalajara 51
Santa Fe 987
Lima 204
Indiferente General 415, 420, 425, 427, 541, 738, 739, 741, 1094, 1202, 1382, 1528, 1561, 1562, 1624, 1801, 1866, 1877, 1963, 2001, 2002, 2003, 2004

Archivo General de Simancas

Registro General del Sello, 26 junio 1523, No. 355.
Estado 368, 373, 378, 511, 514, 515, 517, 518, 519, 811, 834, K1489, K1491, K1642, K1643
Cámara de Castilla 275
Guerra Antigua 62, 302

Archivo Histórico Nacional, Madrid

Ordenes, Santiago, Expediente 8565

Archivo de Protocolos, Seville

Oficio I: 1563, libros 1, 2
Oficio V: 1511, libro único; 1524, libro 1; 1525, libro 4; 1526, libro 1
Oficio VIII: 1563, Register 51
Oficio IX: 1563, libros 2, 4, 5; 1564, libros 2, 4; 1565, libros 2, 3
Oficio XV: 1517, libro 1; 1563, libro 2
Oficio XVI: 1563, libro de julio–septiembre

Oficio XVII: 1562, libro de marzo–junio; 1563, libros de marzo, junio–julio, agosto, septiembre–octubre
Oficio XIX: 1562, libros 1, 2, 3
Oficio XXI: 1562, libro 3 ABCDario; 1563, libro 2

Archivo de Protocolos, Oviedo

Legajo 57, Alonso de Heredia

Archive General de Royaume, Brussels

Etat et de l'audience 427[1]

Published Documents and Guides to Documents

Archivo General de Indias. *O Arquivo das Indias e o Brasil: Documentos para a história do Brasil existente no Arquivo das Indias de Sevilha.* Researched by João Cabral de Mello Neto. Rio de Janeiro, 1966.

Biggar, Henri P., comp. *A Collection of Documents Relating to Jacques Cartier and the Sieur de Roberval.* Ottawa, 1930.

Catherine de Medicis [consort of Henry II, king of France]. *Lettres de Catherine de Medicis.* Edited by Hector de La Ferrière and Gustave Baguenault de Puchesse. 11 vols. Paris, 1880–1943.

Colección de documentos inéditos para la historia de España. Edited by Martín Fernández de Navarrete *et al.* 113 vols. Madrid, 1842–95.

Colección de documentos inéditos relativos al descubrimiento, conquista, y organización de las antiguas posesiones españoles de América y Oceanía, sacados de los archivos del reino, y muy especialmente del de Indias. Edited by Joaquín F. Pacheco, Francisco de Cardenas, and Luís Torres de Mendoza. 42 vols. Madrid, 1864–84.

Colección de documentos inéditos relativos al descubrimiento, conquista, y organización de las antiguas posesiones españoles de Ultramar. Edited by Joaquín F. Pacheco, Francisco de Cardenas, and Luís Torres de Mendoza. 25 vols. Madrid, 1885–1932.

Connor, Jeannette Thurber, ed. *Colonial Records of Spanish Florida.* 2 vols. Deland, Fla., 1925–30.

Davenport, Frances G., ed. *European Treaties Bearing on the History of the United States and Its Dependencies.* 4 vols. Washington, D.C., 1917–37.

Documentary Sources for the Wreck of the New Spain Fleet of 1554. Translated by David McDonald. Prepared by David McDonald and J. Barto Arnold III. Austin, Tex., 1979.

Dumont, Jean, ed. *Corps universal diplomatique de droit des gens . . .* 8 vols. Amsterdam, 1726–31.

Fernández de Navarrete, Martín, ed. *Colección de los viages y descubrimientos que hicieron por mar los Españoles desde fines del siglo XV.* 5 vols. Madrid, 1825.

Fourquevaux, Raimond de Beccarie de Pavie, Baron de. *Dépeches de m. de*

Fourguevaux, ambassadeur du roi Charles IX en Espagne, 1565–1572. Edited by L'Abbé Douais. 3 vols. Paris, 1896–1904.

France, Treaties, etc., 1547–1559 (Henri II). *Traicté de paix fait a Chasteav-Cambresis l'an M.D.LIX, le III d'Avril, et ce qui se passa en la negociation pour la dite paix, Ensemble la Remonstrance faite par Iean Iacques de Mesmes, sur l'inivste occvpation dv royavme de Nauarre par les roys d'Espagne, à qvoy a esté adiovsté l'Instrvction et ambassade dv sievr de Lancosme en Tvrqvie, pour Henry III, roy de France et de Pologne, en l'an M.D.LXXXV.* Paris, 1637.

Fuentes documentales para la historia del Nuevo Reino de Granada desde la instalación de la Real Audiencia de Santa Fe. Edited by Juan Friede. 8 vols. to 1988. Bogotá, 1975–.

Granvelle, Antoine Perrenot de. *Papiers d'état du Cardinal de Granvelle d'après les manuscrits de la bibliothèque de Bessançon.* Edited by Ch. Weiss. 9 vols. Paris, 1841–52.

Great Britain, Public Records Office. *Calendar of Letters and State Papers Relating to English Affairs Preserved Principally in the Archives of Simancas, Elizabeth, 1558–1603.* Edited by Martin A. S. Hume. 4 vols. 1892–96; rpr. Nendeln, 1971.

Hakluyt, Richard. *The Original Writings and Correspondence of the Two Richard Hakluyts.* Edited by E. G. R. Taylor. 2 vols. London, 1935.

Lussagnet, Suzanne, ed. *Les Français en Amérique pendant la deuxième moitié de XVI siècle: Les Français en Floride.* Paris, 1958.

Margaretha of Parma [regent of the Netherlands, 1522–1586]. *Correspondance de Marguerite d'Autriche, duchesse de Parme, avec Philippe II.* Edited by M. Gachard. 3 vols. Brussels, 1867–81.

Menéndez de Avilés, Pedro. "Letters of Pedro Menéndez de Avilés and Other Documents Relating to His Career, 1555–1574." Translated by Edward W. Lawson. 2 vols. Typescript copy at P. K. Yonge Library of Florida History, University of Florida.

Narratives of the Career of Hernando de Soto in the Conquest of Florida. Translated by Buckingham Smith, Edited by Edward Gaylord Bourne. 2 vols. New York, 1904.

Priestley, Herbert I., ed. *The Luna Papers: Documents Relating to the Expedition of Don Tristan de Luna y Arellano for the Conquest of La Florida in 1559–1561.* 2 vols. Deland, Fla., 1928.

Quinn, David B., ed. *The Hakluyt Handbook.* 2 vols. London, 1974.

———, ed. *New American World: A Documentary History of North America to 1612.* 5 vols. New York, 1979.

———, ed. *Roanoke Voyages, 1584–1590.* 2 vols. London, 1955.

———, ed. *The Voyages and Colonising Enterprises of Sir Humphrey Gilbert.* 2 vols. London, 1940.

Quinn, David B., and Neil M. Cheshire, trans. and eds. *The New Found Land of Stephen Parmenius.* Toronto, 1972.

Ruble, Alphonse, Baron de. *Le Traité de Cateau-Cambresis, 2 et 3 avril 1559.* Paris, 1889.
Ruidiaz y Caravía, Eugenio. *La Florida: Su conquista y colonización por Pedro Menéndez de Avilés.* 2 vols. Madrid, 1893.
Smith, Buckingham, ed. *Colección de varios documentos para la historia de la Florida y tierras adyacentes.* London, 1857.
Spain, Ministerio de Fomento. *Cartas de Indias.* Madrid, 1877.
Spain, Sovereigns, etc., 1556–1598 (Philip II). *Negociaciones con Francia, 1559–[1568].* 11 vols. to 1960. Madrid, 1950–.
Wright, Irene A., trans. and ed. *Further English Voyages to Spanish America, 1583–1594.* London, 1951.
Zubillaga, Felix. *Monumenta Antiquae Floridae, 1566–1572.* Rome, 1946.

Sixteenth- and Seventeenth-Century Works: Original and Modern Editions and Translations

Alcoçer, Pedro de. *Historia o descripción de la imperial ciudad de Toledo.* Madrid, 1554.
Alfonse, Jean [Jean Fonteneau]. *La Cosmographie, avec l'espere et regime du soliel et du Nord.* Edited by Georges Musset. Paris, 1904.
Anghiera, Pietro Martiere d'. *De Orbe Nouo Petri Martyris ab Angleria Mediolanensis Protonotarij Cesaris senatoris decades.* Compluti, 1530.
———. *De Orbe Novo: The Eight Decades of Peter Martyr d'Anghera.* Translated by Francis M. MacNutt. 2 vols. New York, 1912.
———. *De orbe novo Petri Martyris Anglerii Mediolanensis, protonotarij, et Caroli Quinti senatoris decades octo.* Paris, 1587.
———. *Decadas del Nuevo Mundo.* Edited by Edmundo O'Gorman. 2 vols. Mexico City, 1964–65.
Barrientos, Bartolomé. *Pedro Menéndez de Avilés, Founder of Florida.* Translated by Anthony Kerrigan. Gainesville, Fla., 1965.
Biedma. *See* Hernández de Biedma.
Carleill, Christopher. *A Breef and Sommarie Discourse upon the entended Voyages to the Hethermoste Partes of America.* London, 1583. In *New American World: A Documentary History of North America to 1612,* edited by David B. Quinn. Vol. III of 5 vols., 27–34. New York, 1979. Also in *The Voyages and Colonizing Enterprises of Sir Humphrey Gilbert,* edited by Quinn. Vol. II of 2 vols., 351–64. London, 1940.
Cartier, Jacques. *A shorte and briefe narration of the two Nauigations . . . to Newe Fravnce.* Translated by Iohn Florio. London, 1580.
Cervantes de Salazar, Francisco. *Life in the Imperial and Loyal City of Mexico in New Spain.* Translated by Mimia Lee Barrett Shepard. Austin, Tex., 1953.
Chaves, Alonso de. *Alonso de Chaves y el libro de su "Espejo de navegantes."* Edited by Pablo Castañeda, M. Cuesta, and P. Hernández. Madrid, 1977.
Chaves, Jerónimo de. *Chronographía o reportório de los tiempos.* Seville, 1581.

Davila Padilla, Agustín. *Historia de la Fundación y discurso de la provincia de Santiago de Mexico de la orden de Predicadores por las vidas de sus varones insignes y casos notables de Nueva España.* Madrid, 1596.

Dee, John. *The Private Diary of Dr. John Dee . . .* Edited by James O. Halliwell. London, 1842.

Eden, Richard. *Decades of the Newe Worlde or West India . . .* London, 1555.

Encinas, Diego de. *Cedulario Indiano.* 4 vols. 1596; rpr. facsimile ed., Madrid, 1945–46.

Fernández de Oviedo, Gonzalo. *Historia general y natural de las Indias.* 4 vols. Madrid, 1851–55.

Garcilaso de la Vega. *The Florida of the Inca.* Translated and edited by John G. Varner and Jeannette J. Varner. Austin, Tex., 1951.

[Gentleman of Elvas.] *Relaçam verdadeira dos trabalhos q[ue] ho governador dõ Fernãdo de souto e certos fidalgos portugueses passarom no descobrimẽto da provincia da Frolida, Agora nouamẽte feita per hũ fidalgo Deluas.* Evora, 1557.

[———.] *True Relation of the Hardships Suffered by Governor Fernando de Soto and Certain Portuguese Gentlemen During the Discovery of the Province of Florida Now Newly Set Forth by a Gentleman of Elvas.* Translated and edited by James A. Robertson. 2 vols. Deland, Fla., 1932–33.

Gilbert, Humphrey. *A discourse for a discoverie of a new passage to Cataia.* London, 1576. In *The Voyages and Colonizing Enterprises of Sir Humphrey Gilbert,* edited by David B. Quinn, Vol. I of 2 vols., 129–66. London, 1940.

Girón, Pedro de. *Crónica del Emperador Carlos V.* Edited by Juan Sánchez Montes. Madrid, 1964.

Gómara, Francisco Lopez de. *Histoire generalle des Indes Occidentales et terres neuues, qui iusques a present ont esté decouuertes.* Translated by Martin Fumée. Paris, 1569.

———. *Historia general de las Indias.* Text modernized by Pilar Guibelalde. 2 vols. Barcelona, 1954.

Hakluyt, Richard. "A Discourse of Western Planting, 1584." In Richard Hakluyt, *The Original Writings and Correspondence of the Two Richard Hakluyts,* edited by Eva G. R. Taylor. Vol. II of 2 vols., 211–326. London, 1935.

———. *Divers Voyages Touching the Discovery of America and the Islands Adjacent.* London: Hakluyt Society, 1850.

Harriot, Thomas. *A Briefe and True Report of the New Found Land of Virginia.* London, 1588. In *The Roanoke Voyages, 1584–1590,* edited by David B. Quinn. Vol. I of 2 vols., 317–87. London, 1955.

Hernández de Biedma, Luís. "Relación de la isla de la Florida." In *Colección de varios documentos para la historia de la Florida y tierras adyacentes,* edited by Buckingham Smith, I, 46–64. London, 1857. Also in *DII,* III, 414–41.

Herrera y Tordesillas, Antonio de. *Historia general de los hechos de los Castellanos en las islas y Tierrafirme del mar oceano.* 17 vols. Madrid, 1934–57.

La Popelinière, Lancelot Voisin, Sieur de. *Les Trois Mondes.* Paris, 1580.

las Casas, Bartolomé de. *Historia.* Translated by André Collard. New York, 1971.

Laudonnière, René Goulaine de. *L'Histoire notable de la Florida située es Indes Occidentales contenant les trois voyages faits en icelle par certains capitaines et pilotes françois . . .* Paris, 1586; rpr. Lyon, 1946. Also in *Les Français en Amérique, pendant la deuxième moitié du XVIe siècle: Les Français en Floride,* edited by Suzanne Lussagnet. Paris, 1958.

———. *Three Voyages.* Translated with introduction by Charles E. Bennett. Gainesville, Fla., 1975.

Lopez de Velasco, Juan. *Geografía y descripción universal de las Indias.* Madrid, 1894.

Martyr, Peter. *See* Anghiera, Pietro Martiere d'.

Núñez Cabeza de Vaca, Alvar. *The Narrative of Alvar Núñez Cabeza de Vaca,* Translated by Fanny Bandelier. With Oviedo's version of the lost joint report presented to the audiencia of Santo Domingo, translated by Gerald Theisen. Barre, Mass., 1972.

Oré, Luís Jerónimo de. *The Martyrs of Florida.* Translation of Oré's *Relación histórica de la Florida* by Maynard Geiger. New York, 1936.

———. *Relación histórica de la Florida.* 1612; rpr. Madrid, 1931–33.

Oviedo, Gonzalo Fernández de. *See* Fernández de Oviedo.

Parmenius, Stephanus Budaeus. *De Navigatione . . . Humfredi Gilberti.* London, 1583. In *The New Found Land of Stephen Parmenius,* translated and edited by David B. Quinn and Neil M. Cheshire. Toronto, 1972.

Peckham, George. *A true reporte of the late discoueries . . . of the Newfound landes by . . . Sir Humfrey Gilbert Knight.* London, 1583.

Ptolemaeus, Claudius. *Geography.* Translated and edited by Edward Luther Stevenson. New York, 1932.

Ramusio, Giovanni Battista. *Navigationi et Viaggi: Venice 1563–1606.* 3 vols. Amsterdam, 1967.

Ranjel, Rodrigo. "Relación." In *Historia general y natural de las Indias,* by Gonzalo Fernández de Oviedo. Vol. I of 4 vols., 544–77. Madrid, 1851–55. Also in *Narratives of the Career of Hernando de Soto in the Conquest of Florida,* translated by Buckingham Smith, edited by Edward Gaylord Bourne. Vol. II of 2 vols., 41–149. New York, 1904.

Ribault, Jean. *The Whole and True Discouerye of Terra Florida: A Facsimile Reprint of the London Edition of 1563, Together with a Transcript of an English Version in the British Museum, with Notes by H. M. Biggar and a Biography by Jeannette Thurber Connor.* Deland, Fla., 1927.

Sacchini, Francisco. *Historiae Societatis Iesu, pars Tertia, sive Borgia.* Rome, 1649.

Santa Cruz, Alonso de. *Crónica del Emperador Carlos V.* 5 vols. Madrid, 1920–25.

———. *Islario general de todas las islas del mundo . . .* 2 vols. Madrid, 1918.

Solís de Merás, Gonzalo. *Pedro Menéndez de Avilés; Memorial.* Translated by Jeannette Thurber Connor. Facsimile reproduction introduced by Lyle N. McAlister. Gainesville, Fla., 1964.

Thevet, André. *Les Singularitez de la France Antarctique.* Anvers, 1558; new edition edited by Paul Gaffarel, Paris, 1878.

Torsay, Hermann Taffin, Sieur de. *La Vie, Mort, et Tombeau de Haut et Puissant Seigneur Philippe de Strozzi* . . . 1582; rpr. Paris, 1608.

Viedma. *See* Hernández de Biedma.

Vitoria, Francisco de. *De Indis (1539); as, On the Indians Lately Discovered.* Translated by John Pawley Bate. In *The Spanish Origin of International Law, Part I, Francisco de Vitoria and His Law of Nations,* by James B. Scott, Appendix A. Oxford, 1934.

Monographs

Almagia, Roberto. *Monumenta Cartographica Vaticana Iussu Pii XII P.M. Consilio et Opera Procuratorum.* 4 vols. Rome, 1944.

Barcía Carballido y Zúñiga, Andrés Gonzalez de. *Chronological History of the Continent of Florida.* Translated by Anthony Kerrigen. Gainesville, Fla., 1951.

Bennett, Charles E. *Laudonnière and Fort Caroline: History and Documents.* Gainesville, Fla., 1964.

Besant, Walter. *Gaspard de Coligny (Marquis de Chatillon), Admiral of France, Colonel of French Infantry, Governor of Picady, Ile de France, Paris, and Havre.* New York, 1891.

Blake, Alan. *A Proposed Route for the Hernando de Soto Expedition from Tampa Bay to Apalachee Based on Physiography and Geology.* Alabama De Soto Commission, De Soto Working Papers, No. 2. University, Ala., 1987.

Bolton, Herbert E. *Coronado: Knight of Pueblos and Plains.* New York, 1949.

The Book of Saints: A Dictionary of Servants of God Canonized by the Catholic Church. Compiled by the Benedictine Monks of Saint Augustine's Abbey, Ramsgate. 4th ed. New York, 1947.

Boyd Bowman, Peter. *Indice geobiográfico de 40.000 pobladores españoles de América en el siglo XVI.* 5 vols. projected. Bogotá and Mexico City, 1964–.

Brevoort, James Carson. *Verrazano the Navigator; or, Notes on Giovanni da Verrazano and on a Planisphere of 1529 Illustrating His American Voyage of 1524.* New York, 1874.

Caldwell, Joseph R., and Catherine McCann. *Irene Mound Site, Chatham County, Georgia.* Athens, Ga., 1941.

Carmona Garcia, Juan I. *El sistema de hospitalidad pública en la Sevilla del Antiguo Régimen.* Seville, 1979.

Chamberlain, Robert S. *The Conquest and Colonization of Yucatán, 1517–1550.* Washington, D.C., 1948.

Chaunu, Pierre, and Huguette Chaunu. *Seville et l'Atlantique.* 8 vols. in 10. Paris, 1955–59.

Cumming, William P. *The Southeast in Early Maps.* Princeton, 1958.

Cumming, William P., R. A. Skelton, and David B. Quinn. *The Discovery of North America.* New York, 1972.

Delaborde, Jules, Comte. *Gaspard de Coligny, Amiral de France.* 3 vols. Paris, 1879–82.

Durant, David N. *Raleigh's Lost Colony.* New York, 1981.

Elliott, John H. *Imperial Spain, 1469–1716.* London, 1963.

Engel, Claire Eliane. *L'Amiral de Coligny.* Geneva, 1967.

Final Report of the United States De Soto Expedition Commission. 76th Congress, 1st Sess., House Document No. 71.

Floyd, Troy. *The Columbus Dynasty in the Caribbean, 1492–1526.* Albuquerque, N.Mex., 1973.

Folmer, Henry. *Franco-Spanish Rivalry for North America.* Glendale, Calif., 1953.

Franklin, Wayne. *Discoverers, Explorers, and Settlers: The Diligent Writers of Early America.* Chicago, 1979.

Ganong, William F. *Critical Maps in the Early Cartography and Place Nomenclature of the Atlantic Coast of Canada.* Edited by Theodore E. Layng. Toronto, 1964.

Gimenez Fernández, Manuel. *Bartolomé de las Casas.* 2 vols. Seville, 1953–60.

Habert, Jacques. *La Vie et les Voyages de Jean de Verrazzane.* Montreal, 1964.

Hanke. Lewis. *The Spanish Struggle for Justice in the Conquest of America.* Boston, 1965.

Hanotaux, Gabriel, and Alfred Martineau. *L'Amérique.* Paris, 1929. Vol. I of Hanotaux and Martineau, *Histoire des colonies françaises et de l'expansion de la France dans le monde.*

Haring, Clarence H. *Trade and Navigation Between Spain and the Indies in the Time of the Hapsburgs.* Cambridge, Mass., 1918.

Harrisse, Henry. *The Discovery of North America.* 1892; rpr. Amsterdam, 1961.

Hemming, John. *The Conquest of the Inca.* New York, 1970.

Hoffman, Paul E. *The Spanish Crown and the Defense of the Caribbean, 1535–1585: Precedent, Patrimonialism, and Royal Parsimony.* Baton Rouge, 1980.

Hudson, Charles. *The Juan Pardo Expeditions.* Washington, D.C., 1990.

Hulton, Paul H., ed. *America, 1585: The Complete Drawings of John White.* Chapel Hill, N.C., 1984.

Israel, Jonathan I. *Race, Class, and Politics in Colonial Mexico, 1610–1670.* London, 1975.

Julien, Charles-André. *Les Voyages de découverte et les premiers établissements: XVe–XVIe Siècles.* Paris, 1948.

Kohl, Johann Georg. *A History of the Discovery of the East Coast of North America.* Portland, Maine, 1869. Vol. I of Maine Historical Society, *Documentary History of the State of Maine.* 24 vols.

Kupperman, Karen O. *Roanoke: The Abandoned Colony.* Totowa, N.J., 1984.

Lamb, Ursula. *Fray Nicolás de Ovando, gobernador de las Indias, 1501–1509.* Madrid, 1956.

Larson, Lewis H. *Aboriginal Subsistence Technology on the Southeastern Coastal Plain During the Late Prehistoric Period.* Gainesville, Fla., 1980.

Le Moyne de Morgues, Jacques. *The Work of Jacques Le Moyne de Morgues, a Huguenot Artist in France, Florida, and England.* Edited by Paul H. Hulton. 2 vols. London, 1977.

Lewis, Clifford M., and Albert J. Loomie. *The Spanish Jesuit Mission in Virginia, 1570–1572.* Chapel Hill, N.C., 1953.

Lorant, Stefan, ed. *The New World: The First Pictures of America, Made by John White and Jacques LeMoyne and Engraved by Theodore de Bry, with Contemporary Narratives of the French Settlement in Florida, 1562–1565, and the English Colonies in Virginia, 1585–1590.* Rev. ed. New York, 1965.

Lowery, Woodbury. *Spanish Settlements Within the Present Limits of the United States.* 2 vols. New York, 1901–1911.

Lyon, Eugene. *The Enterprise of Florida: Pedro Menéndez de Avilés and the Conquest of 1565–1568.* Gainesville, Fla., 1976.

———. *Santa Elena: A Brief History of the Colony, 1566–1587.* Columbia, S.C., 1984.

McCann, Franklin T. *English Discovery of America to 1585.* New York, 1952.

Manzano y Manzano, Juan. *La incorporación de las Indias a la Corona de Castilla.* Madrid, 1948.

Martín Gamero, Antonio. *Historia de la ciudad de Toledo.* 2 vols. Toledo, 1862.

Merki, Charles. *L'Amiral de Coligny: La Maison de Chatillon et la Revolte protestante, 1519–1572.* Paris, 1909.

Milanich, Jerald T. *Hernando de Soto and the Expedition in La Florida.* Miscellaneous Project Report No. 32, Department of Anthropology, Florida State Museum. Gainesville, Fla., 1987.

Miranda Vázquez, Trinidad. *La gobernación de Santa Marta, 1570–1670.* Seville, 1976.

Molinari, Diego Luís. *El nacimiento del nuevo mundo, 1492–1534: Historia y cartografía.* Buenos Aires, 1941.

Mooney, James. *The Siouan Tribes of the East.* Bureau of American Ethnology Bulletin 22. Washington, D.C., 1894.

Morison, Samuel E. *European Discovery of America: The Northern Voyages.* New York, 1971.

Murphy, Henry C. *The Voyage of Verrazzano: A Chapter in the Early History of Maritime Discovery in America.* New York, 1875–76.

Palau y Dulcet, Antonio. *Manual del librero hispano-americano: Bibliografía general español e hispano-americana desde la invención de la imprenta hasta nuestros tiempos . . .* 28 vols. 2nd ed. Barcelona, 1948–77.

Parker, [Noel] Geoffrey. *The Dutch Revolt.* Ithaca, N.Y., 1977.

Parks, George B. *Richard Hakluyt and the English Voyages.* Edited with introduction by James A. Williamson. New York, 1930.

Pigeonneau, Henri. *Histoire du commerce de la France.* 2 vols. Paris, 1885–97.

Price, Richard, ed. *Maroon Societies: Rebel Slave Communities in the Americas.* New York, 1973.

Priestley, Herbert I. *Tristan de Luna, Conquistador of the Old South: A Study of Spanish Imperial Strategy.* Glendale, Calif., 1936; rpr. Philadelphia, 1980.

Quattlebaum, Paul. *The Land Called Chicora: The Corolinas Under Spanish Rule with French Intrusions, 1520–1670.* Gainesville, Fla., 1956.

Quinn, David B. *England and the Discovery of America, 1481–1620.* New York, 1974.

———. *The Lost Colonists: Their Fortune and Probable Fate.* Raleigh, N.C., 1984.

———. *Set Fair for Roanoke: Voyages and Colonies, 1584–1606.* Chapel Hill, N.C., 1985.

Rodriguez Demorizi, Emilio. *Los dominicos y las encomiendas de indios en la isla Española.* Santo Domingo, 1977.

Roncière, Charles G. M. B. de La. *Histoire de la marine française.* 6 vols. Paris, 1899–1932.

Rubio Mañe, J. Ignacio. *Introducción al estudio de los Virreyes de Nueva España, 1535–1746.* 4 vols. Mexico City, 1955–1982.

Santarém, Manuel Francisco de Barros, Vicount de. *Quadro elementar das relações políticas e diplomáticas de Portugal com as diversas potencias do mundo, desde o principio da monarchia portugueza até aos nossos dias.* 18 vols. in 13. Paris, 1842–76.

Sauer, Carl O. *The Early Spanish Main.* Berkeley and Los Angeles, 1966.

Shimizu, J. *Conflict of Loyalties, Politics, and Religion in the Career of Gaspard de Coligny, Admiral of France, 1519–1572.* Geneva, 1970.

Simpson, Lesley B. *The Encomienda in New Spain: The Beginning of Spanish Mexico.* Rev. ed. Berkeley and Los Angeles, 1966.

South, Stanley. *Exploring Santa Elena, 1981.* Columbia, S.C., [1982].

Southey, Robert. *History of Brazil.* 3 vols. 1810–19; rpr. New York, 1969.

Stick, David. *Roanoke Island: The Beginnings of English America.* Chapel Hill, N.C., 1983.

Stokes, I. N. P. *The Iconography of Manhattan Island, 1498–1909.* 6 vols. 1915–28; rpr. New York, 1964.

Swanton, John R. *Early History of the Creek Indians and Their Neighbors.* Bureau of American Ethnology Bulletin 73. Washington, 1922.

Taylor, Eva G. R. *Tudor Geography, 1485–1583.* London, 1930.

Thomazi, August A. *Les Flottes de l'or: Histoire des galions d'Espagne.* Paris, 1937.

El tratado de Tordesillas y su proyección. 2 vols. Valladolid, 1973.

Trudel, Marcel. *Les Vaines Tentatives, 1524–1603.* Vol. I of *Histoire de la Nouvelle-France.* Montreal, 1963. 3 vols. to 1973.

Tucherman, Bryant. *Planetary, Lunar, and Solar Positions, A.D. 2–1649.* Philadelphia, 1964.

Ullivarri, Saturnino. *Piratas y corsarios de Cuba: Ensayo histórico.* Havana, 1931.

U.S. Department of Agriculture. *Soil Survey, Georgetown County, South Carolina,* 1982.

U.S. Department of Commerce, NOAA. *Comparative Climatic Data for the United States Through 1978.* 1979.

———. *Pilot Chart for the North Atlantic, June, 1966.* 1966.

———. *United States Coast Pilot, Atlantic Coast: Cape Henry to Key West.* 16th ed. 1978.

———, Environmental Data Service. *Climatological Data, Georgia,* 75, Nos. 9–11. 1971.

Voegelin, Charles F. *Map of North American Indian Languages.* New York, 1944.

Weddle, Robert S. *Spanish Sea: The Gulf of Mexico in North American Discovery, 1500–1685.* College Station, Tex., 1985.

Whitehead, Arthur W. *Gaspard de Coligny, Admiral of France.* London, 1904.

Willan, Thomas S. *The Early History of the Russia Company, 1553–1603.* Manchester, Eng., 1956.

Wright, Irene A. *The Early History of Cuba, 1492–1586.* New York, 1916.

———. *Historia documentada de San Cristóbal de La Habana en el siglo XVI.* 2 vols. Havana, 1927.

Wroth, Lawrence C. *The Voyages of Giovanni da Verrazzano, 1524–1528.* New Haven, 1970.

Articles

Bourne, Edward G. "The History and Determination of the Line of Demarcation Established by Pope Alexander VI Between the Spanish and Portuguese Fields of Discovery and Colonization." In *Annual Report for 1891* of the American Historical Association, 101–30. Washington, D.C., 1892.

Canter, Juan. "Notas sobre la edición principe de la *Historia* de López de Gómara." *Boletín del Instituto de Investigaciones Históricas* (Buenos Aires), I (1922), 128–45.

Chapelle, Baron de La. "Jean Le Veneur et le Canada." *Nova Francia,* VI (September–December, 1931), 342.

Chardon, Roland. "The Linear League in North America." *Annals of the Association of American Geographers,* LXX (1980), 129–53.

Crawford, James M. "Southeastern Indian Languages." In *Studies in Southeastern Indian Languages,* edited by James M. Crawford, 1–120. Athens, Ga., 1975.

Cumming, William P. "The Parreus Map (1562) of French Florida." *Imago Mundi,* XVII (1963), 27–40.

DePratter, Chester, Charles Hudson, and Marvin Smith. "The Route of Juan

Pardo's Exploration in the Interior Southeast, 1566–1568." *Florida Historical Quarterly,* LXII (1983), 125–58.

Destombes, Marcel. "La Cartographie florentine de la Renaissance et Verrazano." In *Giovanni da Verrazzano: Giornante commemorative, Firenze—Greve in Chianti, 21–22 ottobre 1961,* 19–40. Florence, 1970.

Flannery, Regina. "Some Notes on a Few Sites in Beaufort County, S.C." In *Anthropological Papers,* No. 21, pp. 143–53. Bureau of American Ethnology Bulletin 133. Washington, D.C, 1943.

Fogelson, Raymond D. "Who Were the Aní Kutánî? An Excursion into Cherokee Historical Thought." *Ethnohistory,* XXXI (1984), 255–63.

Hoffman, Bernard G. "Account of a Voyage Conducted in 1529 to the New World, Africa, Madagascar, and Sumatra, Translated from the Italian, with Notes and Comments." *Ethnohistory,* X (1963), 1–79.

Hoffman, Paul E. "The Chicora Legend and Franco-Spanish Rivalry in *La Florida.*" *Florida Historical Quarterly,* LXII (1984), 419–38.

———. "Diplomacy and the Papal Donation, 1493–1585." *The Americas,* XXX (1973), 151–83.

———. "Legend, Religious Idealism, and Colonies: The Point of Santa Elena in History, 1552–1566." *South Carolina Magazine of History,* LXXXIV (1983), 59–71.

———. "The Narrow Waters Strategies of Pedro Menéndez." *Florida Historical Quarterly,* XLV (1966), 12–17.

———. "New Light on Vicente Gonzalez's 1588 Voyage in Search of Raleigh's English Colonies." *North Carolina Historical Review,* LXIII (1986), 199–223.

———. "A New Voyage of North American Discovery: The Voyage of Pedro de Salazar to the Island of Giants." *Florida Historical Quarterly,* LVIII (1980), 415–26.

Hudson, Charles, Marvin Smith, David Hally, Richard Polhemus, and Chester DePratter. "Coosa: A Chiefdom in the Sixteenth-Century Southeastern United States." *American Antiquity,* L (1985), 723–37.

Konetzke, Richard. "Legislación sobre immigración de extranjeros en América durante la época colonial." *Revista internacional de sociología* (Madrid), XI–XII (1945), 269–99.

Lechner, J. "El concepto de 'policía' y su presencia en la obra de los primeros historiadores de Indias." *Revista de Indias,* XLI (1981), 395–410.

Lyon, Eugene. "St. Augustine 1580: The Living Community." *El Escribano,* XIV (1977), 20–33.

Mattingly, Garrett. "No Peace Beyond What Line?" *Transactions of the Royal Historical Society* (London), 5th ser., XIII (1963), 145–62.

Miller, Carl F. "Revaluation of the Eastern Siouan Problem, with Particular Emphasis on the Virginia Branches—the Occaneechi, the Saponi, and the Tutelo." In *Anthropological Papers,* No. 52, pp. 115–212. Bureau of American Ethnology Bulletin 164. Washington, D.C., 1957.

Myer, William E. "Indian Trails of the Southeast." In *Forty-second Annual*

Report, 1924–1925, of the Bureau of American Ethnology. Washington, D.C., 1928.

Quinn, David. B. "A Portuguese Pilot in English Service." In *England and the Discovery of America, 1481–1620,* 246–63. New York, 1973.

Reitz, Elizabeth. "Availability and Use of Fish Along Coastal Georgia and Florida." *Southeastern Archaeologist,* I (1982), 65–68.

Roncière, Charles G. M. B. de La. "Colonies éphémères." In *L'Amérique,* by Gabriel Hanotaux and Alfred Martineau. Paris, 1929. Vol. I of Hanotaux and Martineau, *Histoire des colonies françaises et de l'expansion de la France dans le monde.*

Ross, Mary. "French Intrusions and Indian Uprisings in Georgia and South Carolina, 1577–1580." *Georgia Historical Quarterly,* VII (1923), 251–81.

Shea, John G. "Ancient Florida." In *Narrative and Critical History of the United States,* edited by Justin Winsor. Vol. II of 8 vols., 231–83. Boston, 1884–89.

Skelton, Raleigh A. "The Influence of Verrazzano on Sixteenth Century Cartography." In *Giovanni da Verrazzano: Giornante commemorative, Firenze—Greve in Chianti, 21–22 ottobre 1961,* 55–69. Florence, 1970.

Stevenson, E. L. "Early Spanish Cartography of the New World with Special Reference to Wolfenbüttal-Spanish Map and the Work of Diego Ribero." *Proceedings of the American Antiquarian Society,* n.s. XIX (1909), 369–419.

Thrower, Norman J. W. "New Light on the 1524 Voyages of Verrazzano." *Terrae Incognitae,* XI (1979), 59–66.

Vigneras, Louis-André. "The Cartographer Diogo Ribeiro." *Imago Mundi,* XVI (1962), 76–83.

———. "Is There a 'Verrazano River' on Juan Vespucci's 1526 Mappemonde?" *Terrae Incognitae,* VII (1976), 65–67.

———. "A Spanish Discovery of North Carolina in 1566." *North Carolina Historical Review,* XLVI (1969), 398–414.

Wenhold, Lucy L., trans. "Manrique de Rojas' Report on French Settlement in Florida, 1564." *Florida Historical Quarterly,* XXXVIII (1959), 45–62.

Unpublished Works

Baker, Stephen. "Cofitachequi: Fair Province of South Carolina." M.A. thesis, University of South Carolina, 1974.

Hernández, Mirtha A. "Fray Antonio de Montesinos and the Laws of Burgos." M.A. thesis, Louisiana State University, 1977.

Hoffman, Paul E. "A Best Text of the Ayllón Place Name List." Baton Rouge, 1980. Typescript in collection of the author.

Hudson, Charles, and Gerald Milanich. "Hernando de Soto and the Indians of Florida." Forthcoming.

Judge, Joseph R. "A Memorandum on the Voyage of Discovery of 1521 by Pedro de Quexo and Francisco Gordillo to South Carolina." Washington, D.C., 1979. Typescript in collection of the present author.

Index